The War against Catholicism

Recent Titles

For a complete list of titles, please see www.press.umich.edu

The War against Catholicism

Liberalism and the Anti-Catholic Imagination in Nineteenth-Century Germany

Michael B. Gross

The University of Michigan Press   *Ann Arbor*

First paperback edition 2005
Copyright © by the University of Michigan 2004
All rights reserved
Published in the United States of America by
The University of Michigan Press
Manufactured in the United States of America
⊗ Printed on acid-free paper

2011   2010   2009   2008   6   5   4   3

A CIP catalog record for this book is available from the British Library.

Library of Congress Cataloging-in-Publication Data

Gross, Michael B., 1961–
    The war against Catholicism : liberalism and the anti-Catholic
imagination in nineteenth-century Germany / Michael B. Gross.
        p.   cm. — (Social history, popular culture, and politics in
Germany)
    Includes bibliographical references and index.
    ISBN 0-472-11383-6 (cloth : alk. paper)
        1. Kulturkampf—Germany.   2. Anti-Catholicism—Germany—History—
19th century.   3. Liberalism—Germany—History—19th century.
4. Catholic Church—Germany—History—19th century.   5. Germany—
Politics and government—1871–1888.   I. Title.   II. Series.

    DD118.G76   2004
    322'.1'094309034—dc22   2004000607

ISBN 0-472-03130-9 (pbk. : alk. paper)

ISBN 978-0-472-11383-5 (cloth : alk. paper)
ISBN 978-0-472-03130-6 (pbk. : alk. paper)

For Anne

Contents

Acknowledgments

It is a pleasure to acknowledge my gratitude to all those who over the course of several years helped make this work possible. This book began as a doctoral dissertation at Brown University directed by Volker R. Berghahn. I am grateful for his encouragement, for our rich conversations, and for his example as a scholar and gentleman. I would like to thank Mary Gluck for encouraging me to explore the questions of cultural and intellectual history that made this study possible in the first place. I am grateful also to David Kertzer for lending his interdisciplinary perspective and for his careful reading of my work. At different stages of this work I was fortunate to receive the counsel and in various forms the criticism of David Blackbourn, Larry Eugene Jones, Jürgen Kocka, Jonathan Sperber, James Retallack, and Ronald J. Ross. I would like to thank specifically Margaret Lavinia Anderson for carefully reading a final draft of the manuscript and offering timely corrections and comments. I particularly thank Helmut Walser Smith for his thoughtful critique of my work, generous advice, and continuous encouragement at crucial stages. In addition, I would like to thank the anonymous readers at the University of Michigan Press for their helpful criticism of the manuscript. Many of these scholars have generously saved me from making mistakes, some have not agreed with everything I have said, and none bears responsibility for any faults. All have helped make this work more than it otherwise would have been.

In addition to the archived state documents, the research material for the subject of this book—anticlerical and anti-Catholic, liberal, Catholic, and Protestant books, pamphlets, newspapers, journals, and other documents from nineteenth-century Germany—at one time, judging by the card catalogs and microfiche inventories, amounted to a virtual mountain of material. In the course of the last century this mountain was whittled down as these materials were first under the

National Socialist regime sometimes restricted or confiscated by the Gestapo for reasons known to themselves, later stored during the Second World War in mine shafts to avoid incineration in Allied bombing raids and then often lost, or finally in Berlin toward the very end of the war blown apart by approaching Red Army tanks and artillery. On many occasions my access to the material that survived was due to patient librarians and archivists willing to bear with my requests that they search again for materials miscataloged, misplaced, or marked *Kriegsverlust* and forgotten. Without their assistance and the efforts of others at libraries and archives in Germany this book would not have been possible.

I would, therefore, like to thank the archivists and librarians of the Archiv und Bibliothek des Diakonischen Werkes der EKD in Berlin, especially Dr. Leonhard Deppe for his hospitality, which extended beyond his responsibilities in the library; the Landesarchiv, Berlin; the Geheimes Staatsarchiv Preußischer Kulturbesitz, Berlin; the Landeshauptarchiv, Koblenz; the Hauptstaatsarchiv, Düsseldorf; the Stadtarchiv Düsseldorf; the Hauptstaatsarchiv, Aachen, particularly Dr. Herbert Lepper; the Staatsbibliothek Preußischer Kulturbesitz, Haus 1, Unter den Linden, and Haus 2, Potsdamer Str., Berlin; the Niedersächsische Staats- und Universitätsbibliothek, Göttingen; the Universitätsbibliothek, Freie Universität Berlin; the Öffentlichesbibliothek, Aachen; the Universitätsbibliothek, Düsseldorf; and Landes- und Stadtbibliothek, Düsseldorf. In addition, I would like to thank librarians at the New York Public Library, Central Research Library; and the John D. Rockefeller, Jr., Library, Brown University. Finally, I would like to thank the staff of Joyner Library at East Carolina University, particularly Patricia Guyette and Elizabeth Winstead of Interlibrary Services for their efficiency and Diana Williams and Michael Reece in the Office of Digital Projects for preparing the illustrations.

The research for this work was generously funded by several scholarly institutions and foundations. Support early on provided by the Volkswagen Stiftung through the German Historical Institute enabled me to receive paleographic training at the Karl August Bibliothek, Wolfenbüttel, and to tour archives in Germany. For grants that made the research possible, I am grateful to the German Academic Exchange Service (DAAD) and to the Berlin Program for Advanced German and European Studies of the Social Science Research Council and the Freie Universität Berlin. As a Fellow in the Berlin Program, I was fortunate to be part of an intellectually inspiring, interdisciplinary cohort of scholars. A Lawrence F. Brewster Scholarship from the Department of

History, East Carolina University, freed time from teaching responsibilities and provided funding for travel, research, and writing. A College Research Award from East Carolina University also enabled me to return to Germany for additional research. I would like to gratefully acknowledge this support from East Carolina University as I encourage the university in its responsibility to support and fund future researchers and authors.

I thank also Geoff Eley, who as editor of the University of Michigan Press series Social History, Popular Culture, and Politics in Germany offered his interest, critical comments, and encouragement. I was fortunate to have at the Press the assistance of Christopher Collins, Sarah Mann, and the editorial staff. I should add that, unless otherwise indicated, all translations are my own. My colleagues in the Department of History at East Carolina University provided a collegial home, and I particularly thank Michael Palmer for his counsel, for ongoing encouragement, and for arranging time free from other responsibilities for completing the final revisions.

I give further thanks to Alexandra Staub and Dmitri Bezinover for their hospitality during a memorable summer in Berlin, and I thank Elizabeth Bachhuber and Christof Rihs for providing a warm refuge in Düsseldorf during a particularly dark winter. They gave me a home and family when I most needed them, and I continue to benefit from their stimulating insights about Germany, past and present. For offering along the way encouragement, sympathy, good humor, and other forms of sustenance I thank Michael Bassman; Susan, Melissa, David, and Patricia Bunnell; Eric and Janet Gross; Manik Hinchey; Birgit Jensen; David Scialdone; and my friends at the Berlin Stammtisch. I cherish their friendship. I would also like to thank my professional colleagues and friends with whom I communicate via email and telephone until we finally see each other again, usually at the annual conferences of the German Studies Association. Their camaraderie and our discussions together have kept me going in more ways than they might recognize.

I give special thanks to Carol Hager, who lifted me up, dusted me off, and set me on my feet when I needed it. Kerry McNamara has been there since the early years and was a constant friend during the research and writing. During the final phase of revision, Thomas Midyette, Charles Dupree, and Bets and David Crean kept pointing to the most important things. The memories of John Gross and Bodo Nischan lent perspective, and the impending arrival of Jessica Gross provided the final impetus to complete the manuscript. I especially thank my parents, Frank Robert and Jean Pichotta Gross, for their support during every stage of this book but even more for offering me their living examples of integrity and dedication. I thank above all my very best friend, Anne Bunnell. She patiently lived with this project from the very beginning and during stages of writing and revision let me get away with less of the cooking and housework. More important, she brought to this work balance and faith and to my life innumerable blessings. This book is for her.

Abbreviations

Bd.	Band
Best.	Bestand
Bl.	Blatt or Blätter
BM	Bürgermeister
HSTAD	Hauptstaatsarchiv Düsseldorf
Kr.	Kreis
LR	Landrat
LRA	Landratsamt
LHAK	Landeshauptarchiv Koblenz
Nr.	Nummer
OP	Oberpräsident or Oberpräsidium
OPR	Oberpräsident or Oberpräsidium der Rheinprovinz
P	Präsidium
PB	Präsidialbüro
PD	Polizei Direktor
Pf.	Pfarrer
PP	Polizei Präsident or Polizeipräsidium
RA	Regierung Aachen
RBA	Regierungsbezirk Aachen
RBD	Regierungsbezirk Düsseldorf
RBT	Regierungsbezirk Trier
RD	Regierung Düsseldorf
RK	Regierung Köln
RP	Regierungspräsident or Regierungspräsidium
SBHA	*Stenographische Berichte über die Verhandlungen des preußischen Landtages. Haus der Abgeordneten*

Introduction

For obvious and irrefutable reasons, anti-Judaism in the nineteenth century and particularly anti-Semitism after the 1870s have received considerable attention from historians of modern Germany. The long and shameful record of anti-Judaism and the origins of modern anti-Semitism have undeniable importance for the history of Germany and indeed of Europe. Yet the nineteenth century in Germany with its particular confessional divide, modern rationalizing culture, and secularizing social currents was arguably more a century of anti-Catholicism. It was anti-Catholicism in Germany in the nineteenth century that culminated in what contemporaries called the Kulturkampf (cultural struggle) of the 1870s, a campaign sponsored by liberals and prosecuted by the state intended to break the influence of the Roman Catholic Church and the religious, social, and political power of Catholicism. The attack on the church included a series of principally Prussian, discriminatory laws that made Roman Catholics feel understandably persecuted within a predominantly Protestant nation. The Society of Jesus (the Jesuits), along with the Franciscan, Dominican, and other religious orders, was expelled from the German Empire, the consequence of two decades of anti-Jesuit and antimonastic hysteria. The Prussian state imposed its own authority over the education and appointment of Catholic clergy. Other state legislation authorized the seizure of church property, the expulsion of recalcitrant priests, and the removal of the financial support of those members of the clergy who refused to align themselves with state policies. Roman Catholics within Germany immediately recognized that these measures were an attack not merely on the church but on the entire Catholic way of life. State authorities believed they had no choice but to call upon the army to put down spontaneous riots by Catholics rebelling all over Germany in protest against the closing of monasteries, the imprisonment of priests, the arrest of bishops, and the confiscation of church property by the state. By the end of the decade over eighteen hundred Catholic priests had either been incarcerated or exiled, and Catholic church property worth some sixteen million marks had been taken over by the state.[1]

With the founding of the German Empire in 1871, Jews in Germany, meanwhile, finally achieved complete emancipation. This, of course, did not always mean that Jews were free from discrimination, but it did mean that Jews enjoyed equal legal status in a state that protected its citizens from arbitrary authority and guaranteed the rule of law. With considerable success, German Jews now increasingly moved into respectable commercial, professional, and academic positions and established themselves in German society as attorneys, journalists, physicians, and academics in numbers clearly disproportionate to the size of the Jewish population within the empire. At the same time during the first decade of the empire, contemporary critics continuously complained about the social, cultural, and professional underachievement of the Catholic population. Catholics and the Catholic Church in Germany now also faced a barrage of discriminatory Kulturkampf legislation that seemed constantly to remind them that they were not welcome. In modern Germany, an *Ausnahmegesetz* (exceptional legislation outside normal civil-juridical procedure) that abrogated citizen rights and a state-sponsored domestic war were unleashed first against Roman Catholicism.

While majorities could be found in the Prussian parliament and in the Reichstag to pass discriminatory legislation against Roman Catholics, the emancipation of Germany's Jews, who constituted less than 1 percent of the population and therefore were scarcely capable of defending themselves against opposition, was not revoked. The Kulturkampf, even when most of its legislation lapsed in the 1880s, left a long legacy among German Roman Catholics, the bitter feeling that they had been branded as pariahs and had, for the sake of survival, to establish a separate Catholic subculture within the population. Liberals, the purported champions of tolerance, freedom, and equal rights before the law and as such the leadership of those who had insisted on Jewish emancipation, were the greatest enemies of Catholicism in the nineteenth century and the most dedicated prosecutors of the anti-

---

1. David Blackbourn, *The Long Nineteenth Century: A History of Germany, 1780–1918* (New York: Oxford University Press, 1998), 262.

Catholic attack. By the 1870s liberals in Germany conceived of the anti-Catholic campaign as nothing less than a war to save the new empire from its most powerful enemy within its own territorial borders.

This study explores why the hatred of Roman Catholicism and Catholics was of such paramount importance to liberals, the self-avowed heirs of the Enlightenment, proponents of a modern industrial society, and loyal defendants of the modern nation-state. It examines more specifically the peculiarities of the liberal anti-Catholic imagination and the forms of intolerance developed and practiced by liberals against priests, monks, nuns, and the Catholic population in Germany. The anti-Catholicism of the nineteenth century and the anti-Catholic legislation of the 1870s emerge under close examination not, as so often understood, as contradictions of liberal principles, attempts to preserve the autonomy of the secular state, or campaigns to ensure the Protestant identity of the nation. The intolerance of Catholics that culminated in the Kulturkampf and the attempt once and for all to break the power of Roman Catholic faith and the influence of the Roman Catholic Church were instead embedded in a more pervasive and complex array of imperatives and anxieties specific to liberal identity and the liberal program for political citizenship, economic development, moral order, and public and private life in modern Germany.

German Catholicism and Liberalism in Historical Perspective

From the 1960s to the late 1980s almost an entire generation of social historians of Germany trained their attention on the society, culture, and politics of the working class in the nineteenth century. Toward the end of the 1980s, as historians began to look for new approaches to understand modern society, attention shifted to an exploration of the politics and social-cultural world of the German *Bürgertum.* Meanwhile, the history of German Roman Catholics during the nineteenth century remained for the most part unexamined or confined to *Kirchengeschichte,* often narrow studies of the institution of the church itself, despite the fact that, demographically, Catholics constituted one-third of the social and cultural life of the empire. Though once neglected, the broader religious, social, and political dimensions of German Catholicism have been rediscovered. Wolfgang Schieder's pathbreaking article on the Catholic revival in the Rhineland with the

Trier pilgrimage of 1844 and then Jonathan Sperber's equally important book on the resurgence of popular Catholicism in the Rhineland
and Westphalia in the second half of the century initiated a wave of
interest in the subject.[2] Since these works, the study of German
Catholicism in its rich social, cultural, and political aspects has become
a major field within the historical literature of modern Germany.

Now historians can look back with some justified satisfaction on
almost a generation of exemplary scholarship on nineteenth-century
German Catholicism: Thomas Mergel's study of Catholic middle-class
society in the Rhineland, Otto Weiss's exhaustive study of the
Redemptorists in Bavaria, Irmtraud Götz von Olenhusen's work on
Catholic women and study of the culture of clerical ultramontanism in
Freiburg, Margaret Lavinia Anderson's works on Catholic piety and
political culture, and David Blackbourn's articles on political Catholicism and especially his study of Marian apparitions are only a few
notable examples.[3] As the study of Catholicism in Germany has developed a substantial body of literature, historians of Catholicism have

2. Wolfgang Schieder, "Kirche und Revolution: Sozialgeschichtliche Aspekte der Trierer
Wallfahrt von 1844," *Archiv für Sozialgeschichte* 14 (1974): 419–54; and the critical response
by Rudolf Lill, "Kirche und Revolution: Zu den Anfängen der katholischen Bewegung im
Jahrzehnt vor 1848," *Archiv für Sozialgeschichte* 18 (1978): 565–75; Jonathan Sperber, *Popular Catholicism in Nineteenth-Century Germany* (Princeton: Princeton University Press, 1984).

3. Thomas Mergel, *Zwischen Klasse und Konfession: Katholisches Bürgertum im Rheinland, 1794–1914* (Göttingen: Vandenhoeck und Ruprecht, 1994); Otto Weiss, *Die Redemp-
toristen in Bayern (1790–1909): Ein Beitrag zur Geschichte des Ultramontanismus* (St.
Ottilien: Eos Verlag, 1983); Irmtraud Götz von Olenhusen, ed., *Wunderbare Erscheinungen:
Frauen und katholische Frömmigkeit im 19. und 20. Jahrhundert* (Paderborn: F. Schöningh,
1995); idem, *Klerus und abweichendes Verhalten: Zur Sozialgeschichte der katholischer
Priester im 19. Jahrhundert; Die Erzdiözese Freiburg* (Göttingen: Vandenhoeck und
Ruprecht, 1994); Margaret Lavinia Anderson, *Windthorst: A Political Biography* (Oxford:
Oxford University Press, 1981); idem, *Practicing Democracy: Elections and Political Culture
in Imperial Germany* (Princeton: Princeton University Press, 2000); David Blackbourn, *Class,
Religion, and Local Politics in Wilhelmine Germany: The Centre Party in Württemberg before
1914* (New Haven: Yale University Press, 1980); idem, *Marpingen: Apparitions of the Virgin
Mary in Nineteenth-Century Germany* (New York: Alfred A. Knopf, 1994).

Other major works representing the range of topics in the literature on Catholicism in nineteenth-century Germany include but are not limited to Wolfgang Altgeld, *Katholizismus,
Protestantismus, Judentum: Über religiös begründete Gegensätze und nationalreligiöse Ideen in
der Geschichte des deutschen Nationalismus* (Mainz: Matthias Grünewald Verlag, 1992); Olaf
Blaschke and Frank-Michael Kuhlemann, eds., *Religion im Kaiserreich: Milieus—Mentalitäten—Krisen* (Gütersloh: Chr. Kaiser, 1996); Werner K. Blessing, *Staat und Kirche in der
Gesellschaft: Institutionelle Autorität und mentaler Wandel in Bayern während des 19. Jahrhunderts* (Göttingen: Vandenhoeck und Ruprecht, 1982); Ellen Lovell Evans, *The German Center Party, 1870–1933: A Study in Political Catholicism* (Carbondale: Southern Illinois Univer-

been able to take stock of some of their predominant conclusions in order to direct or redirect further research, an indication of both the vitality and significance of the field. Recently, Oded Heilbronner has argued that historians may have brought the study of Catholicism out of the ghetto of historiographical ostracization, but in doing so they have ironically also confined the nineteenth-century Catholic population to a social and cultural ghetto, one that was willfully circumspect and antimodern, at variance with the progressive, main currents of life in Germany.[4] This current historical evaluation of nineteenth-century Catholicism is an echo of the attitudes of liberal contempories who, as

sity Press, 1981); Horst Gründer, "Nation und Katholizismus im Kaiserreich," in *Katholizismus, nationaler Gedanke und Europa seit 1800,* ed. Albrecht Langer (Paderborn: F. Schöningh, 1985), 65–88; Rudolf Lill, "Die deutschen Katholiken und Bismarcks Reichsgründung," in *Reichsgründung 1870/71: Tatsachen, Kontroversen, Interpretationen,* ed. Theodor Schieder and Ernst Deuerlein (Stuttgart: Seewald Verlag, 1970), 345–66; Wilfried Loth, *Katholiken im Kaiserreich: Der politische Katholizismus in der Krise des wilhelminischen Deutschlands* (Düsseldorf: Droste Verlag, 1984); Rudolf Morsey, "Die deutschen Katholiken und der Nationalstaat zwischen Kulturkampf und Ersten Weltkrieg," *Historisches Jahrbuch* 90 (1970): 31–64; Anton Rauscher, ed., *Katholizismus, Bildung und Wissenschaft in 19. und 20. Jahrhundert* (Paderborn: F. Schöningh, 1987); Ronald J. Ross, *Beleaguered Tower: The Dilemma of Political Catholicism in Wilhelmine Germany* (Notre Dame: University of Notre Dame Press, 1976); idem, *The Failure of Bismarck's Kulturkampf: Catholicism and State Power in Imperial Germany, 1871–1887* (Washington, D.C.: Catholic University of America Press, 1998); Wolfgang Schieder, ed., *Volksreligiosität in der modernen Sozialgeschichte* (Göttingen: Vandenhoeck und Ruprecht, 1986); and Helmut Walser Smith, *German Nationalism and Religious Conflict: Culture, Ideology, Politics, 1870–1914* (Princeton: Princeton University Press, 1995).

4. Oded Heilbronner, "From Ghetto to Ghetto: The Place of German Catholic Society in Recent Historiography," *Journal of Modern History* 72 (2000): 453–95. For an example that emphasizes the "backward antimodernism" of the Catholic clergy, see the study by Urs Altermatt, a historian who has considerably shaped the field of modern Catholic Germany, "Katholizismus: Antimodernismus mit modernen Mitteln?" in *Moderne als Problem des Katholizismus,* ed. Urs Altermatt et al. (Regensburg: Verlag F. Pustet, 1995), 33–50. See also the similar perspective in Martin Baumeister, *Parität und katholische Inferiorität: Untersuchungen zur Stellung des Katholizismus im deutschen Kaiserreich* (Paderborn: F. Schöningh, 1987). Karl-Egon Lönne's discussion of the ultramontane milieu mentality indicates how prevalent this point of view has become in recent studies. Karl-Egon Lönne, "Katholizismus-Forschung," *Geschichte und Gesellschaft* 26 (2000): 137–44. Other reviews of the development of the historiography of Catholicism in modern Germany include Margaret Lavinia Anderson, "Piety and Politics: Recent Work on German Catholicism," *Journal of Modern History* 63 (1991): 681–716; Michael Klöcker, "Das katholische Milieu: Grundüberlegungen—in besonderer Hinsicht auf das Deutsche Kaiserreich von 1871," *Zeitschrift für Religions- und Geistesgeschichte* 44 (1992): 241–62; and Eric Yonke, "The Catholic Subculture in Modern Germany: Recent Work in the Social History of Religion," *Catholic Historical Review* 80 (1994): 534–45.

I shall show, continuously complained of the Catholic population's *Bildungsdefizit* (educational deficit) and backwardness.

In comparison to the body of research now available on Catholicism, little careful and sustained research has been devoted to modern German Protestantism and Protestant piety. David Blackbourn's complaint that "the subject of popular Protestantism in the nineteenth century still awaits its historian" remains for the most part unanswered.[5] Yet if research on Protestantism lags behind research on Catholicism and for that matter Judaism in Germany, historians have recently begun to plow new terrain in the history of religion as they move beyond the traditional focus on one religious denomination, whether Protestant, Catholic, or Jewish. Though usually the religious populations have been studied separately, historians are abandoning older habits, crossing over confessional borders to examine the ways the different religious populations in Germany cohabited and reciprocally shaped religious, social, cultural, and nationalist attitudes and practices.[6]

At the same time, antireligious attitudes, particularly the study of the other side of the Catholic revival in the nineteenth century, the dramatic and parallel resurgence of anticlericalism and anti-Catholicism, have remained largely unexamined despite their breadth and depth and their larger meaning for German society and culture. Those studies that have explored anti-Catholicism in the nineteenth century have predominantly confined themselves to the period of the Kulturkampf itself.[7] Much of this historiography has concentrated on the national political dimensions of the church-state conflict.[8] Studies focused on

5. David Blackbourn, "Progress and Piety: Liberals, Catholics, and the State in Bismarck's Germany," in David Blackbourn, *Populists and Patricians: Essays in Modern German History* (London: Allen and Unwin, 1987), 143–67, quotation at 160.

6. This is one of the virtues among others of Smith, *German Nationalism.* See also the collection of essays in Helmut Walser Smith, ed., *Protestants, Catholics, and Jews in Germany, 1800–1914* (Oxford: Berg, 2001), particularly Helmut Walser Smith and Chris Clark, "The Fate of Nathan," 3–32.

7. For important exceptions, see Ross, *Beleaguered Tower;* and Smith, *German Nationalism.* Margaret Lavinia Anderson examines anti-Catholic sentiments in Wilhelmine politics in "Interdenominationalism, Clericalism, Pluralism: The Zentrumsstreit and the Dilemma of Catholicism in Wilhelmine Germany," *Central European History* 21 (1988): 350–78. Konrad Jarausch cites rising prejudice toward ultramontane Catholics among Protestant university students in *Students, Society, and Politics in Imperial Germany: The Rise of Academic Illiberalism* (Princeton: Princeton University Press, 1982), 377–79.

8. For an exhaustive review of the older literature, see Rudolf Morsey, "Bismarck und der Kulturkampf: Ein Forschungs- und Literaturbericht, 1945–1957," *Archiv für Kulturgeschichte* 39 (1957), 232–70; and idem, "Probleme der Kulturkampf-Forschung," *Historisches Jahrbuch* 83 (1964), 217–43. See also the extensive bibliographic notes in Rudolf Lill, "Der Kul-

Otto von Bismarck as first minister of Prussia and chancellor of the empire have argued that the Kulturkampf was part of a manipulative strategy to ally liberal members of the Prussian parliament and the Reichstag with the state and imperial governments. By offering the Catholics as a target for liberal hostility, the chancellor hoped to divert attention away from the demand for constitutional-political reform. Josef Becker's work exemplifies much of this instrumental and top-down perspective, arguing that "the chancellor imagined himself a 'political chess player,' holding together the splintering inclinations of the liberal parties in the empire by means of a slogan appealing to wide circles, a sort of outcry against popery, in order to corrupt liberalism, the strongest parliamentary force, through the Kulturkampf and to divert it from its constitutional-political goals."[9] Studies that, on the other hand, stress the role of liberal politicians have also for the most part studied the church-state conflict as an aspect of parliamentary politics. Gustav Schmidt, for example, argues that liberal parliamentarians saw the Kulturkampf as an opportunity to solidify their political program, to force the chancellor to depend on liberal support, and to break the political power of the clergy in order to ensure parliamentary majorities.[10]

Other works even as they moved beyond parliamentary politics have retained the traditional focus on Bismarck at the center of the church-state conflict. Heinrich Bornkamm, for example, in his account of the ostensibly ideological origins of the conflict, concluded finally, "the Kulturkampf, despite all associated influences, was Bismarck's per-

turkampf in Preußen und im deutschen Reich (bis 1878)," in *Handbuch der Kirchengeschichte*, ed. Herbert Jedin (Freiburg im Breisgau: Herder, 1973), 28–47. The most extensive treatment of the Kulturkampf remains Johannes B. Kissling, *Geschichte des Kulturkampfes im deutschen Reiche*, 3 vols. (Freiburg im Breisgau: Herder, 1911–16).

9. Josef Becker, *Liberaler Staat und Kirche in der Ära von Reichsgründung und Kulturkampf: Geschichte und Strukturen ihres Verhältnisses in Baden, 1860–1876* (Mainz: Matthias Grünewald Verlag, 1973), 375–76. See also Michael Stürmer, *Regierung und Reichstag im Bismarckstaat, 1871–1880: Cäsarismus oder Parlamentarismus* (Düsseldorf: Droste Verlag, 1974), 87.

10. Gustav Schmidt, "Die Nationalliberalen—eine regierungsfähige Partei? Zur Problematik der inneren Reichsgründung, 1870–1878," in *Die deutschen Parteien vor 1918: Parteien und Gesellschaft im konstitutionellen Regierungssystem*, ed. Gerhard A. Ritter (Cologne: Kiepenheuer und Witsch, 1973), 208–23. Dieter Langewiesche's account of the Kulturkampf also argues that the campaign was in part an attempt to bind Bismarck to the liberals. Dieter Langewiesche, *Liberalismus in Deutschland* (Frankfurt am Main: Suhrkamp Verlag, 1988), 182. As Jonathan Sperber notes, these two explanations—one specifying the role of the state, the other the motivation of the liberals—are not mutually exclusive. Each could have promoted the church-state conflict in order to increase its influence over the other. Sperber, *Popular Catholicism*, 208.

sonal work."[11] Studies that opened up the deeply nationalist character of the Kulturkampf see it as primarily an attempt by Bismarck to "Germanize" the Catholic peripheral populations, particularly the Polish-speaking nationalist population in the east.[12] Marjorie Lamberti argues Bismarck conceived of school reform under the Kulturkampf as a weapon to combat the political activity of the Catholic clergy in the Polish-speaking areas of Posen, Upper Silesia, and West Prussia.[13] Studies of the Catholic Church and local and regional studies have more successfully moved beyond the focus on Bismarck at the center of the Kulturkampf. Christoph Weber's wide-ranging institutional study of the church has taken the historiography of the Kulturkampf into the inner politics of the church hierarchy and the Vatican.[14] Norbert Schloßmacher's study of Düsseldorf, Karl Rohe's study of the Ruhr area, and Ute Olliges-Wieczorek's study of Münster are examples of works that examine the Kulturkampf at the level of local and regional politics and political organization.[15] Together they have been able to demonstrate the distinctive politicizing effects of the Kulturkampf on municipal affairs and the Catholic Center Party. Meanwhile, in an especially rich local and regional study of Constance, Gert Zang and others broke new ground with a structural and socioeconomic analysis of liberalism and the Kulturkampf in the Grand Duchy of Baden prior to the church-state conflict in Prussia and the empire.[16] With a sustained campaign against the Catholic Church and particu-

11. Heinrich Bornkamm, "Die Staatsidee im Kulturkampf," *Historische Zeitschrift* 179 (1950): 41–72, 273–306; the quotation is from the edition appearing as *Die Staatsidee im Kulturkampf* (Darmstadt: Wissenschaftliche Buchgesellschaft, 1969), 59. See also Adolf Birke, "Zur Entwicklung und politischen Funktion des bürgerlichen Kulturkampfverständnisses in Preußen-Deutschland," in *Aus Theorie und Praxis der Geschichtswissenschaft: Festschrift für Hans Herzfeld zum 80. Geburtstag,* ed. Dietrich Kurze (Berlin: de Gruyter, 1972), 257–79; and Winfried Becker, "Kulturkampf und Zentrum: Liberale Kulturkampf-Positionen und politischer Katholizismus," in *Innenpolitische Probleme des Bismarck-Reiches,* ed. Otto Pflanze (Munich: R. Oldenbourg, 1983), 47–71.

12. Lech Trzeciakowski, *The "Kulturkampf" in Prussian Poland* (New York: Columbia University Press, 1990); Richard Blanke, "The Polish Role in the Origin of the Kulturkampf in Prussia," *Canadian Slavonic Papers* 25 (1983): 253–62; Zygmunt Zielinski, "Der Kulturkampf in der Provinz Posen," *Historisches Jahrbuch* 101 (1981): 447–61.

13. Marjorie Lamberti, "State, Church, and the Politics of School Reform during the Kulturkampf," *Central European History* 19 (1986): 63–81.

14. Christoph Weber, *Kirchliche Politik zwischen Rom, Berlin und Trier 1876–1888: Die Beilegung des preußischen Kulturkampfes* (Mainz: Matthias Grünewald Verlag, 1970).

15. Norbert Schloßmacher, *Düsseldorf im Bismarckreich: Politik und Wahlen, Parteien und Vereine* (Düsseldorf: Schwann, 1985); Karl Rohe, *Vom Revier zum Ruhrgebiet* (Essen: Hobbing, 1986); Ute Olliges-Wieczorek, *Politisches Leben in Münster: Parteien und Vereine im Kaiserreich (1871–1914)* (Münster: Ardey Verlag, 1995).

16. Gert Zang, ed., *Provinzialisierung einer Region: Regionale Unterentwicklung und liberale Politik in der Stadt und im Kreis Konstanz im 19. Jahrhundert. Untersuchungen zur*

larly its charitable organizations, which liberals believed drained economic capital and encouraged moral dependence, Constance liberals
launched a progressive program for social improvement, commercial
development, and political autonomy. In a collection of essays important not only for the Kulturkampf but for the history of German liberalism, the campaign against the church takes on larger cultural-politi-
cal life and social and economic dimensions that are often sorely
lacking in narrow political interpretations of the church-state conflict.

Even this cursory review suggests the volume and range of work on
the Kulturkampf. But even as historians have acknowledged the
importance of this work, they have continued to regard the Kulturkampf as an underresearched topic and enduring riddle in the history of nineteenth-century Germany. The most recent account continues to point out that the Kulturkampf itself "remains among the least
understood problems of modern German history."[17] Parallel to the
work on the Kulturkampf, there has been a persistent sense that many
rich and interesting questions about the conflict have not been pursued.[18] The best recent work on the anti-Catholic campaign has, therefore, opened up fresh perspectives, training attention on previously

Entstehung der bürgerlichen Gesellschaft in der Provinz (Frankfurt am Main: Syndikat, 1978).
For work on the Kulturkampf in Baden, see also Becker, *Liberaler Staat und Kirche;* Lothar
Gall, *Der Liberalismus als regierende Partei: Das Grossherzogtum Baden zwischen Restaura-
tion und Reichsgründung* (Wiesbaden: F. Steiner, 1968); idem, "Die partei- und
sozialgeschichtliche Problematik des badischen Kulturkampfes," *Zeitschrift für die
Geschichte des Oberrheins* 113 (1965): 151–96.

17. Ross, *Failure of Bismarck's Kulturkampf,* 3.

18. Examples that run parallel to the development of the historiography of nineteenth-century Germany: "The statement . . . that the Kulturkampf for historical research remains 'the
most perplexing chapter' of Bismarckian domestic politics continues to be true." Birke,
"Funktion des bürgerlichen Kulturkampfverständnisses," 257. "The central significance that
the Kulturkampf had for the full, domestic development of Germany has not been at all
understood to its full extent." Gall, "Problematik des badischen Kulturkampfes," 151.
"Despite an abundance of sources that has been available for decades, research on the Kulturkampf . . . to this day has not yet attained a satisfactory result. A 'definitive' general
account ['*abschliessende*' *Gesamtdarstellung*] of this fundamental and significant political,
diplomatic, and spiritual struggle is still missing." Morsey, "Bismarck und der Kulturkampf," 232. "The history of the Prussian-German Kulturkampf is one of those themes
that still has not been thoroughly researched, placed in its larger historical context, and
examined for its effects on the inner disposition of German Catholics in Wilhelmine Germany." Idem, "Probleme der Kulturkampf-Forschung," 217. More recently: The Kulturkampf "remains remarkably under-researched." Blackbourn, "Progress and Piety," 143.
"The popular-cultural aspects of the Kulturkampf and the sometimes near-utopian aspirations invested in it by liberal activists are a neglected dimension in the literature." Geoff Eley,
"Notable Politics, the Crisis of German Liberalism, and the Electoral Transition of the
1890s," in *In Search of a Liberal Germany: Studies in the History of Germany Liberalism from
1789 to the Present,* ed. Konrad H. Jarausch and Larry Eugene Jones (New York: Berg, 1990),
187–216, quotation at 194 n. 17.

unexamined social and cultural dimensions of anti-Catholicism and the anti-Catholic campaign. David Blackbourn broke new ground initially with an important article on the culture of anticlericalism that pitted liberal "progress" against Catholic "backwardness," arguing that the Kulturkampf was more than an episode in church-state relations or Bismarckian political calculations.[19] He broke ground again with his elegant exploration of the cultural meaning of apparitions of the Virgin Mary in the town of Marpingen under the repressive legislation and state coercion of the Kulturkampf.[20] In a work that brings theories of nationalism to the social history and politics of religious conflict in imperial Germany, Helmut Walser Smith examines the Kulturkampf as an attempt to impose on the German population a high culture based on "enlightened Protestantism."[21] By doing so, he has developed an argument that consciously takes distance from the Kulturkampf understood primarily as a liberal or state-sponsored attack on the church. From a social-historical perspective, Ronald J. Ross's study of the failure of state power to prosecute successfully the campaign against the church captures the popular dimensions and social depth of a conflict that had been largely passed over as shallow or unremarkable.[22] Recently, Margaret Lavinia Anderson in her rich and important work on the democratic franchise in imperial Germany has stressed that the Kulturkampf cannot be understood with the politics left out. The Kulturkampf, however much it owed to the clash between radical anticlericalism and fervent ultramontanism, should not be separated from the anxiety that accompanied the introduction of Germany's democratic suffrage.[23] Arguing that the Kulturkampf was predominantly a political not a cultural struggle, Anderson, in fact, brings the historiographical perspectives on the Kulturkampf almost full circle by reasserting the primacy of politics.

Together these recent works demonstrate that histories of modern Germany that either dismiss the Kulturkampf as marginal or accept the Kulturkampf narrowly as an attack directed merely against the institution of the church, clericalism, and the Center Party and not more broadly as a campaign against Catholicism as a way of life are untenable. The Kulturkampf struck deep into the Catholic population,

---

19. Blackbourn, "Progress and Piety."

20. Blackbourn, *Marpingen.*

21. Smith, *German Nationalism.*

22. Ross, *Failure of Bismarck's Kulturkampf.*

23. Anderson, *Practicing Democracy.* See also idem, "The Kulturkampf and the Course of German History," *Central European History* 19 (1986): 82–115.

both its piety and consciousness, so much so that Catholics in response formed a relatively closed subculture. Catholics read their own newspapers, borrowed books from their own libraries, shopped at their own cooperatives, joined their own associations, belonged to their own trade unions, lived in their part of town, subscribed to their own brand of nationalism, and clung to their own worldview. For all their considerable virtues, however, these works also remain bound to the traditional research on anti-Catholicism inasmuch as they examine anti-Catholicism and the campaign against the Catholic Church only after the founding of the empire. Studies focused on the period of the Kulturkampf itself, as important as that period was, enter the history of anti-Catholicism in the nineteenth century in medias res. While most accounts of the Kulturkampf give the impression that the anti-Catholic campaign arose spontaneously and suddenly at the beginning of the 1870s and therefore provide little sense of the wide and deep-running anti-Jesuit, antimonastic, and anti-Catholic hysteria prior to German unification, the groundwork that made the Kulturkampf possible was, in fact, prepared over a period of decades. In contrast to previous work, one of the aims here is to expand the chronological horizon of the Kulturkampf.[24] The anti-Jesuit paranoia, rabid antimonasticism and anticlericalism, and fervent anti-Catholicism that explain the passion of the Kulturkampf developed along with the dramatic revival of popular Catholicism during the 1850s and 1860s. This book argues that grappling with the significance of the anti-Catholic campaign requires an exploration of anti-Catholicism in Germany after the Revolution of 1848 and, therefore, a vision trained on the period well before the inception of Kulturkampf legislation.

Moving the exploration of anticlericalism and anti-Catholicism back to the 1848 Revolution, 1850s, and 1860s opens up the opportunity to reevaluate the nature of German liberalism in the second half of the nineteenth century. By focusing on the liberal obsession with anti-Catholicism particularly in the years before the unification of Germany and the unleashing of the Kulturkampf, this work develops new perspectives on liberalism and liberals in Germany. Over the past three

---

24. Work on the period before the Kulturkampf is of limited usefulness: Adelheid Constabel, ed., *Die Vorgeschichte des Kulturkampfes: Quellen aus dem Deutschen Zentralarchiv* (Berlin: Rütten und Loening, 1956), though valuable, is only a compilation of source material. Erich Schmidt, *Bismarcks Kampf mit dem politischen Katholizismus: Pius IX. und die Zeit der Rüstung 1848–1878* (Hamburg: Hanseatische Verlagsanstalt, 1942), and Erich Schmidt-Volkmar, *Der Kulturkampf in Deutschland 1871–1890* (Göttingen: Musterschmidt, 1962), by the same author, were written by a member of the SS and exhibit a tendency to accept without critical circumspection the judgment of Catholics as "enemies of the empire."

decades, a considerable amount of work has been devoted to the study of the nature and development of liberalism in nineteenth-century Germany. Conceptually much of this can be traced back to a major historiographical debate that opened in the mid-1970s.[25] In a seminal essay, Lothar Gall stressed the importance of the 1848 Revolution in the transformation of liberalism as a political movement. Gall posited that preindustrial German liberalism as a result of the revolution underwent a transition from a constitutional movement committed to a *bürgerliche Gesellschaft* or "classless society of burghers" that was dominated by a large if internally differentiated *Mittelstand* (shopkeepers, artisans, and independent farmers) to a bourgeois ideology that was devoted to economic development and free-market capitalism. As an ideology of bourgeois class interests committed to the preservation of the status quo, liberalism became increasingly vulnerable during the period before the founding of the empire since it was unable to secure support from newly emerging social forces like the labor movement in the 1860s. Provocatively, Gall went so far as to suggest that the character of liberalism had changed so fundamentally that it might not be possible to speak of liberalism at all in Germany after 1850.[26] On this reading, the period coinciding with Germany's industrialization appears as the beginning of the end

25. See the excellent historiographical review in the introduction to Jan Palmowski, *Urban Liberalism in Imperial Germany: Frankfurt am Main, 1866–1914* (Oxford: Oxford University Press, 1999), 1–37, and specifically for the different arguments concerning the change of liberalism, 38–42. See also Hartwig Brandt, "Forschungsbericht: Zu einigen Liberalismusdeutungen der siebziger und achtziger Jahre," *Geschichte und Gesellschaft* 17 (1991): 512–30; Hellmut Seier, "Liberalismus und Bürgertum in Mitteleuropa 1850–1880: Forschung und Literatur seit 1970," in *Bürgertum und bürgerlich-liberale Bewegung in Mitteleuropa seit dem 18. Jahrhundert,* ed. Lothar Gall (Munich: R. Oldenbourg, 1997), 132–229.

26. Lothar Gall, "Liberalismus und 'bürgerliche Gesellschaft': Zur Charakter und Entwicklung der liberalen Bewegung in Deutschland," *Historische Zeitschrift* 220 (1975): 324–56. Gall's thesis, which ran throughout his subsequent work, was an application to German liberalism in general of his groundbreaking regional study of liberalism in Baden from 1848 to 1871, a study in which he carefully described the liberal abandonment of previously cherished ideals in the years before the founding of the empire. Idem, *Der Liberalismus als regierende Partei;* idem, "Liberalismus und Nationalstaat: Der deutsche Liberalismus und die Reichsgründung," in *Bürgertum, liberale Bewegung und Nation: Ausgewählte Aufsätze,* ed. Dieter Hein, Andreas Schulz, and Eckhardt Treichel (Munich: R. Oldenbourg, 1996), 190–202; idem, "'Südenfall' des liberalen Denkens oder Krise der Bürgerlich-Liberalen Bewegung?" in *Liberalismus und imperialistischer Staat: Der Imperialismus als Problem liberaler Parteien in Deutschland, 1890–1914,* ed. K. Holl and G. List (Göttingen: Vandenhoeck und Ruprecht, 1975), 148–58. The idea of a preindustrial liberalism committed to a classless society of citizens is elaborated in the collection of articles in Wolfgang Schieder, ed., *Liberalismus in der Gesellschaft des deutschen Vormärz* (Göttingen: Vandenhoeck und Ruprecht, 1983).

of liberalism; liberalism was not, after all, the ideological path breaker toward modern industrial society.

At the same time, in a thesis even more sharply formulated than Gall's, Michael Gugel argued that in the middle of the century German liberalism lost its original progressive, emancipatory character and became an exclusive, *bürgerlich* class movement. Facing the social consequences of industrialization, namely, the rise of the working class and the demise of the petite bourgeoisie, liberals either rejected or at least reinterpreted their original goals in favor of a defense of their social status. According to Gugel, the liberal political strategy during the constitutional conflict that dominated Prussian political life from 1861 to 1866 is best understood not by the allure of Realpolitik ideology but as a recalculation of socioeconomic interests.[27] Recent local and regional studies of voluntary associations central to the Bürger as a social group have given further specificity and empirical ballast to Gall's thesis. For example, Michael Wettengel's study of the Rhein-Main area argues that the experience of the 1848 Revolution was, at least in the Duchy of Hesse, the Duchy of Nassau, and the Free City of Frankfurt, the decisive break point in the trajectory of liberalism. Here, according to Wettengel, liberals faced with the failure of the revolution and under the pressure of the reactionary decade of the 1850s jettisoned the idealism of the Vormärz and became hard-nosed realists as they constituted new and modern political parties.[28]

Together Gall and Gugel unleashed a spirited debate concerning the course and fate of liberalism in the nineteenth century. Wolfgang J. Mommsen soon argued that both Gall and Gugel idealized the political and social program of preindustrial liberalism and, by limiting the character of early liberalism to a "constitutional movement," masked or distorted liberal social and economic interests.[29] Mommsen pro-

---

27. Michael Gugel, *Industrieller Aufstieg und bürgerliche Herrschaft: Sozioökonomische Interessen und politische Ziele des liberalen Bürgertums im Preußen zur Zeit des Verfassungskonflikts 1857–1867* (Cologne: Pahl-Rugenstein Verlag, 1975).

28. Michael Wettengel, *Die Revolution von 1848/49 im Rhein-Main-Raum: Politische Vereine und Revolutionsalltag im Grossherzogtum Hessen, Herzogtum Nassau und in der Freien Stadt Frankfurt* (Wiesbaden: Historische Kommission für Nassau, 1989), 504. See also Frank Möller, *Bürgerliche Herrschaft in Augsburg 1790–1880* (Munich: R. Oldenbourg, 1998) by one of Gall's students and also a study of voluntary associations, though the argument ultimately does not fit easily into Gall's periodization.

29. Wolfgang J. Mommsen, "Der deutsche Liberalismus zwischen 'klassenloser Bürgergesellschaft' und 'organisierten Kapitalismus': Zu einigen neuern Liberalismusinterpretationen," *Geschichte und Gesellschaft* 4 (1978): 77–90.

posed that the crisis that changed liberalism into a socially conservative ideology came not in 1848–49 or even 1866–67 or 1878–79 but rather only later in the 1880s with the second thrust of industrial development, protective tariff policy, and the dramatic rise of the working class. Under the conditions of "high capitalism," liberalism began its demise, the liberal movement disintegrated, and the classical liberal program lost its persuasive appeal. Meanwhile, in the first synthetic evaluation of German liberalism since Friedrich C. Sell's comprehensive treatment of the theme in 1953, James J. Sheehan examined "the relationship between liberalism and German society" throughout the nineteenth century.[30] In a study of liberal elites, changing social conditions, party politics, election returns, and city and regional contexts, Sheehan explored, as he argued, "the way in which the historical situation narrowed liberals' choices and often precluded alternatives that might have enabled them to save themselves and their ideals."[31] Sheehan described an early liberalism that was not simply dominated by the *Honoratioren* (notables) of the *Bildungsbürgertum*—intellectuals, civil servants, and the economic bourgeoisie—but also included a broadly based and socially diverse Mittelstand. Sheehan supported Gall's argument to the extent that he showed that the social heterogeneity of liberalism in the prerevolutionary period as well as its ideals meant that it was not a class-based movement. Sheehan, however, argued that liberalism began its decline not with the 1848 Revolution but with the founding of the empire in the 1870s. Although liberalism was once a movement of political opposition, liberals now advocated Bismarck's Kulturkampf, foreign policy, and social-economic programs; no longer a movement of the Mittelstand, liberalism alienated Catholics, workers, and ethnic minorities. Sheehan concluded, "By the 1890s,

30. James J. Sheehan, *German Liberalism in the Nineteenth Century* (Chicago: University of Chicago Press, 1978), 2. Sheehan's book was the culmination of a series of interrelated arguments he had been developing over the previous decade: idem, "Deutscher Liberalismus im postliberalen Zeitalter, 1890–1914," *Geschichte und Gesellschaft* 4 (1978): 29–48; idem, "Liberalism and the City in Nineteenth Century Germany," *Past and Present* 51 (1971): 116–37; idem, "Liberalism and Society in Germany, 1815–48," *Journal of Modern History* 45 (1973): 583–604; idem, "Partei, Volk, and Staat: Some Reflections on the Relationship between Liberal Thought and Action in Vormärz," *Sozialgeschichte Heute,* ed. Hans-Ulrich Wehler (Göttingen: Vandenhoeck und Ruprecht, 1974), 162–74; idem, "Political Leadership in the German Reichstag, 1871–1918," *American Historical Review* 74 (1968): 511–28. Sell described the history of German liberalism, tied as it was to the history of Germany as a whole, as a "tragedy" that culminated in 1933, an assessment that was enormously important for subsequent studies of liberalism. Friedrich C. Sell, *Die Tragödie deutschen Liberalismus* (Stuttgart: Deutsche Verlags-Anstalt, 1953).

31. Sheehan, *German Liberalism,* 3.

their dreams emptied by frustration, dissension, and defeat, the liberals receded to the fringes of political life."[32]

As historians continued to debate the location of the "decisive" turning point in the course of German liberalism, the debate itself took a turn with a stimulating critique by David Blackbourn and Geoff Eley of dominant interpretations in current German historiography. They together exposed as a myth the established notion of a *Sonderweg* or unique course of German historical development and, as they did so, pushed the watershed for German liberalism even further back in the nineteenth century.[33] The significance of the Sonderweg debate has been well rehearsed. As is well known, historians who advocate the Sonderweg thesis argue that an insufficient legacy of liberalism in general and the abortive Revolution of 1848 in particular meant that Germany in the second half of the nineteenth century failed to establish within society the liberal and democratic foundations that developed in other Western countries at that time. According to these historians, preindustrial elites retained their privileged positions within a political autocracy. At the same time, the liberal desire for political reform was silenced by the national unification they themselves had been unable to achieve; culturally and socially the bourgeoisie was feudalized and then distracted by a "social imperialist" policy of manipulation from above.[34] Blackbourn and Eley contend that this interpretation of German deviant develop-

---

32. Ibid., 273. After his initial reply to Gall's thesis, Mommsen seemed to agree with Sheehan that the period 1870 to 1890 was decisive in the transition of liberalism: "The period between about 1870 and 1890 must be seen as the final phase in the history of bourgeois liberalism, at any rate at the level of the state." Wolfgang J. Mommsen, "Society and State in Europe in the Age of Liberalism, 1870–1890," in *Imperial Germany, 1867–1918: Politics, Culture, and Society in an Authoritarian State* (London and New York: Arnold, 1995), 57–74, quotation at 65. This essay was first published as "Gesellschaft und Staat im liberalen Zeitalter: Europa 1870–1890," in *Der autoritäre Nationalstaat: Verfassung, Gesellschaft und Kultur des deutschen Kaiserreiches* (Frankfurt am Main: Fischer Taschenbuch, 1990), 86–108.

33. David Blackbourn and Geoff Eley, *The Peculiarities of German History: Bourgeois Society and Politics in Nineteenth-Century Germany* (Oxford: Oxford University Press, 1984), published originally as David Blackbourn and Geoff Eley, *Mythen deutscher Geschichtsschreibung: Die gescheiterte bürgerliche Revolution von 1848* (Frankfurt am Main and Berlin: Ullstein Materialien, 1980).

34. The most prominent proponent of the Sonderweg interpretation was Hans-Ulrich Wehler in *Das deutsche Kaiserreich, 1871–1918* (Göttingen: Vandenhoeck und Ruprecht, 1973), appearing in English as idem, *The German Empire, 1871–1918,* trans. K. Traynor (Leamington Spa: Berg, 1985), and idem, *Deutsche Gesellschaftsgeschichte,* vol. 3, *Von der "Deutschen Doppelrevolution" bis zum Beginn des Ersten Weltkrieges, 1849–1914* (Munich: C. H. Beck, 1987–96). Other influential work that developed this approach included Ralf Dahrendorf, *Society and Democracy in Germany* (New York: W. W. Norton, 1967); and Barrington Moore, *The Social Origins of Dictatorship and Democracy* (Boston: Beacon, 1966).

ment rested on a normative, ahistorical, and misconceived comparison with the French, English, and American experiences.

Just as important, Blackburn and Eley argue that the fixation of historians on the defeat of the 1848 Revolution has blinded them to the considerable accomplishments of German liberals in the nineteenth century. Despite the political failures of the 1848 Revolution, the compromise of constitutional reform, and the realignment with protective tariffs, German liberals nonetheless waged an economic, social, and cultural "silent revolution." They achieved many of their most important objectives in the domain of civil society, particularly during the 1850s and 1860s, and successfully established the "hegemony of the bourgeoisie." Only in the 1890s, according to Blackbourn and Eley, did the traditional solidarities of liberal *Honoratiorenpolitik* (politics of notables) finally give way to a new style of mass, nationalist politics.[35] Faced with the more complex and fragmented array of political constituencies in the final decade of the century, the National Liberals, unlike the Conservatives and the Catholic Center Party, failed to create popular organizations that included workers, the peasantry, and the Mittelstand. The liberal parties ultimately proved, Blackbourn and Eley argue, unable to keep pace with the dramatic rise in voter turnout that favored the parties to the right.[36]

Historians have by now criticized the German Sonderweg from different theoretical, methodological, and empirical perspectives so successfully that the interpretation no longer dominates contemporary

For one of the first essays critical of the notion of a Sonderweg, see Thomas Nipperdey, "Wehler's 'Kaiserreich': Eine kritische Auseinandersetzung," *Geschichte und Gesellschaft* 1 (1975): 539–60. Among the best surveys of the debate are Roger Fletcher, "Recent Developments in West German Historiography: The Bielefeld School and Its Critics," *German Studies Review* 7 (1984): 451–80; Robert G. Moeller, "The Kaiserreich Recast? Continuity and Change in Modern German Historiography," *Journal of Social History* 17 (1984): 655–83; and James Retallack, "Social History with a Vengeance? Some Reactions to H.-U. Wehler's 'Das Deutsche Kaiserreich,'" *German Studies Review* 7 (1984): 423–50.

35. Blackbourn and Eley also reevaluate the Sonderweg and posit the 1890s as a major shift in political alignments in, respectively, Blackbourn, *Class, Religion, and Local Politics;* Geoff Eley, *Reshaping the German Right: Radical Nationalism and Political Change after Bismarck* (New Haven: Yale University Press, 1980); and idem, "Notable Politics." See also the collection of essays in Richard J. Evans, *Society and Politics in Wilhelmine Germany* (London: Croom Helm, 1978).

36. Jonathan Sperber's examination of elections throughout the imperial period substantiates Blackbourn's and Eley's identification of the 1890s as a decade of considerable movement between parties, marking a break from Bismarckian election patterns. At the same time he concludes in contrast to Blackbourn and Eley that voter turnout declined during the Reichstag elections of the 1890s. Jonathan Sperber, *The Kaiser's Voters: Electors and Elections in Imperial Germany* (Cambridge: Cambridge University Press, 1997).

German historiography.[37] Even so, it continues to serve as a conceptual touchstone, often implicit, that historians use to order debate about fundamental aspects of nineteenth- and twentieth-century German society, politics, and culture, particularly the course of liberalism.[38] In a comprehensive examination of liberalism as ambitious as Sheehan's, Dieter Langewiesche focuses not on a special variant of German liberalism but on liberalism in Germany, a reorientation consciously recorded in the title of his book.[39] In this work and in a string of subsequent essays, Langewiesche argues that liberalism in Germany can be understood only if every change is not equated with a deviation from its original goals.[40] He emphasizes continuities within liberalism over the course of the century: early liberalism may have shifted from a utopian vision of a classless society of citizens to an increasingly bourgeois ideology at midcentury, but at the same time basic tenets, including optimism; an orientation to the future; and a commitment to progressive reform, most notably education, remained intact. In Langewiesche's nuanced evaluation, liberalism was not characterized by a simple linear demise; despite failures beyond 1871 liberal ideas continued to pervade German society and influenced the prevailing political culture. Liberal parties helped lay the legal, social, and economic foundations of the nation-state and helped establish the infra-

37. Even Jürgen Kocka and Hans-Ulrich Wehler, two principal proponents of the Sonderweg thesis, have retracted much of their original point of view. Jürgen Kocka, ed., *Bürgertum im 19. Jahrhundert: Deutschland im europäischen Vergleich* (Munich: Deutscher Taschenbuch Verlag, 1988), 58; idem, "Germany before Hitler: The Debate about the German *Sonderweg,*" *Journal of Contemporary History* 23 (1988): 3–16. Hans-Ulrich Wehler, "Deutsches Bildungsbürgertum in vergleichender Perspektive: Elemente eines 'Sonderwegs'?" in *Bildungsbürgertum im 19. Jahrhundert: Politischer Einfluß und gesellschaftliche Formation,* ed. Jürgen Kocka (Stuttgart: Klett-Cotta, 1989), 215–37.

38. For a general reappraisal of German liberals, see Elizabeth Fehrenbach, *Verfassungsstaat und Nationsbildung 1815–1871* (Munich: R. Oldenbourg, 1992); for liberal achievements, particularly the rule of law in civil society, see Michael John, *Politics and the Law in Late Nineteenth-Century Germany: The Origins of the Civil Code* (Oxford: Oxford University Press, 1989); and for a regional study that challenges the traditional concept of "unpolitical" liberals, Rudy Koshar, *Social Life, Local Politics, and Nazism: Marburg, 1880–1935* (Chapel Hill: University of North Carolina Press, 1986).

39. Langewiesche, *Liberalismus in Deutschland.*

40. These essays include Dieter Langewiesche, "Bildungsbürgertum und Liberalismus im 19. Jahrhundert," in *Bildungsbürgertum und Liberalismus im 19. Jahrhundert. Part 4, Politische Einfluß und gesellschaftliche Formation,* ed. Jürgen Kocka (Stuttgart: Klett-Cotta, 1989), 95–121; idem, "German Liberalism in the Second Empire, 1871–1914," in *In Search of a Liberal Germany: Studies in the History of German Liberalism from 1789 to the Present,* ed. Konrad H. Jarausch and Larry Eugene Jones (New York: Berg, 1990), 217–35; idem, "The Nature of German Liberalism," in *Modern Germany Reconsidered, 1870–1945,* ed. Gordon Martel (London: Routledge, 1992), 96–116.

structures necessary for modern life in the cities. In fact, politically left liberalism experienced a remarkable revival in the first years of the twentieth century before the collapse of the empire in 1918. Only during the Weimar years was liberalism discredited before, according to Langewiesche, it was finished off by the Nazi rise to power in 1933.

Similarly, Konrad H. Jarausch and Larry Eugene Jones have also revised the account of liberal development through the nineteenth century to the post-1945 period.[41] Together they argue that the course of liberalism is not characterized by one decisive break; rather it exhibits an uneven pattern with "peaks of success" and "valleys of disappointment and failure" that do not coincide with previous evaluations. From the French Revolution through the Vormärz, liberal ideas, according to Jarausch and Jones, emerged in a network of voluntary progressive associations in German society. The Revolution of 1848 marked not the ultimate failure of liberalism but a temporary setback from which the liberal movement recovered by the end of the reactionary 1850s. The period from the beginning of the so-called New Era in 1858 to Bismarck's "second founding" of the empire in 1878–79 witnessed not the compromise of liberals with the authoritarian state but the first triumph of liberalism during which liberals were able to launch much of the major legislation including the Kulturkampf of the new empire.

Bismarck's break with the National Liberals at the end of the 1870s initiated, Jarausch and Jones argue, a period of fragmentation and decline that lasted until the 1890s. With the turn of the century came not liberal isolation and dissolution in the face of mass, nationalist organizations but a second wave of liberal achievements that culminated in 1919 with the founding of the Weimar Republic. During this period, the progressive parties revitalized themselves by reaching over class and religious lines to social democratic and Catholic constituencies. This period of success was followed by the chaotic course of social, political, and economic developments specific to the Weimar period that together devastated the social basis of the German liberal parties and finally provided the Nazi Party with its electoral triumph. Liberalism experienced a third wave of accomplishment in the postwar period with the establishment of liberal ideas and practices in the

---

41. Jarausch and Jones, "German Liberalism Reconsidered: Inevitable Decline, Bourgeois Hegemony, or Partial Achievement?" in *In Search of a Liberal Germany: Studies in the History of German Liberalism from 1789 to the Present,* ed. Konrad H. Jarausch and Larry Eugene Jones (New York: Berg, 1990), 1–23.

social, economic, and political life of the Federal Republic of Germany. Ultimately, Jarausch and Jones argue that evaluating the course of liberalism requires standards that include not just the electoral performance of its parties but its social and cultural dimensions as well.

The debate concerning the fate of liberalism in Germany seems to have no immediate end in sight; recent research on liberalism at the local level promises to ensure that the debate will only continue. For example, in a study of Frankfurt am Main during the second empire Jan Palmowski evaluates liberals as they actually exercised power at the municipal level of government, the only level at which liberals across Germany had any real political power throughout the empire.[42] He identifies the late 1860s and 1870s as the crucial watershed that witnessed the fundamental politicization of urban government: during this period, which included the founding of local liberal parties, politics took on the characteristics that lasted in their essentials well into the Weimar Republic. As urban liberal leaders pushed through major reforms, they proved themselves politically astute, innovative, and prepared when necessary to compromise—behavior, Palmowski argues, that indicates their vitality, proves their realism, and refutes the image of German "unpolitical" notables.

In short, historians of German liberalism have argued for a fundamental change in liberal ideology after midcentury while disagreeing as to precisely when this transition took place. In a series of often mutually contradictory accounts, they have located the "decisive" turning point(s) and period(s) of success and failure in virtually every decade from the Revolution of 1848 to the Weimar Republic. Most argue that change for either better or worse was due to one or more seminal events: the defeat of the Revolution of 1848, the years of repression in the conservative decade of reaction, capitalist economic prosperity, the constitutional conflict of the mid-1860s, the success of Bismarck's "Blood and Iron," the allure of Realpolitik, and Bismarck's break with the National Liberals in 1878–79. Clearly all of these events had a major impact on liberals, liberal practice, and liberal theory in the second half of the nineteenth century. But we miss an important part of the development of liberalism as a political ideology, as a social vision, and as a self-identity as long as the issues and terms remain fixed on middle-class prosperity with the economic boom of the 1860s, the con-

---

42. Palmowski, *Urban Liberalism.*

stitutional battle, the success of the wars of unification, the split of the liberals with the "second founding" of the empire, and the fate of Honoratiorenpolitik. As important as these factors were in themselves, liberalism in the second half of the century cannot be understood with reference alone to political and economic pressures.

If so, then Dagmar Herzog's study of religious politics in prerevolutionary Baden, exploring liberalism from a decidedly different angle, opens up opportunities to reevaluate liberalism in Germany.[43] Rooted in feminist theory and literary criticism, Herzog focuses on the discursive relationships that tied together and reshaped controversies over ecclesiastical authority, Jewish emancipation, and women's rights. In reaction to Catholic conservatives' intransigent policy regarding clerical celibacy and marriage between Protestants and Catholics, many liberals embraced the cause in general of religious dissenters and in particular the antiultramontane *Deutschkatholiken* (German Catholics). Support of the religious rights of Deutschkatholiken and opposition to Catholic hard-line orthodoxy, not commitment to universal equality, compelled liberals to accept Jewish emancipation. However, the terms in which liberals accepted Jewish emancipation contributed to the persistence of anti-Jewish prejudice. The liberal paradox is likewise evident in the attitudes of Deutschkatholiken toward women's rights. The *deutschkatholisch* attitude, like the mainstream liberal notion of gender equality, was undermined by an insistence on gender difference that excluded women from genuine emancipation.[44] Not only salient political and economic themes, therefore, but also private matters of intimacy such as faith, marriage, and sex reshaped the liberal political agenda in prerevolutionary Baden. These arguments may together amount to a reorientation of the more traditional study of liberalism. Since they are, however, limited to the Vormärz and to Baden, it remains to be seen whether they apply generally to liberalism in Germany in the nineteenth century. Indeed, since Herzog focuses on Deutschkatholiken, a small minority among liberals in the duchy, it is not clear that her conclusions are representative of liberalism even in Baden in the Vormärz.[45]

43. Dagmar Herzog, *Intimacy and Exclusion: Religious Politics in Pre-Revolutionary Baden* (Princeton: Princeton University Press, 1996).

44. "Liberalism," Herzog concludes, "was part of the problem." Ibid., 82. See also 58.

45. Baden may also be an unlikely place for a case study of Deutschkatholiken. Most of the early deutschkatholisch congregations were located in Saxony, and the largest congregation was, in fact, located in Breslau in Prussia, where some one thousand people signed a

The perspective according to which modern liberal ideology masks a deep authoritarian strain that can be traced to the totalizing utopian project of the Enlightenment bears on anti-Catholicism in the nineteenth century and offers ways to rethink particularly the Kulturkampf. Ultimately, most historians have tried to account for the Kulturkampf by explaining it away: the Kulturkampf with its intolerance and state coercion, they argue, amounts to a mistake along the liberal trajectory of the nineteenth century.[46] They dismiss the Kulturkampf as a betrayal of the ideal of universal rights, a moment of liberal absentmindedness or acquiescence to Bismarckian manipulation during which, in either case, liberals abandoned their cherished principles. Even on its own terms the explanation for the Kulturkampf as a liberal "accident" seems unsatisfactory on three counts. First, the liberal hatred of Catholics that culminated in the Kulturkampf was too deep, too intense, and too abiding to be simply a mistake. Second, accounting for the Kulturkampf as a misguided departure from the presumably normative course of liberalism forecloses further critical inquiry into the origins of the Kulturkampf and the nature of liberalism. Finally, as recent scholarship has emphasized, presupposing a normative course as against a deviant one for the development of German liberalism in the nineteenth century is ahistorical: liberal ideology was what it was in any given historical period, not what it should have been. The Kulturkampf was not due to the liberals' insufficient commitment to their own creed. Nor was it the case that German liberals

declaration of membership at the congregation's founding in early 1845 and over eight thousand belonged by 1847. Herzog also gives considerable space to Louise Dittmar, herself an exceptionally radical feminist for the time, and since she did not live in Baden and she did not publish her works there (she merely gave several addresses at the small Monday Club at the very end of the Vormärz in 1847), it is unlikely that Dittmar had a major impact on the formulation of Badenese prerevolutionary liberalism. Fundamental questions therefore remain regarding the formation of liberal identity and ideology in nineteenth-century Germany.

46. As examples, see Bornkamm, *Die Staatsidee im Kulturkampf,* 18; Gordon A. Craig, *Germany, 1866–1945* (New York: Oxford University Press, 1978), 77–78; Hajo Holborn, *A History of Modern Germany, 1840–1945* (Princeton: Princeton University Press, 1982), 2:264; Lill, "Der Kulturkampf in Preußen," 38; Otto Pflanze, *Bismarck and the Development of Germany* (Princeton: Princeton University Press, 1990), 2:178; Schmidt, "Die Nationalliberalen," 214. For exceptions, see the comments in Geoff Eley, "Bismarckian Germany," in *Modern Germany Reconsidered, 1870–1945,* ed. Gordon Martel (London: Routledge, 1992), 1–32; idem, "State Formation, Nationalism, and Political Culture in Nineteenth-Century Germany," in *Culture, Ideology, and Politics: Essays for Eric Hobsbawm,* ed. Raphael Samuel and Gareth Stedman Jones (London: Routledge, 1982), 277–301; and Smith, *German Nationalism,* 37–41.

were endowed with an inadequate Enlightenment legacy. On the contrary, the German liberals who were *Kulturkämpfer* (culture warriors) against the Catholic Church and Catholicism were passionately dedicated to their ideals and incessantly referenced the Enlightenment for inspiration and orientation. From the perspectives of cultural studies, the issue is rather that intolerance, specifically anti-Catholic intolerance, was, I argue, integral to liberalism in the second half of the nineteenth century.

Understanding why this was so requires recognizing a specific cognitive process of identity formation that placed anti-Catholicism at the center of liberal ideology and practice in the second half of the century. After the defeat of the 1848 Revolution, when liberals faced oppression and ultimately worried about their own continued relevance in the conservative decade of reaction, they found themselves in a crisis of purpose and identity that required critical reevaluation, associational reorganization, and cultural-ideological reorientation. In the context of the dramatic Catholic missionary campaign and the revival of popular Catholicism taking place all over Germany, the liberal response was to develop new anticlerical and anti-Catholic rhetorical metaphors and practices that by means of differentiation and contrast proved powerful ways to define and assert the bourgeois claim to social hegemony. During the New Era after 1858, the liberals' stigmatization of Jesuits, priests, monks, and Catholics as stupid, medieval, superstitious, feminine, and un-German helped orient their vision of German society toward modern rationalism, bourgeois individualism, high industrialization, free-market capitalism, the unified nation-state, and gender-specific public and private spheres. By examining the formation of liberal identity and the liberal prescription for German society after the defeat of the revolution and during the resurgence of popular Catholicism, this book identifies the moral, social, and cultural imperatives behind the Kulturkampf of the 1870s. The Kulturkampf emerges in this light not as an exception to liberal principles but as the culmination of liberal demands for a modern German political, economic, social, and sexual order. Anti-Catholic intolerance was not derivative but constitutive of liberalism; it was not an ancillary expression but, on the contrary, at the core of liberalism in Germany.

Outline of the Argument

Two conceptual precepts inform the course of this work. First, liberalism is understood here not simply as a political movement and set of economic principles but more broadly, as Konrad Jarausch and Larry Eugene Jones have argued, as also a body of cultural attitudes and social practices. As culture, "liberalism existed as a powerful cluster of related ideas and principles that helped legitimate bourgeois claims to social and political hegemony."[47] At the center of this cluster was the idea of the individual free from any restriction to the development of personality. "Directed against the unholy trinity of feudalism, absolutism, and religious orthodoxy, this ideal posited the cultivation of human reason and the development of the human intellect as the highest goal of all cultural activity."[48] Different aspects of German liberalism—a belief in a bürgerlich social order, a constitutional though not necessarily parliamentary state, a historically grounded belief in civil and human rights, a belief in reform within rather than emancipation from the state, a belief in private property and rights—were all embraced by the idea of *Bildung,* the cultivation of the human intellect and spirit. For German liberals Bildung was the defining characteristic of men as individuals and as members of civil society. As one historian has argued, German liberals believed "only the *Gebildete* [cultivated man] was competent to participate 'reasonably' in public discourse, and only the Gebildete could become an 'autonomous personality'— the highest credo in liberal thinking."[49] Living a liberal life, however, entailed more than simply the cultivation of intellect and independence. It was also, according to Dieter Langewiesche, a historically specific "style of thinking" characterized by an "affinity for the new, an orientation toward the future, a belief in progress toward more freedom, rights, and reason."[50] If liberalism was a culture of rationalism, individualism, independence, Bildung, and progress—the principles in general of liberal modernity—then this study examines liberalism as a historically specific cognitive style in nineteenth-century Germany, a psychological and rhetorical disposition that was, I argue, anti-Catholic.

Second, this study accepts the assumption that words and deeds can produce meanings and identities that transcend in often unexpected

---

47. Jarausch and Jones, "German Liberalism," 22.

48. Ibid.

49. Gangolf Hübinger, *Kulturprotestantismus und Politik: Zum Verhältnis vom Liberalismus und Protestantismus im wilhelminischen Deutschland* (Tübingen: J. C. B. Mohr, 1994), 8. See also Margret Kraul, "Bildung und Bürgerlichkeit," in *Bürgertum im 19. Jahrhundert: Deutschland im europäischen Verlgeich,* ed. Jürgen Kocka and Ute Frevert (Munich: Deutscher Taschenbuch Verlag, 1988), 3:45–73.

50. Langewiesche, "Bildungsbürgertum und Liberalismus," 96.

and unwelcome ways the intentions of their original authors and actors. By tracing the management of images in anti-Catholic texts or mob attacks against Jesuits and monasteries, it is possible to trace liberals working through who they were and what they wanted the German nation to be morally, socially, economically, and culturally. It is also possible, however, to uncover within anti-Catholic discourse and practice the deep level of dysphoria that characterized German liberals' cognitive relationship to Roman Catholics. The confrontation with the resurgence of popular Catholicism after 1848 betrayed complex anxieties among liberals about their capacity to establish a unified, rationalized, scientific, and industrial German nation. In the liberal imagination, the Catholic revival represented a new age of mass culture, political democratization, and women's emancipation, an age seemingly hostile to independent character, Honoratiorenpolitik, and the rational public sphere. The specific terms of anti-Catholicism as an act of creative imagination shaped an identity that was, I argue, riddled with insecurities about the reemerging women's movement; the rise of socialism; the masculine public persona; and, ultimately, the viability of liberalism itself. Liberal men made their own identity, but they did not make it just as they pleased.

These issues and arguments are addressed in thematic chapters organized roughly chronologically from the Catholic Church's reaction to the 1848 Revolution through the dissolution (for all practical purposes) of the liberal and state campaign against the church at the end of the 1870s. Chapter 1 examines the ultramontane Catholic revival that was the context for unprecedented levels of liberal anti-Catholic hysteria. It traces the response of Catholic Church authorities to the chaos they believed had been unleashed by the liberal-sponsored 1848 Revolution against throne and altar, the pillars of social, political, and religious order. In the wake of the revolution, with a feverish crusade of missions and the development of new forms of piety, the Catholic Church dramatically reawakened and mobilized popular Catholicism. While I examine the role of the missions in the Catholic resurgence throughout Germany, the concentration is primarily on the Rhineland, a region that due to its heavily Catholic population has been the focus of previous research on the popular revival.[51] I revisit this region using different source material in order to

---

51. Erwin Gatz, *Rheinische Volksmission im 19. Jahrhundert: Dargestellt am Beispiel des Erzbistums Köln* (Düsseldorf: L. Schwann, 1963); Bernhard Scholten, *Die Volksmission der*

revise previous conclusions about the conduct of the missionary campaign and its impact on popular Catholic culture. In contrast to Jonathan Sperber's work on Rhineland-Westphalia, for example, I show that as the campaign continued into the late 1860s the number of missions did not abate but in fact increased, that the missions were better organized and more systematic than in the 1850s. More important, the church's campaign appears not merely as a bulwark against religious indifference and political radicalism; with their dynamic sermons that pounded audiences with the threat of infernal damnation, hellfire, and brimstone, the missions were instruments of psychological and public terror, traumatizing their audiences and driving them back into the church. By moving beyond the biased reports of clergymen, I also show, again in contrast to Sperber, that though the missions had a profound impact on religiosity, *alltäglich* (everyday) patterns of popular, rural culture remained resilient despite the church's efforts to improve moral conduct.[52]

Chapter 2 examines the impact of the Catholic missions on Protestants and Protestant religious authorities, a topic that has been passed over in the social and religious history of modern Germany. The missions were remarkable "intraconfessional zones" where the different religious populations mixed and reconfessionalized in unprecedented ways. Contrary to the largely unquestioned assumption by historians that the Protestant population was undergoing an unrelenting process of secularization throughout the century (not simply in Germany but across Europe), the evidence indicates that one of the unexpected results of the Catholic missionary campaign was the heavy attendance of Protestants and with it the reawakening of popular Protestant religiosity. At the same time, the response of the Protestant leadership to the Catholic missions and revival was the development of militant anti-Catholicism and anti-Jesuit hysteria in particular. Within this context the chapter explores with close readings of important liberal prescriptive texts how anti-Catholicism could be used to rehabilitate and reorient German liberalism after the shattering events of 1848 and 1849, in the following decade of state repression and during a new age of industrial development. The chapter finally examines the polarization of liberalism and Catholicism by the late 1860s and argues that the Kulturkampf was not simply the expression of traditional Protestant

Redemptoristen vor dem Kulturkampf im Raum der Niederdeutschen Ordensprovinz (Bonn: Hofbauer-Verlag, 1976); Sperber, *Popular Catholicism.*
    52. Ibid., 56–63, 91–98.

anti-Catholicism but a more specifically liberal project for social and cultural reform.[53]

Chapter 3 is a more focused examination of the culture of anticlericalism and anti-Catholicism, concentrating on the relationship between the meaning of antimonasticism and anticonvent hysteria and the liberal reconstruction of self and nation. Liberals like state authorities looked with alarm yet fascination on the dramatic increase in the number of male and female religious orders during the postrevolutionary period. As purported relics from the feudal period in an age that, liberals believed, was supposed to be modern, progressive, and scientific, monasteries and monks across the German landscape served in the imagination as historical artifacts that could orient the middle class culturally in the direction of industrialization, capitalism, productive labor, and nation building. I also look for the production of identity and meaning in the proliferation in widely read liberal journals and newspapers of lurid stories about sexual atrocities in convents. These stories on the one hand serviced bourgeois demands for morbid and prurient entertainment. On the other hand, and more important, fantasies about sexual intrigue in convents and nuns secretly hidden away to rot in dungeons ultimately reveal the complex anxieties that haunted liberals in an age of militant ultramontanism and the authoritarian state. At the end of the 1860s, an attack against a Dominican residence in an industrial suburb of Berlin, a series of antimonastic rallies, and antimonastic petitions delivered to the Prussian parliament expressed by means of contrast liberal expectations for the modern nation-state. The more closely we examine the German liberal relationship to monasteries and more broadly clerics and Catholicism in the nineteenth century, the more we recognize that anti-Catholicism was a rich and elaborate ritual of identity.

Chapter 4 examines the links between anti-Catholicism, prescriptions for public conduct and private domesticity, misogyny, and the Kulturkampf in liberal discourse. For liberal men, the reemergence of the women's movement in the mid-1860s, what contemporaries called the *Frauenfrage* or "women's question," and the demand by women for access to the public were inextricably linked to mass Catholic resurgence. In public Catholics seemed to undermine the principle of separate spheres reserved, according to liberal social and sexual ideology, for feminine domesticity and public masculinity. In this light, the attack on Catholicism emerges as an attempt during a period of dra-

53. This contrasts with Smith, *German Nationalism,* 17–49.

matic change to maintain the social and political status quo between men and women. Helmut Smith reminds readers in his study of nationalism and religious conflict that the Kulturkampf is perhaps best understood as a kaleidoscope changing shape with each shift of perspective.[54] If Smith viewed the Kulturkampf as an episode in the process of German nation building, I turn the lens a notch farther and see a war incited by the women's question, the question concerning the role of women in society and their access to public life, education, professional opportunities, and ultimately politics. Exploring the Kulturkampf as a *Geschlechterkampf,* a contest between men and women, for access to the public sphere allows for a dramatically different evaluation of the origins and meaning of liberal anti-Catholicism, one that moves beyond studies that have argued that the church-state conflict was at bottom a clash between the "modern" outlook of liberal nationalists and "backward" Catholics, an attempt to preserve the autonomy of the state, or a campaign to stem the tide of political Catholicism, though, to be sure, the Kulturkampf was in some measure all of these as well.

The final chapter examines two seminal debates during the Kulturkampf, one concerning the ideological background that defined the legal relationship between church and state and the second concerning the enactment of anti-Jesuit legislation meant to break finally the Catholic missionary campaign that had continued unabated since 1848. As leading liberal legal scholars engaged the *Kirchenfrage,* the question concerning relations between the church and the state, they established the theoretical principles that abrogated the autonomy of the Catholic Church in Prussia guaranteed in the constitution of 1850. They went so far as to argue that the imperatives of freedom and progress ultimately justified, if deemed necessary in the campaign against the political power of Catholicism, amending the constitution in order to rescind the citizen rights of the Catholic population. In the debate concerning the Jesuit law, the exceptional legislation closing the Society of Jesus and suspending the residence rights of German citizens, progressive and national liberals argued that they were pursuing a campaign based on their historical responsibility in the name of freedom, modern culture, and the preservation of the modern state. In their prosecution of Kulturkampf legislation, liberals imagined that civilization itself weighed in the balance and that duty, therefore, demanded of them no less than a war against the Catholic Church. Ultimately this book argues that the Kulturkampf, the culmination of

54. Ibid., 19–20. A kaleidoscope as a metaphor for the Kulturkampf is original to Pflanze, *Bismarck and the Development of Germany,* 2:179.

over twenty years of fervent liberal anti-Catholicism, should be understood not simply as an attack on the Catholic Church as most scholarship has argued but, rather, as a more complex (and, therefore, arguably more interesting) attempt during a period of dramatic pressures for change to preserve an entire moral, political, social, and sexual order. Anti-Catholicism, far from the marginal status to which it is usually consigned, emerges as a central theme in nineteenth-century German politics, society, and culture.

An identity that could manifest such religious disdain, social arrogance, and masculine bravado does not perhaps lend itself well to disinterested analysis. I have tried, nonetheless, to balance this work with an appreciation for the historical specificity of time and place. The period in Germany that this work examines was marked by political revolution, by profound social trauma, by blood shed in warfare for national unification in the form of the empire. This was an age of great surges forward in industry and the economy; the time of the breakthrough of the Industrial Revolution and free-market capitalism; and, despite setbacks and crises, a period of accelerated growth and booming prosperity. It might seem a paradox, but it was, I shall argue, surely no mere coincidence that during this period Catholicism and liberalism were the movements with the greatest vitality and momentum. Despite their incompatibility, the age belonged as much to the one as to the other. Anti-Catholic progressives like Rudolf Virchow and Hermann Schulze-Delitzsch and national liberals like Rudolf von Gneist and Heinrich von Sybel exhibited an irony consonant with their age. Though rabidly intolerant, they were not without redeeming virtues. They were principled, public men who believed in science, progress, and freedom; in the value of the individual and the rule of law; in service to humanity as well as the nation. They were idealists who shouldered together the burdens of remaking a world but shared no less the optimistic conviction despite personal sacrifice that it was worth doing and that it could be done for the better. They were, in short, visionaries of a modern age shaped by humanism and the Enlightenment, an age that could only be by definition, they believed, beyond and without Catholicism.[55] They had apparently very little if any sense that their idealism was their limitation, that they were paradoxically as much bound to as repulsed by Catholicism. This is ultimately, therefore, a study of the problem of anti-Catholicism as a prescription for modernity.

55. For an eloquent statement concerning the current inclination to chastise German liberals and to sentimentalize the Catholic victims of the Kulturkampf, see Blackbourn, *Marpingen*, xxxiv.

CHAPTER 1

Revolution, the Missionary Crusade, and Catholic Revival

In 1848 the European world of the nineteenth century shuddered again. Liberal revolutions, the hallmarks of a modern age of change, erupting in France and the Austrian Empire and in the German and Italian states, rocked the traditional pillars of church and state in Restoration Europe.[1] Liberal nationalists and radical democrats, shouting in assemblies, armed on the barricades, and fighting in the streets, demanded a new kind of citizenship with a voice in government, the establishment of constitutions, and the curtailment of monarchical power. In the German states at the height of the revolution, the liberal and democratic representatives of the demand for change met at the National Assembly convened in the Free City of Frankfurt. In the heady and hopeful months of spring and summer, they planned the political reform and national unification of Germany. In the fall, how-

---

1. For accounts of the revolutions in Europe in 1848 see Priscilla Robertson, *Revolutions of 1848: A Social History* (Princeton: Princeton University Press, 1952); Jonathan Sperber, *The European Revolutions, 1848–1851* (Cambridge: Cambridge University Press, 1994); and Peter N. Stearns, *1848: The Revolutionary Tide in Europe* (New York: W. W. Norton, 1974). For the revolution in Germany see Theodore S. Hamerow, *Restoration, Revolution, Reaction: Economics and Politics in Germany, 1815–1871* (Princeton: Princeton University Press, 1958); Carola Lipp and Wolfgang Kaschuba, *1848—Provinz und Revolution: Kultureller Wandel und soziale Bewegung im Königreich Württemberg* (Tübingen: Tübinger Vereinigung für Volkskunde, 1979); Thomas Nipperdey, *Germany from Napoleon to Bismarck, 1800–1866*, trans. Daniel Nolan (Princeton: Princeton University Press, 1996), 562–63; P. H. Noyes, *Organization and Revolution: Working-Class Associations in the German Revolution of 1848–1849* (Princeton: Princeton University Press, 1966); Jonathan Sperber, *Rhineland Radicals: The Democratic Movement and the Revolution of 1848–1849* (Princeton: Princeton University Press, 1991); Veit Valentin, *Geschichte der deutschen Revolution 1848–1849* (Cologne: Kiepenheuer und Witsch, 1970); Günter Wollstein, *Deutsche Geschichte 1848/49: Gescheiterte Revolution in Mitteleuropa* (Stuttgart: Kohlhammer, 1986).

ever, their work was interrupted when angry crowds stormed the assembly in an effort to oust conservatives and radicalize the revolution. When Prussian troops intervened to restore order, radical democrats threw up barricades throughout the city. Fighting again raged in the streets until the radicals were subdued with artillery barrages and infantry assaults. The violence left some eighty radicals and two conservative members of the National Assembly dead. The street battles and bloodshed in Frankfurt were only part of the wave of democratic demonstrations and radical movements breaking out all across western Germany. In Düsseldorf and Cologne, the largest cities in the Rhineland province of Prussia, red republicans influenced by the revolutionary theories of Karl Marx and Friedrich Engels unleashed anarchy and murder. A short-lived insurrection then erupted to the south in the Grand Duchy of Baden.[2] These were the indications that the revolution, even according to its liberal and democratic fathers, had taken the turn toward lawless terror.

Meanwhile, not much farther up the River Main from the National Assembly in Frankfurt, in the city of Würzburg, a wholly different kind of meeting was taking place in the Kingdom of Bavaria. Here the bishops and archbishops of the dioceses of the Roman Catholic Church convened to assess the tumultuous events erupting across Germany. Together they planned a counterrevolution. The Catholic bishops believed that the revolutions were not merely the result of political movements and social unrest. The revolutions were both cause and effect, they reasoned, of a failure of religion and morality that threatened the church as much as monarchical authority. Ecclesiastical authorities believed that religious and moral erosion was a predictable part of the wear and tear of the everyday business and concerns of life. According to Cardinal von Geissel of Cologne, the trend toward secularization and amorality lay "in the weakness of human nature." "Over the course of time, customs, even if holy and honorable," he explained, "lose the impression with which they were born. The strength of religion and the necessity to live by it have not diminished. But the spirit and heart, overcome by worldly sins, have become worn out and cold. The Christian life has become tepid and deadened."[3]

2. Sperber, *European Revolutions*, 212–15.

3. Cardinal von Geissel, Hirtenschreiben, Erlassen beim Beginn der Fastenzeit, Köln, 25 Jan. 1853, in *Aktenstücke zur Geschichte der Jesuiten-Missionen in Deutschland, 1848–1872*, ed. Bernhard Duhr (Freiburg im Breisgau: Herdersche Verlagshandlung, 1903), 188 (hereafter cited as *Aktenstücke*). This is a rich, indispensable, and neglected collection of church documents, clerical letters, missionary reports, Catholic and Protestant eyewitness accounts,

Church bishops believed, however, that the roots of the crisis ran far
deeper. The people had been "blinded" and "bewildered," "bewitched"
and "bedazzled" by modern and fashionable philosophies: materialism, rationalism, liberalism, and democracy, all propagated, church
leaders claimed, by an endless number of anti-Christian and antisocial
newspapers.[4] Expressing the anxieties of church leaders, Bishop Nikolaus von Weis of Speyer argued to the king of Bavaria that philosophical poisons had brought the country to the edge of ruin: "The belief in
a personal God, creator and keeper of all things, has been frequently
and systematically undermined and destroyed by a false-philosophy
[*Trugphilosophie*]. . . . Christianity has been attacked at its deepest
foundations and has lost its influence on many souls. . . . With the
weakening or destruction of faith in divinely revealed Christianity, the
authority of the church and no less the secular authority have also been
undermined. Both support themselves on the authority and order of
God."[5] Against the storm of "evil powers" and "the spirit of darkness"
that "daily deliver a terrible waste," Bishop Weiss argued that a mighty
dam had to be erected. Otherwise there would be an "unspeakable confusion and a terrible ruination of civil society itself."[6] In a second letter, the bishop argued that the depravity of the Zeitgeist could be
judged by the fact that it was "a mark of enlightenment to eschew religion, to embrace unholy indifference, to deny God and the immortality of the soul as absolute in the life hereafter, and to limit the entire
destiny of man to the pursuit of pleasures on earth."[7] These were sentiments indicative of the culture of crisis that permeated the entire

liberal and conservative newspaper articles, and government and miscellaneous documents
concerning the Jesuit missionary campaign. Also valuable though much less extensive for the
Franciscan missions are the documents collected in Autbert Groeteken, ed., *Die Volksmissionen der norddeutschen Franziskaner vor dem Kulturkampf (1848–1872)* (Münster: Alphonsus
Buchhandlung, 1909) (hereafter cited as *Volksmissionen der norddeutschen Franziskaner*). A
compilation of Protestant declarations attacking the missions and Catholic popular petitions in
defense of the Jesuits can be found in Christoph Moufang, ed., *Aktenstücke betreffend die
Jesuiten in Deutschland* (Mainz: Franz Kirchheim, 1872). For the perspective of a Jesuit active
in the missionary campaign see the biography by Johannes Mundweiler, *P. Georg von Waldburg-Ziel: Ein Volksmissionär des 19. Jahrhunderts* (Freiburg im Breisgau: Herdersche Verlagshandlung, 1906), which includes extensive excerpts from Waldburg-Ziel's diary.
    4. See, for example, Bischof Nikolaus von Weis an den König Max von Bayern, 24 July
1851, *Aktenstücke*, 72–79; Rundschreiben des Bischofs Johann Georg von Münster an die
Geistlichkeit über die Missionsvereine, 31 Dec. 1852, *Aktenstücke*, 181; Bischof Nikolaus von
Weis an den König Max von Bayern, 3 March 1865, *Aktenstücke*, 337.
    5. Bischof Nikolaus von Weis an den König Max von Bayern, Speyer, 24 July 1851, *Akten-
stücke*, 72.
    6. Ibid.
    7. Bischof Nikolaus von Weis an den König von Bayern, 3 March 1865, *Aktenstücke*, 337.

Catholic Church in Germany after the revolution. In 1850 a low-level parish priest in Bonn, a stronghold of liberalism, reported to his bishop, "a significant part of the population has unfortunately . . . not been spared by the spirit of the age, which characterizes itself as the enemy of religion, truth, and morals."[8] Less the consequence of daily life, it was the philosophical poisons of the age, parish clergy believed, that were throwing the German population into ruin.

Whatever the ultimate cause of the revolution, [the bishops who assembled at Würzburg in the fall of 1848 agreed that the church could not stand idly to the side and watch Germany slide into chaos. They therefore committed the church to an extraordinary campaign of "missions for the people" (*Volksmissionen*) to restore faith, obedience, and order among Catholics throughout Germany] The missionary campaign unleashed by the bishops and undertaken by the principal religious orders in Germany was systematic and dramatic, extending across the German states and continuing for over two decades. With hellfire and brimstone sermons that promised damnation for the unrepentant and salvation for the obedient, the missions attracted unprecedented crowds; inculcated a new commitment to church and faith; and rallied the Catholic population in an anti-Enlightenment campaign against materialism, liberalism, and rationalism. However, the Catholic revival that followed in the path of the missionaries was neither smooth nor uniform everywhere. The missionaries not only faced adversaries among state officials, Protestant Church leaders, and liberal and democratic opponents. Just as important, they often encountered pockets of resistance within the Catholic laity and sometimes within the church leadership itself, among the older parish clergy who resented the heavy-handed intrusion of the missionaries. At the same time, the life-style and habits of leisure of the Catholic rural peasantry proved to be remarkably resilient when challenged by the missionaries' attempts to inculcate new sobriety and moral reform. The pace of Catholic repietization also varied by region and in rural and urban areas. It was nonetheless clear to everyone, Roman Catholic and non-Catholic alike, those who greeted the Catholic revival as salvation and those who feared it would ruin Germany, that by the end of the 1860s the church and Catholicism had been reborn as a popular and powerful religious movement with a faithful laity and a new militancy.

8. Pf. von Bonn an den Erzbischof Johannes von Geissel, 28 Aug. 1850, *Aktenstücke,* 34.

The Missionary Crusade

After the German bishops of the Catholic Church met in Würzburg, they quickly prepared their parish clergy for the new missionary crusade to restore Catholicism. In a pastoral letter in early 1850, for example, the bishop of Münster instructed the priests in his diocese, "Among the means approved and recommended by the church to awaken the spirit of penance, to root out corruption, and to stimulate fervor, there is no better, none so reliable based on the recommendation of the church and the experience of the centuries, as the holding of so-called missions for the people. . . . There has never been a time more than our own when such extraordinary means have been necessary, a time of religious indifference and immorality in which more than ever before divine and human laws are being trampled under foot."[9] Later in a letter to the king of Prussia justifying the need for the missions, the clergy of the Diocese of Münster cataloged a depressing array of sins they believed characterized the spirit of the age: "Indifference, depravity, an undermined sense of right, irresolute faith, indecision, treason and fraud, insolence, a spineless anything-goes, and an almost thorough self-interest and selfishness in religious and political matters is the signature of our time which we clergy encounter among the masses."[10]

With the banning of the Jesuit order by papal decree in 1773 the popular missions had disappeared in central Europe. When the order was revived in 1814 with the defeat of Napoleon and the restoration of the monarchical regimes of Europe, state authorities within the German Confederation looked upon the Jesuits with deep suspicion, and the Prussian government did not allow the order within state territorial borders. In Westphalia secular clergy (i.e., clergy living and ministering to the laity "in the world") attempted to revive the missions shortly before the outbreak of revolution. If Roman Catholic authorities were initially equivocal toward or even condemned the revolution, the church nonetheless quickly emerged as one of its principal beneficiaries. The "decree constitution" imposed by the reactionary Brandenburg ministry in the fall of 1848 and then the Prussian constitution of

9. Rundschreiben des Bischofs Johann Georg (Müller) von Münster an sämtliche Herren Pf. des Bistums Münster, 4 Feb. 1850, *Aktenstücke, 8*. See also Karin Jaeger, "Die Revolution von 1848 und die Stellung des Katholizismus zur Problem der Revolution," in *Kirche zwischen Krieg und Friede: Studien zur Geschichte des deutschen Protestantismus,* ed. Wolfgang Huber and Johannes Schwerdtfeber (Stuttgart: Ernst Klett Verlag, 1976), 243–91.

10. Immediatvorstellung der zehn Landkapital des Dioezese Münster an den König von Preußen für die Jesuiten, Münster, 16 Oct. 1852, *Aktenstücke,* 167.

1850 not only granted the church's freedom and independence. They also established a parliament within which Catholic material, political, and spiritual interests could be articulated and defended at the national level. Perhaps even more important for the long-term development of political Catholicism was the push the revolution gave to Catholic associational life and the Catholic press. The Piusverein, founded in Mainz in March 1848, was followed by numerous sister associations in almost every part of Germany; older Catholic organizations like the Bruderschaften and Schützvereine were revitalized, and Germany's Catholic bishops set up the National German Bishops' Conference to pursue political and ecclesiastical issues. The *Rheinische Volkshalle* (replaced by the *Deutsche Volkshalle*) and the *Deutsche Volksblatt* were published in Cologne and Württemberg respectively, and in Mainz the *Mainzer Journal* soon established itself as the most important Catholic periodical. The revolution provided, therefore, opportunities to mobilize, consolidate, and coordinate Catholic opinion in ways hitherto unavailable or unimaginable.[11]

At the same time, additional concordats and conventions between the church and states throughout Germany brought to an end state interference in the ecclesiastical affairs of the Vormärz. In particular, the new political order and church-state agreements guaranteed to the church the right of religious orders to settle freely on German territory and to hold their missions. Now sanctioned by the state, members of the Society of Jesus gathered in Cologne in July 1849. In response to the Würzburg conference they agreed to take up the call of the German bishops and organized an extensive missionary campaign. Jesuits already in the German states were quickly joined by additional members of their order from the United States, Australia, England, France, and Belgium. Other religious orders, including the Redemptorists and Franciscans and to a lesser extent the Capuchins and Lazarists, joined the crusade and organized their own popular missions.[12] In general,

11. Simon Hyde, "Roman Catholicism and the Prussian State in the Early 1850s," *Central European History* 24 (1991): 95–121.

12. Accounts of the Jesuit order and its missionary activities include the work by the Jesuit Bartholomew J. Murphy, *Die Wiederaufbau der Gesellschaft Jesu im Deutschland im 19. Jahrhundert: Jesuiten in Deutschland, 1849–1872* (Frankfurt am Main: Peter Lang, 1985). Enno Kopperschmidt, *Jesuiten Arbeiten: Zur Geschichte des Jesuitenordens in Deutschland von 1866 bis 1872* (Munich: Ludendorff, 1940) is a biased account published by the ultranationalist Lundendorff publishing house during the Nazi period. The accounts of the Redemptorist missions by the Redemptorist Bernhard Scholten, *Volksmission der Redemptoristen;* and idem, *Die Volksmission der Niederdeutschen Redemptoristen und Oblaten während des Kaiserreichs (1873–1918)* (Bonn: Hofbauer-Verlag, 1978) are narrow, institutional accounts. For a more interesting study of the Redemptorist popular missions in Bavaria see the the-

after the revolution and into the early years of the reactionary 1850s, the state greeted the church as a partner against revolutionary agitation, and it granted the church the autonomy it needed to pursue this task.[13]

Starting in 1849 teams of missionaries swept across Germany visiting thousands of villages and towns and major cities from Trier in the Rhineland to Danzig on the Baltic Sea during all seasons of the year. The missions continued uninterrupted for a twenty-three-year period ending in 1872 with the closing of the Jesuits and other religious orders during the Kulturkampf. The role of the missionaries in changing the face of Roman Catholicism in Germany and establishing new patterns of piety—as well as the fervor with which they undertook their crusade—can hardly be overestimated.[14] However, the missions held by the Catholic religious orders across Germany not only revived and reshaped popular German Catholicism. Aside from the brute force of the state, they were also the most important element in the process of counterrevolutionary rollback during the decade of reaction. They initiated a counterrevolutionary, antiliberal, anti-Enlightenment mass religious and cultural movement that served not only the interests of the church but also those of the monarchical state in the conservative decade of reaction.[15]

During the period between the revolution and the founding of the German Empire, the intensity of the missionary crusade as a whole did not slacken. The missions were, in fact, more numerous as well as bet-

matically broader, richly detailed, and more critical work by Otto Weiss, *Die Redemptoristen in Bayern.* For the missions, see 977–1017. See also the work by P. Klemens Jockwig, "Die Volksmission der Redemptoristen in Bayern von 1848 bis 1873: Dargestellt am Erzbistum München und Freising und an den Bistümern Passau und Regensburg; Ein Beitrag zur Pastoralgeschichte des 19 Jahrhunderts," in *Beiträge zur Geschichte des Bistums Regensburg,* ed. Georg Schwaiger and Josef Staber (Regensburg: Verlag des Vereins für Regensburger Bistumsgeschichte, 1967), 41–407. The single source concerning the activities of the Lazarists is Leonhard Dautzenberg, *Geschichte der Kongregationen der Mission in der deutschen Provinz* (Graz, 1911). For the popular missions in the Rhineland see Gatz, *Rheinische Volksmission.*

13. For an account of the cooperation and tensions between the Catholic Church and the Prussian state in the Rhineland, see Weber, *Kirchliche Politik.* For an account of church-state cooperation but at the same time the missions as an instrument of counterrevolution at variance with the counterrevolutionary agitation of the state, see Sperber, *Popular Catholicism,* 99–114. See also idem, "Competing Counterrevolutions: Prussian State and Catholic Church in Westphalia during the 1850s," *Central European History* 19 (1986): 45–62.

14. For the revival of popular Catholicism in Germany after 1850 see Sperber, *Popular Catholicism.* For the popular missions see 56–63. For recent debates on the periodization and interpretation of the Catholic revival in Germany see Anderson, "Piety and Politics."

15. Sperber, "Competing Counterrevolutions." But for a rebuttal see Hyde, "Roman Catholicism and the Prussian State."

ter organized and attended, in the late 1860s than they were during the postrevolution period of reaction.[16] The figures indicate levels of Jesuit, Franciscan, and Redemptorist missionary activity between 1848 and 1872 when the missions were finally brought to a halt by Kulturkampf legislation. Figure 1 gives the number of Jesuit missions held throughout the German states. Figure 2 indicates the number of Franciscan missions in the Prussian dioceses of Breslau, Cologne, Münster, and Osnabrück as well as missions held in the Austrian dioceses of Königsgratz and Olmütz. Between 1849 and 1872 the Franciscans held an additional 20 missions in Paderborn and 30 missions in both Trier and Lüttich dioceses. Figure 3 indicates the number of Redemptorist missions in the Dioceses of Cologne, Limburg, Münster, Paderborn, and Trier. Between 1850 and 1872, the Redemptorists also held 15 missions in the Diocese of Osnabrück, and in addition between 1848 and 1872 they held approximately 700 missions in Bavaria. Figure 4 totals Jesuit, Franciscan, and Redemptorist missionary activity between 1849 and 1872. The Lazarists held an average of 8 to 10 missions each year during this period.[17] Meanwhile, the Capuchins added at least 152 missions from 1853 to 1872.[18] Based on these statistics and excluding hundreds of shorter follow-up missions (*Missionserneuerungen*), the total number of missions by Catholic religious orders held throughout Germany between 1848 and 1872 was at the very least about 4,000.

The missions concentrated on dense Catholic areas. They were also thorough. Within twenty years, for example, every parish in the dioceses of the Rhineland and Westphalia received at least 1 mission, and many received several. Together the Jesuits, Franciscans, and Redemptorists held a mission in almost every one of the 360 parishes in the Diocese of Münster. In the Diocese of Regensburg in Bavaria 88 missions were held from 1850 to 1857, and 67 missions were held from 1860 to 1867. So frequent were the missions in that diocese that the bishop had to assure state authorities there that the frequency of missions was not having a significantly detrimental impact on the region's agricultural productivity.[19]

16. This is in contrast to Sperber's assessment of the missionary activity in the Rhineland. Sperber, *Popular Catholicism,* 57.

17. Scholten, *Volksmission der Redemptoristen,* 108.

18. Ibid., 112.

19. Bischof von Senestrey an den Staatsminister von Gresser, 28 Sept. 1867, *Aktenstücke,* 361–62. An average of 11 missions were held in the Diocese of Regensburg from 1850 to 1857 (16 missions in 1853, 19 in 1854, 18 in 1855, and 15 in 1856), and an average of 8 or 9 missions per year were held from 1860 to 1867.

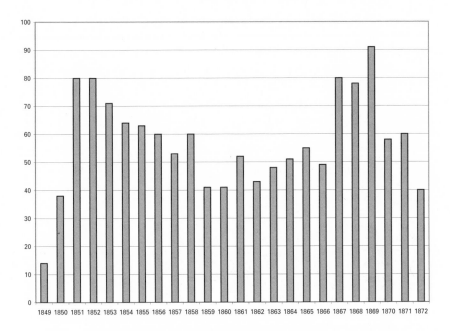

Fig. 1.   **Jesuit missionary activity, 1849–72, dioceses of the German states. (Data from Scholten,** *Die Volksmission der Redemptoristen,* **103 n. 9.)**

The missionaries concentrated their efforts on the towns and villages of the countryside where in 1850 two-thirds of the population still lived. The Jesuits, however, also brought the Catholic revival to large, secularizing cities, including those with slim Catholic minorities like Hamburg, Bremen, and even Berlin. Missionaries usually worked in groups of three, but they might include as many as eight. The missions typically lasted for two weeks. Not only missionaries but also the Catholic laity were on the move all over Germany. From the surrounding areas and from neighboring towns and villages hundreds or thousands of Catholics led in processions by their parish priests journeyed to the mission sites.[20] Towns bulged to four or five times their normal populations. Visitors from outside the community found accommodations in lodges, stayed overnight in the churches, or slept in the churchyards. In 1851, when the Jesuit mission came to the small town of Gabsheim near Mainz, three thousand Catholic pilgrims descended on a popula-

20. See Pf. Huschenbett an Bischof Konrad Martin, 20 Jan. 1859, *Aktenstücke,* 276; Pf. Klütsch an Bischof Wilhelm (Arnoldi) von Trier über die vom 17. Februar bis 2 März abgehaltene Mission, 3 March 1856, ibid., 248.

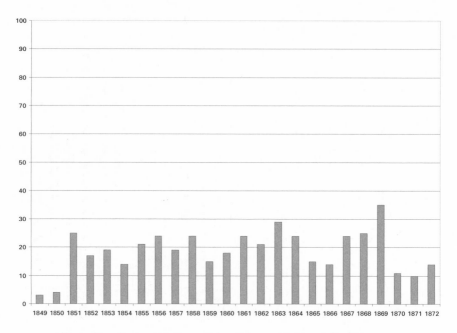

Fig. 2.   Franciscan missionary activity, 1849–72, Dioceses of Breslau, Cologne, Münster, Osnabrück, Königsgratz, and Ölmutz. (Data from Groeteken, *Die Volksmissionen der norddeutschen Franziskaner*, 110–33.)

tion of six hundred. "All the houses and huts were filled with lodgers," reported one Catholic newspaper.[21]

Church authorities did not impose the popular missions on an unwilling population. During the Vormärz many German lay Catholics had crossed from Baden into Alsace and from the western Rhineland into Belgium to participate in the missions held near the borders. Many Catholics were eager now for the missions to be held on German territory. When Franz Joseph Buß, professor of theology at Freiburg University and representative to the National Assembly, finally abandoned the revolution and returned to Baden in the late summer of 1850, hundreds of Catholic men asked him to add his voice to the call for missions to restore faith and morality among the people.[22] Wherever a mission was held, it was an enormously popular, all-

21. *Katholische Sonntagsblatt,* 16 Feb. 1851, *Aktenstücke,* 44.
22. Franz Joseph Buß, *Die Volksmissionen: Ein Bedürfnis unserer Zeit* (Schaffhausen: Hurter, 1850), 152.

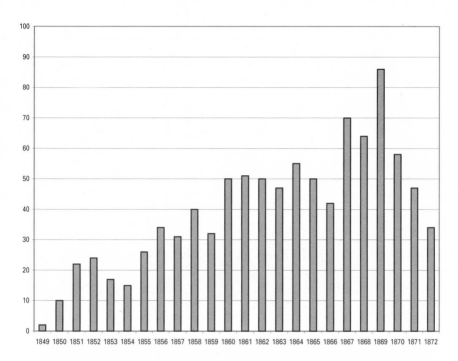

Fig. 3.   Redemptorist missionary activity, 1849–72, Dioceses of Cologne, Limburg, Münster, Paderborn, and Trier. (Data from Scholten, *Die Volksmission der Redemptoristen,* 151.)

consuming event. Work in the fields was suspended, and housework stopped. Factories, businesses, shops, theaters, and schools shut down.[23] Both Catholic and Protestant factory owners shortened or canceled the workday, ordered their workers to go to the missions, and compensated them with full wages.[24] When the Redemptorist mission came to the industrial town of Bottrop near Bochum in 1868, mine and

23. Mission Pf. Nieters an den Bischof Paulus Melchers von Osnabrück, Emden, 5 April 1864, *Aktenstücke,* 318; Pf. Köester an das Bischöfl. General Vikarat Münster, Ölde, 20 Feb. 1850, *Aktenstücke,* 10; Die Missionen im Münsterlände, Oldenburg, 10 Nov. 1850, *Aktenstücke,* 95; Scholten, *Volksmission der Redemptoristen,* 143, 155.

24. Stadtdechant Dilschneider an Kardinal Johannes von Geissel, Aachen, 20 May 1851, *Aktenstücke,* 64; Dekan Rietz an das Generalvikariat Kulm, Mühlbanz, 21 July 1859, *Aktenstücke,* 280.

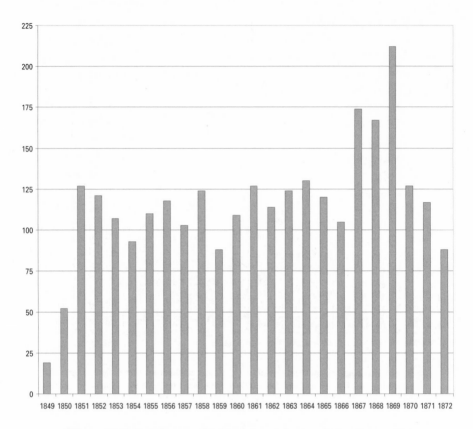

Fig. 4.   Jesuit, Franciscan, and Redemptorist missionary activity, 1849–72. (Data from Groeteken, *Die Volksmissionen der norddeutschen Franziskaner,* 110–33; and Scholten, *Die Volksmission der Redemptoristen,* 103 n. 9, 115.)

factory managers were delighted.[25] In an industrial age requiring new forms of discipline, employers recognized the value of sermons that extolled the virtues of authority and obedience. On the other hand, if the Protestant factory owners in Aachen refused to suspend or to shorten the workday when the mission arrived, Catholic workers literally took matters into their own hands. They simply reset the work clocks so that there would be sufficient time for them to attend the sermons.[26]

The missionaries were part of a well-organized, systematic effort

25. Scholten, *Volksmission der Redemptoristen,* 129.
26. Ibid., 140.

involving cooperation at all levels of the church hierarchy. Bishops plotted the movement of the missions throughout their dioceses, and parish priests prepared their congregations weeks in advance. Local carpenters built extra confessionals. Churches were emptied of their pews to allow for the maximum amount of room. Still, people stood "from the entrance to the steps of the altar, man to man, and head to head."[27] People flooded the churches at four or five in the morning and remained until far into the night. Thousands more often stood outside in the churchyard, straining to hear the sermons and to find a way to enter. When the mission came to Cologne in 1850, as many as sixteen thousand people filled the cathedral.[28] Where the churches were not large enough, sermons and masses were held outside in the churchyard, at the marketplace, or in the town square. Men and women from all social classes participated: according to the Catholic journal *Sion* in 1853, "City as well as country people took the greatest interest. Men and women from all social strata, military and civil officials, university professors, especially the aristocracy eagerly attended."[29] The police commissioner at Koblenz confirmed in his report to the district governor that people "from all classes of the Catholic population" were attending the missions.[30]

The Promise of Hell

The missionaries held mass, heard confessions, and performed exorcisms at an intense pace for two weeks, but the sermons were the most important instrument of the missionaries in their crusade to restore Catholic faith. The sermons, held three times a day at dawn, in the afternoon, and in the evening, lasted two hours each.[31] The secular priest Joseph Hillebrand, the indefatigable director of missions in the Diocese of Paderborn, has left a rich collection of mission sermons.[32] They indicate that the missionaries concentrated on the major aspects of church doctrine: the origins of man, the sacraments, the Ten Commandments, sin and repentance, the judgment after death, the threat of

27. Pf. Koop an Bischof Konrad Martin, Arnsberg, 9 Dec. 1858, *Aktenstücke*, 273.

28. Murphy, *Der Wiederaufbau der Gesellschaft Jesu*, 93.

29. Bericht der Zeitschrift *Sion*, Nr. 25, 27 Feb. 1853, *Aktenstücke*, 197.

30. LHAK, Best. 403, OP der Rheinprovinz, Nr. 7511, "Die Jesuiten, 1855–1865," PD Junker to RP, Koblenz, 28 Feb. 1856, Bl. 99–106.

31. HSTAD, RD, PB, Nr. 1252, "Katholische Orden und Missionen: Betr. vor allem Niederlassungen und Missionsveranstaltungen des Jesuitenordens," Bd. 1, 1852–87, BM to LRA, Hüls, 17 Jan. 1872, Bl. 15.

32. Joseph Hillebrand, *Missionsvorträge*, 2 vols. (Paderborn: F. Schöningh, 1870).

damnation, the need for confession, the incarnation of Christ, and the incontestable authority of the church. At the same time, the sermons introduced powerful new forms of popular veneration including the crucifix and the Virgin Mother of Christ (whose Immaculate Conception became dogma in 1854). The objective of the missionaries also included the reform of popular culture. They ranted against alcohol consumption and tavern life, dancing, playing cards, gambling, reading novels, foul language, and sexual license.[33] The sermons struck at radical political movements that threatened traditional authority and order. The uprisings of 1848 and 1849 were singled out and denounced as sins, the consequence of depravity and religious indifference. Rationalism, materialism, the Enlightenment, democracy, and socialism were attacked as the work of Satan. All of this was music in the ears of state authorities in the years of conservative reaction. Following the mission in Düsseldorf in 1851, the police commissioner had the Jesuits' sermons printed and circulated in order to restore order in a city that had once been a center of democratic radicalism during 1848 and 1849.[34]

It was, however, the sermons delivered on the themes of sin, hell, and repentance that had the most impact on listeners. According to a *Bürgermeister* (mayor or principal magistrate) in the Ruhr region of Westphalia, Jesuits delivered some sermons that "appealed to understanding and sound reason and took great pains to avoid exciting the mind."[35] Rural parish priests, with their closer ties to peasant sensibility, however, encouraged the missionaries to give "not especially learned, scientific, but on the contrary more powerful, forceful sermons emphasizing sin and repentance."[36] Missionaries therefore adopted a theatrical style that looked like a tantrum. They screamed, pounded the pulpit, stomped their feet, jumped up and down, and thrashed about. According to one disturbed witness, "The preacher

33. For a list of forty-two sermons delivered at a mission at Danzig see *Über die von Missions-Priestern aus dem Orden der Gesellschaft Jesu in Danzig gehaltenen Missionen* (Paderborn: F. Schöningh, 1852), 7–12. See also the list in K. A. Leibbrand, *Die Missionen der Jesuiten und Redemptoristen in Deutschland und die evangelische Wahrheit und Kirche* (Stuttgart: E. Schweizerbart'sche Verlagshandlung, 1851), 30–34.

34. Sperber, *Popular Catholicism*, 60.

35. HSTAD, RBD, P, Nr. 1252, "Katholische Orden und Missionen: Betr. vor allem Niederlassungen und Missionsveranstaltungen des Jesuitenordens," Bd. 1, 1852–87; BM, Hüls, to LA, Kempen, 17 Jan. 1872, Bl. 15; BM Schwartz, Brügger, to LRA, Kempen, 19 March 1857, Bl. 10.

36. Pf. Cruse an Bischof Konrad Martin, 24 April 1868, *Aktenstücke,* 377.

breaks the staff of God's wrath over everyone. He shouts with his hands balled into fists. He violently swings his body, working on one side of the pulpit then the other. He thumps his feet, smacks his hands together, stretches his arms high over his head then out over the rails."[37] The missionaries terrorized their audiences with furious and graphic depictions of infernal horror and the promise of eternal damnation for unrepentant sinners. Here is a typical example of the way the missionaries repeatedly beat the image of hell into the heads of their listeners.

> Hell is a gruesome dungeon in which sinners languish for all eternity. Hell is the state of excommunication, where horror and misery reign. Hell is the place where fire and brimstone burn forever. Hell is the place of constant despair and everlasting damnation. Hell is the place of wailing and darkness, the shadow of death and chaos, confusion and terror.[38]

The number of sermons on hell in Hillebrand's collection attests to the power the missionaries believed the threat of damnation had over their audiences. The grim and exhausting catalog of titles includes "The Judgment of Damnation," "There Is a Hell," "What Does It Mean to Be Damned?" "Hell," "The Sinner in Hell and the Sinner on Earth," "The Sorrow of the Damned," "The Fear of Hell," "The Eternal Fires," "The Rich Man in Hell," "The Gradations of Punishment in Hell," "Eternal Punishment in Hell," "The Danger of Going to Hell," "The Fruits of Considering Hell," and "The Belief in Hell and the Behavior of Christians." Other sermons devoted to the themes of sin, death, and final judgment also emphasized the promise of damnation for unrepentant sinners and drew pictures of infernal horror. Fire and brimstone were, in fact, invoked so often in the sermons that the missionaries found themselves dubbed "the hell-preachers." As one disgusted critic complained, "What do the Jesuits preach?—Hell and damnation and damnation and hell!"[39] Among the Catholic laity in the Diocese of Paderborn, Hillebrand himself became popularly known as *Höllebrand* (Hellfire).

    Those who denied the existence of hell did so, according to the missionaries, for various reasons: because they were "materialists, athe-

---

37. *Die Jesuitenansiedlung in Westfalen und das Westfälische Junkerthum. Beiträge zur Geschichte der Volksverdummerung in Preußen* (Bremen: A. D. Giesler, 1850), 14.

38. Hillebrand, "Was ist ein Verdammter," *Vorträge* 2:267.

39. *Jesuitenansiedlung in Westfalen,* 14.

ists, or wrongdoers and usurers, or whores and adulterous, or completely hardened sinners."[40] And those who sought solace in the belief that the fires of hell were a mere metaphor without real consequence were, the missionaries warned, deluded. The missionaries told their listeners that the five corporeal senses like the human soul were eternal and that hell was a real, physical, endless furnace ruled by Satan and stoked by his angels, a woeful abode, and the just end for anyone who transgressed God's laws on earth: "Everything endures pain in the flames: the evil tongue, the lusting eyes, the imprudent ear, the unchaste body, the impure heart. All suffer. The entire body is gripped and consumed with fire."[41] With all their senses listeners were told to imagine themselves already in hell: to see the flames and suffering souls; smell the smoke, sulfur, and burning flesh; taste their own tears and feel the worm of conscience slithering through their bodies; hear the frightful shrieks and blasphemies of the damned. "Endless burning in the fire pits, hearing without end the howls and shrieks of the damned, eternally suffering the scorn of the all-powerful and just God. That is the horrible, hopeless condition. . . . Forever! Eternity without end!"[42] At the hell sermons it was, therefore, not simply the promise of horror itself that was powerful but the way the torture could be internalized. Hell was not where one looked upon the fate of others. In the Catholic imagination it was a place prepared and waiting for oneself, in a lake of fire, flesh crackling, charred black, melting but not dying.

The pressure broke down men and women. They panicked, panted, wailed, and raised their arms above their heads, dropped to their knees, and "wept like children."[43] But there was nowhere to go. The missionaries admonished "sinners!" to "leave the path of ruin!" and confront the choice "repent or hell!"[44] The hellfire sermons reflected the moral dimensions of Catholic eschatology practiced for centuries,

---

40. Hillebrand, "Es gibt eine Hölle," *Missionsvorträge*, 2:256.

41. Idem, "Was ist ein Verdammter," *Missionsvorträge*, 2:272.

42. Quoted in Scholten, *Volksmission der Redemptoristen*, 172 n. 34.

43. *Allgemeine Zeitung*, Nr. 316, 1852, *Aktenstücke*, 174; Bericht eines Augenzeugen, Münnerstadt, 29 Feb. 1852, *Aktenstücke*, 114; *Volksmissionen der norddeutschen Franziskaner*, 11.

44. Hillebrand, "Die Furcht vor der Hölle und die Bewahrung vor der Hölle," *Missionsvorträge*, 2:288. For a study of the centrality of the threat of damnation in hell in Catholic life and moral behavior see Andreas Heller, "'Du kommst in die Hölle . . .' Katholizismus als Weltanschauung in lebensgeschichtlichen Aufzeichnungen," in *Religion und Alltag: Interdisziplinäre Beiträge zu einer Sozialgeschichte des Katholizismus in lebensgeschichtlichen Aufzeichnungen*, ed. Andreas Heller and Therese Weber. (Vienna: Böhlau Verlag, 1990), 28–55.

and the link of sin to suffering was an ancient, fundamental aspect of Christian sensibility. Especially in rural towns and villages, the melodrama of the sermons was, however, no less a psychological shock, an explosion of the quiet and boring routines of peasant *Alltag*. The emotional susceptibility of the participants to the sermons was due in part to their physical exhaustion and mental fatigue. For many parishioners the pace of the missions was frantic. At large missions in cities, crowds hurried back and forth between churches to hear one sermon after another and hardly stopped to rest or eat.[45] Men and women went for days without hot food, eating instead what they could, when they could. Peasants at the Jesuit mission in Reissing in the Diocese of Regensburg in 1856 went day after day without sleep. As the local priest reported to his bishop, "The parishioners were on their feet day and night. A large part of the night had to be used in order to be able to devote oneself on the one hand to the agricultural work and on the other hand to the mission."[46] Those who fainted due to stress and hunger and sleep deprivation under the bombardment of the sermons or collapsed for lack of oxygen were dragged to the first-aid stations located at the church portals.

Prepared by three days of sermons on the themes of sin, judgment upon death, punishment in hell, purgatory, and the need for repentance and confession, men and women gathered before dawn in front of the church doors eager to repent their sins.[47] When the Jesuit mission came to Aachen people stood in a rainstorm through the night. They continued to wait as long as twelve to fifteen hours in seemingly endless lines for their turn in the confessional. Teams of as many as thirty to forty priests gathered from the neighboring parishes and demanded complete and detailed "life confessions" of every penitent, each of which lasted about twenty minutes.[48] So desperate were they not to miss their turn in the confessionals at the Aachen mission, factory workers and peasants broke into a bloody brawl.[49] The Jesuits' chief instrument was the sermon, but the Redemptorists concentrated

45. Bericht der Zeitschrift *Sion*, Nr. 25, 27 Feb. 1853, *Aktenstücke*, 197–98.

46. Pf. Obelt an Bischof von Valentin von Regensburg, Reissing, 30 June 1856, *Aktenstücke*, 256.

47. See the order of sermons recorded with brief summaries in *Über die von Missions-Priestern aus dem Orden der Gesellschaft Jesu in Danzig gehaltenen Missionen*, 7–12.

48. See Pf. Koop an Bischof Konrad Martin, Arnsberg, 9 Dec. 1858, *Aktenstücke*, 273; Pf. Zehrt an Bischof Konrad Martin, Heiligenstadt, 15 May 1859, *Aktenstücke*, 277; Pf. Cruse an Bischof Konrad Martin, Büderich, 24 April 1868, *Aktenstücke*, 377. To ensure anonymity and encourage repentance, local priests did not hear confession during the missions.

49. Mundweiler, *Waldburg-Zeil*, 84.

their efforts on confession. One of them found it difficult to find the words to describe the scene before him when the confessionals were finally opened during the mission in the Diocese of Limburg.[50] Men and women burst into tears when they missed the chance to confess their sins and returned to the lines the next day. After exiting the confessional, the particularly exuberant went back to the end of the line to confess all over again. The emotional purgation of confession and the relief, if not euphoria, of forgiveness and redemption were intense personal and collective religious experiences not readily imaginable today. Clearly the missionaries' objective was an emotional, not intellectual, response to the sermons. Not simply the number of people but the volume of weeping and shrieking at the missions was, therefore, the measure of their success.[51] The missionary and parish reports repetitiously emphasize, even celebrate, the amount of "wailing and sobbing," "mourning and weeping," and "tears of remorse and love" in order to prove to ecclesiastical superiors the success of the missions.

The mission culminated on the final day in a large festive procession and the planting of a large permanent cross in the town square or in front of the church. At the mission in Mergentheim in the Diocese of Rothenburg, over thirty thousand attended. The scene was repeated at Meudt in the Diocese of Limburg.[52] Crowds threw blossoms in the path of the missionaries on the way to the local railway station. Amid cheering crowds they boarded the train and moved on to repeat their work at the next mission site. The missionaries paid for the relentless tempo of the missions—the strain of constant travel, preaching, offering mass, hearing confessions for hours on end, performing exorcisms, and organizing sodalities—with their health. Many lost their voices, collapsed, and broke into fever.[53] Hillebrand's own record offers at least one indication of the strenuous pace of the missionary work. From 1846 to 1856 he held 155 missions (excluding shorter follow-up missions) in Paderborn, a large diocese that stretched in western Prussia through Westphalia almost to the border of Hanover. According

50. Scholten, *Volksmission der Redemptoristen,* 214.

51. Trevor Johnson, "Blood, Tears, and Xavier-Water: Jesuit Missionaries and Popular Religion in the Eighteenth-Century Upper Palatinste," in *Popular Religion in Germany and Central Europe, 1400–1800,* ed. Bob Scribner and Trevor Johnson (New York: St. Martin's Press, 1996), 183–202, esp. 195; William Christian, "Provoked Religious Weeping in Early Modern Spain," in *Religious Organizations and Religious Experience,* ed. John Davis (London: Academic Press, 1982), 97–114.

52. Mission, Mergentheim, 22 Mai bis 5 Juni 1853, *Aktenstücke,* 207; Scholten, *Volksmissionen der Redemptoristen,* 124.

53. Bericht des *Schwäbisch Merkur,* 11 June 1857, *Aktenstücke,* 262.

to one calculation, he delivered 3,852 sermons, heard 194,634 "life confessions," recruited 109,656 people in alcohol abstinence sodalities, and enrolled 26,679 young women in religious associations, though such statistics may invite some incredulity.[54] In any case, Hillebrand utterly exhausted himself, so much so that it came as a surprise to no one when in 1863 at the age of fifty he finally collapsed and was unable to recover and continue his work. Another missionary nearly died from overexertion, and bishops worried that the missionaries had so physically and emotionally spent themselves that they would never fully recuperate.[55]

Protestant leaders and social activists like Heinrich Johann Wichern, working in the inner mission movement among the working class in large cities like Berlin and Hamburg, were aghast by what they believed was a campaign of calculated coercion. One indignant Protestant pastor claimed that Protestant clergy would never manipulate their congregations with the brute force of terror and the threat of punishment in hell. The Catholic missionaries, however, "conjure up images of hell with great diligence and energy, and they routinely do it in the evening hours when the heart is especially susceptible. The speakers really know how to paint a picture for the people, that much one must grant them. Hellfire runs through their sermons like a bloody thread." He likened the Catholic missionaries roaming across Germany to the Methodist preachers and their "practice of shock and fear" (*Erschütterungs- und Angstpraxis*) taking place at revivalist meetings at the same time in the United States.[56] A democratic critic argued it was even worse: not only did the Jesuits stupefy and coerce the people, but they wrecked their physical health too. Almost two-thirds of the inhabitants of Münster, he explained, were bedridden following the mission held there in 1850. In their weakened condition, crammed together head to head in the dank, overcrowded cathedral, they had contracted the "Jesuit disease," a severe strain of influenza that coupled missions with pathology. He believed the founding of a permanent Jesuit residence near Münster meant no relief was in sight. Ultimately, he likened the "Jesuit disease" to a new strain of cholera that

54. *Aktenstücke,* xii–xiii n. 1.

55. For examples, see Bericht der Zeitschrift *Sion,* Nr. 25, 27 Feb. 1853, *Aktenstücke,* 198; Der Provinzial P. Behrens S.J. [Society of Jesus] an den Bischöfl. Missionär Hillebrand in Paderborn, Münster, 29 Sept. 1856, *Aktenstücke,* 259; Pf. Zehrt an Bischof Konrad Martin, 15 May 1859, *Aktenstücke,* 277; Pf. Herrmann an den Bischof von Ermland, Gr.-Köllen, 14 July 1863, *Aktenstücke,* 313.

56. Leibbrand, *Missionen der Jesuiten und Redemptoristen,* 30–31, 43.

"now threatens to become endemic like the Asiatic cholera in Europe."[57] Protestants and liberals also complained that the missions contributed to mental illness, induced "religious insanity," or caused psychological malaise that might lead finally to suicide.[58] They repeatedly charged the Jesuits with preying on those of frail constitution, on the mentally and physically "weaker sex," and on the peasantry. During what one historian has called "the cholera years," with the emergence of a new medical science including hygienic rationalization and psychological asylums, the Jesuit problem was best grasped as a pathological problem, a viral infection or mental illness attacking the psychological, physical, and social health of the nation.[59] Given the lessons wrought from the ravages of typhoid and cholera, the epidemiological analogy also proffered a solution: quarantine or extirpation. Catholic Church authorities, meanwhile, countered that the reports in liberal newspapers of hysteria and psychological distress induced by the sermons were merely attempts to discredit the missionary campaign. But it is telling that the Jesuits themselves began to open their missions with the warning that anyone prone to anxiety or depression should avoid their sermons.[60]

Intrachurch Conflicts

Hundreds of reports and letters written by parish priests to ecclesiastical authorities effusively sing the praises of the missionaries and their work. They no doubt pleased the bishops who had summoned the missionary campaign and looked with satisfaction on its success. Bound by duty and faith to preserve at least the appearance of unanimity, local clergy rarely alluded in their reports to any tensions that might have been engendered by the visits of the missionaries to their parishes. State reports on the missions, however, offer another perspective.

57. *Jesuitenansiedlung in Westfalen,* 19–20.

58. Dr. Hubert Joseph Reinkens verteidigt die Jesuitenmission in Schlesien, Breslau, 22 July 1852, *Aktenstücke,* 146; Pf. Weckesser an das bischöfl. Ordinariat zu Speyer, Maikammer, 29 July 1852, *Aktenstücke,* 152. Also Bericht des katholischen Pfarramts Thennenbronn an das Dekanat Triberg zu Dauchingen, Thennenbronn, 9 Dec. 1862, *Aktenstücke,* 304.

59. See also the discussion in Blackbourn, *Marpingen,* 258. For a social and cultural analysis of the cholera epidemics see Richard J. Evans, *Death in Hamburg: Society and Politics in the Cholera Years, 1830–1910* (New York: Penguin Books, 1987).

60. See Mission Bericht des katholischen Pfarramt. Thennenbronn, 9 Dec. 1862, *Aktenstücke,* 304. For the context of gender and "religious madness" see Ann Goldberg, *Sex, Religion, and the Making of Modern Madness: The Eberbach Asylum and German Society, 1815–1849* (Oxford: Oxford University Press, 1999).

However much local priests valued the restoration of piety among their parishioners, state accounts suggest that parish clergy resented being upstaged in their own congregations by the ascetic, zealous, and heavy-handed missionaries. A report of the district governor in Aachen to the Rhenish provincial governor in Koblenz in 1859 records the animosity and insecurity suppressed beneath the surface.

> Off the record, the secular clergy bitterly complain about the way the missions devalue the priest. The missionaries are usually sent to the parish with foreign encouragement, if not without the consent of the parish priest. The parish priest believes he is overshadowed by the sermons and lectures of the missionaries and by their austere appearance. He thinks he is far more undervalued than he deserves. It hurts him even more to be displaced in the confessional and in the confidence of his parishioners. . . . The priest endures it and remains silent, and he cannot do otherwise. But, if he were allowed to speak, he would come forward against the tendency encouraged and cultivated by the diocesan authorities, with the help of the monastic clergy, to reintroduce asceticism and formalism in church life.[61]

The *Landrat* at Malmedy near Cologne recognized that "the local clergy is in general no friend of the Jesuits and dislikes their visits" and reported that the parish priests were offended by the Jesuits' "far-reaching ambitions that disrupt their comfortable, quiet lives."[62] Bishops could empathize with the parish clergy. They too were not always happy with the attention and authority the missionaries now commanded within the church and in the life of the church. To the surprise and no doubt ironic delight of the anticlerical critics of the missions, the Redemptorists like the Jesuits and other missionaries threatened to undermine not secular state but episcopal authority.[63]

Ultimately, ecclesiastical authorities, however, worried that secular clergy had become too settled in their routines and immersed in the day-to-day realities of pastoral care in the world. The bishops doubted their routines of pastoral practice were equal to the challenge of reli-

---

61. LHAK, Best. 403, Nr. 7511, RP, Aachen, to OP Pommer-Esche, Koblenz, 13 Sept. 1859, Bl. 367–77.

62. HSTAD, RA, PB, Nr. 1239, "Missionaren, Jesuiten, Lazaristen: Ordenstätigkeit derselben in Kirche und Schule, 1835–1916," LA to RP Kühlwetter, Aachen, 13 Aug. 1859, Bl. 156.

63. Anderson, "Piety and Politics," 700; Weiss, *Redemptoristen in Bayern*, 787–821.

gious revival. They suspected that given the events of 1848–49 local clergy had after all failed at some fundamental level to control their congregations and uphold religious and secular authority. The missionary campaign was meant, therefore, not just to repietize the laity but to rehabilitate the religious commitment and institutional discipline of the parish clergy. As the bishop at Speyer argued, "the secular clergy from time to time need religious renewal not less but even more than the people so that they do not become secularized by their constant contact with the world." In contrast, the regular clergy (i.e., clergy who swore vows to live according to monastic regulations) had the complete confidence of the church leadership. "They are especially prepared and ready for [the missionary campaign]. They are devoted by an uninterrupted inner spiritual life to attend to sin-worn souls and to renew the spirit of penance and piety with their teachings and lives."[64] The social status of the Jesuits and monastic clergy relative to the clergy "in the world" contributed to the resentment felt by the parish clergy and their sense of insecurity. Parish priests seldom had an advanced education and were often themselves sons of peasants. The Jesuits by contrast were the elite in the church and German Catholic society. They were well-educated, well-traveled, exercised considerable ecclesiastical influence, and often came from prominent or aristocratic families. In an age when patterns of deference to Honoratioren were still intact, the Jesuits appeared in humble rural communities as more impressive and venerable representatives of Catholic religious and social power. It irked local priests, who after all had for years, some for a lifetime, dedicated themselves to their congregations, to find their own spiritual advice, penance, and absolutions overruled by outsiders and superiors within the church.[65]

The tension between secular parish clergy and the missionaries was a reflection of deeper conflicts within the church over shifts in authority and the nature of the Catholic revival. At the same time that the missions were sweeping through the German states, there was also dramatic growth in the number of new monastic orders and religious congregations in Germany. Secular parish clergy recognized that the

---

64. Bischof Nikolaus von Weis an den König von Bayern, 3 March 1865, *Aktenstücke,* 337.

65. For the development of the ultramontane clergy and frictions with older clergy see also Götz von Olenhusen, *Klerus und abweichendes Verhalten;* idem, "Klerus und Ultramontanismus in der Erzdiözese Freiburg: Entbürgerlichung und Klerikalisierung des Katholizismus nach der Revolution von 1848/49," in *Religion und Gesellschaft im 19. Jahrhundert,* ed. Wolfgang Schieder (Stuttgart: Klett-Cotta, 1993), 113–43; idem, "Die Ultramontanisierung des Klerus: Das Beispiel der Erzdiözese Freiburg," in *Deutscher Katholizismus im Umbruch zur Moderne,* ed. Wilfried Loth (Stuttgart: W. Kohlhammer, 1991), 46–75.

missionary crusade and the Catholic revival brought an increase in the stature and influence of monastic clergy and a movement toward the centralization of authority within the church. The missionaries and the regular orders to which they belonged enthusiastically embraced ultramontanism, an unwavering dedication to the absolute and incontestable authority of the pope in Rome. With their new radical ultramontanism, the Franciscans, Redemptorists, Dominicans, and Jesuits, their detractors sarcastically claimed, wanted to be more Catholic than the pope himself. Ultramontanism continued to gain ground in the church throughout the 1850s and 1860s and finally culminated in the promulgation of the dogma of papal infallibility at the Vatican Council in 1870. But to the traditional local clergy, and many episcopal authorities too, the new culture of ultramontanism often seemed coercive and repressive. Only grudgingly did they yield to the new ultramontanism and the increasing prominence of the regular clergy within the church, a fact not missed by Prussian state authorities. In 1858, as the report to the provincial governor of the Rhineland explained, "The parish clergy is still warding off, as much as possible, a larger increase of the monastic clergy. But it is not possible to judge how long this will be possible."[66] Parish priests who had joined the clergy during the Vormärz and were accustomed to the more subdued sermon styles and patterns of worship of that period were often out of step with the more flamboyant Catholicism that emphasized sensational preaching, fire and brimstone, and Marian devotion.[67]

At least as serious as the social gap and the issue of ecclesiastical authority was the tension between older, secular clergy and younger, regular clergy. The generational contest between parish and regular clergy, a competition for authority that the monastic orders were winning, was obvious even to the Landrat at Aachen: "The local, older clergy," he reported to the district governor, "are not especially fond of the monastic clergy. The latter seems to attract the younger clergy. It has to be expected that, if the younger clergy climb to the top of the parishes, the missions and with them the activities of the monastic clergy will increase."[68] The district governor reported to his superior, "The younger clergy, already educated in [asceticism and formalism], will not tolerate any resistance."[69] A conflict between mere youth and

66. LHAK, Best. 403, Nr. 7511, RP, Aachen, to OP Pommer-Esche, Koblenz, 13 Sept. 1859, Bl. 367–77. See also PD Junker, Koblenz, to RP, Koblenz, 28 Feb. 1856, Bl. 99–106.

67. Sperber, *Popular Catholicism,* 58.

68. HSTAD, RA, P, Nr. 1239, LA to RP, Aachen, 21 Aug. 1859, Bl. 160.

69. LHAK, Best. 403, Nr. 7511, RP, Aachen, to OP Pommer-Esche, Koblenz, 13 Sept. 1859, Bl. 367–77. See also PD Junker, Koblenz, to RP, Koblenz, 28 Feb. 1856, Bl. 99–106.

age within the church was, however, hardly the issue. At bottom was again a conflict between two different paths of devotion and service and experience within the church, between secular priests in and of the world, tied to life and relationships in their parishes on the one hand and monks detached from the world, fiercely loyal to their respective orders, and utterly devoted to the pope on the other hand. Finally, to this picture of conflict between traditional local clergy and the younger evangelical missionaries must be added the tension between the religious orders themselves. Redemptorists in Bavaria apparently both feared and despised the Jesuits.[70] Clergy in closed, monastic orders like the Redemptorists and presumably the Dominicans and Franciscans too, with their reputation for extreme asceticism, exaltation of blind obedience, and mortification of the flesh, were at loggerheads with the Jesuits, who were much more comfortable, even enjoyed, being in the world.

Hostilities between missionaries of different orders did not necessarily translate into practical problems. At the level of organization and logistics, the religious orders could simply avoid one another as they went about their work. This was hardly an option, of course, for secular clergy, who by necessity and duty were bound to cooperate with the missionaries. Yet the parish clergy embraced the missionaries. The slights they endured and the resentments they harbored for the missionaries all paled next to their common high purpose. Secular clergy recognized immediately that the missions were the only apparent answer to many of the problems of pastoral care they had been encountering in the Vormärz, and they, therefore, eagerly accepted their role in the missionary crusade. They gave advance notice from their pulpits and heightened the anticipation of their congregations for the forthcoming mission. They cleared arrangements with civil officials, and they managed the beautification of the church, the clearing of pews, the building of additional confessionals, and the reception of the missionaries. Priests led their congregations from outlying parishes into the towns that had been selected as mission centers, listened for hours on end to confessions, and facilitated affairs during the course of the mission. The Jesuits themselves recognized that their efforts would have been fruitless without the dedication of the secular priests.[71] Missionary reports to bishops often singled out individual parish priests for comment and praise.

70. Anderson, "Piety and Politics," 698; Weiss, *Redemptoristen in Bayern,* 813–14.
71. Sperber, *Popular Catholicism,* 97.

Meanwhile, the other authority in the community, the Bürgermeister, felt little reason to resent the missionaries. He was, in fact, often an enthusiastic advocate of the missions. Whether Catholic or Protestant, he welcomed the opportunity to bolster civic order and authority with sermons extolling the virtues of obedience, duty, reconciliation, and peace. The Bürgermeister of Milbringen, for example, personally welcomed the Jesuits when they arrived at his town in 1867. He made an appointment to discuss with the missionaries the "reigning, principal evils" of his town and was then well pleased to hear them singled out and castigated in the sermons.[72] Civil magistrates were delighted to see their communities socially rehabilitated by the missions. During the missions long and bitter feuds were resolved between neighbors, and family quarrels were laid aside . As late as 1871 on the eve of the Kulturkampf, the Bürgermeister of Croev in the Diocese of Trier argued to the Landrat in Wittlich that the missions were "good and useful, indeed, even necessary."[73]

The Impact of the Missions

Parish reports and diocesan accounts unanimously proclaimed the crusade to revive Catholicism in Germany a triumphant success. With the arrival of the missions, according to reports from the parish priests at Warburg to their bishop of Paderborn in 1851, the church had entered nothing less than "a new epoch."[74] The parish priest at Niederembt in his report to the archbishop at Cologne in 1858 proclaimed "a new life for the church."[75] While some local clergy reported initial resistance among some parishioners, the priest at Neunburg vorm Wald in the Diocese of Regensburg reported to his bishop that the Jesuits had ultimately conquered all opposition. By 1869 they could, he believed, proclaim in the immortal words of Julius Caesar announcing his victory at Zela, "Veni. Vidi. Vici."[76] According to the priest at Cochem in the Diocese of Trier, after the mission in 1864 only ten of the five hundred parishioners who had stopped attending mass refused to return to the

72. LHAK, Best. 442, Nr. 3963, "Wirken und Verhalten der katholischen Missionen und Jesuiten, 1859–1900," BM, Milbringen, to LRA, Merig, 7 April 1867.

73. LHAK, Best. 442, RBT, Nr. 3963, BM to LRA, Wittlich, 3 Oct. 1871, Bl. 447.

74. Die Pf. Willmes und Pees an den Bischof Drepper von Paderborn, Warburg, 27 Dec. 1852, *Aktenstücke*, 180.

75. Pf. an das Erzbischöfl. Generalvikariat, Köln, 8 Nov. 1858, *Aktenstücke*, 272.

76. Pf. Fell an den Bischof Ignatius vom Regensburg, Neunburg vorm Wald, July? 1869, *Aktenstücke*, 396.

fold.[77] Men and women who had not confessed or taken the Eucharist for fifteen or twenty years received the sacraments in the confessional and at the altar. "The indifference that ran like a thread through the so-called educated strata and also infected the working class many times," according to the priest at Worbis in the Diocese of Paderborn in 1859, was transformed into religious conviction.[78] In the small town of Jücken in the Diocese of Cologne, young people of the upper class, "who had become indifferent and morally depraved as a result of reading and traveling," now recanted their ridicule of religion and declared their loyalty to the church.[79] "Where the spirit of the time had poisoned everything and had threatened to destroy the last roots of Christianity," the bishop of Eichstätt joyfully declared in 1853, "a fear of God and Christian propriety blossomed again"; those "bedazzled by the arrogance of a false Enlightenment were awakened again to belief in God by the power of the divine word."[80] According to the report of a parish priest to his superior in Regensburg, even a year after the missionaries had come to Offenstetten in the Diocese of Regensburg in 1867, his congregation was still attending mass on Sunday with more intense and heartfelt attention.[81] According to the report of a proud priest about the mission at Gmünd in 1850, a sermon on the existence and eternity of hell "destroyed with a few blows the web of the modern Enlightenment and skepticism."[82] Such triumphalist and celebratory reports by Catholic Church leaders about the missionary campaign could be cited and quoted by the hundreds.

The objective of the missions, however, was not only to indoctrinate religiosity but also to improve individual and social morality. The missionaries believed that the one was necessarily bound to the other. Sermons on the doctrines of sin and repentance, therefore, hammered away at alcohol consumption and sexual license and exhorted listeners to resolve family feuds, to mend broken friendships, to return stolen property, and to live righteous lives. The missionaries who preached that hell was a real place, not a metaphor, wanted not only to exert control over the laity but to save others from infernal damnation and

---

77. Dechant Schnorfeil an das Generalvikariat in Trier, Cochem, 18 April 1864, *Aktenstücke,* 319.

78. Pf. Huschenbett an Bischof Konrad Martin, Worbis, 20 Jan. 1859, *Aktenstücke,* 276.

79. Pf. Döhler an den Erzbischof Paulus von Köln, Jücken, 21 Jan. 1868, *Aktenstücke,* 373.

80. Fasten-Hirtenbrief des Bischofs Georg (v. Öttl) von Eichstätt, Eichstätt, 23 Jan. 1853, *Aktenstücke,* 186.

81. Pf. Rosmann an den Bischof von Regensburg, Offenstetten, 8 Nov. 1867, *Aktenstücke,* 363.

82. Quoted in Leibbrand, *Die Missionen der Jesuiten und Redemptoristen,* 30–31.

in the process to transform themselves and society for the better in this life. In reply to hostile liberal and progressive critics and the concern of secular authorities that the missions drained away otherwise productive social and economic resources, the bishop of Regensburg argued to the Bavarian state minister in 1867 that the missions, on the contrary, positively served the interests of society. He explained that the sermons emphasizing moral character, modesty, and self-discipline rescued households from bankruptcy and bolstered the economy: "Luxury, excess, and waste are the principal problems leading to the financial ruin of families, and lying and fraud undermine social trust, the foundation of credit. But the missions have swept away these vices wherever they have free access. The uprooting of these vices and the planting of their opposite virtues have dried up the sources that have led to the sad demise of so many of our farmers today."[83] The missions not only saved souls, church leaders argued, they also encouraged sound fiscal management and rehabilitated the moral and social foundations of the capital credit and investment necessary for economic expansion and the recovery of agricultural production.

The missions also set up religious sodalities with the dual aim of sustaining the religious revival and socially rehabilitating the community. The new sodalities established after 1850 represented a revolution in the associational life of German Catholics.[84] Catholic communities set up elaborate networks of association along gender, class, and generational lines. In Aachen, for example, seven different devotional confraternities were founded for men, journeymen artisans, students, youth from the "educated classes," young female servants, factory workers, and working women.[85] Members of these new religious associations took oaths to God to morally improve their individual lives. Those who joined the sodalities and religious brotherhoods vowed to stop drinking. Members of the new Catholic youth groups promised to avoid unsupervised contact with persons of the opposite sex. Young men and women swore to enter into relationships only with the

---

83. Bischof v. Senetrey an den Staatsminister v. Greßer, Regensburg, 28 Sept. 1867, *Aktenstücke,* 362.

84. Sperber, *Popular Catholicism,* 73–98; idem, "The Transformation of Catholic Associations in the Northern Rhineland and Westphalia, 1830–1870," *Journal of Social History* 15 (1981): 253–63; Oded Heilbronner, "In Search of the (Rural) Catholic Bourgeoisie: The Bürgertum of South Germany," *Central European History* 29 (1996): 191–93. See also the articles in Otto Dahn, ed., *Vereinswesen und bürgerliche Gesellschaft in Deutschland* (Munich: R. Oldenbourg, 1984).

85. LHAK, Best. 403, Nr. 7511, RP to OP Pommer-Esche, Koblenz, 21 Feb. 1860; RP to OP, Koblenz, 9 Sept. 1857, Aachen, Bl. 91.

expressed intent of marriage and with the approval of their parents.[86] Men and women dedicated themselves to more austere, morally sober lives. They agreed to eschew public entertainment and did so apparently with conviction. Following the mission at Münster, the theater halls stood practically empty; only those not from the city attended.[87] The parish priest at Darfeld took pleasure in reporting to his bishop at Münster in 1851 that during the year following the mission the moral behavior of the community had significantly improved. There was no longer any boozing and nightly romping. Girls were even wearing their hats more modestly, without bands and flowers.[88] Parish reports concerning the religious and moral impact of the missions paint a picture of unqualified success and an impressive example of the religious and social control exercised by the church.

The reports of parish secular clergy, eager as they were for the revival both to succeed and to meet the expectations of their authorities regarding the religious and moral rehabilitation of their congregations, are themselves, however, not disinterested information.[89] Assessing the impact of the missions on popular behavior requires, therefore, at least some qualification of the triumphalist appraisals of the missionary and parish reports. First of all, the missions were not everywhere equally well received. In the village of Öfft, for example, hard on the French border in the Rhineland, the congregation broke into a riot of protest when the parish priest announced that the Redemptorist missionaries were coming.[90] When in 1861 the missionaries came to Niederau, a small town near Aachen, while the factory workers attended the sermons, the peasants refused to show up. They did not care at all about moral or religious improvement.[91] Especially in the cities, not all Catholics greeted the Jesuits with open arms. Missions

86. Dechant Händly an den Bischöflichen Kommissar Nolte in Heiligenstadt, Neustadt, 14 May 1850, *Aktenstücke*, 25; Pf. Spithöver an Bischof Johann Georg von Münster über die Mission, 18 July 1850, *Aktenstücke*, 32; Pf. Feuslageden Bischof von Münster über den Segen der im März 1850 gehaltenen Volksmission, Darfeld, 16 April 1851, *Aktenstücke*, 62; *Kölnische Zeitung*, Nr. 274, 15 Nov. 1851.

87. *Jesuitenansiedlung in Westfalen*, 18–19.

88. Pf. Fenslage an den Bischof von Münster über den Segen der im März 1850 gehaltenen Mission, Darfeld, 16 April 1851, *Aktenstücke*, 63.

89. For all its virtues, Sperber's study of the missions and the Catholic revival in the Rhineland and Westphalia accepts too uncritically church reports and sources regarding the impact of the missions on the moral behavior of Catholics. Sperber, *Popular Catholicism*, chap. 2.

90. Scholten, *Volksmission der Redemptoristen*, 119 n. 48.

91. Sperber, *Popular Catholicism*, 62, and for other examples of popular opposition to the missions, 62–63.

held in urban areas drew massive audiences, but in relative terms they, in fact, were less successful than those held in small towns and villages in rural areas. At the height of the missionary campaign in 1868, the mission in Aachen pulled an impressive throng of 20,000, yet the total Catholic population was 73,000. When the mission came to Cologne in the same year, 30,000 of a population of 100,000 attended.[92] On the other hand, by nineteenth-century standards crowds of 20,000 and 30,000 were spectacular sights and were proof of the new mass power of Catholicism. Even so, the *Rheinisches Kirchenblatt* noted that in Cologne the "affluent part" of the population stayed away from the mission or came only to see enough to be able to participate in a conversation about it.[93] The lower attendance among the total Catholic urban populations was an indication of the secularization under way in cities. In the small towns and peasant villages of the rural areas, where clerical monitoring of individuals within the community was possible and personalized patterns of authority and deference were more entrenched, almost everyone attended the missions.

In addition, educated, secularizing, middle-class Catholics were more inclined to resent the missionaries' antiliberal, antirational, antimaterialist message that struck at the heart of their social-cultural identity as members of the Bürgertum. Middle-class Catholics may have appreciated the Jesuits' campaign for social order and moral sobriety among the lower classes, but they also distrusted their heavy-handed manner and were embarrassed by the unseemly spectacle of men and women at the sermons moaning, swooning, and sobbing. Throughout the period of the missionary campaign Catholic liberals found themselves increasingly torn between their membership in the middle class on the one hand and loyalty to the Catholic Church on the other.[94] They were wary of an ultramontane Catholicism that they often regarded as the imposition of a foreign and centralizing authority and that seemed especially strong among "ignorant" peasants and privileged aristocrats. The prominent role of the Jesuits in the Catholic revival placed a further strain on their relationship with the church. In 1858, to cite one example, Cologne's liberal-Catholic patrician Eberhard von Groote railed against the Jesuit "parasites in the ecclesiastical

---

92. Scholten, *Volksmission der Redemptoristen,* 241.
93. Ibid., 242.
94. Mergel, *Zwischen Klasse und Konfession.* See also idem, "Ultramontanism, Liberalism, Moderation: Political Mentalities and Political Behavior of the German Catholic Bürgertum, 1848–1914," *Central European History* 29 (1996): 151–74.

hierarchy."[95] By the Kulturkampf of the 1870s liberal Catholics—like secular and Protestant liberals—had become fervently anti-Jesuit. In 1872 all the liberal Catholics in the National Liberal Party and the Liberale Reichspartei in the Reichstag threw their votes behind the anti-Jesuit legislation that brought a halt to the missionary campaign. It was, in fact, Eduard Windthorst, an Old Catholic progressive from Berlin and nephew of the Catholic Center Party leader, Ludwig Windthorst, who led the attack against the Jesuits in the Reichstag.[96] Even Ludwig Windthorst had never made a secret of his personal distaste for the Jesuits, though he believed the anti-Jesuit law was an abuse of state power and an intolerable attack on the autonomy of the Catholic Church.[97]

Meanwhile, missions encountered organized opposition from secular liberals, democrats, and socialists. In Düsseldorf radicals bitterly contested the missions. Radicals blanketed the city walls with posters decrying the missions, harassed the missionaries with letters, and held demonstrations during the sermons.[98] Democrats set up placards that read: "Citizens!! As you know, the Jesuits are preaching here. Go and hear them. Then you can convince yourselves how these wretched swindlers are using the pure democratic teachings of Jesus to stultify the people and to win them for the monarchy by the grace of God."[99] Liberal newspapers repeatedly argued that the missions spread nothing but stupidity, superstition, and dogma. In return the Catholic Church and Catholic press accused liberals and democrats of hypocrisy. In 1850 the Catholic Sonntagsblatt in Münster attacked those liberal and democratic newspapers that, while proclaiming freedom and claiming to represent "the rights of the people," spread lies about the missions. The paper implored all those who had seen the missions in Münster to judge for themselves whether they had really harmed the interests of the people; undermined freedom; or endangered the welfare of the individual, the family, and society.[100]

Especially in the first years of the missionary campaign, the elite, intellectually sophisticated Jesuits also seriously miscalculated their

95. Mergel, Zwischen Klasse und Konfession, 399.

96. Michael B. Gross, "Kulturkampf and Unification: German Liberalism and the War against the Jesuits," Central European History 30 (1997): 545–66, esp. 550–51.

97. Anderson, Windthorst, 128, 166.

98. Bürger von Düsseldorf (934 Unterschriften) an den Provinzial der deutschen Ordensprovinz, Düsseldorf, 30 July 1851, Aktenstücke, 79–80.

99. Sperber, Popular Catholicism, 62.

100. Bericht eines Augenzeugen, Sonntagsblatt, 17 March 1850, Aktenstücke, 14.

audience. Their sermons on matters of doctrine and dogma often flew hopelessly over the heads of their listeners from humble, rural communities. The Catholic *Schwäbische Chronik,* for example, estimated that in 1850 hardly a tenth of the audience at the Jesuit mission in Constance right on the Swiss border understood one particular sermon. The preacher naively assumed that his listeners were "familiar with the learned tools of the trade and philosophical-technical terms which he pulled out of his sleeve sentence after sentence." The paper complained that prodigious scholarly training was required "to follow the compilation of his thoughts, the swift and precise development of his philosophical argument, the chain of extensive conclusions, and the series of logical proofs until they finally became cogent and effective."[101] This particular Jesuit, a professor of dogmatic theology at the University of Louvain in Belgium, was more suited for the university lecture hall. When he delivered his sermons again to an educated audience in the university city of Bonn, the audience reportedly listened with appreciation.[102] If the highly intellectual content of the sermon was difficult enough for common folk to follow, the problem of understanding the preacher, himself originally Swiss but now from the Walloon, Francophone region of Belgium, was merely compounded by the fact that those who came from the adjacent territories to attend the mission at Constance spoke *schwäbisch,* low Alemannic, or high Alemannic dialects. This is the kind of problem the missionaries repeatedly faced. In different regions and in the countryside where highly idiomatic dialects were spoken in peasant communities, sermons delivered by Jesuit elites in High German on the intricate nuances of theology, dogma, and doctrine were often simply too difficult to understand. That French or Polish not German was the native language of many of the Jesuits only further detracted from the comprehensibility of the sermons. The language and intellectual gaps between the Jesuits and the Catholic popular and peasant population were, therefore, additional factors that limited the capacity of the missionaries to dictate from above the reform of religious and popular culture.

Finally, the campaign to reform the social and moral conduct of Catholics was limited by indigenous and resilient features of popular culture. To take one illuminating example, the missionaries and mission sodalities endlessly attacked dancing, *the* form of popular entertainment in the nineteenth century. Church authorities were obsessed with the

101. *Schwäbische Chronik,* Nr. 220, 13 Sept. 1850, *Aktenstücke,* 33–34.
102. Murphy, *Wiederaufbau der Gesellschaft Jesu,* 108.

problem of dancing because they believed it was the *occasio proxima* for more serious sin. Their suspicions were not without justification. By the nineteenth century, premodern, highly ritualized, communal dancing among the rural peasantry had given way to couples dancing together of their own choosing. Dance movements were also less stylized, freer, more spontaneous and sensual, often lewd. Sex was a prevalent topic of conversation at village dances, and scabrous, sexual themes often provided the lyrics for folk songs. Dancing, therefore, was part and parcel of the culture of sexual permissiveness in rustic working-class life: it provided the medium for romantic (or not-so-romantic) courtship and facilitated sexual liaisons. No wonder almost all parish priests in Bavaria believed the *Freinächte,* the nights on which dances were held, were the occasion for sex and followed by rising illegitimacy rates.[103]

To the Bavarian cleric, recreational dancing, implicated as it was in the sexual life of his village, was intractable precisely because dancing was also embedded in popular religious life. Dancing was woven into the communal celebrations of the annual liturgical cycle. The traditional dance of the Minneburg took place on the first Sunday of May, and the "bonfire dance" on the Feast of St. John. In rural communities, spinners celebrated the Feast of St. Agatha with food and dancing. Every occupational group and guild had a patron saint and a day set aside for his or her celebration with dancing. The occasion for dancing was also provided by the sacramental rites of passage at baptism, confirmation, marriage, and death. In 1852 the careful calculation of the chancery at Munich determined that marriages, *Kirchenweihen* (church festivals), guild patron-saint festivals, and holy feast days provided the occasion for holding most of the 4,842 dances in the Diocese of Munich in one year alone. That impressive number did not even include those dances held in the cities of Munich and Landshut![104] Dancing in rustic and village culture was, despite the protests of the church, not sacrilegious conduct in popular culture but, to the contrary, an ongoing ritual that linked, celebrated, and facilitated at once both sexual and religious life.

If, however, the proud priest of Darfeld is to be believed, the missionaries' attack on dancing was a sweeping success: the town had abruptly stopped dancing, and even a year after the mission people no longer danced *even at the height of Carnival.* The population, he

103. J. Michael Phayer, *Sexual Liberation and Religion in Nineteenth-Century Europe* (London: Rowman and Littlefield, 1977), 82–93.

104. Ibid., 89.

claimed, simply no longer felt the least desire to dance.[105] Even if this was the case, his parish was the exception, certainly not the rule. Dancing remained inextricably laced into the fabric of the sexual and religious life of rural communities throughout central Europe, and attempts to reform such basic components of popular culture were limited at best. The report of the parish priest of Rees in the Diocese of Münster reflected more accurately the norm: those in his parish who joined the new devotional confraternities merely promised to abstain from dancing. "To really prohibit dancing," he candidly acknowledged, "doesn't lie within our power."[106]

If the missions and new sodalities could not stop dancing, there is also reason to doubt that the missions were able to reduce substantially the amount of cavorting at the tavern, gambling, drunkenness, foul language, and extramarital sexual activity. While research is not conclusive, illegitimacy rates throughout Germany probably did not decline during the 1850s and 1860s in the wake of the missions; even where and when the rates appear to decline it would be difficult to attribute that decline with any assurance to changes in moral conduct rather than to social, economic, and demographic factors. Jonathan Sperber argues that the illegitimacy rates in selected areas of Rhineland-Westphalia dropped with the religious revival, but, even as he indicates, the records of vital statistics are sparse. Most of the statistics for the period of the 1840s and 1850s are missing in his tabulation, yet they are necessary in order to gauge with confidence any decline during the period of missionary activity.[107] Alcoholism also remained an intractable problem throughout the century. The Jesuits, always more at home in the cities than the countryside, in particular recognized that they could not simply dictate but often had to accommodate certain features of rural popular culture. Parish priests cited the persistence of drunkenness and alcoholism as one reason the missions were necessary in the first place, and the Redemptorists and Hillebrand tirelessly campaigned against alcohol abuse. The Jesuits, however, seldom preached against drinking, directing their audiences' attention instead to what they considered the more important issues, namely, religious indoctrination and catechism.[108] Research on the

---

105. Pf. Feuslage an den Bischof von Münster über den Segen der im März 1850 gehaltenen Volksmission, Darfeld, 16 April 1851, *Aktenstücke,* 62.

106. Pf. Hartmann an den Bischof von Münster, Rees, 6 Feb. 1851, *Aktenstücke,* 50.

107. Sperber, *Popular Catholicism,* 93.

108. Scholten, *Volksmission der Redemptoristen,* xxii.

peasantry in Bavaria and on the lack of impact of the Redemptorist missionary campaign on peasant moral behavior and the illegitimacy rate in Bavaria has also suggested that peasant culture and value systems remained remarkably detached from those prescribed to them by church authorities.[109]

In the wake of the missions both rising church attendance and persistent or rising illegitimacy rates or for that matter dancing, drinking, fistfighting, gambling, cursing, swearing, and foul language in Catholic rural communities would, therefore, not be a contradiction. The most stalwart peasant may have been reduced to tears at the hellfire sermons, confessed his sins, accepted the Eucharist, and even joined a confraternity, but one cannot deduce from this his subsequent moral conduct. He himself recognized that his behavior and "religiosity" or "irreligiosity" were not the same thing. He might drink, utter obscenities, dance, and enjoy the pleasures of the Freinacht and on Sunday morning still take his seat in church with the rest of his community. The rural peasant found that he could join religious faith to his life without fundamentally changing it in other respects, and this, indeed, was one of the reasons for the phenomenal success of the Catholic revival.

The Response of the State

Prussian state authorities may have been unsettled by the overt power of the missions, the Catholic popular revival, and specifically the mass appeal of the Jesuits, but they also welcomed the missionaries' demand for social discipline, call for obedience to the monarchy, and attack on moral laxity.[110] Given its dense Catholic population and its radical legacy from 1848, the Rhineland was designated by episcopal authorities for intense missionary activity. Over a twenty-year period the missionaries repeatedly crisscrossed the province. By the time of German unification every parish in the dioceses of the Rhineland received at least one mission, and many received several.[111] The Rhineland provides, therefore, an instructive case with which to register and evaluate the reaction of Prussian state administrators and authorities to the missions. Here the missions from the moment of their inception were intensely scrutinized by state officials. Rhenish government infor-

109. W. Robert Lee, *Population Growth, Economic Development, and Social Change in Bavaria, 1750–1850* (New York: Oxford University Press, 1977), 384; Weiss, *Redemptoristen in Bayern*, 1021–23; and the critical comments by Anderson, "Piety and Politics," 700.

110. LHAK, Best. 403, Nr. 7511, RP, Aachen, to OPR, Pommer-Esche, Koblenz, 13 Sept. 1859, Bl. 367–77.

111. Sperber, *Popular Catholicism*, 57.

mants, Bürgermeister, Landräte, and police commissioners routinely submitted detailed reports about the missionary activity to district governors throughout the decade of reaction. District governors reported to the provincial governor, who in turn both channeled information to and received instructions from the reactionary ministry in Berlin. In these reports government officials closely monitored and evaluated the missions, teachings, and pastoral activities as well as the movements of the individual missionaries, particularly the Jesuits. Their reports record the Janus-faced attitude of authorities toward the missionary work in Prussia. On the one hand, municipal officials and district and provincial governors—especially in the years immediately following the revolutions of 1848 and 1849 but also throughout the 1850s—welcomed the reinforcement the missionaries gave to state and municipal authority. For the most part reports from local-level administrators and authorities repeatedly stated that the sermons of the Jesuits and other missionaries did not attack Protestantism and bolstered state authority. On the other hand, many state authorities at the same time insisted that the missionaries threatened confessional peace and undermined the ultimate authority of the state.

In Berlin, Minister of Interior Ferdinand von Westphalen, Minister of Education and Ecclesiastical Affairs Karl Otto von Raumer, and the other Protestant ministers of the reactionary period responded to the Jesuit missions with hostility. In the postrevolutionary period, conservative authorities understandably looked askance on popular gatherings. They not only believed that the missions were trying to convert Protestants to Catholicism just as they had done during the Counter-Reformation of the sixteenth century. They, no doubt, also feared public assemblies that looked with their unbridled passions suspiciously like the unruly mobs of the 1848 Revolution. Already in early 1851, therefore, Berlin took action against the missionary campaign. In February the minister of the interior and the minister of education and ecclesiastical affairs issued a directive stating that punitive action against foreign missionaries should be taken if they committed a "criminal offense" or incited "politically dangerous or other excesses" that could lead to the disruption of public peace.[112] In the decrees of 22 May 1852 (the "Raumer decrees") the ministers banned the holding of missions in Catholic parishes in predominantly Protestant provinces "since there is the suspicion that other goals are being pursued here

---

112. Die Minister v. Raumer und v. Westphalen an die Oberpräsidenten, Berlin, 25 Feb. 1851, *Aktenstücke,* 52.

than an influence on the Catholic parishes."[113] One week later Berlin prepared to go a step further in the predominantly Catholic Rhineland. Hans von Kleist-Retzow, the Rhenish provincial governor, was informed in Koblenz that in the Rhineland missionary proselytizing might constitute such a threat to religious and civil peace as to warrant prohibition of the missions altogether.[114] Local and regional officials, however, balked. The Landrat of district Aachen warned his superiors that banning the missions in the province would only provoke a Catholic backlash against the government.[115] Despite his hatred for the Jesuits and their missions, the district governor at Aachen, Friedrich Kühlwetter, could only concur. In his report to Provincial Governor Kleist-Retzow he advised against banning the missions, and authorities in Berlin backed down from the plan to prohibit the missions in the Rhineland. Meanwhile, in response to the decree of May 1852, sixty-two deputies in the lower house of the Prussian parliament formed the "Catholic *Fraktion,*" the first political stirrings of the Catholic Center Party that was to emerge with the founding of the German Empire. The Catholic deputies demanded that the government respect the church's right to the religious freedoms guaranteed by the constitution of 1850: the right to independent administration of church affairs free from government interference and the right of religious orders to settle in Prussia. The Catholic Fraktion stood firm, and the Prussian government backed down from enforcing the decree.[116]

To be sure, the missionaries did sometimes incite interconfessional hostility as they tried to instruct their audience on matters of Catholic doctrine. During the spring of 1856, the Bürgermeister of Duisberg submitted a detailed report to the Landrat about the sermons given in his town. One Jesuit, he reported, spoke about the necessity of the Roman Catholic priesthood for the administering of the sacraments. The missionary had not directly referred to Protestantism, but the implication was clear enough. Anyone, he said, could simply give a piece of bread to someone else and say "do this in memory of me." "But this," the Jesuit argued, "is not a sacrament. The sacrament requires a properly ordained priest." At the end of the mission the well-

---

113. Erlaß der preuß. Minister v. Raumer und v. Westphalen über die Missionen, Berlin, 22 May 1852, *Aktenstücke,* 128.

114. HSTAD, RA, P, Nr. 1239, letter to OP Kleist-Retzow, Koblenz, Berlin, 29 May 1852, Bl. 26.

115. HSTAD, RA, P, Nr. 1239, LA, Kr. Aachen, to RP, RBA, Kr. Aachen, 11 June 1852.

116. Sperber, *Popular Catholicism,* 61.

known Jesuit missionary Peter Roh delivered a sermon on the hierarchy of the Catholic Church. Catholics, he argued, were like members of an army with officers and generals. By contrast, Protestants, he argued, had no such hierarchy and were, therefore, no better than "free-schoolers." Father Roh then attacked the Lutheran Bible, claiming that Luther had deliberately falsified many sections in his translation in order to undermine the Catholic Church and promote the interests of his own church. The Jesuit spiced his attack with sarcasm, mocking the name "Dr. Martin Luther" by pronouncing it slowly and laboriously. Now the Protestant Church refused, he argued, to correct Luther's mistakes. The Bürgermeister reported that Roh told his audience that the Protestant Church believed its followers had become so accustomed to the errors that "it is better to leave them in their errors (I was told, he said 'in their idiocy') than to correct the mistakes."[117] The incident, however, contrasts sharply with Father Roh's reputation. Previously he had been known not only for his oratorical skill but also for his tact and restraint. He was the one often entrusted with missions held in towns with heavily Protestant populations such as Heidelberg and Breslau.[118] According to the conservative *Neue Preußische Zeitung,* for example, the Protestants attending the sermons at Breslau in 1852 were moved only by the eloquence of the Jesuits' sermons including one by Peter Roh. His sermons attacked the current "philosophical-religious" errors and moral depravities of the current age. They made no attack on Protestantism, and there was, according to the paper, no irritation noticeable among the attending public.[119]

During 1855 and 1856 the Jesuits had turned toward a more polemical and incendiary style, and, to be sure, this conjured up images of Counter-Reformation bombast and zealotry. However, it was more often the case, according to the reports from administrators and authorities at different levels—Bürgermeister, Landräte, police commissioners, district governors—as well as articles from both liberal and conservative newspapers, that the Jesuit missionaries continued to avoid any polemic against or even reference to Protestantism. The liberal *Vossische Zeitung,* certainly no friend of the Jesuits, was impressed that the sermons from the pulpit in Flötenstein in the Diocese of Kulm

117. HSTAD, RD, P, Nr. 1252, BM, Duisburg, to LA Keshler, Duisberg, 1 June 1856, Bl. 72–74.

118. Gesuch des Erzpriesters Theil im Namen der Archpresbyteriatsgeistlichen der Stadt Breslau um eine Volksmission, Breslau, 23 Oct. 1852, *Aktenstücke,* 169.

119. Urteil der *Neuen Preuß. (Kreuz-) Zeitung,* Nr. 263, 12 Nov. 1852, *Aktenstücke,* 171–72.

in 1858 were free of dogmatic statements and confessional provoca-
tions. The Jesuits' restrained style, according to the paper, was especially appreciated by the non-Catholics in attendance. These sermons
were, in fact, so spiritless and unoriginal that it seemed even to the *Vossische Zeitung* a relief when another Jesuit delivered a subsequent sermon with more passion.[120] In August 1859 the Landrat at Düren in his
report concerning the Jesuit mission to District Governor Friedrich
Kühlwetter in Aachen had to admit that the sermons "were concerned
only with the foundation of Catholic dogma, with the urgency of the
commandments of the church and morality, somehow without show-
ing any animosity toward non-Catholics."[121] Two weeks later the district governor reported to Provincial Governor Kleist-Retzow in
Koblenz that all the reports he had received from Bürgermeister, Landräte, and the police commissioner had stated that all the sermons had
avoided confessional polemics.[122] Such assurances, however, did little
to assuage the Rhenish provincial governor. An intransigent East
Elbian and Pietist personally weary of all popular festivities of any
kind, Provincial Governor Kleist-Retzow remained opposed throughout the reactionary period to the missions. Even as late as January
1872, however, when the Jesuit missions had become a matter of hysterical debate throughout the empire and only months before the Jesuit
order was banned, the Bürgermeister of Hüls in the Düsseldorf district
reported to the district Landrat at Kempen that at the mission held in
his town not one word in the sermons could have been taken as an
affront to non-Catholics.[123]

Government reports throughout the period of reaction also stated
repeatedly that the sermons steered clear of political polemics. To the
extent the sermons did have a political content, according to officials,
they bolstered the authority of the state. In the postrevolutionary
period, state authorities could not have been more pleased by a counterrevolutionary sermon in 1852 that preached that "state relations are
divine decrees, obedience to authority a service to God, sacrifice for the
fatherland a divinely inspired sacrifice, that authority is a sublime
height established by God, in which subjects are deeply invested in

120. Bericht der *Vossische Zeitung,* Nr. 171, 1858, *Aktenstücke,* 270.

121. HSTAD, RA, PB, Nr. 1239, Bericht, Düren, to RP Kühlwetter, Aachen, 31 Aug. 1859,
Bl. 164.

122. LHAK, Best. 403, Nr. 7511, RP, Aachen, to OP, Koblenz, 13 Sept. 1859, Bl. 367–77;
see also RP, Aachen, to OP Kleist-Retzow, Koblenz, 26 July 1856, Bl. 157–59.

123. HSTAD, RD, P, Nr. 1252, BM, Hüls, to LA, Kempen, 17 Jan. 1872, Bl. 15.

accordance with the will of God."[124] In 1853 the Landrat at Geilenkirchen reported to District Governor Kühlwetter in Aachen, "In political respects [the Jesuits] have exercised no influence except to admonish the people to obey the king and the authorities."[125] In the same year even the governor of the district of Minden, otherwise no friend of Catholicism, admitted,

Up until now nothing of a politically damaging nature has been observed about the Jesuits. On the contrary, it appears their sermons have had a laudable effect. They have brought forth an energetic expression of loyal behavior from the inhabitants of Paderborn in recent times. It appears believable, as people maintain, that the Jesuits' lectures frequently discuss the obedience due the laws and the authority of the state especially when one considers that the democratic party, which has entirely different goals in mind, has never found any encouragement from the Jesuits.[126]

In 1856, despite the common allegation that the Jesuits were spreading anti-Prussian propaganda, the police commissioner at Trier reported that the Jesuits had, in fact, exerted no "anti-Prussian influence" on the population.[127] Again in 1857 the Bürgermeister of Brügger reported to the Landrat of district Kempen that at the missions held in his town "not a single word was expressed against the state or against other confessions."[128] Later in 1866, according to the report of the Landrat at Wittlich to the district governor in Trier, the sermons held at the mission in Monzel had "absolutely no political color and contained even less of an attack on the state government."[129]

Despite the benefits that such sermons gave to the authority of the state, and contrary to government reports concerning the confessionally and politically unpolemical character of the Jesuit sermons, gov-

124. Bericht des Erzbischöfl. Ordinariats vom 11 Nov. 1852 an den König von Bayern, *Aktenstücke*, 174.

125. HSTAD, RA, PB, Nr. 1239, LA, Geilenkirchen, to RP Köhlwetter, Bezirk Aachen, 15 July 1853, Bl. 63.

126. Quoted in Sperber, *Popular Catholicism*, 61.

127. LHAK, Best. 403, OPR, Nr. 7511, report of PD Tillgen, Trier, 24 June 1856, Bl. 147–48.

128. HSTAD, RD, P, Nr. 1252, BM Schwartz, Brügger, to LA, Kempen, 19 March 1857, Bl. 104.

129. LHAK, Best. 442, RBT, Nr. 3963, LA, Wittlich, to RP Gärtner, Trier, 20 Nov. 1866, Bl. 385–86.

ernment authorities insisted that the Jesuits threatened the state and religious peace. In Aachen, for example, where the Jesuits were especially active, the district authorities alarmingly reported in 1856 that the Jesuits were winning "more and more influence. Their sermons are the best attended of the entire city."[130] Here the congregation was purportedly making large financial contributions to help with the building of a permanent Jesuit settlement. Police Commissioner Hirsch in Aachen informed District Governor Kühlwetter that the Jesuits were "sparing no means to achieve their goals." In congregational assemblies in the parish churches, the police commissioner reported, the Jesuits were "applying all their oratorical skill to win over the members for themselves."[131]

Well into the 1860s, government officials maintained their belief in the Jesuit threat by insisting on its insidious character. In 1865 Police Commissioner Hirsch expressed a central theme in the anti-Jesuitism of government authorities when he explained to his superior that the means by which the Jesuits exerted and spread their control in political affairs was indirect and covert: "Even if it is undoubtable, that the order in public affairs (e.g., in the elections for Bürgermeister and municipal commissioners) exercises at least indirectly its influence through the all-powerful clerical party here, there is nevertheless no positive proof for it."[132] It followed that allegations concerning the Jesuit danger could not be subject to evidence and verification with surveillance reports. By arguing that although the Jesuits' attempts to gain control over the Catholic population for both religious and political ends were undetectable or unprovable, they were no less real, state officials were free to develop an array of Jesuit threats.

On one level, the anti-Jesuitism of Prussian state authorities during the period of reaction represented anxieties about un-German or anti-Prussian "ultramontanism" and the reassertion of Austrian influence in central Europe. Reports from the provincial governor of the Rhineland only fueled these fears. According to Police Commissioner Junker in Koblenz in his report to the district governor in 1856, for example, the Jesuits represented a foreign and Austrian presence that compromised Prussian state security. Junker offered his superiors a reading list about the missions in case the state wanted to pursue the assumption "that the Jesuit order has a more ultramontane than German and more Austrian than

130. LHAK, Best. 403, Nr. 7511, Aachen, 15 May 1856, Bl. 131; HSTAD, RD, P, Nr. 1252, Bl. 66.

131. LHAK, Best. 403, Nr. 7511, PP Hirsch, Aachen, to RP Kühlwetter, Aachen, 10 Oct. 1865; HSTAD, RA, P, Nr. 1239, PP, Aachen, to RP Kühlwetter, Aachen, 10 Oct. 1865, Bl. 195–98.

132. HSTAD, RA, P, Nr. 1239, PP, Aachen, to RP Kühlwetter, Aachen, 10 Oct. 1865, Bl. 195–98.

Prussian character." According to the police commissioner, the Jesuits were inculcating pro-Austrian *grossdeutsch* sentiments among the population. "That the Austrian state principle," he argued, "has been predominant in the order for centuries and that this does not agree with the Prussian [principle], is hardly disputable."[133] Similarly, the Landrat at Malmedy, district Aachen, reported in 1859, "Jesuit ultramontanism is represented here in abundance and is throwing itself on Austria."[134]

On another level, the Jesuit order represented, according to Prussian authorities, a rogue "state within the state," a hostile camp inside the nation or parasite in the body of Prussia. Authorities believed that the Jesuit order preyed upon religiously devout, wealthy widows, secretly soliciting large donations and amassing large sums of cash in order to establish permanent residence in the Rhineland. In 1857, District Governor Eduard von Möller in Cologne alarmingly reported directly to Minister of the Interior Ferdinand von Westphalen in Berlin that the Jesuits were purchasing property in his district.[135] In 1858 both Möller and District Governor Kühlwetter in Aachen reported to provincial governor of the Rhineland Kleist-Retzow that Jesuits had acquired property and were building a monastery and a church in Bonn and a residence in Aachen, the latter with funds donated by private persons.[136] Subsequently, however, the Landrat in district Erkelenz reported to District Governor Kühlwetter that there was no increase in bequests to the so-called dead hand—religious orders, monasteries, churches, hospitals, and orphanages administered by religious orders—sinkholes for otherwise productive capital.[137] The Landrat of district Düren also reported that bequests to the "dead hand" had been insubstantial during the last decade and had not significantly increased in the past few years.[138] Nevertheless, Kühlwetter's report two weeks

133. LHAK, Best. 403, Nr. 7511, PD Junker, Koblenz, to RP, Koblenz, 28 Feb. 1856, Bl. 99–106.

134. HSTAD, RA, P, Nr. 1239, LA to RP Kühlwetter, Aachen, 13 Aug. 1859, Bl. 156. Of course, pro-Austrian comments such as those expressed by Father Hillebrand, not a Jesuit but the indefatigable director of the missions in the Diocese of Paderborn, did nothing to alleviate the concerns of state officials. In a sermon after the Corpus Christi celebration in Lichtenau in 1854, he asked his audience to pray, "May the Lord God uphold the House of Austria, bulwark and protector of the Catholic Church for many years." Quotation from Sperber, *Popular Catholicism,* 104.

135. LHAK, Best. 403, Nr. 7511, RP Moeller, Köln, to Königlichen Staats-Minister und Minister des Innern Westphalen, Berlin, 13 June 1857.

136. LHAK, Best. 403, Nr. 7511, RP, Köln, to OP Kleist-Retzow, Koblenz, 7 May 1858, Bl. 267–69; RP, Aachen, to OP Kleist-Retzow, Koblenz, 5 Aug. 1858, Bl. 301–6.

137. HSTAD, RA, P, Nr. 1239, LA, Erkelenz, to RP, Aachen, 21 Aug. 1859, Bl. 160.

138. HSTAD, RA, P, Nr. 1239, LA, Düren, to RP Kühlwetter, Aachen, 31 Aug. 1859, Bl. 164. See also LHAK, Best. 442, RBT, Nr. 3963, BM to LA, Milbringen, 7 April 1867.

later to the new Rhenish provincial governor, Pommer-Esche, dismissed these reports and doggedly argued that this was only as it appeared on the surface. "Evidently, the donations are of a form that elude monitoring; false names are used, donations are made from hand to hand, and collections are made without attracting attention." Was it not a "public secret," he asked, that the Jesuits already owned considerable property and that the persons in whose name the property was purchased were only being used as front men?[139] Though such allegations could not be substantiated, the conviction that the Catholic Church was draining productive capital in an age devoted to industrial expansion was shared by many Prussian civil servants. In 1865 Police Commissioner Hirsch in Aachen argued, "Only rarely does news about the donations and bequests flowing to the Jesuits come to public attention since the order has purposely avoided acquiring property through the arrangement of testaments." Instead straw men were set up secretly to funnel money to the Jesuits.[140] Such reports preserved the notion of capital squandered on the Jesuits and other religious orders, promoting their interests at the expense of productive economic development and capitalist expansion.

While the reactionary ministry in Berlin had backed down, retracting the antimissionary decree of 1852, many authorities in the Rhineland especially after 1855 continued to push for suppression of the Jesuits and the missions. They were frustrated throughout the latter half of the 1850s by Berlin's apparent unwillingness or legal incapacity to act decisively in the face of the Jesuit menace. The efforts of District Governor Möller in Cologne illustrate both the obstinacy and exasperation of Rhineland authorities. In December 1858 he warned Provincial Governor Pommer-Esche about the Jesuit settlements in Bonn and Aachen. Here, he argued, the Jesuits were "digging themselves in more and more firmly; they have begun to accumulate a considerable means at their disposal." The district governor could only once again unequivocally state "that the Jesuit settlements are not to be tolerated." In the hopeless bureaucratese typical of a Prussian civil servant he argued, "It is desirable to be rid of them. We can raise from the side of the state government no doubts; just as little does it need to

139. LHAK, Best. 403, Nr. 7511, RP, Aachen, to OP Pommer-Esche, Koblenz, 13 Sept. 1859, Bl. 367–77.

140. LHAK, Best. 403, Nr. 7511, PP Hirsch, Aachen, to RP Kühlwetter, Aachen, 10 Oct. 1865; HSTAD, RA, P, Nr. 1239, PP to RP Kühlwetter, Aachen, 10 Oct. 1865, Bl. 195–98.

be doubted that *their removal* is gladly seen as altogether necessary *by all sensible patriots*" (emphasis in original).[141]

District Governor Möller believed the various constitutional rights and legal obstacles preventing state action against the Jesuits should be either circumvented or abrogated, and he searched tirelessly for ways to do so. As early as August 1853 he had argued to the provincial governor that the Jesuit settlements were not protected by the Law of Association and Assembly of 11 March 1850, guaranteeing the right of association and freedom from state interference. In October 1853 he argued again that the Jesuit institutions were not legally sanctioned by the state. He took up the cause again in August 1857, arguing that the Jesuit order lay outside the legal organization of the Catholic Church and therefore was not protected by the right of association of religious corporations. Finally in his report of December 1858 he carefully spelled out an interpretation of the pertinent articles of the constitution of the Prussian state that stipulated that the Catholic Church was free to administer its own affairs only so long as the state specifically affirmed those associational laws that allowed it to do so.[142] Frustrated yet tireless, Möller continued to demand in subsequent reports to the Rhenish provincial governor in Koblenz that the state eliminate the Jesuit menace. Even many good priests, he argued, "passionately complain about the weakness of the government," which permitted "the unlawful efforts of a party antagonistic to the Prussian state within the Catholic Church."[143] Although in 1852 District Governor Kühlwetter in Aachen had advised Berlin not to ban the missions in the Rhineland, by 1859 he had joined Möller's efforts to put pressure on superiors in the governmental hierarchy. He believed it was now necessary to resolve any ambiguity on the part of the state regarding the Jesuit question: "It seems high time," he argued, "for the state government to decide whether the Jesuit order should be tolerated or not."[144] In a subsequent report in 1860, he argued that legislation existed that prohibited Jesuits and other monastic clergy in Prussia that did not belong to specific dioceses.[145]

According to Prussian government officials, the Jesuits and other orders leading the missions practiced monasticism, a form of associa-

141. HSTAD, Best. 403, Nr. 7511, RP Möller, Köln, to OP, Koblenz, 14 Dec. 1858.
142. Ibid.
143. LHAK, Best. 403, Nr. 7511, RP Möller, Köln, to OP, 27 Sept. 1859, Bl. 385–87.
144. LHAK, Best. 403, Nr. 7511, RP, Aachen, to OP, Koblenz, 13 Sept. 1859, Bl. 367–77.
145. LHAK, Best. 403, Nr. 7511, RP to OP, Aachen, 21 Feb. 1860, Bl. 395–403.

tion so peculiar that it could not be protected by laws that guaranteed freedom of public association. According to a report from the Department of the Interior in the district of Aachen to Provincial Governor Pommer-Esche in 1859, monasteries represented a grotesque aberration of human life, entailing a suppression of the individual and a violent contortion of personality: "The vows of poverty, chastity, and unqualified obedience established under the abdication of all personal freedom and independence, impossible in a mere association, can only be realized in the polarized expression of the person." The report argued that, because religious orders had an effect on public affairs "like schools, churches, missions, welfare for the poor and sick, and burial," they should be considered political associations and were bound, therefore, by the more stringent laws regulating such associations.[146] By 1860, according to reports of the Department of the Interior in the district of Aachen, the majority of state authorities believed that the Jesuit and monastic orders were not legally protected associations. One report argued that since religious orders were hardly associations in any normal sense, they could not find refuge in the Law of Association and Assembly. As evidence it offered the depressing example of life in a Trappist monastery: the Trappists' "primary activity consists of communal prayer in choir and silent contemplation; apart from that they regularly spend many hours of the day in physical work, namely, in agriculture. Characteristically the order is under the absolute rule of the most stringent silence which may only be interrupted with the greeting *memento mori*."[147]

Throughout the 1850s, during the period of reaction, despite most reports that the Jesuit sermons were not offensive to Protestants and that they always upheld Prussian (not to mention Protestant) state authority, government officials and authorities argued that the Jesuits threatened confessional peace and state authority.[148] By insisting that there was far more to the Jesuits' activities and influence than met the eye, they developed notions of a Jesuit conspiracy: Jesuits exercising political power through the clerical parties, Jesuits as agents of anti-Prussian and pro-Austrian intrigue, Jesuits quietly assembling large

146. LHAK, Best. 403, Nr. 7532, "Die Auseinandersetzung des Staates mit der Kirche, 1855–1869," Abteilung des Innern, Aachen, to OP, Koblenz, 24 Nov. 1859, Bl. 113–22.

147. LHAK, Best. 403, Nr. 7532, Abteilung des Innern, Aachen, to OP, Koblenz, 8 Nov. 1860, Bl. 171–75.

148. In the provincial and district archive files on the Jesuits and religious orders, the missionary campaigns, and the Catholic Church, regular government reports on the missions in the Rhineland either stopped or more likely no longer exist after the end of the 1850s.

sums of cash and property to augment their own power within the
state. Authorities feared that the Jesuits were generating a religiously
fervent and organized Catholic public with serious political implications. Such beliefs were expressed in the authorities' arguments that the
Jesuit order and other religious orders were political associations that
covertly and indirectly had an influence on political elections and public affairs. Local and district authorities in the Rhineland, where the
impact of the missionary crusade and the Catholic revival was especially dramatic, repeatedly demanded that the state take action against
the Jesuits and their missions. They were already doing so some twenty
years before the founding of the empire, the initiation of the Kulturkampf, and the implementation of the law of 1872 that banned the
Jesuits and monastic orders from German territory.

CHAPTER 2

Protestantism, Anti-Catholicism, and the Reconstruction of German Liberalism

Within the Catholic population, the missionaries and particularly the Jesuits were revered for having such a large role in the restoration of religious faith and for delivering to Catholicism in Germany a new lease on life. Catholics, however, were not the only ones drawn to the missions, and the missions had a religious significance beyond their impact on Catholics and Catholicism in the German states. Even though the missions did not intend to attract and convert non-Catholics, they nonetheless drew huge numbers of Protestants from all over Germany. In towns like Unterkochen bei Ellwangen in the Diocese of Rothenburg in 1854, a quarter of the participants at the mission were Protestant.[1] In 1860 in Lüdenscheidt in the Diocese of Paderborn, half of those attending the Franciscan sermons were Protestants. The parish priest thought that "their attitude showed that they were deeply moved."[2] At the evening sermons of the mission in Emden in the Diocese of Osnabrück in 1862, "the educated part of the Protestants, namely the civil officials, were always represented in large numbers."[3] All this belongs to a remarkable story passed over by historians accustomed to assuming that if not the Catholic than at least the Protestant population of Germany was headed down the secular road of the nineteenth century. For example, one important historian of Catholicism

---

1. Bericht des P. v. Zeil in seinem Tagebuch, 1–12 Oct. 1854, *Aktenstücke,* 232.

2. Pf. Baumhöer an Bischof Conrad Martin, Lüdenscheid, 26 April 1860. *Volksmissionen der norddeutschen Franziskaner,* 62.

3. Pf. Nieters, Emden, an den Bischof Paulus Melchers von Osnabrück, Emden, 5 April 1864, *Aktenstücke,* 319.

in Germany concluded that after 1850 although Catholicism was an expanding milieu, the Protestant milieu was in retreat.[4]

Yet the church's missionary crusade had an impact on Protestantism, however much unintended, no less important than its impact on Catholicism. Without recognizing the revival of Protestantism, we cannot fully appreciate in general the social and cultural history of Germany and in particular the rise of confessional conflict between the 1848 Revolution and unification. It was the Protestant revival unleashed by the missions and in response to the missions and the revival of the Protestant animus for Catholicism that provided the religious context for the attack on Catholicism in the 1870s. Not only in towns and villages but also in predominantly Protestant, secularizing cities the number of Protestant participants at the missions was also high. Despite the vitriolic barrage of articles against the missions and the Jesuits in the local newspapers, when the missionaries came to Bremen in 1863 the Protestant churches stood empty while their congregations attended their sermons.[5] Protestants from all social walks of life were attracted to the missions, and Protestant interest in the missions even reached up to the highest levels of the monarchy. Among the attentive participants at the mission in Bonn in 1851 was no less than Prince Friedrich Wilhelm, student at the university and heir to the Prussian throne. He was especially taken by the power and the eloquence of the Jesuit sermons. To the embarrassment and frustration of state authorities and the Protestant church leadership critical of the missions, Friedrich Wilhelm's attendance was publicly approved by his father, Prince Wilhelm, future king of Prussia and as such supreme bishop of the Protestant Church and later emperor of Germany.[6] The missions were, therefore, remarkably mixed and emotionally charged events, not only religiously but socially, and as such they quickly became a threat to Prussian conservatives and state authorities intent now on a decade of reaction, order, and control after the convulsions of the revolution.

Protestant pastors and church leaders responded to the Catholic revival and, more important, to the competition posed by the attractiveness of the missions for their own congregations with a flood of anti-Catholic, anticlerical, and anti-Jesuit sermons and pamphlets. The

4. Sperber, *Popular Catholicism*, 294.
5. *Bremer Bürgerfreund*, 28 May 1863, *Aktenstücke*, 306.
6. *Aktenstücke*, 57 n. 1; Gatz, *Rheinische Volksmission*, 97; Murphy, *Der Wiederaufbau der Gesellschaft Jesu*, 108–9.

anti-Catholic vitriol of the Protestant leadership served to preserve and demarcate Protestant identity as it exacerbated tensions between Protestants and Catholics. At the same time, in general the Catholic missionaries on confessional matters exercised polemical restraint, proving themselves consistently tolerant of Protestants and Protestantism. Indeed, part of the appeal of the missionary sermons was precisely their general Christian inclusiveness and applicability.

Just as important, the missions and the religious revival, both Catholic and Protestant, provided the context for the rehabilitation of liberalism in Germany after the defeat of 1848 and during the new age of industrialization. During the decade of reaction and into what contemporaries called the New Era of the 1860s, liberals developed new anti-Catholic and anticlerical representations and images. Often couched within a broad discourse of cultural Protestantism, anti-Catholicism became a powerful way to reorient liberalism toward postrevolutionary, middle-class priorities, including constitutional reform, educational progress, free-market economics, and industrial development. The Roman Catholic Church leadership responded to liberal anti-Catholicism and anticlericalism with the attempt to drive liberal ideology from its ranks, intolerance that made it increasingly difficult for middle-class Catholics to be at once faithful to their church and to liberalism. Attention to the cultural and economic agenda of anti-Catholicism and identifying the social dimensions of the Kulturkampf are important because they reveal that the antichurch campaign of the 1870s was neither simply nor primarily Protestant but more specifically a middle-class, liberal movement for modernity and hegemony in Germany.

The Protestant Revival

Scores of parish reports, Catholic newspapers, and state surveillance reports indicate that not just Protestants but also Jews were drawn to the missions. A few examples make the case: in 1853 at the mission in Dortmund, a local priest reported to his bishop that "Protestants of all classes are appearing in large numbers and repeatedly; Jews are also coming."[7] At the evening sermons of the mission at Oberwesel in the Diocese of Trier in 1856 not only "many Protestants from the vicinity

---

7. Pf. Wiemann an Bischof Drepper von Paderborn, Dortmund, 20 March 1853, *Aktenstücke*, 203.

but even their pastors and even Jews" attended.[8] A report to the bishop of Paderborn in 1858 concerning the mission in Arnsberg stated that "a great number of the local Protestants and even the Jews attended the sermons almost without interruption."[9] The parish priest at Neheim in the Diocese of Paderborn reported that all the Protestants and all the Jews in the town attended the sermons given by the Franciscan mission there in 1868.[10] The parish priest at the mission at Allenstein in 1857 reported to his bishop that Jews knelt down together with Catholics and Protestants and wept during the sermons.[11] These were scenes, according to clerical reports, repeated all over the German states.[12] The reports are corroborated by newspaper accounts and government surveillance reports that also record the attendance of Protestants and Jews at the missions. According to the Catholic journal *Sion*, Jewish families attended the sermon given for children at the mission in Würzburg in 1853. A Jewish father told his son, "You hear what the Lord says. Follow."[13] In 1856 at the mission in Trier, the police com-

8. Pf. Klütsch an Bischof Wilhelm (Arnoldi) von Trier über die vom 17 Feb. bis 2 März abgehaltene Mission, Oberwesel, 3 March 1856, *Aktenstücke*, 248.

9. Pf. Koop an Bischof Konrad Martin, Arnsberg, 9 Dec. 1858, *Aktenstücke*, 273.

10. Pf. Münstermann an Bischof Conrad Martin, Neheim, 20 March 1868, *Volksmission der norddeutschen Franziskaner*, 94.

11. Erzpriester Pruss an den Bischof Josef Ambrosius von Ermland, Allenstein, 29 Sept. 1857, *Aktenstücke*, 264.

12. Other clerical sources recording the attendance of not only Protestants but also Jews at the sermons include Pf. Baur an den Bischof von Münster, Cleve, 10 March 1851, *Aktenstücke*, 56; Stadtdechant Dilschneider an Kardinal Johannes v. Geissel, Aachen, 20 May 1851, *Aktenstücke*, 64; Bericht des Pf. Neumann an den Kardinal v. Diepenbrock, Würzburg, 28 Feb. to 7 March 1852, *Aktenstücke*, 121; Bericht des Pf. Walther, Weißenburg (Straßburg), 14 June 1852, *Aktenstücke*, 136; Bericht des Erzbischöfl. Ordinariats vom 11 Nov. 1852 an den König von Bayern, *Aktenstücke*, 176; Erzpriester Pruß an den Bischof Joseph Ambrosius von Ermland, Allenstein, 29 Sept. 1857, *Aktenstücke*, 265; Pf. Endepols an das Erzbischöfl. Generalvikariat Köln, Heinsberg, 5 Aug. 1859, *Aktenstücke*, 280; Die Pf. Pees und Gerken an den Bischof Konrad Martin, Warburg, 17 Dec. 1859, *Aktenstücke*, 282; Dekan Kammer (?) an den Bischof von der Marwitz in Pelpin, Damsdorf, 26 Aug. 1861, *Aktenstücke*, 298; Pf. Stein an P. Zurstraßen, Montabaur, 20 Jan. 1865, *Aktenstücke*, 341; Pf. Antoni an das Generalvikariat in Paderborn, Hultrop, 24 Sept. 1868, *Aktenstücke*, 381; Pf. Kleine an das Generalvikariat in Paderborn, Lippspringe, 13 Feb. 1871, *Aktenstücke*, 405.

13. *Sion*, Nr. 25, 27 Feb. 1853, *Aktenstücke*, 197. Other journal or newspaper reports recording the attendance of Jews at the sermons include *Schwäbische Chronik des Schwäb. Merkur*, Nr. 98, 24 April 1850, *Aktenstücke*, 23; *Augsburger Abendzeitung*, 1 Aug. 1853; *Sion*, Nr. 16 [Beilage], 7 Aug. 1853, *Aktenstücke*, 213–15; *Schlesische Zeitung*, Nr. 596, 1855, *Aktenstücke*, 245–46; "Westf. Kirchenblatt für Katholiken," 31 May 1851, *Volksmission der norddeutschen Franziskaner*, 35; and "Kathol. Missionsblatt," 4 July 1858, *Volksmission der norddeutschen Franziskaner*, 49.

missioner recorded that "a very large number of every confession" attended the sermons.[14] Meanwhile, the police commissioner at Koblenz reported that a Jesuit sermon was heavily attended by Catholics of all classes and by those of the "Protestant confession and the Jewish religion."[15]

If there ever was a time when the different religious populations of Germany crossed over the confessional divide, what the historian Etienne François has called the "invisible boundary," this was it.[16] Especially in light of Gangolf Hübinger's conclusion that the boundaries between the confessions remained all but closed, the missions, as interconfessional "contact zones," offer an important opportunity to move from the traditional study of confessional monocultures to the ways religious populations interacted and mutually shaped interconfessional attitudes.[17] In religiously mixed communities, Jews in villages and rural areas whether they lived as merchants, rabbis, teachers, tailors, or homemakers learned a great deal about the beliefs and practices of Christianity at the missions.[18] Protestants learned firsthand, often against their long-held prejudiced stereotypes, and for themselves, not with the tainted sentiments of their own religious leaders, about the Jesuits, the missionary campaign, and Catholicism.

But the missions with their excitement and their religious fervor not only cut across confessional lines; they generated a remarkable and unprecedented class, gender, and generationally mixed public as well. Here was a spectacular sight. Nowhere else and at no earlier time during the course of the nineteenth century did so many different kinds of people—Catholics, Protestants, and Jews; aristocrats, bourgeois, workers, and peasants; men and women; adults and children—peacefully interact as they did at the missions. This was what so concerned state authorities in the sensitive postrevolutionary years: mixed and excited crowds of hundreds or thousands or tens of thousands that represented a new and potentially even more powerful kind of public agitation.

14. LHAK, Best. 403, Nr. 7511, PD, Trier, 24 June 1856, Bl. 147–48.

15. LHAK, Best. 403, Nr. 7511, PD Junker, Koblenz, to the RP, Koblenz, 28 Feb. 1856, Bl. 99–106.

16. Etienne François, *Die unsichtbare Grenze: Protestanten und Katholiken in Augsburg, 1648–1806,* trans. Angelika Steiner-Wendt (Sigmaringen: Jan Thorbecke Verlag, 1991).

17. Gangolf Hübinger, "Confessionalism," in *Imperial Germany: A Historiographical Companion,* ed. Roger Chickering (Westport, Conn.: Greenwood, 1996), 156–84.

18. See also the comments in Smith and Clark, "The Fate of Nathan," 12; and Steven M. Lowenstein, "Jüdisches religiöse Leben in deutschen Dörfen: Regionale Unterschiede im 19. und frühen 20. Jahrhundert," in *Jüdisches Leben auf dem Lande,* ed. Monika Richarz and Reinhard Rürup (Tübingen: Mohr Siebeck, 1997), 219–30.

Non-Catholics who attended the missions were not interested in leaving their faith. No records in the sources found for this study indicate that Jews converted to Catholicism at the missions. Among Protestants there were instances of conversion to Catholicism or attendance at the confessional following the sermons, but these cases were rare. The intermingling of confessional populations did not lead to significant conversions or the dissolution of confessional consciousness. On the contrary, the consciousness of the other made possible at the missions contributed to the heightened confessional self-consciousness that marked the nineteenth and early twentieth centuries. Protestants and Jews were attracted to the missions because they wanted to participate in the experience of religious revival. Protestants were, in fact, eager for a revival and joined the Catholic missions only because they had none of their own to attend. In 1864 one parish priest reported with a measure of self-satisfaction that Protestants in Hüpstedt in the Diocese of Paderborn confessed, "If only we were so lucky. If only we could have such a mission!"[19]

Even in a Protestant, secularizing city like Hamburg the Catholic missions had an impact. Protestants were so deeply impressed by the mission in 1862 that they occupied every seat in the Roman Catholic church and, in effect, displaced the Catholic parishioners. According to one Protestant observer they believed that the sermons were an especially influential instrument in the Catholic Church that the Evangelical Church should not simply look upon with scorn and envy. Hamburg Protestants, he believed, attended the mission in order to learn from the Catholic Church how the Evangelical Church might organize its own religious revival. The Catholic revival was successful first of all, he argued, because the Catholic Church recognized in this age of religious indifference the need to return the laity to the fundamentals of faith and worship, what he called "the ABCs of Christianity." Second, unlike Protestant sermons, the themes of the missionary sermons also had more popular impact because they were cumulative and cyclical. "We left the church in any case with the wish that those in the Protestant Church, cursing and complaining about the efforts of the Catholics, would instead learn from them a way to revive spiritual life and to promote the kingdom of God." Meanwhile, in this worldly and prosperous Hamburg *Hansastadt,* Protestants, he concluded, had the Catholics to thank for reminding them that there was more to life than

---

19. Pf. Sittel am Bischof Conrad Martin, Hüpstedt, 19 March 1864, *Volksmissionen der norddeutschen Franziskaner,* 85.

buying and selling, socializing and slumber.[20] In the absence of an organized campaign for Protestant revival, Protestants all over Germany continued to be drawn to the Catholic missions for Christian instruction. The liberal-Protestant *Bremer Bürgerfreund* did not disapprove: it was better that secularized Protestants be brought back into the Christian fold by Catholic missionaries than not at all.[21]

Protestants participated in the missions without offense since the sermons predominantly offered general Christian instruction common to both confessions (the immortality of the soul, the Trinity, the Ten Commandments, the divinity of Christ), not exclusively Roman Catholic doctrine and dogma. When in 1852 the missions faced prohibition by the Protestant state, the *Evangelisches Kirchen- und Schulblatt für Schlesien und Posen* argued, "Even we Protestants have no reason to be angry about [the Jesuit missions]; most of their sermons were without confessional impurities."[22] Protestant attendants and Catholic priests too believed that the sermons had much to offer Protestants, not as potential converts to Catholicism but as fellow Christians. The mission at Nordhausen in the Diocese of Paderborn in 1860 "wasn't just a mission for Catholics; it was a mission for thousands of Protestants too" according to the local priest.[23] District officials and provincial authorities in the Rhineland, many of whom had anticipated that the mission sermons would disrupt confessional peace, were impressed by the relative, though not complete, absence of confessional polemics.[24] The missionaries took care to steer clear of topics that would alienate Protestants. To be sure, there were excep-

20. *Boten a.d. Alstertal*, Nr. 16, 1862, *Aktenstücke*, 301.

21. *Bremer Bürgerfreund*, 28 May 1863, *Aktenstücke*, 306.

22. *Evangelisches Kirchen- und Schulblatt für Schlesien und Posen*, Nr. 20, 13 May 1852, *Aktenstücke*, 126.

23. Pf. Baumhoer an den Bischof Konrad Martin, Nordhausen, 24 April 1860, *Aktenstücke*, 283.

24. HSTAD, Best. RD, P, Nr. 1252, "Katholische Orden und Missionen: Betr. vor allem Niederlassungen und Missionsveranstaltungen des Jesuitenordens," Bd. 1, 1852–87; BM Schwartz, Brügger, to LRA, Kempen, 19 March 1857, Bl. 10; HSTAD, Best. RA, P, Nr. 1239, "Missionaren, Jesuiten, Lazaristen: Ordenstätigkeit derselben in Kirche und Schule, 1835–1916," LR, Düren, to RP Kühlwetter, Aachen, 31 Aug. 1859, Bl. 164; LHAK, Best. 422, RBT, Nr. 3963, "Wirken und Verhalten der katholischen Missionen und der Jesuiten, 1850–1900," LR, Wittlich, to PR Gärtner, Trier, 20 Nov. 1866, Bl. 385–86; LHAK, Best. 403, OPR, Nr. 7511, "Die Jesuiten, 1855–65," RP, Aachen, to OPR Pommer-Esche, Koblenz, 13 Sept. 1859, Bl. 367–77; PD Tilligen, Trier, 24 June 1856, Bl. 147–48; and RP, Aachen, to OPR Kleist-Retzow, Koblenz, 26 July 1856, Bl. 157–59. But for a sarcastic attack by a missionary on Luther's translation of the Bible, see HSTAD, Best. RD, P, Nr. 1252, Duisberg, 1 June 1856, BM to LR Keshler, Bl. 72.

tions, but the zealotry and ultramontanism of the missionaries did not automatically mean intolerance. This was primarily the case because the church leadership, the missionaries, and the parish clergy never considered the missionary campaign a continuation or revival of the Counter-Reformation of the sixteenth century. To the contrary, even the Redemptorists, who as a whole delivered even more fervent sermons than the Jesuits, believed that polemicizing against Protestantism would have been a "sin against truth and charity."[25]

Those missionaries who did provoke controversy were immediately disciplined by the bishops, and the bishops continued to work diligently throughout the campaign to maintain harmonious relations between Protestants and Catholics. A specific incident serves to make the general point. At the celebration of Ascension Day in 1855, during a mission held in Neufalz near Breslau in the predominantly Protestant province of Silesia, a young, eager, and inexperienced Jesuit ignited interconfessional controversy with a sermon that included the enormously sensitive topic of mixed marriages. To his confessionally mixed audience, he exclaimed, "If Catholic parents who are in mixed marriages don't baptize and raise their children Catholic, then the parents and the children are damned." The local Protestants were outraged, and the following Sunday the Protestant pastor immediately counterattacked the Jesuit's sermon from his own pulpit. Copies of his sermon were quickly published under the title "Words of Reassurance in the Face of the Denunciation of our Evangelical Confession" and then distributed throughout the community. The local Catholic priest, Father Plüschke, then joined the fray. He claimed that the Protestant pastor had exploited an unfortunate incident to attack and spread lies about the Catholic Church. At his own pulpit, he held up and then with dramatic flourish ripped to shreds a copy of the pastor's "diatribe" against Catholicism in front of his sobbing congregation.[26] Higher authorities and cooler heads in the church, however, knew full well that the success of the missions depended on prudence and restraint regarding interconfessional matters. For Bishop Förster of Breslau, therefore, the mission in Neufalz had been nothing less than a disaster. In his letter to Father Plüschke he angrily argued that "with a single, careless assertion from a missionary—an assertion that has no foundation—all the old prejudices and the old hatred of the Jesuits have been reawakened

---

25. Weiss, *Redemptoristen in Bayern,* 1096–97, 1107.
26. Pf. Plüschke an Fürstbischof Förster in Breslau, Neufalz, 31 May 1855, *Aktenstücke,* 238–39.

and their pious activities hindered perhaps for a long time." The bishop of Breslau reprimanded the priest for having thrown oil on fire and instructed him to reestablish confessional harmony in his community.[27] Interconfessional marriages remained, however, a particularly inflammatory issue. A year after the incident in Neufalz, the Bürgermeister of Duisburg reported to the Landrat at Kempen that some in his town suspected a Catholic husband spurred on by the Jesuit sermons had so castigated his Protestant wife that she attempted suicide. She then fell into a fever and died.[28]

Some Protestants did disapprove of the missions when they arrived. Most attending the mission in Dortmund in 1853 simply sneered during the sermons (though three did convert to Catholicism).[29] A group of Protestants in Langenschwalbach in the Diocese of Limburg attacked and broke up the mission in 1856. In 1864 at Neustadt in the Pfalz, with a population of eight thousand including over five thousand Protestants and over two hundred mixed marriages, the Bürgermeister (himself Protestant) advised the district administration that a proposed mission would be considered, among other things, an "anachronism." He believed that "there is no soil here for a mission" and that "it will certainly not have any great moral influence."[30]

Yet almost everywhere else the missionaries were welcomed with enthusiasm by the Protestant population. When the Jesuits came to Damsdorf in the Diocese of Kulm in 1861, Protestants delivered flowers to the missionaries' rooms and decorated the church and pulpit with garlands and oleanders.[31] A Protestant layman eagerly defended the Jesuit mission when it came to Danzig in 1852.[32] At the Franciscan mission in Neheim the Protestant factory owner contributed to the missionaries travel-expense account.[33] One priest reported that at a mission in Ratibor in the Diocese of Breslau, Protestants were so "deeply

27. Fürstbischof Förster an Pf. Plüschke, Breslau, 11 June 1855, *Aktenstücke,* 240.

28. HSTAD, Best. RD, P, Nr. 1252, BM, Duisburg, to LR Keschler, Kempen, 1 June 1856, Bl. 72–74.

29. Pf. Wiemann an Bischof Drepper von Paderborn, Dortmund, 20 March 1853, *Aktenstücke,* 203.

30. Das Bürgermeisteramt an das königliche Bezirksamt, Neustadt a.d.H., 13 Dec. 1864, *Aktenstücke,* 329; and Das Bürgermeisteramt Neustadt a.d.H. an das königliche Bezirksamt Neustadt a.d.H., 12 Jan. 1865, *Aktenstücke,* 328.

31. Dekan Kammer (?) an den Bischof von der Marwitz in Pelpin, Darmsdorf, 26 Aug. 1861, *Aktenstücke,* 299.

32. *Über die von Missions-Priestern aus dem Orden der gesellschaft Jesu in Danzig gehaltenen Missionen.*

33. Pf. Münstermann an Bischof Conrad Martin, 20 March 1868, *Volksmissionen der norddeutschen Franziskaner,* 94.

moved" and "gripped" by the sermons that they wanted to be heard in confession.[34]

Of course, not all Protestants who attended the Catholic missions did so because they wanted to be part of a religious revival. The director of a *Gymnasium* in Danzig took his Protestant pupils to the mission sermons held in the winter of 1853 not for Christian instruction but because they served as models of eloquent and persuasive oratory.[35] For young Protestant seminarians at the University of Heidelberg, the visit of the mission in 1851 was also the occasion for an extracurricular exercise. They went ready to take copious and critical notes on Jesuit sermons and on matters of Roman Catholic doctrine and dogma.[36] Others went to the missions simply because they were curious. One Protestant author argued that the Jesuits in Hildesheim were mistaken to imagine that Protestants had come to them to listen with any sincere reverence. They went, he insisted, merely to see for themselves what all the fuss was about. The missions and sermons had, no doubt, a certain attraction as spectacle and entertainment. As a Protestant critic of the missions explained in 1851, "Protestants are already attracted to the mission sermons by natural curiosity; why shouldn't people go when something so spectacular is taking place in their neighborhood? Many want to see what these monks—now so new to us—are pushing."[37] At the same time, however, the missions, roving over large sections of Germany, especially in the Rhineland, a seat of democratic radicalism during 1848 and 1849, tapped into the energies and mass mobilization that had been both cause and effect of the revolution. The critic alluded to as much when he observed that "in the same places where they had made such racket shortly before the revolution, thousands pawed at the pulpits and confessionals of the Jesuit missionaries."[38] The Jesuits used the opportunity following the revolution, he argued, "to extend extensively and intensively the boundaries of their area and their influence." "The Jesuits," he concluded, "have always understood very well how to travel with the wind."[39]

The Catholic missions, therefore, created a rift within Protestantism between the laity, who generally approved of and willfully flocked to the missions, and their church authorities, who worried that they were

34. Pf. Heide an den Kardinal von Diepenbrock, Ratibor, 26 June 1852, *Aktenstücke,* 145.
35. Bericht des Protestanten Richard Wulckow, *Aktenstücke,* 140.
36. *Augsburger Allgemeinen Zeitung,* 22 Aug. 1851, *Aktenstücke,* 87.
37. Leibbrand, *Missionen der Jesuiten und Redemptoristen,* 58–59.
38. Ibid., 8.
39. Ibid., 24.

losing their influence over their own congregations. As a result, Protestant pastors began working harder to educate their congregations about the differences between the Protestant and Catholic faiths. As one Protestant pastor explained: "So Protestants have also drawn a profit from the Jesuit missions. Many Protestant Christians are now better informed about the doctrinal differences and show more interest in church matters than they did before. In a word, their indifference, which was the result of a long period of peace in church affairs, has come to an end."[40]

At the same time, the Catholic missionary campaign was an issue to which state officials in Berlin and the Protestant leadership reacted with equal measures of disgust and alarm. As mentioned in the previous chapter, in May 1852 Minister of Interior Ferdinand von Westphalen (himself Catholic but no friend of the Jesuits) and Minister of Educational and Ecclesiastical Affairs Karl Otto von Raumer in Berlin issued decrees placing the Jesuits under police surveillance, prohibiting Catholic seminarians from studying in Rome, and banning the missions in predominantly Protestant areas. The Raumer decrees were immediately met by Catholics with a wave of antigovernment demonstrations across the German states since they seemed to infringe on the church's constitutionally guaranteed freedom and to return to the state the right of the Vormärz period to supervise ecclesiastical affairs. The Catholic majority in the Rhenish provincial parliament resolved in a petition to the king that the decrees be revoked. The Conference of Catholic Bishops in Cologne condemned the decrees as unconstitutional, while the Catholic press unleashed a salvo of antigovernment criticisms.[41]

As the Catholic popular and ecclesiastical protests continued, the official Protestant response to the state decrees took shape at the fifth annual Evangelical Kirchentag convened in Bremen in September 1852. All other issues at the conference became irrelevant as it immediately became a referendum on the Catholic Church's missionary campaign and a crucial moment that determined the fate of not only the Catholic but also the Protestant revival. Anti-Catholic passions ran high. Red-faced Pastor Ledderhose from Brombach swore, "No flirting with the Roman church! Hate, irreconcilable hate for the infernal system of Romanism!" Ledderhose believed that the Catholic "Church

40. *Die Jesuitenmissionen in Hildesheim und damit Zusammenhängendes: Worte der Belehrung und Mahnung an den protestantischen Bürger und Landmann* (Hanover: Hermann Heuer, n.d.), 15.
41. Hyde, "Roman Catholicism and the Prussian State," 111.

was an abomination from hell." He was not alone. Pastor Krummacher from Duisburg pointed out that the Jesuits were doing the work of the devil, sowing division within Christianity so that he might more easily destroy it. Superintendent Dr. Sander from Elberfeld demanded that the "Protestant state" rise against the Jesuits, "who have been destroying the new Protestant life everywhere it has not been protected by princes, as a glance at France, Italy, Austria, Bohemia, etc., demonstrates." Professor Piper from Berlin reminded his colleagues that the goal of the missions was not so much the revival of Catholicism as the "destruction of Protestantism." Superintendent Wachnagel from Elberfeld concluded, "No union is possible with the Catholics until the pope himself becomes Protestant."[42] Piper introduced a resolution supporting the state decrees restricting the missions and calling on the state to ban the activities of the Society of Jesus.

But cooler-headed and more calculating Protestant authorities had already grasped that curtailing the missions and banning the Jesuits would not serve their own best interests. The leading Protestant defender of the Catholic missions was surprisingly none other than Ernst Wilhelm Hengstenberg. As a theologian at the University of Berlin, editor of the prestigious *Evangelische Kirchenzeitung,* and no friend of Roman Catholicism, he had tirelessly dedicated his talents and energies to Protestant throne and altar. Hengstenberg was well recognized for his efforts to purge Protestantism of the influences of rationalism and neohumanism. He worked continuously to join Protestantism to the campaign to root out all forms of opposition to the will of the monarchy. It was a matter of course that he agreed with other Protestant clergy that the Jesuits were destroying science and Bildung with what he called "barbarity." Their sermons, he complained, were without any morally edifying content and always catered to the base instincts of the lower classes. It was precisely for these reasons that the Jesuits' power, he warned, should not be underestimated since it was directed not only at the Catholic but also at the Protestant population.

A conservative idealist with an acute sense of pragmatism, Hengstenberg was, however, not blind to the fact that the Protestant Church benefited from the missions. He believed that the new challenge posed by the missions and the temptation they presented to Protestants would only lift the Protestant Church up out of its slumber. He argued that confessional coexistence was fortunately sanctioned by the terms

---

42. Verhandlung des fünften deutschen evangelischen Kirchentages in Bremen, 15 Sept. 1852, *Aktenstücke,* 159–60.

of the Peace of Westphalia of 1648 ending thirty years of bloody war between Catholics and Protestants across Europe. Not a plea for tolerance, this was a reminder that confessional conflict, like temptation, sin, and the struggle between good and evil, was the necessary condition of humankind in the world. This condition was no less necessary for the spiritual growth of the entirety than it was for the individual: it exposed humanity's defects, self-delusion, and false sense of security and ultimately proved to humanity that it could find salvation only in God. "Prayer, contemplation and temptation," Hengstenberg explained, "are the components of Lutheran theology. The devil's temptations ultimately serve the sacred, the angels, the Lord Himself."[43] For the same reason that God does not kill the devil, he argued, the state must not ban the Catholic missions. For Hengstenberg the Catholic Church and the Jesuits, however evil, were mere servants of the higher cause against spiritual atrophy and religious indifference; within this manly and muscular Christianity, he recognized that it was precisely the contest between the churches that promised to justify and strengthen Protestant conviction.

According to the theology of conservative Protestantism, therefore, state-sponsored intervention against Catholicism, in fact, ran counter to the ultimate divine plan for the world and the interests of Protestantism. Protestants must welcome the good fight with Roman Catholicism as the opportunity to fortify their faith, bolster their resolve, and improve the Evangelical Church. Hengstenberg's eloquent exegesis on the Protestant condition of faith in the world carried the day: Professor Piper bowed to Hengstenberg's persuasion, backed down, and withdrew his resolution. Not only did the Protestant Church leadership now agree to tolerate, however reluctantly, the Catholic missions, it also cut support out from underneath the Prussian state's antimissionary decrees. Government officials on the scene in the Rhineland also warned state authorities in Berlin that prohibiting the missions would only incite the Catholic population. Without broader support the state government was now isolated. After all, as noted, even members of the royal family had approved of and attended the Catholic missions. Berlin state authorities ultimately climbed down from enforcing the decrees when after the Catholic success in the elections in the autumn it faced concerted opposition in the Prussian parliament from the Fraktion of Catholic deputies, the forerunner to the

43. *Aktenstücke,* 157–58.

Center Party, under the leadership of the fraternal duo August and Peter Reichensperger.

Now already in 1852 was an indication of the reasons conservative Protestant leaders, though anti-Catholic, would nonetheless for their own theological and pragmatic reasons refuse to join liberals and the state in support of the Kulturkampf legislation of the 1870s. Protestant leaders could agree that lack of Christian faith, rather than the power of Roman Catholicism or the missions, was the most serious threat to society. Catholic and Protestant leaders could also recognize godlessness as the common enemy and Christianity as the common cause that together might promote a measure of mutual forbearance for reasons of faith and religious pragmatism. Religious leaders, Catholic and Protestant, argued at the same time that the churches must be left free from state regulations in order to attend to their respective evangelical responsibilities. More to the point, the ecclesiastical leadership of both confessions insisted that the state must recognize that it had no appropriate role to play in the great contest between the Catholic and Protestant faiths in Germany. It was in this spirit that Protestant pastors, theologians, and other religious leaders now unleashed a deluge of anti-Catholic and hysterically anti-Jesuit literature that pitted Protestantism against Catholicism in an uncompromising theological and moral battle to the bitter end.[44] They furiously devoted themselves throughout the 1850s and 1860s and into the 1870s to the inculcation of Protestant consciousness and the preservation of Protestant identity. Primarily for this reason, within the Christian revival, despite the remarkable intermingling of the religious populations at the missions, Protestant and Catholic identities became polarized and rigid.

There was, therefore, not only a Catholic popular revival but also considerable indication of a remarkable revival of Protestant confessionalism under way in the 1850s and 1860s incited quite unintentionally by the Catholic Church and the Catholic missions. The reawakening of Protestant confessionalism took place in Catholic churches and

---

44. See, for example, Hermann Reuter, *Über die Eigenthümlichkeit der sittlichen Tendenz des Protestantismus im Verhältniß zum Katholicismus* (Greifswald: König. Univ.-Buchdruckerei, [1859]); I. F. Sander, *Der Beruf der Protestanten, Rom gegenüber, in dieser Zeit: Sendschreiben an die evangelischen Gemeinden* (Leipzig: Gebhardt und Reisland, 1853); Erich Stiller, *Grundzüge der Geschichte und der Unterscheidungslehren der evangelisch-protestantischen und römisch-katholischen Kirche* (Hamburg: Robert Kittler, 1855); Adolf Stöber, *Evangelische Abwehr, katholischer Angriffe* (Strasbourg: J. Kräuter, 1859); and G. Vintzelberg, *Protestantismus und Katholicismus oder die Werthschätzung des evangelischen Glaubens* (Fehrbellin: Im Selbstverlage des Verfassers, 1862).

churchyards, where Protestants and Catholics stood literally side by side at the missions, listened, and indeed knelt and wept together at the sermons. The Protestant revival was unplanned, reactive, and more muted than its confessional rival. The meaning of Protestant attendance at the missions was admittedly more ambiguous than Catholic participation, and the popular Protestant revival, like the Catholic revival, was a highly complex process with variations with respect to class, region, and gender that still remain to be better understood. More detailed statistical evaluations are required to complement the anecdotal accounts offered here. The increase in confessional polemic must also be weighed against an actual increase in Protestant religious commitment and practice. Ultimately, the episode of Protestant revival gave way to the currents of secularization that only increased after the 1870s. As historians have argued, Protestantism was susceptible to continuing migration, urbanization, industrialization, the shortage of churches in large cities, the spreading culture of science and progress among the middle class, and the development of a large social-democratic working-class subculture.[45] But the eager participation of Protestants at the missions and the campaign by Protestant religious elites to reawaken Protestant identity during the 1850s and 1860s does challenge the assumption of an uninterrupted secularization of Protestants throughout the nineteenth century.

At the same time, Protestant Church authorities believed the period of interconfessional peace during the Vormärz was over and found themselves now in the middle of a "Kriegszustand," a state of war, with the Catholic Church. In fact, many argued, either for rhetorical effect or because they believed it, that they faced an hour darker than any since the Counter-Reformation. With their backs against the wall, or so they feared, Protestant Church leaders called for an end to divisive intraconfessional rivalry between Lutherans, Calvinists, and

---

45. Hugh McLeod, *Piety and Poverty: Working-Class Religion in Berlin, London, and New York, 1870–1914* (New York: Holmes and Meier, 1996). In his work on Catholics and Protestants in Münster and Bochum from 1830 to 1933, Antonius Liedhegener has examined the process of Protestant secularization and the Catholic religious revival in response to modernity. Antonius Liedhegener, *Christentum und Urbanisierung: Katholiken und Protestanten in Münster und Bochum 1880–1933* (Paderborn: F. Schönigh, 1997). Lucian Hölscher has meticulously studied the process of Protestant secularization in Hanover starting in the mid-1870s. Lucian Hölscher, "Die Religion des Bürgers: Bürgerliche Frömmigkeit und protestantische Kirche im 19. Jahrhundert," *Historische Zeitschrift* 250 (1990): 595–630; Lucian Hölscher and Ursula Männich-Polenz, "Die Sozialstruktur der Kirchengemeinde Hannovers im 19. Jahrhundert: Eine statistische Analyse," *Jahrbuch der Gesellschaft für niedersächsische Kirchengeschichte* 88 (1990): 159–211.

Pietists, and between liberal and orthodox Protestants, for the sake of a united front against the Roman enemy.[46] The feverish anti-Catholicism and anti-Jesuitism of Protestant Church authorities in the 1850s and 1860s helped create the general popular anti-Catholic context for the more specific liberal and state-sponsored attack on the Roman Catholic Church in the 1870s.

Jesuitphobia and the Protestant Church Leadership

Protestant Church authorities believed that the Catholic missions and the Jesuits—with whom the Franciscan, Redemptorist, Capuchin, and Lazarist missionaries were immediately lumped—threatened both Protestantism and the modern, autonomous state. With the start of the missions, the Jesuits were vehemently attacked by Protestant pastors, theologians, and other religious leaders in sermons from the pulpit, in public speeches, in newspapers, and in pamphlet literature. They can be read together not simply as a registry of hostility and anxiety but also as a body of work with shared patterns that can be laid out and traced.

For centuries, in the popular Protestant imagination, the Jesuits had represented everything that was most wicked in the Roman Church. Much of this hysteria involving Jesuit conspiracies against monarchs and the state and stories of sexual intrigue provided the basic stock of the Protestant anti-Jesuit polemic of the post-1848 period. This discourse drew on a tradition of anti-Jesuit diatribe that ascribed enormous powers to the Jesuit order, a rogue society in the church, engaged, both liberals and Protestants believed, in a colossal and fantastic conspiracy to conquer the world. Jesuits never stopped short of blackmail and murder to attain their goals, and always they operated with stealth and cunning. According to formulas that date back to the Counter-Reformation, for example, Jesuits secretly concocted deadly serums and administered them to those monarchs of Europe who stood in the way of their ambitions for world rule. Jesuits pursued an evil opportunism based on the logic "the end justifies the means" and justified and defended their methods with the obfuscating and self-

---

46. See, for example, Th[eodor] Kliefoth, *Wider Rom! Ein Zeugniß in Predigten* (Schwerin: Stiller'schen Hofbuchhandlung, 1852); Daniel Schenkel, *Das gegenwärtige aggressive Verfahren der römisch-katholischen Kirche in ihrem Verhältnisse zum Protestantismus* (Darmstadt: C. W. Leske's Separat-Conto, 1857); idem, *Deutschlands Erb- und Erzfeind: Mahnruf an das deutsche Volk* (Coburg: F. Streit's Verlagsbuchhandlung, 1862); Heinrich Wiskemann, *Die Lehre und Praxis der Jesuiten in religiöser, moralischer und politischer Beziehung von ihrem Ursprung an bis auf den heutigen Tag* (Cassel: J. Georg Luckhardt, 1858).

serving casuistry of Escobar. In anti-Jesuit discourse, women were a particular focus of anxiety since they were purportedly the vulnerable link in the family. In the confessional Jesuits allegedly used intimacy and the exchange of confidences to win women over and seduce the wives of statesmen. Once in the grip of the Jesuits, women were used to spy on their husbands and gather information and feed it to the Jesuits. Through women, Jesuits supposedly exerted influence on the decisions made by their husbands. Jesuits also captured girls for work in convents or young men for service in the order. Those who hated Jesuits believed this kind of criminality was an immutable law of history. The Jesuits' own illusive and obfuscatory credo, "Jesuitae sint, ut sint, aut non sint!" (Let the Jesuits be so that they may or may not be!), repeatedly invoked in anti-Jesuit polemics, was cited as proof of their deception and reactionary fanaticism.[47]

In the postrevolutionary period, however, Protestant pastors, church officials, and social and religious observers also transformed with new inflections and new emphases the discourse of anti-Jesuitism and with it the patterns of anti-Catholicism. Responding both to the Revolution of 1848 and to the new Catholic revival, they recast or developed new anti-Jesuit and anti-Catholic themes, metaphors, and rhetorical strategies. Jesuits as hunters and trappers with nets and the Catholic Church as a huge web, ensnaring whole populations Protestant as well as Catholic, were prominent tropes in post-1848 Protestant anti-Jesuit and anti-Catholic discourse. A local Protestant pastor in Ellwangen, K. A. Leibbrand, argued that already by 1851 the Jesuit and Redemptorist missionaries had dropped "their nets in more than twenty places."[48] The same fears were repeated at the highest levels of the Protestant Church. According to a member of the Evangelischer Oberkirchenrat, Theodor Kliefoth, in 1852 the Catholic Church had "spread a net of cunning and power" over the Catholic population. With a peculiarly contrived com-

47. See, for example, O. Andreae, *Die verderbliche Moral der Jesuiten in Auszügen aus ihren Schriften* (Ruhrort: Andreae, 1865); and H. A. Bergmann, *Die geheimen Instructionen für die Gesellschaft Jesu. Oder: die Staat und Kirche bedrohenden Pläne des Jesuitenordens* (Erfurt: Hennings und Hopf, 1853), both written by Protestant pastors. See also *Jesuiten und Jesuitereien: Wirkliche Begebenheiten und geschichtliche Thatsachen nebst Gründen der Erfahrung* (Berlin: Verlag der Vereins-Buchhandlung, 1853); and Wiskemann, *Die Lehre und Praxis der Jesuiten.* For a Catholic denial that the "Monita Secreta" ever existed, see *Die Verleumder der Jesuiten in Deutschland* (Cologne: J. B. Bechem, 1853). For the image of the Jesuit in Imperial Germany as androgyne (as bisexual and asexual) see Róisín Healy, "Anti-Jesuitism in Imperial Germany: The Jesuit as Androgyne." In *Protestants, Catholics, and Jews in Germany, 1800–1914,* ed. Helmut Walser Smith (Oxford: Berg, 2001), 153–81.

48. Leibbrand, *Die Missionen der Jesuiten,* 13.

bination of metaphors, he argued that the Catholic Church was like an "organism" that "spreads itself like a net over the people, its ropes pressing into every life and into every heart."[49] He warned that all Germans of every kind were susceptible to the cunning appeal of the Jesuits. They would, he argued, offer to the rich their services. They would offer to the poor generosity, to the ambitious power and praise, and to the humble their affection and friendship. Finally, in an appeal that would appropriate and then destroy the most cherished hopes of liberals, Kliefoth insisted that the Jesuits "will say to the Germans: there will never be a united, free, strong Germany, as long as we are all not a single Roman confession."[50]

Similar metaphors of entrapment and strangulation run throughout the postrevolutionary secular liberal anti-Jesuit and anti-Catholic pamphlet literature. The anonymous *Enthüllung der neuesten Umtriebe der Jesuiten in Deutschland gegen Fürsten und Völker* argued in 1851 that the pomp of the Catholic Church played on the psychology of the population especially now when it was exhausted and bewildered by the traumas of revolution. In the postrevolutionary period, it was, therefore, no wonder that "Catholicism is now casting its nets over the worried and weary people." Because reactionary Jesuits simply used Catholicism to service the interests of the throne and the absolute power of the monarchy, it was "no wonder that they ensnared many statesmen with their nets; no wonder that high-placed Protestant officials in the state and in the church were openly known as 'secret Jesuits.'"[51] According to another anonymous pamphlet, *Die Katholische Religionsübung in Mecklenburg-Schwerin,* appearing in 1851, since 1848 "a new net of Catholic religious practice and Catholic priests" out of proportion to the small number of Catholics in Mecklenburg-Schwerin had spread over the state. Its function could only be to suppress the Lutheran Church and ensnare its members.[52] The author explained that since the history of the missions in Mecklenburg-Schwerin recorded an unbroken chain of excesses and never-ending offenses, the state had the right to impose restrictions on the Catholic Church and the practice of Catholicism. Protestant pastors imagined

---

49. Kliefoth, *Wider Rom!* 101, v, respectively.
50. Ibid., 93.
51. *Enthüllung der neuesten Umtriebe der Jesuiten in Deutschland gegen Fürsten und Völker: Nebst einem Abriß der Gesellschaft des Jesuitenordens* (Leipzig: Christian Ernst Kollmann, 1851), 126–27, 101, respectively.
52. *Die katholische Religionsübung in Mecklenburg-Schwerin* (Jena: Friedrich Frommann, 1852), 87.

the postrevolutionary German landscape covered with a series of webs and nets laid out by roving Jesuits, trapping the exhausted population like booty for the Vatican.

That the Jesuits had taken advantage of the social disorientation caused by the 1848 Revolution in order to reestablish the power of the church and to launch an attack on Protestantism was also a prominent theme among Protestant pastors. Pastor Leibbrand echoed the widely held belief that the Jesuit missionary campaign to restore morality was merely a sham.[53] In the hour of the revolution with the masses swept to and fro by the winds of change, ultramontane authorities in the church had called upon the Jesuits as part of the plan to reassert the power of the pope in the German states. Where the Jesuits set up missions, there the church laid down "roots in the soil of the lives of the people." Leibbrand envisioned Jesuits roaming across Germany like "troops and platoons often with the most sparse equipment." They had swept over the entire southwest corner of Germany; now they were launching a strike to the north. Alternatively, Catholicism was a rising flood tide that threatened to swamp Germany in superstition and stupidity. Catholicism was an ocean that could be contained only by a Protestant dam built to protect the population from intolerance, proselytizing, and conversion.[54]

For pastors like Leibbrand there were no doubts: the Jesuits, *milites papae,* defenders of Roman hierarchy, and the instrument for the worldwide rule of the Roman Church, opposed to all that was holy and Christian, were the "deadly enemy of Protestantism."[55] According to the superintendent of the Elberfeld district synod in an address to Protestant parishes in 1853, the Jesuits, not democrats and liberals, were the true revolutionaries that threatened to smash monarchical and Protestant authority. The Jesuits, he argued, were granted by their superiors any means including exciting the masses to insurrection against the authorities "to destroy the Protestant Church; they have now arisen freely with their missions in our fatherland, in our immediate vicinity."[56] According to *Enthüllung der neuesten Umtriebe der Jesuiten,* however, this could hardly have been a surprise. The goals of the Jesuits for three hundred years had never been other than "to exterminate Protestantism along with its roots."[57] Exploiting the new con-

---

53. Leibbrand, *Missionen der Jesuiten.*
54. Ibid., 36, 63, respectively.
55. Ibid., 26.
56. Sander, *Beruf der Protestanten,* 12.
57. *Enthüllung der neuesten Umtriebe der Jesuiten,* 101.

stitutional rights won for the church during the revolution, the Jesuits had spread not just their missions but also the new ultramontane associations all over Germany. Now the Piusverein, according to the author, had the audacity to plan a conference in Berlin, "the capital of Protestant Germany. Another sign of the times!" The most important cause of the spread of the Jesuits and Catholicism was, he argued, the support of reactionary absolutist governments for the church since they were allies for the subjugation of the people and the reestablishment of "blind, unqualified obedience."[58]

Many liberal Protestant Jesuit-haters believed that the Jesuits had taken advantage of the 1848 Revolution not only to launch an attack on Protestantism and to establish the power of the church but also to assault the virtues of the Enlightenment—light, truth, and reason—and to attack the welfare of the German fatherland. Pastor H. A. Bergmann, like other liberals, was disgusted by the excesses of the revolution. He echoed a widely held belief when he argued in *Die Jesuitenpest* in 1856 that the Jesuits were using the chaos ensuing from the revolution, that "infectious sickness" that had captured hold of the lower classes, to establish and spread their influence. Now the Jesuits were a "pestilence" among the people, waging war against the most sacred liberal beliefs, "against Bildung and the humanity of our time, against light and enlightenment, against the well-being of the people, against the welfare of the state and the happiness of the family."[59] Even in the midst of Protestant states and cities, he argued, the Jesuits were holding their missions, hitching people to the "yoke of slavery" with religious fanaticism and superstition.[60] For Bergmann, as for liberals Protestant and secular alike, Catholicism was a way of life anathema to reason, Bildung, and enlightenment. Catholicism, he argued, survived merely in an empty, outward form, in ostentatious but hollow displays of ceremony and hierarchy. Italy, for example, offered the pathetic spectacle of a country

> covered over with more cardinals, archbishops and bishops, priests, monks, masses, Marian cults, sacred pictures, miraculous

58. Ibid., 115, 127, respectively.

59. H. A. Bergmann, *Die Jesuitenpest,* 2d. ed. (Berlin: Gebauer'sche Buchhandlung, 1856), 54; ibid., 1st ed. 1852, 57–58. Dehumanizing Jesuits by referring to them as a sickness, pestilence, or pollutant was commonly employed in the Protestant polemic. According to one writer, the Jesuits were an "evil, which threatened to pollute the people." *Enthüllung der neuesten Umtriebe der Jesuiten,* 128. See also Magnus Jocham, *Die sittliche Verpestung des Volkes durch die Jesuiten* (Mainz: Franz Kirchheim, 1866), 5–6.

60. Bergmann, *Jesuitenpest,* 7.

relics, indulgences, processions, festivities, fasts, jubilees, celebrations and other kinds of papal rubbish than can possibly be imagined. The most rampant faithlessness, slander, indeed even contempt for the most Holy has emerged here next to the most blind superstition, next to the most un-Christian fanaticism and bigotry in such a way that the danger that threatens the hierarchy at its roots is hardly recognizable.[61]

The problem was not confined to Italy. This, according to the author, was the condition "more or less" of all Catholic countries, and he shuddered when he imagined that the Jesuits might transform Germany, the home of sober Protestantism, into one of them. According to another liberal Protestant the Catholic Church was the most blatant contradiction of "science, Bildung, and the consciousness of the time." Yet all the tortures and persecution of the Inquisition and of the Jesuits, he argued, could not prevent "the increase of light, and no human power, even the power of the Jesuits, will ever manage to return the night that covered the people centuries ago."[62]

Protestant and secular liberals who envisioned the Jesuits as a toxin poisoning the capacity of people to think for themselves, a dark cloud obstructing light, truth, and reason, shared the authority of an Enlightenment vocabulary and tradition of Enlightenment anticlericalism with secular democrats. Radical democrats argued monarchists had joined with the Jesuits in the decisive hour to defeat the revolution. According to one anonymous pamphlet, *Die Jesuitenansiedlung in Westfalen und das Westfälische Junkertum,* Catholic Junkers, in order to preserve their traditional privileges and authority, called upon the Jesuits to join a conspiracy of counterrevolution. The author believed that the Jesuits, working hand in hand with the government and aristocratic reactionaries, had launched a campaign to "reduce the people to idiocy." Together they promoted superstition, blind faith, and religious fanaticism among the people, just as they suppressed Bildung, reason, and enlightenment, the foundations of freedom. The Catholic aristocracy, meanwhile, gladly joined in pilgrimages, revered crucifixes and religious relics, and encouraged hocus-pocus and "similar nonsense" in order to reestablish their hold on the people and resurrect the patriarchal "good old times."[63]

61. Ibid., 57.
62. *Enthüllung der neuesten Umtriebe der Jesuiten,* 128.
63. *Jesuitenansiedlung in Westfalen.*

Though united in their animosity toward the Jesuits and in their fear of the Roman Catholic revival, Protestant Church authorities were at loggerheads about the proper polemical response to the threat and about the Protestant Church's capacity to meet this threat. Many Protestant pastors went into a tailspin of despair. H. A. Bergmann, for example, was especially pessimistic. He believed that while the Jesuits were spreading the rule of the pope, converting Protestants, and reestablishing Catholic predominance in countries throughout Europe, the Protestant Church was meanwhile "almost dead."[64] The Protestant clergy, Bergmann argued, remained naive, indifferent, and silent. Since the Protestant Church was unable or unwilling to meet the challenge of the Catholic revival, he turned and placed his hopes in the resilience of the people, that is, liberal people. If the Jesuit campaign and the Catholic renewal could not be matched with Protestantism, he argued, they must be met, instead, with the power of liberal virtues, the force of Bildung, and the enlightenment of the people, who, cultivating "the deepest contempt and hate in their innermost heart," must exclaim, "Be gone, Satan!"[65]

As a member of the Evangelischer Oberkirchenrat, Theodor Kliefoth, however, could not have disagreed more. He called not for a campaign of Bildung, reason, and enlightenment to meet the Catholic threat but for a steadfast rededication to Protestant theology against the lure of "Rome's agents" whispering in the ears of the German Protestant population. Kliefoth believed that his coreligionists had to attack the Romans with Protestant resolution and the "Protestant truth of God."[66] He argued that using rhetoric that drew on the vocabulary of the Enlightenment and liberalism was misguided. He did so not because such concepts were inherently flawed. Instead, a campaign against Catholicism that emphasized "declarations of 'light,' 'reason,' 'freedom,' and 'enlightenment'" had in the current context become, he argued, useless or disreputable. At another time and in another place one could combat the Catholic Church with such words and phrases, but one could not use them now and here; liberal ideals had been discredited by the violence and ultimate failure of the revolution. In Germany such "high, holy, and sacred words in the last decade have been, on the one hand, so sullied that a national penance must wash them clean again and have become, on the other hand, so hollow that they

64. Bergmann, *Jesuitenpest,* 2d ed., 56.
65. Ibid., 62, 61, respectively.
66. Kliefoth, *Wider Rom!* 101, 93, respectively.

do not mean anything anymore."[67] In this postrevolutionary period he warned against invoking the vocabulary of liberalism since this would only contribute further to the dissolution of its meaning. In the campaign against Catholicism and the Jesuits, he could in 1852 only recommend looking elsewhere for words and ideas that still had the capacity to communicate content and direction.

Anti-Catholicism, Protestantism, and the Reconstruction of Liberalism

The reaction and repression that followed the failure of the Revolution of 1848–49 was for liberals a period of defeat, despair, and disarray as the conservative authorities of the German states retaliated with often brutal force. In the Grand Duchy of Baden, for example, a tenth of the revolutionaries who finally surrendered in the last month of the revolution at the garrison of Rastatt were lined up and shot down. For their roles in the revolution, liberal leaders of the revolution like Wilhelm von Trützschler and Maximilian Dortu were tried by military courts and executed. Gottfried Kinkel and Ludwig von Rango were sentenced to long prison terms. In the regular courts, both Franz Waldeck and Johann Jacoby may have been acquitted of charges of lèse-majesté and high treason, but acquittal did not ensure freedom from continued harassment by state authorities. Franz Ziegler was expelled from the town of Brandenburg, where he had at one time been Bürgermeister, while Hans Viktor Unruh was forced out of his position in the civil service. Herman Schulze-Delitzsch was harassed by the police and not allowed to practice law. Other leading democratic and liberal lights like Carl Schurz, Ludwig Bamberger, Friedrich Kapp, and Stephan Born avoided persecution by fleeing the German states either permanently or temporarily. In Baden alone some eighty thousand "forty-eighters" escaped to the United States, Switzerland, or another refuge, effectively depleting the duchy of its progressive liberal and democratic population. The resurrected German Confederation abrogated the "Fundamental Rights of the German People," and the liberal red-black-gold tricolor was hauled down from the palace in Frankfurt where the Diet of the Confederation sat. The reactionary government censored the press, dissolved political organizations, and discouraged electoral participation. Elections, therefore, were marked by apathy and low voter turnout.[68]

67. Ibid., 101, v, respectively.
68. Blackbourn, *The Long Nineteenth Century,* 162–63; Hamerow, *Restoration, Revolution, Reaction,* 203–4; Sheehan, *German Liberalism,* 75, 84, 92.

The success, meanwhile, of the Catholic missionary campaign and the Catholic revival added to state reaction and persecution another assault on the liberal hopes for social reform and progress. Many liberals believed that political repression only made the spread of Catholicism more likely. When in 1854 Pope Pius IX proclaimed the dogma of the Immaculate Conception of the Virgin Mary, the father and venerable exponent of the *kleindeutsch* school of historiography, Johann Gustav Droysen, wrote bitterly to his colleague Heinrich von Sybel that "idolatry . . . belongs to the mob; the more the wisdom of our governments in Germany turns us into plebeians, the greater the prospects for the Roman Church."[69] After the collapse of the revolution, liberalism was not merely suppressed by state force; it seemed now overrun by a more vigorous and ascendant popular Catholic movement based in religious faith and dedicated to the conservative monarchical order.

Contrary to the view, however, that under the new pressures of the 1850s the revolutionaries of 1848–49 simply retreated from politics to pursue economic activities or settled into private retirement, the majority of the former Paulskirche representatives as well as many other liberal and democratic radicals across Germany either stayed politically active in spite of persecution or returned to political life after imprisonment or emigration.[70] The politicization of German society and culture in the revolutionary era had permanently changed the relationship between state and society, and within the new postrevolutionary world, liberals found opportunities to reengage as advocates for economic, constitutional, and social reform. As part of their commitment to progress, even during the reactionary decade of the 1850s and into the New Era of the 1860s—the period of renewed hopes for social and political change—liberal and progressive reformers lashed out at the Catholic revival with fanatical hostility. In 1853 one of the hundreds of liberal and Protestant anti-Jesuit pamphlets that had emerged with the Jesuit missionary campaign drew attention to a quotation in the *Deutsche Volkshalle,* one of the many new Catholic newspapers founded after the revolution. The paper asserted in the face of government interference and in defiance of liberal-capitalist worldliness that it was "not founded for material reasons. To us all the customs treaties in the world are trivial compared to a single government measure that

---

69. Johann Gustav Droysen to Heinrich von Sybel, 12 Dec. 1854, in *Johann Gustav Droysen Briefwechsel,* ed. Rudolf Hübner (Stuttgart: Biblio-Verlag, 1967), 2:300.

70. Christian Jansen, "Saxon Forty-Eighters in the Postrevolutionary Epoch, 1849–1867," in *Saxony in German History: Culture, Society, and Politics, 1830–1933,* ed. James Retallack (Ann Arbor: University of Michigan Press, 2000), 135–50.

infringes upon the freedom of Catholic beliefs. A single institution of the church [the Society of Jesus] is more dear to our hearts than all the factories of the entire monarchy; and we are convinced that the power of Prussia in Germany depends much less on the tariff line than on the Jesuit line."[71] Such comments confirmed the belief current among secular and Protestant liberals that the Catholic Church and Catholics intended to ensure that Germany remained tied to an antiquated world of religious zealotry, hostile to modern commercial interests and industrial progress.

In the new postrevolutionary world, the conservative political repression and Catholic reactionary fanaticism often seemed hand in hand or one and the same. If, however, postrevolutionary critics like Kliefoth were right, that liberal ideology was exhausted, that words like *light, reason, freedom,* and *enlightenment* had become empty and useless, liberal leaders in the face of their adversaries were left now without even a language of political resistance and social reform. During the period following the revolution and in their efforts to carry forward the campaign to modernize Germany, liberals out of necessity searched for new ways to think about many of their most basic tenets at the most fundamental level of meaning. As they did so, they found that coupling liberalism and anti-Catholicism was an especially powerful way to rehabilitate and voice their program for reform in the postrevolutionary era. Traditionally, historians have argued that anti-Catholic sentiment was the mortar that held the liberal house in Germany together. The Catholic problem provided liberals from the left across to the right a common ground to which they all could continue to return despite their different approaches to and disagreements concerning social reform and state authority, including economic policy, military budgets, and particularly the constitutional crisis of the 1860s. Catholicism was, however, not only a common, liberal problem; unlike with many other problems, liberals of all shades could agree on what should be done about it. More important, the liberals' running battle with Catholicism decisively reshaped German liberalism from a preindustrial, precapitalist movement into an ideology consonant with middle-class industrial development, capitalist expansion, and modern social order after 1848. Recognizing that anti-Catholicism was the central obsession of liberals after

71. Quoted in Bergmann, *Die geheimen Instructionen,* 68.

midcentury, determining their programmatic choices and the character of liberalism itself, helps us identify the historically specific contingency of liberal ideology often missed in other studies of nineteenth-century German liberalism.

Following the defeat of the 1848 Revolution and under the conditions of state repression during the 1850s, German liberals developed models of anticlerical, anti-Jesuit, antimonastic, and anti-Catholic thinking that reoriented and reconstituted German liberalism on a new basis of legitimacy and authority. The cultural anthropological perspective of Clifford Geertz offers one way to identify the value of anti-Catholicism for German liberals in the postrevolutionary period. According to Geertz, thinking, the development of meaning, and the formation of ideas are best understood as a mental procedure of contrasting available representations. "Thinking, conceptualization, formulation, comprehension, understanding," he has argued, "consists not of ghostly happenings in the head but of a matching of the states and processes of symbolic models against the states and processes of the wider world."[72] When liberals matched their idealized beliefs about themselves and their hopes for German society in the postrevolutionary era against stigmatized images of the Catholic clergy, Catholics, and the Catholic Church, they were thinking again about who they were and what they were supposed to be. With Jesuits, monks, nuns, monasticism, Catholicism, and the Catholic Church as rhetorical points of reference, they reinvented the language of liberalism, including individualism, science, education, constitutionalism, and free-market economics. By identifying the ways liberal aspirations were managed in opposition to clericalism, the Catholic Church, and

---

72. Clifford Geertz, "Ideology as a Cultural System," in *Ideology and Discontent,* ed. David E. Apter (New York: Free Press of Glencoe, 1964), 46–76, quotation at 61. A temperate and circumspect use of the methods of discourse analysis in gender and cultural studies offers a similar approach. Joan Wallach Scott has argued that meaning is generated by the juxtaposition of oppositions whereby a "positive definition" is always based on "the negation or repression of something represented as antithetical to it. And categorical oppositions repress the internal ambiguities of either category." Joan Wallach Scott, *Gender and the Politics of History* (New York: Columbia University Press, 1988), 7. From a self-avowed postmodernist perspective, Zygmunt Bauman's work on the sociological significance of the Jewish minority and its relationship to dominant culture in Germany also illuminates just as well the fundamental relationship between Catholics and liberalism. Bauman argues that the invention of dichotomies in the attempt to control ambivalence is specific to the modern, liberal vision of social order. Zygmunt Bauman, *Modernity and Ambivalence* (Ithaca: Cornell University Press, 1991).

Catholicism, it is possible to trace the reconstruction of German liberalism after 1848, broadly understood.

For example, in 1855 the philosopher and theologian Christian Carl Josias Bunsen in his introduction to *Die Zeichen der Zeit* used anti-Catholicism to make some sense of the postrevolutionary period, a period of such disorientation that it required first of all, he believed, a more concerted effort at honest self-reflection: "What do the signs of the times mean? Is it ebb tide or flood? Are we in Germany and in Europe going backward or forward?" he asked.[73] A Protestant liberal, Bunsen in 1848 had placed his hopes in the Frankfurt National Assembly and the unification of Germany under the leadership of Prussia.[74] Now the Nachmärz was a world at the crossroads. Those in it, he believed, found themselves faced with clear and urgent choices: either prostration before clericalism or the assertion of national self-determination. "Which," he asked his readers, "will triumph, church or state? Clergy or nation? *Pfaffenthum* or *Volksthum?*"[75] That his book was an immediate success, selling out within the first month, and that already by the third month a third edition had to be printed to keep up with demand demonstrates that Bunsen's questions were of urgent concern to many Germans in the postrevolutionary period.[76] Bunsen's way forward coupled liberal social and political ideals with the authority of cultural Protestantism in a desperate battle against the Jesuits' plan to destroy Germany. What interests us is the pattern of relentless and crude oppositions in a diatribe that pitted the evils of "Jesuitism" and its campaign to stupefy the people against the virtues of Protestantism and the enlightenment of Bildung. Bunsen saw in the Jesuits—at the very time that they were holding their missions and repietizing the Catholic population of Germany—the "complete inversion" of both divine and human plans for world history and world order. The "Jesuitical view of the world" was, he argued, "the murderer of the

---

73. Christian Carl Josias Bunsen, *Die Zeichen der Zeit: Briefe an Freunde über die Gewissenfreiheit und das Recht der christlichen Gemeinde* (Leipzig: F. A. Brockhaus, 1855), 1:3.

74. Two addresses sent to the Frankfurt National Assembly conveyed Bunsen's hopes for a united and constitutional Germany and establish his liberal credentials: "Die deutsche Bundesverfassung und ihr eigenthümliches Verhältnis zu den Verfassungen Englands und der Vereinigten Staaten" (London, 7 May 1848); and "Vorschlag für die unverzügliche Bildung einer vollständigen Reichsverfassung während der Verweserschaft" (Frankfurt am Main, 5 Sept. 1848).

75. Bunsen, *Zeichen der Zeit,* 1:3.

76. See the preface to the English translation, Christian Carl Josias Bunsen, *Signs of the Times: Letters to Ernst Moritz Arndt on the Dangers to Religious Liberty in the Present State of the World,* trans. Susanna Winkworth (London, 1856), v.

principle of personality bestowed by and belonging to God."[77] Ignatius Loyola, the founder of the Society of Jesus, never sought truth for itself, argued Bunsen, but rather as a means of ruling by the strangulation and murder of individuality. Ultimately, "Jesuitism" was at its essence, according to Bunsen, a form of "drill, not Bildung; an enslavement, not a liberation," which encouraged "among the people, not independence and prosperous development, but a ruinous fluctuation between anarchy and despotism, like that between skepticism and superstition."[78]

Not just an attack on the freedom of the individual, Bunsen argued, "Jesuitism" was "irreconcilably hostile to freedom, science, and humanity."[79] For Bunsen and for German liberals, the Jesuits were the precise antithesis of liberal-minded Germans. In contrast to "Jesuitism," Germany, Bunsen believed, demanded respect for the individual and for science, for unfettered progress and freedom. The reestablishment of the Jesuit order was at the same time nothing less than a declaration of war against Protestantism. A mighty *Gotteskampf* (holy war) between Protestantism and the Jesuits was, therefore, inevitable. With solemn conviction, however, Bunsen explained that "the contradiction between the oppression of conscience and freedom is eternal, but the banner of the free and moral person waves victoriously over the battlefield, and on it is written in letters of fire: *In hoc signo vinces,*" the words that appeared to Constantine on the Christian cross before his victory at Milvian Bridge in C.E. 312. While there was hope yet for Protestant Germans, Bunsen conceded little beyond "laboring for the kingdom of God among us" could be done to rescue "our [Catholic] brethren" from the Jesuits.[80] Bunsen's anti-Catholicism indicates how readily liberals drew upon Protestantism as a cultural resource, evoking common Protestant sentiments and employing Protestant symbolism to motivate programs for social and political progress.

This was even more the case after 1857 when in Prussia the transfer of the conduct of government from Friedrich Wilhelm IV, declared hopelessly insane by a regency council, to his brother Prince Wilhelm brought an end to the postrevolutionary period of reaction. He dismissed the reactionary ministers and in their place appointed a new ministry more sympathetic to the moderate liberal opposition. The

---

77. Bunsen, *Zeichen der Zeit,* 2:277–78, 283–83, respectively.
78. Ibid., 2:282–83.
79. Ibid., 2:277–78.
80. Ibid., 2:286, 284, respectively.

move signaled, contemporaries believed, a New Era awakening hopes
among liberals for new reforms after a decade of reaction. Adolf
Diesterweg, a progressive liberal, 1848 revolutionary, and authority on
educational reform, immediately published *Pädagogisches Wollen und
Sollen,* a major work of pedagogical theory that proposed a sweeping
educational, social, economic, and moral reform.[81] Diesterweg's progressive program was based on what he called the "Grundprincipien
des Lebenskampfes" (basic principles of the struggle for life) in the
contest between Catholicism and Protestantism. At stake in this struggle was a comprehensive catalog of choices: "monarchical absolutism"
or a "free constitution"; "protective tariffs" or the "free market";
"guilds" or "free competition"; "patronage" or "self-regulation";
"censorship of the press" or "freedom of the press"; a "state church" or
"freedom of conscience"; "stagnation" or "progress"; "subjection to
authorities in thought and in deed" or "free research and thinking for
yourself." In 1859 in his essay "Bischof und Pädagog," Diesterweg reit-
erated the choices between, on the one hand, "Catholic" "absolute
rule," "bureaucratic administration," "compulsory guilds," and the
"system of protective tariffs" and, on the other hand, "Protestant"
"constitutional freedom," "self-management," "the free market," and
"free competition."[82] These "oppositions," as Diesterweg called them,
were reducible to the most basic opposition: "authority or freedom,
Catholicism or Protestantism."[83] Diesterweg's arguments on pedagogy
move from one litany of stark contrasts to another. Absent in his for-
mulations is any common ground, any possibility for compromise that
might contribute to ambiguity. The force of Diesterweg's argument
derives from this clarity of irreconcilable antagonisms. For Diesterweg, the opposition between the "principle of Catholic inertia" and the

---

81. Adolf Diesterweg, *Pädagogisches Wollen und Sollen: Dargestellt für Leute, die noch
nicht fertig sind, aber eben darum Lust haben, nachzudenken* (Leipzig, 1857). In 1848 Diesterweg had seen the revolution as the opportunity to rid Germany of "Pfaffentum" once and for
all. The *Rheinischen Blätter* ran an address to all teachers summarizing with excerpts an article by Diesterweg: "Now is the time, to say it in a word, to make an end of Pfaffentum, to
extricate it root and branch wherever we have it in our power." *Rheinische Blätter* 38 (1848):
2, 15, quoted in Hugo Gotthard Bloth, *Adolf Diesterweg: Sein Leben und Wirken für Pedagogik und Schule* (Heidelberg: Quelle und Meyer, 1966), 160.

82. Adolf Diesterweg, "Bischof und Pädagog," in *Sämtliche Werke,* ed. Robert Alt, Hans
Ahrbeck, Rosemarie Ahrbeck, Ruth Hohendorf, Gerda Mundorf, Günter Schulze, and Leo
Regener (Berlin: Volkseigener Verlag, 1976), 347–85. The article appeared originally in *Päd-
agogisches Jahrbuch für Lehrer und Schulfreunde* 9 (1859): 89–156.

83. Diesterweg, *Pädagogisches Wollen und Sollen,* 81–83.

"principle of Protestant movement" applied to all realms of human interaction, including religion, society, politics, and education.[84] In the realm of religious activity the principle of Protestant movement was in agreement with "rationalism as a method, with the primacy of reason," and in contradiction to "supernaturalism," "the imprisonment of reason by belief." In the spiritual realm, Diesterweg argued, Protestantism was in agreement with "self-determination, spontaneity," and in contradiction to "the rule of dark feelings, with passive devotion, blind obedience." In matters of political life, Protestantism was in agreement with "the principle of self-government and what goes with it" and in contradiction to "the absolutist, the aristocratic, and its consequences."[85]

Diesterweg's "Bischof und Pädagog" also developed a series of Catholic pedagogical principles in opposition to Protestant principles. According to Diesterweg,

The differences (in part absolute, in part relative opposition) between Catholic and Protestant principles of education require no detailed explanation. The following are self evident:

1. education to promote belief in the authorities;
2. education to promote unqualified belief in the church, the pope, and the anointed priests;
3. the renunciation of one's own inquiry into matters of church dogma—renunciation of reason;
4. the subordination of the Holy Scripture to catechism, interpretation of the same through the infallibility of the pope;
5. the adherence to church practices necessary for salvation (genuflection, making the sign of the cross, spraying holy water, praying with the rosary, confession, fasting, pilgrimages, penance, mortification, *opera operata*);
6. the belief in superstition and miracles, etc.;

compare to

1. the Protestant freedom of belief and conscience;
2. the right (or the duty) of one's own inquiry into the Scriptures;

84. Ibid., 83.
85. Ibid., 40.

3. the recognition of individual convictions;
4. the agreement between belief and reason;
5. the attribution of all phenomena to laws (natural and spiritual);
6. an education for free self-determination; and with all that follows from these principles and is harmonious with it. *Summa:* an upright life dedicated to a firm belief in the common good.[86]

Diesterweg throughout his construction of oppositions borrowed legitimacy from Protestantism as a resource of cultural value to revive key words in the vocabulary of liberalism: *progress, rationalism, individualism, Bildung,* and *constitutionalism,* and ultimately the principles of free trade that became increasingly current among liberals in the late 1850s and during the 1860s.[87] According to Diesterweg, Protestantism like liberalism rested on the presupposition of tolerance; Catholicism, however, led only to intolerance. But the Protestant tolerance of Catholics, he argued, must have its limit. Catholic monks and monasteries served as an example: "No hostility to hoods, cowls, and bald heads so long as they leave us alone and do not molest us. Peace—but not at any price!"[88] In the face of the Catholic missionary campaign against Protestantism and the attempt to win over the Protestant population, the intolerance of intolerance, he argued, was justified. This conflict between the confessions could be reduced in its essentials to the questions "going forward or going backward?" and "more light or more darkness?" Despite the attempts of the Catholic clergy to lock the wheels of progress, the struggle, Diesterweg argued, offered the sanguine assurance of the "unfettered progress of light and enlightenment."[89] The appeal of the anti-Catholic model for thinking about liberal identity and liberal principles apparent in Diesterweg's program for reform was, however elegant the idealism, precisely its crude and formulaic character. The cognitive model could be effortlessly and seemingly endlessly applied to the broad array of programs that constituted the liberal prescription for progress in Germany.

For example, at the start of the New Era, in *Das gegenwärtige aggressive Verfahren der römisch-katholischen Kirche,* Daniel Schenkel, a dedicated and prolific anti-Catholic, sketched out the contours of the

86. Diesterweg, "Bischof und Pädagog," 364.

87. For liberal advocacy of free trade beginning in the 1860s, see Langewiesche, "German Liberalism," 225.

88. Diesterweg, "Bischof und Pädagog," 364.

89. Ibid., 378.

liberal-Protestant polemic against Catholicism. For Schenkel as for other liberal Protestants, the Catholic attack on Protestant Germany was part of a daring and comprehensive "system of power," an inevitable, enduring, and constant threat: "If the Roman Catholic Church behaves aggressively against the Protestant Christians, . . . it is forced to do so," he explained, "by an inner necessity, because it cannot do otherwise, even if it wanted."[90] Establishing a separate society within society, splitting Germans into two separate and irreconcilable populations, the Roman Church demanded that Catholics avoid all religious and civil community with Protestants. Most recently, Catholics were not only segregated from Protestants in schools and universities but even in cemeteries. The Catholic Church had intruded also into the "sacred lap of family life," demanding that all children in confessionally mixed marriages be raised Catholic. There was no aspect of life, according to Schenkel, that was now not a matter of confessional allegiance. The Roman Catholic Church wanted not only to establish a distinctly Catholic history and philosophy, but even Catholic mathematics and ultimately even a Catholic culinary art, he argued. Schenkel believed that according to the plans of the Catholic Church, "there would no longer be an area of human thought, cognition, research, knowledge, and business in which the Catholic Christian would not think, do research, know, and conduct business differently than the Protestant Christian." "Protestant scholarship and science" could be compared to "Catholic science without shame." In contrast to the Catholic Church that denied any freedom to its adherents, Protestantism had discovered that there could be no true knowledge without the freedom of thought. "Science and art, the life of the state and of the people, customs and traditions, business and shipping, agriculture and commerce," all human activities had been transformed with the Protestant Reformation of the sixteenth century.[91]

Throughout Schenkel's argument, Catholicism is depicted as backward and past oriented while Protestantism is progressive and future oriented; Protestantism is easily consonant with liberalism, but Catholicism is anathema to liberal ideals. Catholicism, Schenkel argued, belonged to a time in history when it had been necessary to Christianize the heathen masses as quickly as possible. However pow-

---

90. Schenkel, *Das gegenwärtige aggressive Verfahren,* 3. Schenkel thought that "the aggressive behavior of the Roman Catholic Church against the evangelical Christians is a necessary emanation of its being; it must hold itself not only justified but also obligated for this." Ibid., 7.

91. Ibid., 13–14, 23, respectively.

erful and important Catholicism may once have been, now, in this modern age of progress, "it no longer has any roots in the spirit and needs of our century, and it no longer carries within itself the fresh buds of the future. The view, on which Roman Catholicism rests, belongs to a bygone period of world history." Monks, monasteries, and religious orders were at best obsolete and useless. "Currently no one would dare assert that the Roman Catholic clergy is at the lead of the spiritual movement of this century, and that the powerful impulses which the Christian peoples employ to solve their world-historical problems come from the monks and fraternal orders." Catholicism, he argued, was strongest in precisely those areas where spiritual and ethical development was weakest. "Conversely the progress of Protestantism goes hand in hand with the progress of civilization, with the increasing spread of Bildung and knowledge," leaving behind their Catholic counterparts to atrophy.[92]

The Jesuits were a particularly fanatical obsession in Schenkel's anti-Catholic diatribe. They were "the most terrible and irreconcilable enemy of Protestantism," an enemy, cloaked in secrecy, "that has embraced faithlessness and mindless hedonism with open arms." According to Schenkel, while the Jesuit missions seemed to be held in Catholic areas for the benefit of the Catholic population, they were, in fact, usually held in Protestant areas for the purpose of converting Protestants to Catholicism. Even in Berlin, "the metropolis of German Protestantism," missions were being held to convert the Protestant inhabitants. The more Protestants were ignorant of the basic truths of their own belief, Schenkel argued, the greater the danger of their falling into the Jesuit "catch net" of propaganda.[93] In 1862 Schenkel further expounded his anti-Jesuitism in Die kirchliche Frage und ihre protestantische Lösung. It was precisely the Jesuit order, he explained, that eradicated any capacity for reform and progress in the Catholic Church. The Jesuits recognized that with the Counter-Reformation decrees of the Council of Trent (which met from 1545 to 1563), "medieval Catholicism closed up its system and exhausted its spiritual capacity."[94] From then on, from the standpoint of the order, there was only one command for Catholics in the church, obedience to the papal seat and its dictates, and only one sin, "the emancipation of the indi-

92. Ibid., 22.
93. Ibid., 19.
94. Daniel Schenkel, Die kirchliche Frage und ihre protestantische Lösung im Zusammenhange mit den nationalen Bestrebungen und mit besonderer Beziehung auf die neuesten Schriften von Döllinger und Bischof von Kettelers (Elberfeld: R. L. Friederichs, 1862), 138.

vidual from hierarchical authority." The Jesuit order dedicated itself to the global, supranational rule of the pope and to the subordination of the state to his commands. "With admirable perseverance," Schenkel continues, "it always pursued the same goal: the suppression of freedom and independence of the human spirit. It acquired an art with which to still the capacities of human intellect without developing the spirit, to train human willpower without building character."[95] Without any moral direction or scientific capacity, Jesuits had also lost themselves in a dark cave of medieval scholasticism and casuistry. As the agents of ultramontanism, the vassals and servants of an international, religious world monarchy seated in Rome, the Jesuits whipped up pro-Austrian sentiment among Roman Catholics and undermined Prussian nationalist leadership in Germany. Schenkel's demonization of the Jesuits culminates in the assertion that the Jesuit order, the encapsulation of all that was worst in Catholicism, was, in fact, ultimately dependent on Protestantism for its existence. "It scrapes together a bare existence only with the help of its opposite, Protestantism, which it persecutes with the glowing hate . . . of a crippled rival."[96] Protestantism was the result of national conscience; "Jesuitism" the product of the suppression of conscience. Protestantism rested on the spiritual freedom and the unbound love of truth; "Jesuitism" chained the spirit to the slavery of obedience. True to form, Schenkel's anti-Jesuitism was a ritualized performance, a demonstration of the rhetorically contingent, mutually referential meanings of "Jesuitism" and Protestantism consonant with the basic tenets of the language of liberalism: progress, freedom, individuality, science, and a united Germany under Prussian hegemony.

In step with this kind of Protestant liberal, anticlerical, and anti-Jesuit literature, leading lights of German *Kulturprotestantismus* coupled Protestantism and liberalism in new, national-level, anti-Catholic organizations. They included notables like Rudolf von Bennigsen, Johann Caspar Bluntschli, Johannes Miquel, and Daniel Schenkel himself who joined together in the Nationalverein (National Association) founded in 1859 with headquarters in Frankfurt. Soon afterward Protestant theological moderates like Michael Baumgarten, Willibald Beyschlag, and Richard Rothe set up the Deutscher Protestantenverein (German Protestant Association) at the University of Halle in 1863. These associations of middle-class Protestants were designed to bring together political, civic, and academic notables from across the

95. Ibid., 138, 140, respectively.
96. Ibid., 141–42.

German states; to pursue liberal and nationalist goals; and to form a united front in the war against the Church of Rome. At its height the Nationalverein numbered over twenty-five thousand, and while it remained closed to the wider public, it had considerable success mobilizing popular opinion. The bishop of Mainz, Wilhelm Emmanuel von Ketteler, a leader of the clerical counterattack against liberalism, understood its formidable influence and charged in 1862, "the Nationalverein is an anti-Catholic association, an association that from the standpoint of rationalistic Protestantism is hostile to the proper place of the Catholic Church in Germany, an association that is an insult and an impairment to us Catholics in our belief and in our rights."[97] Meanwhile, Daniel Schenkel repeated in his manifesto of the Deutscher Protestantenverein the widely held view that while Protestantism, "the essential lever of cultural progress," was the foundation for religious, moral, and intellectual freedom, Roman Catholicism was, by contrast, an attack on the cultural development and on the moral and scientific progress of the century.[98]

The historian Adolf M. Birke has argued that German liberals as the heirs of the Enlightenment saw the "Catholic principle" as the embodiment of theological, spiritual, and political reaction, wholly irreconcilable with the modern Zeitgeist.[99] The church's effort to revive Catholicism intensified a popular piety and mobilized a mass culture that stood in sharp contrast to the belief in progress and science. Bildung, the cultivation of intellect and spirit, was likewise claimed by liberals as Protestant. It was the hallmark of the individual Bürger as opposed to the superstition and dogmatism of the Catholic "mob." The contemporary historian Johann Gustav Droysen, who believed that the nation was not simply a political power but also an agent of morality, culture, and progress, helped inculcate a worldview that during the decade of the founding of the empire became the conviction of Protestant liberals: Catholicism was synonymous with ignorance, submission, and plebeianism.[100] That Catholicism was fit only for the ignorant mob, not

97. Wilhelm Emmanuel von Ketteler, "The Nationalverein," excerpted in Schenkel, *Die kirchliche Frage,* 105.

98. Daniel Schenkel, *Der deutsche Protestantenverein und seine Bedeutung in der Gegenwart nach den Akten dargestellt* (Wiesbaden: C. W. Kreidel, 1868), 98. Quoted in Adolf M. Birke, *Bischof Ketteler und der deutsche Liberalismus: Eine Untersuchung über das Verhältnis des liberalen Katholizismus zum bürgerlichen Liberalismus in der Reichsgründung* (Mainz: Matthias Grünewald Verlag, 1971), 52.

99. Ibid., 43–44.

100. See Langewiesche, *Liberalismus in Deutschland,* 68; Smith, *German Nationalism,* 27–28.

for educated Protestant individuals, Droysen had already confirmed in a trip to Bavaria in 1852: "There is no question," he explained in a letter to his brother Karl, "that this heathenish Catholicism is better suited to and accepted by the masses than Protestantism, which really demands from every individual an improvement, a personal elevation, and ennoblement."[101] In 1864 Pope Pius IX issued one of the most important documents of Vatican history. In the Syllabus of Errors the pope rejected as one of the "principal errors" of the century the notion that "the Roman Pontiff can and ought to reconcile himself and come to terms with progress, liberalism, and modern civilization." It was this document that reminded the eminent liberal *Kulturprotestant* Heinrich von Treitschke "what good luck it is to be Protestant. Protestantism has the capacity for endless, continuing Bildung."[102]

This increasingly close identification of liberalism with a Protestant legacy of anti-Catholicism at midcentury was one important step in the reconstitution of liberalism as anathema to Catholicism. Prominent anti-Catholic reformers like Christian Bunsen, Adolf Diesterweg, and Daniel Schenkel aligned a broad social, educational, political, and economic program with a cultural tradition of Protestantism in the effort to reconstitute and motivate their prescription for the German nation after the defeat of 1848–49. Together they represent a significant Protestantization of German liberal aspirations for reform. Even as many liberals claimed Protestantism as their cultural heritage, liberalism, however, had virtually no claim on Protestant religious institutions. The Protestant Church leadership, most pastors, and the theological professoriate were conservative agents of antiliberalism, committed to the tradition of monarchical authority. Leading liberal dissidents in establishment Protestantism were disciplined, eventually forced out of, or left on their own accord the traditional Protestant religious institutions.[103]

For example, Enlightenment metaphors of darkness and light were central to the anti-Jesuit discourse of the clerical leadership of the Friends of Light and their "free congregations," a religious dissenting movement that joined Protestantism to liberal rationalism as it rebelled against the conservative theology and structure of the established Evangelical Church. In A. L. Stachelstock's *Licht und Finsterniß oder die*

101. Johann Gustav Droysen to Karl Droysen, 17 Sept. 1852, in Hübner, *Briefwechsel,* 2:130.

102. Both quotations in Langewiesche, *Liberalismus in Deutschland,* 181.

103. Andrew C. Gould, *Origins of Liberal Dominance: State, Church, and Party in Nineteenth-Century Europe* (Ann Arbor: University of Michigan Press, 1999), 84–85.

freien Gemeinden und die Jesuiten, which appeared in 1861, Germany is the battleground for a campaign of the modern heirs of the Enlightenment against the reactionary "Jesuitism" of the Middle Ages. Stachelstock considered himself a "lightning bolt of truth": Germans, he claimed, stood in face to face, life or death combat with the Jesuit proponents of obfuscation, treachery, and dogma.[104] Jesuits are "the men of darkness," "black brutes," winged hunters in the cold night—bats and screech owls—that must be driven out of Germany with all means of light: candles, night lamps, torch fires, and the break of dawn, the metaphors of spiritual illumination, reason, and intellect. The defeat of the Revolution of 1848, the hope for a liberal, enlightened, and modern Germany, Stachelstock argued, was smashed by the "Loyolaites," medieval agents of reaction: "It is as if all of hell opened up to repeat once again if only as farce the Walpurgisnacht of the Middle Ages." During the decade of reaction following the revolution a new Holy Roman Empire had been established in Germany with priests spreading superstition and stupidity. According to Stachelstock, "reaction and the single-minded *Priesterschaft* along with their dependents wrapped the unbiased point of view in gloom by casting suspicion upon and screaming about the revolutionary liberalism of the free congregations."[105]

Now, Stachelstock argued, the current period stood in sharp contrast to the period of reaction. Germans found themselves at the "dawn of a beautiful time," a new day of free, fresh air. There was, however, much work to be done. Stachelstock called upon his readers to join him in the fight "to defend the freedom to know, to think, and to defend our state against the insane self-conceit of orthodoxy and the ruinous phantasmagoria of Jesuitism."[106] While, according to Stachelstock, the Mittelstand could be counted upon to despise the Jesuits, large numbers from the upper and lower strata of the population had been seduced by the order, caught in its net of religious fanaticism. The Jesuits had been able to establish a network of informants and lackeys. Male and female house servants, for example, who fell under their sway in the confessional became tools, "secret spies" who passed information to the Jesuits. Nevertheless, Stachelstock insisted that Germans despite their long imprisonment could stand on their own feet and despite the long night could still open their eyes to the sun. In order to save themselves from the Jesuits, Germans had to embrace the

104. A. L. Stachelstock, *Licht und Finsterniß oder die freien Gemeinden und die Jesuiten* (Altona: Verlagsbureau, 1861).

105. Ibid., 10, 33–34, respectively.

106. Ibid., 12, 16–17, respectively.

Enlightenment, for only the Enlightenment had the virtues and power to defeat the Jesuit menace. "Who," he asked, "wrested power from the hands of the Jesuits? . . . . Who brought an end to the most non-sensical and unreasonable dogmas? Who allowed us to free ourselves from the belief in interminable damnation in hell? Who saved us from the torture that the servants of the Inquisition had practiced with such virtuosity?" "The Enlightenment, again the Enlightenment, and always the Enlightenment!"[107]

Of particular concern to Stachelstock were the illicit business prac-tices of the Jesuits or what he called "Jesuit economics." Stachelstock pointed to the alleged illegal trade of the Jesuits in Spanish America and the West Indian colonies and to what he claimed had been the Jesuits' fraudulent bankruptcy of France. He argued that the "Loy-olaites" had carried these practices into modern times. According to Stachelstock, the millions that the Jesuits had amassed were not obtained simply through deceit and begging but by usury and through currency-exchange businesses and stock-market investments, all man-aged with exceptional cunning and diligence. Immediately after they reestablished themselves in France, for example, the Jesuits had started a booming wine business. The wine business was only surpassed by the lucrative retail trade conducted by the missionaries. Stachelstock argued missionary work was the occasion for "horse-trading" and exploitation. At stalls set up at the entrance of churches, the mission-aries presented a grotesque spectacle, lining their pockets with the pro-ceeds from the gullible, all too eager to buy up hymnals, missionary lit-erature, religious pamphlets, rosaries, crucifixes, sacred hearts, rings, skulls, scapularies, religious pictures, figurines, "and other hocus-pocus" sold in all sizes and at all prices. The Jesuits preferred to hold their missions in the large cities and avoided the poor villages since "there was nothing for them to fish for there."[108] The Jesuits also con-ducted a lucrative business renting or subrenting to speculators church pews during the missions, and in France, where the order was illegal, capital and property were siphoned through front men to the Jesuits.

The "Jesuit economy," Stachelstock argued, particularly exploited women. Although Jesuits otherwise favored the company of young women, in their retail trade they preferred to employ old women as their agents. These women peddling religious figurines were an espe-cially exasperating display of stupid idolatry: "'Hey! Hey!' called one

107. Ibid., 16–17.
108. Ibid., 74.

of these mission entrepreneurs to another, who had staggered and dropped a figurine from her arms, 'don't let the good Lord fall in the mud!' What priests and what gullibility! What men and what gods!"[109] According to Stachelstock, Jesuits continued their exploitation of women with a lucrative factory-based industry that concealed their enormous greed behind a facade of magnanimity. The church established and administered female religious orders, congregations for girls from all social strata, and philanthropic institutions for servant girls; however, Stachelstock explained, these girls were not just held to rigid moral rules and piety but, in reality, also subjected to a regime of hard labor in "work convents." Here the girls produced for the profit of the Catholic Church goods for the commercial market. They received as daily wages only the minimal amount needed to support their lives.

There was more at stake in this attack on "Jesuit economics" than mere derision. According to Stachelstock, the Jesuit system coupling exploitation and philanthropy threatened bürgerlich competitors. The cheap labor of girls in the "work convents," for example, undercut the business interests of the Bürgertum: "In this way the work convents could bring their products to the market at prices that were not possible for bürgerlich factory owners who had to pay their workers proper daily wages." The businessman or middle man who dealt in "convent goods" was, therefore, soon the most dangerous competition for everyone else, and many businessmen felt they were victimized by "the hypocritical form of religion and philanthropy."[110] In many industrial towns, "work convents" quickly captured all the female workers in the vicinity. According to the argument, they drove wages so low that girls from the lower classes could no longer manage an existence by "honest means" and "forced by poverty, fell into the arms of depravity." "Work convents" ultimately destroyed the virtue of women, driving them into prostitution. Legitimate bürgerlich economics, based on a free, self-regulating labor market, stood in contrast to illicit, exploitive, and destructive "Jesuit economics." According to Stachelstock, the "Götterdämmerung," the final reckoning with the Jesuits, was coming and none too soon. While arguing "never before have the oppositions appeared so sharp and divisive," he assured his readers that truth would in the end prove victorious despite the recalcitrance of the "Dunkelmänner" (men of darkness).[111]

109. Ibid., 75.
110. Ibid., 87.
111. Ibid., 88, 103–4, respectively.

"Jesuit economics" was the bleak alternative to the liberal economic principles emerging during the 1850s and 1860s. Their political hopes dashed during the revolution, squeezed by state reaction and threatened by the Catholic revival, liberals began to emphasize the importance of and need for economic reform and industrial growth. They now developed the reassuring promise of economic advancement and material achievement. This was the age of the new aggressive entrepreneur and the impressive economic boom, the period during which German economic power first became apparent. By 1856 the liberal *National Zeitung* announced the new spirit that characterized the time: "What idealistic efforts strove in vain to do, materialism has accomplished in a few months."[112] The Bremen businessman Wilhelm Kiesselbach criticized the older brand of liberalism for not recognizing that "a politically independent Bürgertum must be based on economic independence."[113] When liberal political activities resumed with the New Era, liberal leaders continued to emphasize economic issues. The leaders of the new Kongress deutscher Volkswirte (Congress for German Political Economy), which held its first general meeting in 1858, contrasted their plans for the economic foundation for progress and more practical orientation toward national issues with what they considered to have been the heady and misguided idealism of the Frankfurt National Assembly. The Kongress deutscher Volkswirte was only one of many new participatory organizations devoted to economic issues and the advocacy of specific economic interests. By the 1860s, liberal popular periodicals and academic journals also gave much more attention to economic matters. Publications such as Bluntschli's *Staatswörterbuch* devoted more room to the economy than they had before 1848. The post-1848 edition of the *Staatslexikon,* the most important model of Vormärz liberalism, now gave more attention to commercial and industrial affairs, deleting the earlier entry "Secret Societies" and replacing it with "Joint Stock Companies."[114]

With the new devotion to economic affairs, liberals developed a growing faith in the principles of a free economy. Liberals increasingly insisted that the regulation of industry and trade was only counterproductive and ultimately destructive. Releasing the resources of society, many believed, would yield prosperity and progress. The virtues of an

112. This and the following are based on Sheehan, *German Liberalism,* 79–94, quotation at 84.

113. Quoted in ibid., 88.

114. Ibid., 84. See also James J. Sheehan, *German History, 1770–1866* (Oxford: Oxford University Press, 1989), 731–35.

unharnessed market were enthusiastically endorsed not only by commercial and industrial entrepreneurs but also by intellectuals, bureaucrats, small manufacturers, and craftsmen who believed they stood to gain as they pursued their respective interests in a deregulated economy. The brief depression from 1857 to 1859 did nothing to blunt the general enthusiasm for laissez-faire economics. In early 1861, the liberal group in the Prussian parliament known as Young Lithuania adopted a program that was a typical repudiation of the regulation of industrial production: "We shall recommend the liberation of trade bonds which still exist in our customs duties and consumption taxes to the detriment of the broad masses, and we shall also support a revision of the manufacturing laws, so that regulations which are oppressive and which remind us of the antiquated guild system are repealed, and after the abolition of police concessions free scope is given to all industrial energies."[115]

It would be a mistake, however, to conflate liberalism after 1850 with laissez-faire economics or the specific interests of the capitalist bourgeoisie. Not all liberals endorsed without qualification a free economy, and most continued to stress the idealism and the principles of education, "independence," and culture, the heritage of Vormärz liberalism. Nevertheless, an age of *Gewerbefreiheit* and *Handelsfreiheit,* deregulation and free trade, had arrived. Throughout the late 1850s and early 1860s, state after state pursued arrangements that facilitated the exchange of goods within the Zollverein (German Customs Union), removed restrictions on economic activity, rebuffed the arguments of guild organizations, and embraced the factory system. Between the opening of the New Era in 1858 and the end of the war with Denmark in 1864, sixteen of the German states had accepted capitalism. By 1866 the number increased to over twenty, and by 1869 the number was thirty.[116] By 1857 new, large banking houses—Schaafhausen, the Darmstädter, Disconto Gesellschaft, Berliner Bank, and Credit Anstalt in Leipzig—were set up to meet the demand for investment capital and to participate in the formation of corporations. During the 1850s and 1860s almost three hundred joint stock companies were established with a combined capital of over twenty-four hundred million marks.[117]

In the summer of 1866, Prussia's decisive victory over Austria categorically foreclosed any hopes for a grossdeutsch solution to the Ger-

115. Quoted in Hamerow, *Restoration, Revolution, Reaction,* 244–45.
116. Ibid., 246–48.
117. Sheehan, *German History,* 735–76.

man national question, a German state unified under the aegis of the House of Habsburg. The fact that Prussia and Austria had come to blows made German Catholics apprehensive. Many Catholics had placed their sympathy with the Austrian monarchy and its population, which was 95 percent Catholic. Now with the Austrian defeat they were thrown into despair. The life hopes of August Reichensperger, a leading Catholic politician and spokesman, came crashing down. He wrote in his diary, "Everything that belonged to my ideals has collapsed."[118] The prominent Catholic politician Hermann von Mallinckrodt could only think, "The world stinks."[119] Even worse, Cardinal Antonelli exclaimed, "The world is collapsing!" and it was his apocalyptic conclusion that was repeated by Roman Catholics across Germany.[120] Catholics, who had been in the majority in the German Confederation that had endured since 1815, now found themselves a minority within the North German Confederation: within the new confederation there were twenty million Protestants and eight million Catholics. Catholics, therefore, believed they were among the losers of 1866.[121]

The Catholic response is understandable given the exaltation of the victory in Prussia as a vindication of liberalism and Protestantism. Unlike Pietists and conservative Lutherans, Protestant liberals welcomed the defeat of the Catholic Habsburg as the foundation for the German nation. Their achievement, they believed, was the triumph of Prussian progressiveness and virility over the backward, internally weak Catholic monarchy; Prussia's new hegemony in central Europe was celebrated as the guarantee of the cultural legacy of the Reformation, the Enlightenment, philosophical idealism, and bourgeois neohumanism.[122] According to Johann Gustav Droysen, for example, the

---

118. Entry for 16 October 1866, quoted in Lill, "Die deutschen Katholiken und Bismarcks Reichsgründung," 346.

119. Quoted in Eda Sagarra, *A Social History of Germany, 1684–1914* (New York: Holmes and Meier, 1977), 230.

120. Hübinger, "Confessionalism," 161.

121. Ibid. See also Adolf M. Birke, "German Catholics and the Quest for National Unity," in *Nation-Building in Central Europe,* ed. Hagen Schulze (Leamington Spa: Berg, 1987), 51–63, esp. 59.

122. For the shock and disappointment of the Catholic population, the reaction of political Catholicism to the defeat of Austria, and the significance of the victory for Protestant Prusso-German nationalism, see Birke, "German Catholics"; Walter Bussmann, "Preußen und das Jahr 1866," *Aus Politik und Zeitgeschichte: Beilage zur Wochenzeitung "Das Parlament"* 24 (1966): 19–27; Karl-Georg Faber, "Realpolitik als Ideologie: Die Bedeutung des Jahres 1866 für politisches Denken in Deutschland," *Historische Zeitschrift* 203 (1966): 1–45; Fritz Fischer, "Der deutsche Protestantismus und die Politik im 19. Jahrhundert," *Historische Zeitschrift* 171 (1951): 473–518; Lill, "Die deutschen Katholiken und Bismarcks

victory was a "triumph of the true German spirit over the false, the spirit of 1517 and 1813 over the Roman spirit."[123] The military campaign against Austria, he believed, was the final act in the campaign of Protestant national freedom against the rule of Rome.

For like-minded liberals, the Jesuits' persistent missionary campaign on Prussian soil seemed all the more impossible to reconcile with the quick and decisive triumph on the fields at Königsgratz. The victory over Austria was, therefore, an important moment in the reconstruction and dissemination of anti-Catholicism. As one observer commented in 1866, "the reproaches, which for a long time have been made against the Catholic Church, that it makes the people stupid, makes them useless for bürgerlich life, destroys the mind, places obstacles in the way of progress in science and culture, seem at present to be all consuming. The main reason for these accusations and complaints is the fact that the Jesuits may hold missions in almost all the dioceses of Germany, preach, and hear confession."[124] The continuation of the Catholic missionary crusade despite the defeat of "Catholic Austria" broadened and deepened anti-Catholicism. No longer predominantly in the pamphlet literature of Protestant pastors and theologians or among liberal intellectuals, politicians, and social observers, the problem with Catholicism was now a ubiquitous topic in all reaches of German society, culture, and politics.

Catholic Antiliberalism, Liberal Catholics, and the Kulturkampf

While leading liberal authors used diatribes against "Jesuitism" and Catholicism to revive or reorient basic liberal tenets during the New Era, authorities of the Catholic Church and in the Catholic press defined Catholicism in diametrical opposition to liberalism. By the

Reichsgründung"; H. Müller, "Der deutsche politische Katholizismus in der Entscheidung des Jahres 1866," *Blätter für pfälzische Kirchengeschichte und religiöse Volkskunde* 33 (1966): 46–75; W. Real, "Die Ereignisse von 1866–1867 im Lichte unserer Zeit," *Historisches Jahrbuch* 95 (1975): 342–73; and George C. Windell, *The Catholics and German Unity, 1866–1871* (Minneapolis: University of Minnesota Press, 1954).

123. Quoted in Wolfgang Hartwig, "Von Preußens Aufgabe in Deutschland zu Deutschlands Aufgabe in der Welt: Liberalismus und borussianisches Geschichtsbild zwischen Revolution und Imperialismus," *Historische Zeitschrift* 231 (1980): 265–324, quotation at 316. (In 1517 Martin Luther nailed his theses to the church door at Wittenberg initiating the Protestant Reformation. In 1813 the Prussian army defeated Napoleon at Leipzig and drove him out of Germany.) Similarly, Droysen argued, "with this victory we finally became master of the miserable situation of 1519" (the year Charles V, king of Spain and devout Catholic, became emperor of the Holy Roman Empire). Quoted in Smith, *German Nationalism*, 28.

124. Jocham, *Die sittliche Verpestung des Volkes*, 5–6.

early 1860s ultramontane newspapers were arguing that, though misguided, the hostility of the liberals and progressives and Freemasons toward Catholicism was understandable. However, according to church authorities, the position of the liberal Catholic had become so self-contradictory as to be incomprehensible; subscribing to both liberalism and Catholicism was simply an impossibility. As early as 1862, for example, the *Freiburger Katholisches Kirchenblatt* declared in a notice under the heading "The Liberal Catholic":

> We can grasp that there are Carbonari, nationalists, Voltaireans, free thinkers who are assaulting the bulwarks of the Catholic Church. They all have one goal, one motive: it is *general subversion*—the revolution! When they therefore inscribe on their banners, "Death to the Pope!" they are only following the logic of their convictions. But what we cannot accept, what is beyond our ability to comprehend, is the so-called *liberal* Catholic. (Emphasis in the original.)[125]

According to the paper, the "hypocritical freedom of false liberalism" consisted of "saying anything, writing anything, doing anything for the purpose of slander." By contrast, a "real Catholic" accepted without question what the church both taught and condemned. Obeying the traditions of Christian history as directed by Rome was the hallmark of the "good Catholic," as the paper explained; a "liberal Catholic" was a "bad Catholic," who excluded himself or herself by choice from the community of the Catholic Church.[126] The Syllabus of Errors in 1864 established as a matter of doctrine that the church considered liberalism and Catholicism incompatible. This position was further hardened by the church with the announcement of the First Vatican Council in 1869 and the plans to proclaim the infallibility of the pope on matters of dogma and doctrine. In February of that year, a notice drawing the line between "liberal Catholics" and "true Catholics" appeared in *Civiltà Cattolica,* the official journal of the Vatican, founded by Pope Pius IX in 1850 and published by the Jesuits under a director appointed by the pope himself:

> Liberal Catholics are afraid the [Vatican] Council may proclaim the doctrines of the Syllabus and the infallibility of the pope, but they do not give up hope that it will modify or interpret certain

125. *Freiburger Katholisches Kirchenblatt,* 4 (1862): 347. Quoted in Götz von Olenhusen, "Klerus und Ultramontanismus in der Erzdiözese Freiburg," 113.
126. Ibid., 114.

statements of the Syllabus in a sense favorable to their own ideas, and that the question of infallibility will either not be mooted or not decided. True Catholics, who are a great majority of the faithful, entertain opposite hopes. They wish the Council to promulgate the doctrines of the Syllabus . . . [and] will accept with delight the proclamation of the pope's dogmatic infallibility.[127]

This article, representing as it did the pope's own views in an age of mounting ultramontanism, was bound to have a significant impact on the Catholic clergy and laity.

With such crude and uncompromising proclamations pitting "true" and "loyal" against "liberal" and "bad" Catholics, directed not outward against adversaries but inward against the laity itself, the church reached a new level of intolerance, not to mention distrust, within its own ranks. It did much to antagonize middle-class Catholics, and it embarrassed and angered important Catholic political and religious leaders who had, after all, campaigned for Catholic rights under the liberal banner of religious freedom. These included Ludwig Windthorst, the formidable leader of political Catholicism, and Wilhelm Emmanuel von Ketteler, the highly respected bishop of Mainz and politically the most important figure in the German episcopate, both of whom led the surprisingly vocal if short-lived opposition to papal infallibility. They now worried, and rightly so, that the church's exclusion of liberals from Catholicism would undermine their efforts to unify Catholicism in Germany and lead to schism.[128] As the Catholic press announced the new antiliberal discipline, the Katholikentage (which had first convened in 1848 and soon became the national assembly of the German Catholic associations) and priests at the local level brought direct pressure on the laity. Again it was often women who most readily accepted the new orthodoxy and then promoted compliance by exerting their influence on husbands and family in private life. Now, for example, even a prominent notable like the Oberbürgermeister of Bonn, Leopold Kaufmann, experienced the power of the Catholic popular movement. When the mayor proposed marriage to Elisa Michels, the pious daughter of a wealthy merchant in Cologne and fifteen years his junior, he bent to her precondition that he drop his membership in the Freemasons.[129] The close of the liberal and state campaign against the Catholic Church at

---

127. Quoted in Anderson, *Windthorst*, 121.
128. Ibid., 121–22.
129. Mergel, *Zwischen Klasse und Konfession*, 185.

the end of the 1870s did nothing to abate the antiliberal fervor of the church. Even well after the Kulturkampf was over, an entry concerning liberalism in a Catholic Church lexicon in 1891 told its readers that liberalism was responsible for all the ills of the world from its creation to the present day. "The snake in Paradise already spoke the temptations and false promises of liberalism." "The most decisive liberal principles emerged with the Reformation," and "the most progressive socialism" represented its current sad fruit.[130]

As the church stepped up its efforts to purge liberals and liberalism from its own ranks, liberal Catholics found themselves increasingly torn between middle-class membership on the one hand and loyalty to their church on the other. They had always been disturbed by the raw power of the missions to unleash unseemly displays of religious fanaticism, women kissing the Jesuit robes and men reduced to tears in public. Bürgerlich Catholics looked down on the Catholic peasant masses for the same reason the secularized and assimilationist Jewish bourgeoisie looked down on the generation of Yiddish-speaking, bearded and sidelocked *Ostjuden* emigrating from Eastern Europe. Middle-class Jews did so even as this impulse conflicted with the desire to assist fellow Jews obviously in need of philanthropic care.[131] Bürgerlich Catholic prejudice against more common Catholic folk stemmed from a social sense of insecurity: like bürgerlich Jews who wanted to socially integrate, who tried to "fit" and "pass" in the predominantly Protestant culture of the middle class, many middle-class Catholics were self-conscious about their status within that milieu. They married into Protestant families; they shared their professions, their education, their metropolitan lifestyle, and the bourgeois prejudice against the lower classes. Ultimately, however, they worried that the antimaterialist, antiliberal fervor of ultramontane Catholicism and the popular Catholic revival compromised by dint of confessional association their social credentials as members of the Bürgertum.

Politically, Catholics continued to support liberal candidates during

130. H. Gruber, S.J. [Society of Jesus], "Liberalism," in *Kirchenlexikon oder Enzyklopädie der katholischen Theologie und ihrer Hilfswissenschaften,* ed. Wetzer and Welte (Freiburg, 1891), 7:1912f, quoted in Langewiesche, *Liberalismus in Deutschland,* 187.

131. Steven E. Aschheim, *Brothers and Strangers: The East European Jew in German and German-Jewish Consciousness, 1800–1923* (Madison: University of Wisconsin Press, 1982); Sander L. Gilman, *Jewish Self-Hatred: Anti-Semitism and the Hidden Language of the Jews* (Baltimore: Johns Hopkins University Press, 1986); Michael R. Marrus, *The Unwanted: European Refugees in the Twentieth Century* (Oxford: Oxford University Press, 1985); Jack Wertheimer, *Unwelcome Strangers: East European Jews in Imperial Germany* (Oxford: Oxford University Press, 1987).

the conflict over the reform of the military, the budget crisis, and the constitutional battle of the 1860s. In heavily Catholic Westphalia and the Rhineland, Catholic voting for liberals was, in fact, overwhelming; during the Prussian elections, Catholic voting districts (those with populations more than 55 percent Catholic) elected liberal candidates three to one over clerical candidates. Catholic parish clergy on occasion preferred liberal candidates in the 1860s, not just to government and conservative candidates but also to Catholic candidates of the Catholic political Fraktion in the Prussian parliament. It was even possible for Catholics to elect such later prominent liberal Kulturkämpfer as Rudolf Virchow and Carl Hermann Kanngiesser. Deputies with Catholic constituencies also supported liberal positions on key issues in the Prussian parliament. Of deputies from Catholic districts in the Rhineland and Westphalia, 66 percent joined those liberals who rejected the 1866 Indemnity Bill excusing Bismarck for his extraconstitutional collection of taxes (55 percent of all Rhenish and Westphalian deputies rejected the bill though only 25 percent of all deputies did so).[132] But the Syllabus of Errors with its condemnation of progress, rationalism, and liberalism; the promulgation of papal infallibility, construed by liberals as an attack on the autonomy of the individual and the modern state; and the continued antiliberal agitation of the Catholic press and clergy made it increasingly unlikely at the end of the 1860s that bürgerlich Catholics could continue to avoid the question of ultimate loyalty.

By the time of the Kulturkampf, as the historian Thomas Mergel has argued, the Catholic middle class split as its members found new, often tenuous identities relative to Catholicism and liberalism.[133] Some Catholic Bürger prioritized Catholicism while not necessarily becoming antiliberal. These would include those who rose to become politicians in the Center Party, leaders of political Catholicism, and managers of major Catholic newspapers during the Kulturkampf. Other middle-class Catholics emphasized liberalism without completely rejecting Catholicism. Many of them were civil servants, university professors, lawyers, and judges who had a certain connection to the state and the government due to their profession, family tradition, and social attach-

132. Margaret Lavinia Anderson and Kenneth D. Barkin, "The Myth of the Puttkamer Purge and the Reality of the Kulturkampf: Some Reflections on the Historiography of Imperial Germany," *Journal of Modern History* 54 (1982): 647–86, esp. 681, 681 n. 82; Anderson, "The Kulturkampf," 84–88.

133. The ensuing follows Mergel, "Ultramontanism, Liberalism, and Moderation," 165–66; and idem, *Zwischen Klasse und Konfession.*

ment. As social progressives, they recognized the need for modern elementary school reform and, therefore, the need to break the hold of clerical control on education.[134] They believed that Catholic orders and charitable foundations sapped capital that would otherwise finance industrial growth and economic expansion. They also resented the heavy-handed role of the Jesuits, who, they believed, had seized an illegitimate amount of authority within the church hierarchy and undermined the traditional position of the priest in parish life. At the same time, however, they resented what they considered an arrogant and illegitimate attack on the autonomy of the church by liberals and the state.

Another group of Catholic Bürger unequivocally moved over to militant liberal anticlericalism. With the promulgation of infallibility, they openly defied the papacy, rejected Roman Catholicism, and established the Old Catholic Church. Old Catholic Kulturkämpfer now fought ultramontane Catholicism with no less and perhaps more ferocity than did Protestant and secular Kulturkämpfer. It warrants repeating that one of the most unrelenting proponents of Kulturkampf legislation including the Jesuit law was Eduard Windthorst, Old Catholic and no less than the nephew of Ludwig Windthorst, leader of the Center Party. (The latter could himself be at times a difficult friend of the church, berating and defending the Jesuits in the same moment.) Like the Windthorsts, the distinguished Bachem family that published the *Kölnische Volkszeitung* also had its embarrassment: the brother-in-law of Josef Bachem was a Kulturkämpfer and "bootlicker of Bismarck."[135] For its part, the Catholic Church turned its back on and never forgave Catholics who had had any part in the Kulturkampf against the church. Catholic liberals, therefore, often had to take the consequences of their beliefs and actions literally to the grave. When Max von Forckenbeck—a national liberal; president of the Reichstag at the height of the Kulturkampf; and, he believed, a good Catholic his entire life—died in 1892, his family members received the condolences and gratitude of the most prominent dignitaries and officials of the state. But the establishment of the Church of Rome denied his family the right to give him a Catholic burial.[136]

Such cases serve as reminders that the prosecution of the Kulturkampf bridged the confessional divide as it cut through Catholic middle-class families. Historians have shown that the Kulturkampf was hardly the arid affair confined to verbal duels over policy between

134. Mergel, "Ultramontanism, Liberalism, and Moderation," 169.
135. Ibid. idem, *Zwischen Klasse und Konfession,* 264–65.
136. Langewiesche, *Liberalismus in Deutschland,* 187.

church and state officials and deputies in parliamentary chambers that it has often been made out to be.[137] The passions and pressures of the Kulturkampf permeated daily life. Between Catholics and Protestants it warped popular perceptions, poisoned friendships, and wrecked social and business associations. Among middle-class Catholics, however, it cut deeper into private life, often straining marriages between liberal husbands and pious wives and souring relations between brothers and sisters, in-laws and cousins. At the same time, well into the next century and beyond, liberal Catholics felt torn now by their faith, believing as they did that they were never fully at home in their own church.

Electoral behavior with the founding of the empire and during the Kulturkampf offers another indication of how Catholics decided the dilemma politically between liberal and Catholic identity. Most liberal Catholics may not have gone as far as Eduard Windthorst in his enthusiastic leadership of the attack on the Roman Church during the Kulturkampf. But as one historian who has carefully examined the elections of the empire has calculated, Catholics did make up a sizable percentage of those voting during the first two (universal male) Reichstag elections for the liberal enemies of political Catholicism.[138] According to these tabulations, in 1871 between the signing of the Treaty of Frankfurt, which brought the war against France to victorious conclusion, and the start of the Kulturkampf, 23 percent of Catholic voters supported the Center Party in Prussia, 28 percent supported the Center in the non-Prussian states (including those with heavily Catholic populations in Hesse, Baden, Bavaria, and Württemberg), and 25 percent supported the Center across Germany. At the same time, 11 percent of Catholic voters in Prussia, 34 percent of Catholic voters in the non-Prussian states, and 21 percent of Catholic voters in all of Germany supported the liberal parties. They voted for National Liberal and Liberale Reichspartei candidates who were anticlerical, favored the creation of the kleindeutsch empire under the hegemony of Prussia, and enjoyed the backing of the governments of the south German states.

In the 1874 elections in Prussia, the Kulturkampf brought with it a

---

137. Anderson, *Windthorst;* Blackbourn, *Marpingen;* Ross, *Failure of Bismarck's Kulturkampf.*

138. Sperber, *Kaiser's Voters,* 157–71. Jürgen Winkler's calculations for voting according to confession are close to Sperber's calculations. Jürgen Winkler, *Sozialstruktur politische Tradition und Liberalismus: Eine empirische Längsschnittstudie zur Wahlentwicklung in Deutschland 1871–1933* (Oplanden: Westdeutscher Verlag, 1995), 125–28, 169.

profound change in the percentage of Catholics voting for the Center Party. In Prussia, as the antichurch campaign reached its climax with the closing of the Jesuit and other religious orders, the imprisonment of bishops, and the banning of priests from their parishes, the percentage of eligible Catholics voting for the Center doubled, jumping from 23 percent in 1871 to 45 percent. But the percentage of Catholic voters supporting the liberal parties remained constant at 11 percent in Prussia in the middle of the Kulturkampf. Those numbers dropped to 18 percent in the non-Prussian states and 14 percent in all of Germany. Catholic eligible voter turnout reached a remarkable 80 percent, a height not to be reached again until 1907. The historian Thomas Nipperdey has estimated that at the same time the proportion of practicing Catholic adult males climbed to almost 90 percent across Germany.[139] If so, then the point is that across Germany the percentage of Catholic males estranged from the church, the percentage of Catholics voting liberal, and an estimate of the middle-class percentage of the Catholic population roughly correlate. Noteworthy is that the correlation is especially accurate for Prussia, where the confrontation between liberals and Catholics, state and church was most intense. In the non-Prussian German states, where bishops were not imprisoned and vacant parishes were supplied with priests, the public practice of Catholicism continued with minimal state interference.

Beyond matters of social-cultural prejudice; a distaste for the exuberant piety of Catholic common folk; anti-Jesuit sentiment; and resentment toward neo-orthodox, heavy-handed ultramontanism, middle-class Catholics had other good reasons, they believed, to vote for the liberal parties rather than for the Center Party. Since the Center as a political party did not simply represent Catholic confessional interests, middle-class Catholics did not reject the party for reasons solely having to do with matters of faith and church. The party may have been imbued with a specifically Catholic confessionalism in its politics, but the leadership of the party was thoroughly laicized and jealously guarded its autonomy from the church in Germany and from Rome. It was the party's lay leadership that decided the social and economic policy of the party in accordance with the political realities specific to the individual German states; like the leadership of other parties, therefore, it pursued policies that reflected the interests of its primary constituency. In the case of the Center the constituency that

---

139. Thomas Nipperdey, *Religion im Umbruch: Deutschland 1870–1918* (Munich: C. H. Beck Verlag, 1988), 23.

overwhelmingly provided the rank and file of party support was Mittelstand shopkeepers, craftsmen, small businessmen, and peasants. For the sake of this support, the party advocated for agricultural tariffs, for antimargarine laws, and for restrictions on meat importation. More important, the party campaigned for the restoration of the guild system and other anti-industrial legislation meant to protect the traditional position of craftsmen. Even though Ludwig Windthorst and those close to him tried to subdue the more ardent anti–free market and procorporatist demands of others in the party, most leaders of the party employed anti-industrialist and anticapitalist rhetoric in order to attract agrarian, petit bourgeois, and working-class votes.[140] Protectionist legislation benefiting the agrarian sector and procorporatist measures on behalf of the guild system meant that the Center shared economic policies with the conservatives, but the Center Party's economic policies had little to recommend themselves to more progressive middle-class Catholics interested in industrial development and capitalist economic growth.

That Catholics voted for the liberal parties and in doing so opposed the clericalism of the Center Party challenges the conclusions of important historians of political Catholicism who have argued that confession was the most significant determinant of political behavior in nineteenth-century Germany, especially during the Kulturkampf. Margaret Lavinia Anderson has argued that by 1873 a Catholic bloc had formed that would continue for the next sixty years. Religion remained, she argues, the most important variable in elections; Catholic voters were lost to liberalism in the late nineteenth century.[141] David Blackbourn has more specifically argued that the Catholic middle class remained loyal to Catholicism and the Center Party during the Kulturkampf. Catholic middle-class leaders "rallied instinctively," he argues, to the defense of the church against state repression: Catholic members of the traditional middle-class professions, lawyers, businessmen, and academics, might have looked askance at papal infallibility, the Jesuits, and popular piety, but their religious loyalties ultimately trumped class loyalties during elections.[142] These arguments are in line with Stanley Suval's influential general study of Wilhelmine

140. David Blackbourn, "Catholics and Politics in Imperial Germany: The Centre Party and Its Constituency," in *Populists and Patricians: Essays in Modern German History* (London: Allen and Unwin, 1987), 188–214; idem, *Class, Religion, and Local Politics.*

141. Anderson, "The Kulturkampf"; idem, *Windthorst.*

142. Blackbourn, "Catholics and Politics," 202; Blackbourn and Eley, *Peculiarities of German History,* 262.

election politics that concluded that religion, ethnicity, nationality, and race—not class—were the more significant lines of political demarcation, and research has maintained in general that confession was the single most important line of cleavage in the German electorate.[143] At the same time, Karl Rohe, in his reexamination of the sociology of elections and political parties in the imperial period, has argued that we must be prepared to think anew, not just in terms of the social characteristics of individuals (e.g., religious identification) but also in terms of cultural characteristics, that is, mentalities and ways of life, if we are to identify and understand voting patterns, particularly those that deviate from the traditional expectations.[144] In the case of most bourgeois Catholic men, we are left in the aggregate with the impression that they were more bound to their middle-class social milieu than to their confessional identification though this does not apply to those bourgeois Catholic women who remained dedicated Catholics.[145] Catholic middle-class men continued to share even during the heat of the Kulturkampf the anticlerical, anti-Jesuit, procapitalist, and industrial culture of the liberal, predominantly Protestant middle class. If so, there was an important dimension of class conflict to the Kulturkampf that arrayed the middle class, including the Catholic middle class, against the aristocrats and popular masses who joined the Catholic revival and defended the church against state repression.

As this chapter has argued, from the 1850s through the 1860s and into the 1870s, Protestant religious elites and church leaders eagerly joined in the attack against the Jesuits, the missionary campaign, ultramontanism, the Catholic Church, and Catholicism. In their attempt to reawaken and preserve Protestant identity in the face of the Roman Catholic revival, they unleashed a torrent of hysterically anti-Catholic sermons, speeches, newspaper and journal articles, brochures, pamphlets, essays, and books that were widely disseminated throughout German society. The Protestant revival and backlash against resurgent Roman Catholicism generated anti-Catholic attitudes that endured throughout the rest of the century and beyond. Specifically, the attempt to revive Protestant identity and the animus toward Catholicism that accompanied it provided the larger context for the Kulturkampf. The Protestant revival concurrent with the Catholic revival

143. Stanley Suval, *Electoral Politics in Wilhelmine Germany* (Chapel Hill: University of North Carolina Press, 1985); Sperber, *Kaiser's Voters,* 274.

144. Karl Rohe, ed., *Elections, Parties, and Political Traditions: Social Foundations of German Parties and Party Systems, 1867–1987* (New York: Berg, 1990), 3.

145. See also Sperber, *Kaiser's Voters,* 279.

has been missed by historians, yet it does much to account for the breadth and depth of the popular anti-Catholic sentiment prominent after midcentury. Without recognition of not only the Catholic but also the popular Protestant revival, it is difficult to account fully for the rise of Catholic and Protestant nationalist conflict in Germany.[146] At the same time, prominent liberals employed the authority of cultural Protestantism to legitimate and mobilize support for their broad prescription for reform after the defeat of 1848–49 from the decade of reaction through the New Era.

Even so, it is important not simply to conflate Protestantism and liberalism after midcentury and to recognize that persistent popular Protestant anti-Catholic culture did not itself define the character of the Kulturkampf. The anti-Catholic fervor of the Protestant religious leadership that added heat to and popularized the campaign against the church was a continuation of the animosity toward Roman Catholicism, the authority of the pope, and missionary proselytizing that was as old as the Reformation of the sixteenth century. Indeed, the Kulturkampf with its coercive legislation represented a fault line over which many Protestant anti-Catholics for religious and confessional reasons were not prepared to step. As we have seen, conservative Protestant leaders who were led by Ernst Wilhelm Hengstenberg and who were as passionate about their anti-Catholicism as anyone else had already rejected state interference in the affairs of the Roman Catholic Church and specifically the missionary campaign in 1852. It should not be surprising, therefore, that later in the 1870s conservative Protestants, deeply offended by the attack on religion by liberals and by their onetime champion Chancellor Bismarck, moved during the course of the Kulturkampf into opposition to the state government alongside Catholics.

When liberals first proclaimed a "great cultural struggle" on the floor of the Prussia parliament, they specified that it was a secular campaign to free society from the fetters of religious power and to compel the state to recognize its duty to make this possible.[147] Liberals always intended the Kulturkampf to be wider and more than another Protestant anti-Catholic campaign in part precisely because they realized such a campaign would narrow and weaken the front against the

146. This is an element that could be joined to the study of nationalist conflict between Catholics and Protestants in Smith, *German Nationalism.*

147. The speech in which Rudolf Virchow proclaimed, "I am convinced that we are engaged in a great cultural struggle," is found in *SBHA* (Berlin: W. Moeser, 1850, et seq.), session 28, 17 Jan. 1873.

Roman Catholic Church, more important because they recognized such a campaign would lack the drive for social predominance and broad progressive reform at the core of their attack on Catholicism. Catholic national liberals (like Max von Forckenbeck), Catholic progressives (like Anton Allnoch), Old Catholic progressives (like Eduard Windthorst), thoroughly secular progressives (like Rudolf Virchow and Hermann Schulze-Delitzsch), and Jewish national liberals (like Ludwig Bamberger and Eduard Lasker) who joined the Kulturkampf did so not because, it goes without saying, they were Protestant.[148] They made common cause with Kulturkämpfer because they were liberal, modern, and middle class. The Kulturkampf should be understood, therefore, as a specifically middle-class, liberal movement that joined with the power of the Bismarckian state to create a socially, culturally, and economically modern nation-state.[149]

---

148. For biographical information including religious affiliations (with designation of both Catholics and Old Catholics) of Prussian parliamentary and Reichstag deputies, see Bernhard Mann, ed., *Biographisches Handbuch für das preußische Abgeordnetenhaus, 1867–1918* (Düsseldorf: Droste Verlag, 1988); and Max Schwarz, ed., *MdR Biographisches Handbuch des Reichstages* (Hanover: Verlag für Literatur und Zeitgeschehen, 1965).

149. These comments contrast again with Smith, *German Nationalism*, which argues that the Kulturkampf was an attempt to consolidate a national high culture based on a literary canon of "enlightened Protestantism." See Smith, *German Nationalism*, 19–37. See also Hartwig, "Preußens Aufgabe."

CHAPTER 3

The Anti-Catholic Imagination: Visions of the Monastery

Not only the Catholic missionary crusade but also ~~the dramatic increase of monastic and conventual religious orders~~ was an indication of the new vitality of Roman Catholicism in the German states. In 1872 Johann Friedrich von Schulte, an Old Catholic and professor of canonical and Germanic law, was one of many liberals who compiled exhaustive statistical surveys of the Roman Catholic religious orders and congregations that had spread across Germany since 1848. He looked with alarm at what he found. Recent official statistics available in 1865 and 1866 and Schulte's own meticulous count recorded together in *Die neuren katholischen Orden und Congregationen besonders in Deutschland* indicated that there had been in the past seventeen years a veritable revolution in the number of monasteries and congregations in Prussia.[1] Before 1848 there had been in the German states only a few male Benedictine, Carmelite, and Franciscan monastic orders. Female congregations and closed orders, hardly worth enumerating, had included only a few Ursuline, Dominican, and Carmelite nunneries.[2] Over a twenty-four-year period, while the Prussian state had been engaged in three successive wars and devoted itself to the establishment

1. Johann Friedrich von Schulte, *Die neueren katholischen Orden und Congregationen besonders in Deutschland* (Berlin: C. G. Lüderitz'sche Verlagsbuchhandlung, 1872). During the Kulturkampf, Schulte was a National Liberal deputy in the Reichstag from 1874 to 1879 representing a voting district in Düsseldorf. See Schwarz, *MdR Biographisches Handbuch,* 199, 299. Schulte was a dedicated Kulturkämpfer and wrote extensively on the problem of the Catholic Church and Catholicism. His works include *Kirchenpolitische Aufsätze aus den Jahren, 1874–1886* (Gießen: E. Roth, 1909); *Die Macht der römischen Päpste über Fürsten, Länder, Völker, Individuen nach ihren Lehren und Handlungen seit Gregor VII: Zur Würdigung ihrer Unfehlbarkeit beleuchtet* (Prague: F. Tempsky, 1871); *Über Kirchenstrafen* (Berlin, 1872).

2. Schulte, *Die neuen katholischen Orden und Congregationen,* 8.

of the empire, Schulte argued, monasteries had been "shooting up everywhere like mushrooms out of the ground."[3] Now, he believed, the body of the nation found itself riddled with pockets of ultramontane fanaticism and anti-Prussian recalcitrance, rogue states within the state.

Monks and monasteries, nuns and nunneries were a singular obsession for liberals like Schulte. Liberals repeatedly counted and recounted the number of monasteries and convents emerging in the German states from 1848 through the founding of the empire up to the closing of contemplative monastic orders on Prussian soil with the Congregations Law of 1875, one arrow in the quiver of Kulturkampf legislation directed at the Roman Church. The ecclesiastical authorities of the Catholic Church in Germany apparently did not feel the need (for they surely possessed the means) to compile periodic and comprehensive statistical accounts of the number, increase, and proliferation of monastic orders and congregations during the nineteenth century.[4] Detailed statistical compilations registering the number of male contemplative monasteries; female closed convents and open congregations devoted to philanthropic work; religious orders; and monks, friars, nuns, sisters, and novices were, however, published in all the major liberal journals and newspapers. They were periodically reviewed and updated, and the amount of attention paid to monitoring empirically the new monasteries and religious orders suggests in itself one level of antimonastic anxiety: to liberals, monasteries and convents seemed to be unfolding like a shroud across the German landscape, supposedly reducing populations within their reach to stupidity and subservience. At the same time liberals concentrated their attention on monasteries and convents because they offered especially productive material for the creative work of the imagination. Liberals fixed on the convent and the monastery as medieval artifacts that seemed to represent the worst of Roman Catholicism, its fanaticism, superstition, submission, and ultimate uselessness, just as they justified now the liberal bourgeois program for social, cultural, economic, and moral reform.

An exploration of the liberal relationship to monasticism and monasteries offers opportunities for deep insight into the cognitive

---

3. Ibid., 14, 49.

4. The Catholic Church in Germany did not compile statistics in the nineteenth century. Relinde Meiwes, *"Arbeiterinnen des Herrn": Katholische Frauenkongregationen im 19. Jahrhundert* (Frankfurt am Main: Campus Verlag, 2000), 74.

practice of anti-Catholicism in the postrevolutionary period. This chapter, therefore, trains analysis on three especially rich and revealing cases involving antimonasticism and anticonvent hysteria from the decades after the Revolution of 1848 to the founding of the empire before the Kulturkampf itself was legislated and directed against the Catholic Church. The antimonasticism prevalent in the most popular liberal family journal of the period reflects the ways liberals could use monks and monasteries as points of reference to which they could repeatedly return as they oriented themselves in the new age of the free market and industrial growth. The sensational story of a Carmelite nun raped and held prisoner in a convent dungeon, which was widely circulated in liberal newspapers, warned young women away from a religious life dedicated to the church. More important, with fantastic convent atrocity stories liberals thematized the complex trauma they themselves experienced as they shaped an anti-Catholic identity following the defeat of the 1848 Revolution. Finally, on the eve of German unification, riots against a settlement of Dominican monks in a suburb of Berlin generated a series of liberal antimonastic rallies and petitions that elaborated by means of contrast the expectation for the modern nation in an age of industry and progress. The unseemly violence of a mob attack helped prominent liberals in the Prussian parliament recognize that their organization and judicious leadership were ultimately required to redress by means of a Kulturkampf the monastic and larger Catholic problem in Germany.

The Monastic Revolution

Prussian state authorities were disturbed by the rapid spread of monasteries and congregations especially in the peripheral, predominantly Catholic areas to the east and west with their suspect Polish and French ethnic populations. In 1873 the official government report in the *Statistische Correspondenz* indicated that the outbreak of monasteries and increasing number of monks and nuns had been particularly dramatic in the Rhine Province. In the Diocese of Cologne in 1850 there had been only 272 monks and nuns. By 1872 the number of monks and nuns in this diocese alone had risen to 3,131. Cologne quickly earned the designation "Rome on the Rhine," an apparent literal case of ultramontanism, a reach of the pope's arm over the Alps. Meanwhile in the three dioceses of Breslau, Posen-Gnesen, and Kulm there had been before 1853 a combined total of only 236 monks and nuns. By 1872 the number had jumped to 1,986. Of particular concern was the presence of foreign monks and nuns who were members of religious orders in regions whose ethnic populations were already accused of insufficient loyalty to the Kaiser and the nation. In six monasteries with 154 monks in the Diocese of Cologne in 1872, 29 were foreigners. In 1871 of the 96 members of two monastic orders in the Diocese of Breslau, 2 were non-Germans, and in four nunneries with 942 members, 49 were not German nationals.[5] At the high point of the missionary campaign and popular antimonastic fervor in 1869, the Prussian parliament deemed the problem important enough to commission its own report on the increase of monks and proliferation of monasteries. Table 1 indicates the number of male orders, monasteries, and regular clergy in Prussia registered by the Prussian parliament.

Schulte accused the Roman Church of spreading its influence and seeking converts by introducing religious orders and establishing monasteries not only in Catholic areas but in Protestant areas of Prussia as well. Table 2 indicates that the male monasteries were, however, located on the periphery of Prussia, in the predominantly Catholic southwest in the Rhineland and to the east in Breslau and Posen. Meanwhile, in the Dioceses of Ermland and Osnabrück, which had relatively small Catholic populations, monasteries were absent. According to Schulte's estimates there were in heavily Catholic Bavaria and in Hesse-Darmstadt an additional 73 male monasteries with over 1,100 members, bringing the total in Germany to 170 monasteries with over 2,200 monks, novices, and lay brothers. The number of monastic clergy in each diocese, Schulte concluded, exceeded the requirements of its population. Table 3 indicates the increases in the number of male monastic clergy for four Prussian dioceses for roughly the decade of the 1860s, increases that Schulte argued were far beyond the relative needs of the dioceses.

If the rapid establishment and spread of male monasteries were alarming, the growth of the female orders and congregations was even more so. In Prussia by 1869 there were now 6 female monastic orders, including Ursuline, Women of the Good Shepherd, Benedictine, Carmelite, Elizabethan, and Clarissen, with a total of 41 closed convents. In addition, there were 690 female religious congregations with 4,497 nuns and 867 novices and lay sisters dedicated to teaching girls

5. Newspaper clipping in HSTAD, Best. RD, Nr. 29314, "Jesuiten," Bd. 3, 1874–1913. For a detailed compilation of the increase in nuns and male monastics in Prussia in the nineteenth century, see Meiwes, *Arbeiterinnen des Herrn*, 73–88.

TABLE 1.   Male Religious Orders in Prussia in 1869

Order	Monasteries	Regular Clergy	Novices or Lay Brothers	Dioceses
Franciscan	30	182	113	Breslau, Posen, Kulm, Cologne, Trier, Fulda, Münster, Paderborn, Hildesheim, Freiburg (in Hohenzollern)
Brothers of Charity	22	205	39	Breslau, Cologne, Trier, Limburg
Jesuit	14	123	0	Breslau, Posen, Cologne, Trier, Münster, Paderborn, Freiburg (in (Hohenzollern)
Lazarist	7	25	8	Kulm, Cologne, Paderborn, Hildesheim
Redemptorist	4	47	16	Cologne, Trier, Münster, Limburg
Dominican	4	17	4	Breslau, Posen, Cologne
Brothers of the Christian Schools	3	47	0	Cologne, Trier
Poor Brothers [of St. Francis]	3	32	1	Breslau, Cologne
Capuchin	3	16	0	Münster
Priests of the Holy Ghost	3	9	21	Cologne, Limburg
Trappist	1	12	23	Cologne
Benedictine	1	12	0	Freiburg (in Hohenzollern)
Congregation of St. Philip Neri	1	10	0	Posen
Augustine	1	3	1	Hildesheim
Total	97	740	226	

Source: "Verzeichniß der Zahl der Klöster," 995–97.

and women and caring for the poor, the orphaned, and the sick.[6] According to Schulte's calculations there were in Bavaria, meanwhile, an additional 182 institutions, including Ursuline, Benedictine, Dominican, Franciscan, and Redemptorist with 2,470 members.[7]

6. See "Übersicht der in Preußen vorhandenen Stationen geistlicher Orden und Genossenschaften," in *SBHA* (Berlin: W. Moeser, 1870), 10. Legis. Per. 3. Session, 1869–70, Anlagen 2, Aktenstück no. 221, 17 Dec. 1869, 1000–1002.

7. See Schulte, *Die neuern katholischen Orden und Congregationen,* 16–18, for a complete

TABLE 2.   Distribution of Male Religious Orders in Prussia in 1869

Diocese	Monasteries	Regular Clergy	Novices and Lay Brothers	Catholic Population
Cologne	28	218	48	1,420,108
Trier	13	140	23	825,882
Breslau	12	86	39	1,539,851
Münster	9	65	0	706,752
Posen	8	49	14	920,307
Paderborn	8	58	0	627,083
Limburg	7	41	40	231,083
Kulm	4	22	41	529,834
Hildesheim	3	10	9	81,170
Freiburg (in Hohenzollern)	3	30	0	63,461
Fulda	2	21	17	152,000
Ermland	0	0	0	268,000
Osnabrück	0	0	0	156,805
Total	97	740	231	7,522,336

Source: "Verzeichniß der Zahl der Klöster," 995–97.

TABLE 3.   Increases in Male Monastic Clergy in Four Dioceses in Prussia, 1859–69

Diocese	Number in Year	Number in Year	Increase
Breslau	81 in 1862	95 in 1869	14 (17.3%)
Cologne	118 in 1862	209 in 1869	91 (77.1%)
Trier	73 in 1859	117 in 1869	44 (60.3%)
Paderborn	44 in 1862	63 in 1868	19 (43.2%)
Totals (approx.)	316 in 1862	484 in 1869	168 (53.2%)

Source: Schulte, *Die neueren katholischen Orden,* 15.

Of the 41 male monasteries and female religious orders and congregations in the Diocese of Cologne, a hotbed of monastic activity, only 4 had been established prior to 1848; all the others had been founded since the revolution. Of the 26 monasteries or orders in the Diocese of Paderborn only 1 Franciscan and 4 female orders existed before 1848; all the remaining had been founded since the revolution. According to Schulte, only since then had the Dominicans, Jesuits, Liguorians, Lazarists, School Brothers, Franciscans, Trappists, and Brothers of the Holy Spirit set up residences. The increase was especially dramatic in predominantly Protestant Prussia relative to Catholic Bavaria. In

statistical breakdown of the number of female monasteries and congregations, their locations, and the number of nuns and sisters.

Bavaria the majority of female religious orders had been established before 1848. In Prussia, however, 90 percent of the female orders had been established since 1849.[8]

Paul Hinschius, professor of law at the University of Berlin and a National Liberal deputy in the Reichstag, was another liberal particularly taken by the rampant spread of monasteries. He was so disturbed, in fact, that he wrote *Die Orden und Kongregationen der katholischen Kirchen in Preußen,* in which he carefully traced the growth of monasteries and religious orders in Prussia since 1848.[9] While there had been 15 settlements of male religious orders in Prussia prior to that year, 13 additional settlements had been established between 1848 and 1855, 9 between 1855 and 1860, 13 between 1860 and 1865, and 21 between 1865 and 1872 (with an additional residence established sometime between 1857 and 1868).[10] Hinschius calculated that a total of at least 57 new male monasteries or residences had been established since 1848. Hinschius also counted year by year the growth of female institutions. According to his account, as of 1872 there were 836 female closed convents and residences in Prussia. Only 67 had existed prior to 1848. During the three years immediately following the revolution, 27 female conventual institutions had been established. From 1851 to 1855, another 85 convents were founded. From 1856 to 1860, there were 146 more founded, and from 1861 to 1865 another 118. Finally, 139 were set up from 1866 to 1870, and in the three years from 1871 to 1873 another 28 were added. At the height of the church-state conflict in 1874, Minister of Educational and Ecclesiastical Affairs Adalbert Falk thought Hinschius's work so important that he made it required reading for state authorities.[11]

Schulte argued that the establishment of large numbers of orders and congregations was due to the resurgence of "Catholic life," the mounting power of the clergy, and the rising tide of ultramontanism after the revolution. He and other liberals also believed that the spread of monasticism was one more link in the chain of reaction against liberals: the growth of monasteries and the rising number of monks, bul-

---

8. Ibid., 23.
9. Paul Hinschius, *Die Orden und Kongregationen der katholischen Kirchen in Preußen: Ihre Verbreitung, ihre Organisation, und ihre Zwecke* (Berlin: Verlag von I. Guttentag, 1874).
10. Ibid., 30.
11. HSTAD, Best. RA, Nr. 10699, "Orden der Gesellschaft Jesu bzw. die Ausführung des Gesetzes 1872, 1872–1883," Ministerium der geistlichen Unterrichts- und Medicinal Angel. to die saemmtliche Koenig. Regierung und Landräte, Berlin, 31 July 1874, Bl. 210.

warks against rationalism, industry, and progress, were ultimately the work of the "conservative circle" that continued to fear and despise liberalism.[12] Yet Schulte disagreed with others who insisted that the charitable institutes were simply sinkholes, draining capital that might otherwise spur economic growth or flushing otherwise productive labor in useless service to the Roman Church. He argued that the female congregations provided valuable social services. They cared for the sick and the orphaned, provided for small children, and undertook the education of girls and young women who would have been abandoned to lives of poverty or prostitution, in either case a burden to the state. Schulte's point was that the problem with female charitable institutes was not inherent to the subject but rather one of proportion. The number of women dedicated to philanthropic work in the religious orders was in excess of the actual need. On the other hand, in contrast to services provided by female philanthropic congregations, he argued, "there existed no need in Germany for the establishment of male orders regardless of the tasks they pursued."[13]

It was clear to liberals that the monastaries had not just dramatically increased. The monastic orders had also become more powerful. Liberals over and over argued that the new monasteries were augmenting their influence by exploiting illegitimately the laws of association and assembly codified in the Prussian constitution of 1850 that guaranteed their independence from state supervision and control. According to liberals, the monastic missionaries condemned the liberal revolution while enjoying the privileges they had been won as a result of that revolution. Equally troubling, previously monks in the religious orders had at least been citizens of German states. Now the membership of the monasteries, like that of the convents, was international. The new, ultramontane monks recognized only the central authority of Rome and therefore represented foreign agents within the state. Most important, the monastic orders, liberal and state observers believed, exercised more influence on the Catholic population than ever before. Protestant as well as Catholic liberals believed, and state authorities agreed, that the monastic clergy had, in fact, established a firmer foundation and exerted more power among the Catholic parishioners than the parish clergy themselves. Completely committed to the bishops and

12. Schulte, *Die neuern katholischen Orden und Congregationen.* See 48–49, quotation at 54.

13. Ibid., 55.

the papacy, members of the religious orders, Schulte argued, were soldiers in "an army of the pope," whose spiritual officers were the Jesuits. According to Schulte, monastics belonged to an army that numbered between forty thousand and fifty thousand soldiers, including regular and secular priests, seminarians, and members of Catholic associations. Military discipline was imposed by monastic superiors with unlimited authority, which they were free to exert with physical force, an infringement, liberals insisted, upon the individual rights of the *Staatsbürger* (state citizen). By 1872, leading liberal antimonastics had developed a case against the religious orders that Prussian state authorities found sufficiently convincing. Because the new congregations and orders were a threat to the state, "hostile to all patriotic sentiment," the guarantee of the Catholic Church's autonomy by the laws of association and assembly had to be terminated and the monasteries and convents brought under the supervision and jurisdiction of the state, in accordance with the Congregations Law of 1875.[14]

Reading the *Gartenlaube:* The Liberal Journal as an Antimonastic Map

During the postrevolutionary period, among the liberal elite the dramatic spread of monasteries along with the missionary campaign, popular pilgrimages to religious sites, and the rise of ultramontanism was cause for alarm. Antimonasticism was a prominent theme in all major liberal broadsheets, including newspapers like the *Breslauer Zeitung, Crefelder Zeitung, Deutsche Allgemeine Zeitung, Kölnische Zeitung, National Zeitung,* and *Vossische Zeitung;* finer literary journals like *Grenzboten* and *Die Gegenwart;* the academic *Preußische Jahrbücher;* and satirical journals like *Ulk, Berliner Wespen,* and *Kladderadatsch.* The liberal illustrated journal the *Gartenlaube* is, however, an especially instructive document of liberal antimonasticism. It was the most widespread family journal as well as the single most successful periodical of any kind in Germany. Since its founding in 1853 the number of subscribers to the journal had risen from 5,000 to no less than 100,000 in 1860, and by 1867 it had reached over 225,000, an impressive statistic by the standards of midcentury journalism.[15] By the founding of the empire, the *Gartenlaube* had become *the* journal of the German mid-

14. Ibid., 49–50 n. 1, 55, 57–58.
15. For circulation figures for the *Gartenlaube* see Friedrich Hofmann, ed., *Vollständiges Generalregister der Gartenlaube* (Leipzig, 1882), ii.

dle-class family, the most representative organ of its tastes and preoc-cupations.[16]

The journal's founder, editor, and owner, Ernst Keil, saw himself as a popular educator in the best tradition of the Enlightenment. Genera-tions of the *Gartenlaube* subsequent to the death of Keil in 1876 are characterized more by the kitsch for which the journal is perhaps bet-ter known. In its first generation, however, the *Gartenlaube* was a ded-icated champion of bourgeois Bildung and the virtues of progress and science. During this period the *Gartenlaube* represented the heartland of liberalism not only politically but socially and culturally. Indeed, the *Gartenlaube* is an ideal example of the nineteenth-century journalism that brought the public sphere into the bourgeois realm of domesticity, literally, as its title indicates, into the family arbor. Reading the *Gartenlaube* was supposed to be a family affair, and its articles and illustrations were designed as the basis for leisurely discussion and entertainment in the circle of family and friends. According to the jour-nal's editors, "It is supposed to be a paper for the home and for the family, a book for large and small, for everyone in whom a warm heart beats against the ribs, who still likes goodness and virtue."[17] At the end of the year, editions of the *Gartenlaube* were typically collected in hefty, leather-bound volumes. As *Hausbücher* these handsome vol-umes were prominently placed in the parlors of middle-class homes not only for ready reference but also as bourgeois accoutrements signifying class status and respectability.

Editions of the *Gartenlaube* from its founding in the early 1850s through the 1870s can be read as an ideological map in which monks and monasteries are key points of reference in the cultural and social terrain of the middle class. Cultural anthropologists and cultural his-torians have recognized that artifacts, documents, and texts are car-tographies that set, plot, reflect, and demarcate the boundaries of social and cultural norms, experience, identity, and ideology. It is in this sense that the *Gartlenlaube* is an antimonastic map of German lib-eralism. Images of monks and monasteries are contoured, shaped, and

16. See Ernest Bramsted, *Aristocracy and the Middle-Classes in Germany: Social Types in German Literature, 1830–1900* (Chicago: University of Chicago Press, 1964), 204. According to Bramsted the *Gartenlaube* was the "most representative family-journal of the liberal bour-geoisie between 1850 and 1900," and "the periodical wanted to be the organ of a middle-class, liberal enlightenment. Its readers were to be informed . . . about the significance of a liberal middle-class in a united fatherland." Ibid., 205.

17. *Gartenlaube* (1853): 1.

positioned on its pages according to procedures of acknowledged and unacknowledged preference and prejudice. In the layout of the journal, images of monasticism are managed relative to those that depict service to the nation in ways that helped the middle class orient culturally and socially in the decades after the Revolution of 1848. Throughout these years the *Gartenlaube* laid out hundreds of illustrations of and articles about monks and monasticism that liberal, bürgerlich families used by means of contrast to identify themselves and each other and to negotiate their way through the decade of reaction, the founding period of the German Empire, and the Kulturkampf. With the use of competing images and stories, the *Gartenlaube* romantically idealized the types of service and leadership required for capitalist industrialization, scientific progress, and the building of the nation.

Editions of the journal throughout the 1850s, 1860s, and 1870s always featured or included articles about Catholicism, church doctrines, popular Catholic superstitions, clericalism, Jesuits, the missionary campaign, ultramontanism, monks, nuns, convents, and monastic life.[18] The first article, for example, in the series Rom am Rhein (Rome on the Rhine), which describes the development of ultramontanism in the Rhineland, calls attention to the church's attempt to assert control over individual rights and marriage.[19] The clergy established in Catholic law that as a condition for all confessionally mixed marriages the couple must promise to raise their children Catholic. This, according to the article, was an assault on personal freedom, and "since the Protestant Church on its side defends the right not to have to make such a pledge, a brazen confessional wall splits those whom love has joined and who have in common the fatherland, Bildung, customs, and all the other relations of life."[20] The Catholic Church with its intolerance, the article explained, simultaneously attacked individual rights and marriage, the foundation of the family. The article also assaulted the pilgrimages that had become more numerous with the revival of popular Catholicism at midcentury. Pilgrims such as the more than

18. Henry Wassermann's examination of the *Gartenlaube*'s positive portrayal of and benevolent attitude toward Jews contrasts sharply with the journal's intolerance of Catholics. Henry Wassermann, "Jews and Judaism in the Gartenlaube," *Leo Baeck Institute Yearbook* 23 (1978): 47–60.

19. The *Gartenlaube* offered the following definition of *ultramontane:* "An ultramontane in our sense is anyone who has his fatherland in Rome, who wants to place all vaterländisch and state interests under the influence and rule of the Roman Church and its interests as represented by the pope." Rom am Rhein, Nr. 1, *Gartenlaube* (1867): 23–25, quotation at 23.

20. Ibid., 24.

one hundred thousand who journeyed from all over Germany to pay homage at Cologne to the relics of the three kings of the Epiphany were denounced for their disorder and "superstitious mischief." Especially unseemly at the site were the displays of gullibility that only lined the pockets of the church: monks blessed and then hustled herbs that they claimed held miraculous powers for warding off evil spirits. Priests turned the site into a market where they set up a lucrative business selling rosaries, sacred pictures, crucifixes, and religious figurines that, apparently even more than the three kings, attracted the attention of the pilgrims.

Jesuits presented a particular problem since they pinched the raw nerve of nationalism. According to another article from the series Rom am Rhein, Jesuits had swept over Germany. In the Rhineland and Westphalia they had set themselves up in Paderborn, Münster, Cologne, Aachen, Bonn, and Koblenz. Making the situation worse, the Jesuits were not primarily German but French, Belgian, and Swiss. "And we do not know whether there is some kind of control over them through the existing laws limiting nationalities and freedom of movement. There is no talk of their applying for citizenship. Only the approval of the generals of their order and their provincial subordinates is needed for their invasion."[21] Not only was he a non-German (a problem for German national security), the Jesuit had also abrogated his own individuality and humanity. "He has to suppress within himself all natural and human emotions. He has to rip from his heart all his parents, brothers and sisters, and friends, and he must with blind obedience follow his superiors." Like zealots, the Jesuits roamed the country doing their work among the people. "Here they make a great impression, preaching, hearing confessions; there they erect stone crosses in public places before which the pious kneel and throw up their arms even many years later. They also carry religious discord into almost completely Protestant areas."[22] During the war with Catholic Austria in 1866, argued the article, the ultramontanism encouraged by the clergy in the Rhineland undermined the Prussian war effort. When asked to give a blessing for the wounded, a priest in a town on the Rhine retorted: "I don't give anything to the Prussians." According to the article, priests instructed Catholics called into the army not to shoot at the Austrians but to fire their rifles overhead or, better, to throw them down when they stood opposite the Habsburg armies. A

21. Rom am Rhein, Nr. 3, *Gartenlaube* (1867): 135–37, quotation at 135.
22. Ibid.

Prussian soldier reported that his confessor denied him absolution when he refused to promise to shoot over the heads of the Austrians. Despite the denials of the church, "In this way [the Roman Catholic clergy] tried to undermine loyalty and to thwart the interests of the state and promote those of Rome."[23]

In the *Gartenlaube* it was antimonasticism, however, that best serviced and represented liberal interests. Its pages were filled with articles describing tours through monasteries, curious monastic rituals, overnight visits to monasteries, and the nefarious intrigues behind monastery walls. In "Ein Besuch in einer Klosterbrauerei" (A visit to a monastic brewery), visitors to a Franciscan monastery were shocked, for example, to discover bustling monastics attending to their improvised beer vat, quaffing steins of brew, and lining up business. The illustration, "In einer baierischen Klosterbräustube" (A monastic brewing room in Bavaria), provides the documentation, and the reader is assured that this is no exaggeration but on the contrary "a thoroughly true, characteristic representation of monastic life" (fig. 5).[24] The drawing, dated 1869, is typical of the repertoire of Eduard Grützner (whose kitsch depictions of beer-guzzling, corpulent monks, incidentally, made him later the favorite artist of Adolf Hitler).[25] At a monastery near Constance, monks were found feasting and drinking without restraint. ("Don't scream, ladies.") In its library, no books about science or art could be found, only records condemning life in this world and, hypocritically, ledgers cataloging the monastery's inventories, wealth, and extensive properties.[26] In "Hinter der Klosterpforte" (Behind monastic gates) the sad case of "Sister X" of Orleans in France is proffered as an admonition. An innocent young woman, her heart shattered by a broken promise of marriage, falls victim to the influence of her confessor, a Jesuit, who is soon able to bring her "fully into his power." He convinces her to visit a monastery without the knowledge of her parents. There she comes under the sway of the nuns, "who play their roles with the most complete mastery" and persuade the girl to break all ties with her family and the world. "At the moment, when Loyola's boys . . . have the audacity to declare a *Vernichtungskrieg* (war of extermination) against all of modern learning," the example of Sister X provided an instructive case in point.[27]

23. Ibid., 136.

24. "Ein Besuch in einer Klosterbrauerei," *Gartenlaube* (1870): 412–15, quotation at 412.

25. Brigitte Hamann, *Hitler's Vienna: A Dictator's Apprentice* (Oxford: Oxford University Press, 1999), 36, 72.

26. "Drei Tage in einem Karthäuserkloster," *Gartenlaube* (1871): 428–30, quotation at 428.

27. "Hinter der Klosterpforte," *Gartenlaube* (1870): 72–74, quotation at 72.

In einer baierischen Klosterbräustube.
Originalzeichnung von Eduard Grützner

Fig. 5. "In einer baierischen Klosterbräustube," *Gartenlaube* (1870): 413. An article in the *Gartenlaube* describes a visit to a monastery in Bavaria. The accompanying illustration, "A Monastic Brewing Room in Bavaria," by Eduard Grützner, was, according to the article, "a thoroughly true, characteristic representation of monastic life."

Articles about monks and monasteries could be cited at length.[28] One, however, is especially instructive and serves to make the argument. The final paragraph of the article "Der Ostermorgen in einem Franziskaner-Kloster" (Easter morning in a Franciscan monastery) offers a reflection on the character of monastic life.

28. Other major articles running in the *Gartenlaube* from the 1860s through the Kulturkampf and indicating the journal's obsession with monasteries include, for example, "Ein ehemaliger Klostergarten" (1860): 308; "Eine Klosterschule" (1860): 507; "Das Renchthal und die Klosterruine Allerheiligen im Schwarzwald" (1861): 605–6; "Aus dem Klosterleben" (1862): 696; Land und Leute, Nr. 17, "Das Gespensterkloster in Schwaben" (1864): 408; "Ein seltner Mönch" (1865): 404–8; "Klosterzelle und Familiestube" (1867): 260–63; "Schwerer Klosterdienst" (1871): 361; "Eine Todtenbeschwörung im Kloster" (1872): 790–91; "Klosterhofe" (1873): 25; Bis zur Schwelle des Pfarramts, Nr. 3, "Im Kloster" (1873): 386–91; "In den Hallen des 'Schweigens' und des 'Mirakels'" (1873): 619–21; Aus dem österreichische Kloster-

Vague, overly emotional fanaticism, bitter experiences, and harsh disappointments of a heart that is not sufficiently strong to bear the repeated blows of fate, deficient strength and courage after failed and smashed hopes in the fight for a new foundation for a bright future—these may well be in most cases the motives that led the way [to life] behind these walls. And then there remains the thought that man is not born to indulge the small joys and sorrows of his own heart in quiet self-confinement, but that he, on the contrary, should if only in small ways and in modest places join in the work of mankind, that he only as a working member of human society can claim and reach that measure of happiness that is allotted to mortals.[29]

The illustration that accompanies the article depicts the portly Franciscan friar on Easter morning, a caricature, effeminate and ultimately pathetic, eagerly accumulating gifts and happy to be in the company of women (fig. 6).

That the monk represented all that the resolute liberal character found contrary as he faced the challenges of a world being remade became unavoidable for readers simply moving their gaze down the page. Immediately following this description of the monk appears Bilder aus der kaufmännischen Welt, Nr. 2, "Im Bankiergeschäft" (Images from the business world, Nr. 2, The banking business). "Business with money!" is the article's joyous opening. With the announcement "Money is recognized as the most significant Großmacht on earth," a reminder of the pragmatic shift to a new Realpolitik of economic interests, the article takes the reader on a tour of a banking house and its staff. In the private rooms, the director receives the reports of his subordinates and approves or denies credit with equal measures of cool detachment. The reader is introduced to the Hauptcassirer, "a man of truly stoic composure. . . . Neither the clang of gold, nor the appearance of such a great sum of cleanly engraved cash can fluster him." Nearby are the Cassendiener diligently counting and packing coins. "These are tried and true men, and although within a

---

leben, Nr. 1, "Das Noviziat und der Aufenthalt im Seminar zu Prag" (1874): 483–85; Aus dem österreichische Klosterleben, Nr. 2, "Häusliche und theologische Erziehung" (1874): 616–18; "Am Klostergarten" (1874): 738; "Klosterzelle und Gedankenhelle" (1879): 740–41.

29. "Der Ostermorgen in einem Franciskaner-Kloster," Gartenlaube (1864): 407–8, quotation at 408.

Fig. 6. "In der Sacristei eines Franciskaner-Klosters am Ostermorgen," *Garten-laube* (1864): 405. On Easter morning effeminate Franciscan friars happily accumulate gifts.

year they count through many millions, they are endowed with strong nervous systems." The position of *Cassenbeamte,* responsible for the quick handling of sums in small amounts with the public, "requires a practiced man." In the *Comptoir* it is hardly allowed to look over the shoulders of the calculators since no one would want to disturb the work: *Herr Hauptbuchhalter* is busy reckoning debits and credits in thick books. No slackers here. These are the exacting and even-keeled empiricists, the lieutenants of financial opportunity and sergeants of capital on whom the industrial-capitalist future depends.[30]

Throughout the journal, an entire vision of a specific social order opens up on a grand scale with recurring and contrasting images of

30. Bilder aus der kaumännischen Welt, Nr. 2, "Im Bankiergeschaft," *Gartenlaube* (1864): 408–11, quotations at 410 and 411.

monks and monastic life. Take, for example, the serialized story "Des Kaufmanns Ehrenschild" (The businessman's badge of honor), which describes the loyalty and solidarity two friends share with each other as public men of business and civil service.[31] Or take another article from the series Bilder aus der kaufmännischen Welt, which introduces a London auction house. The spectacle of a single day of business looks like a scene "out of an Arabian fable." The sales figures in a single year alone, the reader is told, are so vast that they defy any attempt to comprehend them. The article recommends that they might be better grasped by comparing them to "a certain poetic magic . . . like that solitude in a moonstruck forest or the splendor of the sun on an Italian sea."[32]

This flourish of contrived romantic sentiment was typical of articles and illustrations depicting what might have otherwise seemed mundane accounts of middle-class society, expectations, and service. For example, in the article "Der Herr Director" from the series Aus der Beamtenwelt (The world of the civil service) the reader is introduced to the "wondrous nomenclature of *Beamtentum*" from *Subalternbeamte* through *Canzlei-Director* and the higher level of *Canzlei-Rath* to, finally, *Geheimer-Rath* and *Präsident*. This, however, is no banal rehearsal of civil service bureaucracy but rather the chronicle of Herr Canzlei-Director's final hours of life. Despite serious illness he attends to his professional duties into the evening and then goes on to fulfill his obligations at the soiree hosted by a colleague. He returns home to bed and, attended by his wife, realizes he must prepare for his end. Instructing his wife with a final breath, he knows even at this moment where his duty belongs: "I wrote a letter to the Präsident this morning . . . give it to him . . . tomorrow." In the letter he excuses himself from his profession and thanks his Präsident for the many years of dutiful service he was able to offer him. The reader is assured that in the newspaper obituaries Herr Canzlei-Director was praised as a model of civil service. "To the same degree as his devotion he had the trust of his superiors

31. "Des Kaufmanns Ehrenschild," *Gartenlaube* (1861): 561–64.

32. Bilder aus der kaufmännischen Welt, Nr. 1, "Ein Londoner Auctionshaus," *Gartenlaube* (1863): 762–64, quotation at 762. "The power of a metaphor derives precisely from the interplay between the discordant meanings it symbolically coerces into a unitary conceptual framework and from the degree to which that coercion is successful in overcoming the psychic resistance such semantic tension inevitably generates in anyone in a position to perceive it. When it works, a metaphor transforms a false identification . . . into an apt analogy; when it misfires, it is mere extravagance." Clifford Geertz, "Ideology as a Cultural System," in *Ideology and Discontent,* ed. David E. Apter (New York: Free Press of Glencoe, 1964), 46–76, quotation at 59.

and the respect and love of his colleagues. His name will remain forever in most honored remembrance."[33] The four-part story "Ein Beamtenleben" (The life of a civil servant) is a similar account of civic duty and pathos. A *Kreisgerichtsdirector* in the Ministry of Justice is known publicly throughout his district and beyond as a diligent and orderly man, "an excellent judge, industrious, and above all a man of unwavering righteousness and spotless honor." In his private life he quietly endures the certain knowledge that his beloved young daughter will die of a terminal illness. On the very day that he receives notification that he is to be promoted to the prestigious position of *Obergerichtspräsident* his life is suddenly plunged into crisis. His devoted wife and the dutiful mother of his family defaults on a credit payment. She is prepared to leave the family, to sacrifice herself for the sake of his honor. Instead, the *Gerichtsdirector* shoulders the responsibility himself and resigns his position. He, however, is resurrected by his unimpeachable public reputation. At the close of the series, he stands before the Präsident of the Ministry of Justice who pronounces as a judgment, "But you are a man of honor. You cannot be a thief."[34]

Similarly, articles in the series Deutschlands große Werkstätten (Germany's great workshops) celebrate the industrial entrepreneur and his factory. "Bei dem Locomotivenkönig" (The locomotive king) describes "the indescribable," "the great impression" made by the locomotive construction plant in Berlin established by Albert Borsig. "One is filled with genuine respect when one thinks about how this great factory was built from small beginnings and only with the industry and application of a single man."[35] Borsig's iron smelting plant Königin-Marienhütte at Zwickau is "the great triumph of German spirit and energy."[36] Likewise, thanks to the determination and ingenuity of Johann Lothar Faber, a pencil maker near Nuremberg, Germany had now surpassed all other countries in the manufacture of pencils.[37] At the colossal locomotive plant at Chemnitz founded by Richard Hartmann "we see with pride and joy how German industry is increasingly self-confident and energetic, how it promotes the well-

33. "Der Herr Director," *Gartenlaube* (1857): 519–22, quotations at 521 and 522, respectively.

34. "Ein Beamtenleben," *Gartenlaube* (1861): 769–72, 785–88, 815–16, 818–19, quotation at 819.

35. Deutschlands große Industriewerkstätten, Nr. 4, "Bei dem Locomotivenkönig," *Gartenlaube* (1867): 554–58, quotations at 554.

36. Deutschlands große Industriewerkstätten, Nr. 5, "Die Königin-Marienhütte bei Zwickau," *Gartenlaube* (1869): 283–87, quotation at 283.

37. Deutschlands große Industriewerkstätten, Nr. 2, "Die Faber'sche Bleistiftfabrik in Stein," *Gartenlaube* (1865): 748–51.

being, independence, and autonomy of the German people and commands the respect of foreigners."[38] Borsig, Faber, and Hartmann—
energetic, diligent, perseverant, and self-made men—were celebrated
as the German equivalents of England's Samuel Smiles, Josiah Wedge-
wood, and Richard Arkwright. Just as important, such men, the articles argue, in pursuit of their own individual gain never lost sight in the
economic competition with England and the United States of the need
to advance German industrial development by taking advantage of
new ideas and technological inventions in the spirit of the modern age.
And still at the factory in the small village of Griesheim near Darmstadt industrial production is effortlessly wedded to the German
primeval landscape. "We see how in this current time even the romanticism of the forest, which sustains us with *Waldculture,* goes hand in
hand with industry, whose progress rests on the application of science
and the investment of large amounts of capital."[39]

During the 1860s every edition of the *Gartenlaube* featured a story
about an industrial plant; a visit to an industrial exhibition; or the
introduction of a new, steam-driven machine. In these articles industrial mills that billow smoke contrast sharply with images of "Jesuit
economics," "work convents," and "Catholic business" are given
impressive two-page spreads. The industrial iron rolling and hammering plant established in the industrial suburb of Moabit in northwest
Berlin contrasts with the monastery, a useless anachronism in the
modern age of industrial expansion. The plant included huge, steam-
powered hammers and steam-driven machines that produced together
such a deafening thunder that they gave the impression "all the *Lärm-
geister* of hell had been unleashed" (fig. 7).[40] A New Era that included
new hopes not just for political liberalization but also for economic
growth and industrial development was exemplified by the machine
building plant at Chemnitz. The factory employed two thousand
workers; included forty separate buildings with five steam-driven hammers, five huge vertical cranes, and nine mighty steam-powered
machines; and occupied an area of approximately 160,000 square
yards (fig. 8).[41] With the impressive bird's-eye view of the steel casting

---

38. Deutschlands große Werkstätten, Nr. 3, "Die Schöpfungen eines Zeugschmiedege-
sellen," *Gartenlaube* (1866): 59–63, quotation at 63.

39. Deutschlands große Industriewerkstätten, Nr. 3, "Die Griesheimer Klenger," *Gartenlaube* (1867): 132–35, quotation at 135.

40. "Borsig's Etablissement im Moabit bei Berlin Die Gußstahlfabrik des Bochumer Vereins," *Gartenlaube* (1867): 556–57.

41. "Die Königin-Marienhütte bei Zwickau," *Gartenlaube* (1869): 284–85.

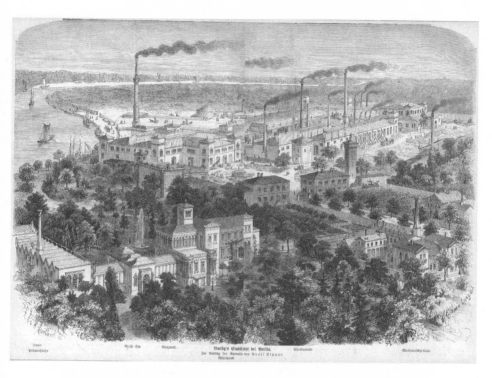

Fig. 7. "Borsig's Etablissement im Moabit bei Berlin," *Gartenlaube* (1867): 556–57. One in the series entitled "Germany's Great Workshops," the illustration of the iron rolling and hammering plant established by Albert Borsig in the industrial suburb of Moabit in northwest Berlin contrasts with the monastery, a useless anachronism in the modern age of industrial expansion.

plant of the Bochumer Association, readers of the *Gartenlaube* could envision huge industrial plants stretching the length and breadth of Germany (fig. 9).[42]

In the layout of the journal the two-page illustration "Der Herrgottshändler" (The merchant of God) contrasts with the illustration "Gußstahlfabrik des Bochumer Vereins" (The Bochum Association steel plant). Now the scene is the impoverished and nomadic Catholic

42. "Die Gußstahlfabrik des Buchumer Vereins," *Gartenlaube* (1875): 544–45.

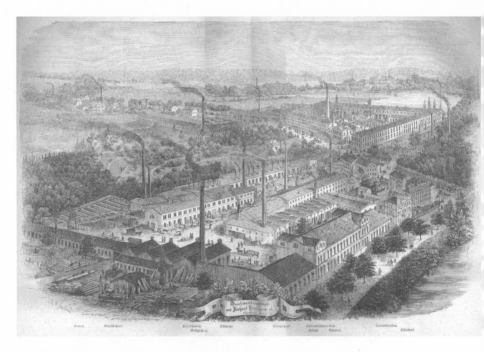

Fig. 8. "Maschinenbauanstalt, Chemnitz," *Gartenlaube* (1866), 60–61. A New Era that included hopes not just for political liberalization but also for economic growth and industrial development was exemplified here by the machine building plant founded by Richard Hartmann at Chemnitz.

family. The father is trying to provide for his barefoot wife, newborn infant, and dirty children in rags by peddling crucifixes, religious trinkets, and figurines. A priest takes a moment to interrupt his hand of cards and literally looks down his nose (fig. 10). In the accompanying poem "Zwei Herrgottshändler" (Two merchants of God) the priest resents not only the intrusion but, more important, the competition: "Leave me alone, you tramp! You're all as stupid as cows. I'm not going to buy God from you. I sell Him myself."[43] This is the world of "Roman Catholic business," and the church demands its monopoly, not the free market of either goods or ideas. The illustration "Arme Leute—fromme Leute" (Poor people—pious people) depicts Catholic

43. "Zwei Herrgottshändler," *Gartenlaube* (1875): 500.

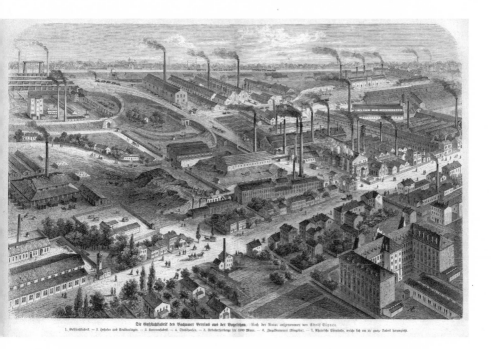

Fig. 9. "Die Gußstahlfabrik des Bochumer Vereins aus der Vogelschau," *Garten-laube* (1875): 544–45. With formidable, two-page illustrations like that giving a bird's-eye view of the steel plant of the Bochumer Association, readers of the *Gartenlaube* could envision huge, industrial plants that spewed smoke and filled the entire German landscape.

family members breaking their backs, faces to the ground, as they haul a cart up a mountain. A church stands below in the valley. A Jesuit and a monk merely move aside. The mother has to carry the baby too. The children are barefoot, and even the grandmother is pulling. The load might bring them all down, but the father does not forget to doff his hat (fig. 11). In the accompanying poem he pleads as they pass, "O, pray for us to Holy Mary that she lighten our cart!" The church authorities respond, "God the Father has laid on the load! Praying is therefore of no use. You have to pull!"[44] The reader can linger on the instructive image of pitiful Catholics trying to climb up and out of

44. "Arme Leute—fromme Leute," *Gartenlaube* (1873): 619.

Fig. 10. "Der Herrgottshändler," *Gartenlaube* (1875): 496–97. The father of an impoverished Catholic family peddles crucifixes, religious trinkets, and figurines. The priest literally looks down his nose and exclaims: "Leave me alone, you tramp! You're all as stupid as cows. I'm not going to buy God from you. I sell Him myself."

their poverty but held back by the freight of their own religious sub-mission. Even the dog has it better.

Imposing illustrations of Germany's great industrial mills make a striking comparison to images of useless monasteries in decay, the vision of an age now over. But in the illustration "Die Ruinen der Abtei Allerheiligen" (The ruins of the abbey All Saints) monastic ruins in the Black Forest of Bavaria also provide an occasion for an excursion by the bourgeoisie at leisure (fig. 12).[45] Ivy now covers the belfry, portals, and arches. Pines have returned to the spot, and the scene

45. See also the accompanying article, "Das Renchthal und die Klosterruine Allerheiligen in Schwartzwald," *Gartenlaube* (1861): 605–6.

„Arme Leute — fromme Leute." Originalzeichnung von Mathias Schmid in München.

Fig. 11. "Arme Leute—fromme Leute," *Gartenlaube* (1873): 619. With the illustration "Poor People—Pious People," readers can linger on the pitiful image of Catholics trying to climb up out of poverty, laboring against the freight of their own religious submission. Even a dog has it better.

makes an appeal to the romantic sentiment. There is a nostalgic evocation of the monastery as material culture from the medieval past that provides readers a holiday from the preoccupations of the industrial age. More emphatic is the illustration "Der Friedhof auf dem Oybin" (The cemetery on the Oybin) accompanying an article about a visit to monastic ruins near the city of Zittau in Saxony on scenic Mount Oybin overlooking the slopes of the Neisse River valley and close on the border with the Austrian Empire (fig. 13). The monastery was built in 1369, dedicated in 1384, and wrecked in 1577 by a bolt of lightning. The church, one "from the better period of Gothic architecture," is

Das Renchthal und die Klosterruine Allerheiligen im Schwarzwald.

Die Ruinen der Abtei Allerheiligen.
Nach der Natur aufgenommen von C. G. Winckler.

Fig. 12.   "Die Ruinen der Abtei Allerheiligen," *Gartenlaube* (1861): 605. Here monastic ruins provide an occasion for an excursion by the bourgeoisie at leisure. The scene offers the monastery as material culture from the Middle Ages that readers could use as a holiday from the preoccupations of the industrial age.

now no more than a hollow shell on a hillock. Tall elms stand at the ruins and provide a shelter of shade. In the cemetery, flora, thick and unchecked, approach the gravestones to claim the dead, and fresh bouquets, "still wet with the tears for loved ones," sweetly scent the air. The monastic ruins in backdrop are a gesture of romantic pathos to the Middle Ages, and a mother and daughter—hand in hand, in the shadows, alone, and a husband and father gone but not forgotten—complete the tender sentiment.[46] This lyrical scene is reminiscent of visits to other cemeteries at monastic tourist sites: the "majestic effects" of the view overlooking the sea at the gravesite by the churchyard at Camposanto, Naples; the church cemetery in Prague, "as profound and

46. "Auf dem Oybin," *Gartenlaube* (1874): 31–35, 47–48, quotation at 47.

Fig. 13. "Der Friedhof auf dem Oybin," *Gartenlaube* (1874): 49. Visions of the monastery like that on Mount Oybin provided a momentary flight from the modern age of "bureaucratic sobriety" (*bureaukratische Nüchternheit*), emotional detachment, and industrial development.

melancholy as a *Nachtfantasie* [fantasy of the night]"; the "imposing and dignified graveyards" at Pisa and Verona; and the expansive cemetery in Munich. But they cannot compare. The author has nowhere else been able to find "a death site that is so full of the magic of luxuriant nature, so infused with the romantic, as that at the small churchyard on Mount Oybin."[47] Visions of the monastery provided the liberal bourgeoisie with both a contrast to and an escape from the modern age of "bureaucratic sobriety" (*bureaukratische Nüchternheit*), emotional detachment, and rational calculation, a flight from the world of huge industrial mills that it had done so much to build.

47. Ibid.

At the same time, readers might consider in another article the scientific conclusions of "the most distinguished and learned of all living national economists" confirming "the fact that precisely the Protestant countries have achieved the highest degree of economic maturity." According to the article, economic growth stagnated in (Catholic) Spain, Italy, and the South American states. In Belgium the clerical party once in power pursued an economic policy according to which "capital was Catholicized and taken out of the hands of Protestants and Jews. The enterprise ended in disaster."[48] Other articles throughout the journal sing the praises of freethinking rationalists, celebrate inventors, and glorify scientists unfettered by religious dogma.

> These people, standing on the firm and unshakable ground of science that they have themselves established on the foundation of nature with cool scientific spirit, with remarkable zeal and industry, and with glowing enthusiasm, place a lever beneath the world as it has hitherto appeared in order to lift it out of its socket with Archimedian strength. They put in its place a new world truth discovered by science, born in an enlightened spirit, and baptized with the fire of an inspired poetical enthusiasm.[49]

The scientist is the Franciscan friar on Easter morning turned inside out.

Articles that model the scientist, the civil servant, and the industrialist contrast with "Ein Besuch im Kloster" (A visit to a monastery). In a monastery near Aachen, microcephalic "ape men" have been discovered. The *Gartenlaube* included a detailed account of these creatures:

> These beings are born with craniums and brains that are much too small. The forehead is at most two fingers high and sharply flattened toward the back. The cranium is only a little larger than the size of a man's fist. The eyebrows protrude forward. Thick lips and jaws, which are armed with large, powerful teeth, jut out even farther. The skull is so small and flat that the ears reach as high as the top of the head. The expression of the eyes and of the whole face is sometimes pleasant, sometimes angry, but almost always more like that of an animal than that of a human being. They

48. "Ein klerikaler Industrie-Ritter," *Gartenlaube* (1870): 425–27, quotations at 425.
49. *Gartenlaube* (1866): 171. Quoted also in Bramsted, *Aristocracy and the Middle-Classes,* 205.

don't speak but rather utter only inarticulate sounds and guttural tones.[50]

Of the two "ape men" who lived alongside the monks at the monastery, only "Emil N.," eighteen years old, has survived in his unfortunate condition. The article includes his portrait, which, the reader is told, is an accurate illustration except that it "gives him perhaps too much of an intelligent expression in his eyes" (fig. 14).[51] The rector of the monastery points upward with his finger and repeatedly asks Emil, "Where is God?" Finally the microcephalic understands, spastically points upward, and blurts unintelligibly. The article includes a second illustration, the grotesque spectacle of Emil dressed in a monastic robe, dancing to music while pointing up to the heavens (fig. 15).[52] The suggestion is, of course, that the microcephalic and his monastic masters merely "ape" each other and, therefore, live equally ridiculous and pathetic lives.

In their study of the popular American journal of nature and science *National Geographic,* cultural anthropologists Catherine A. Lutz and Jane L. Collins have examined the meanings produced by the layout—choices regarding the format, size, order, and placement—of photographs. Design principles, they argue, that determine the sequencing of images in the journal give priority to thematic content over other considerations, including aesthetics. Editors recognize that the juxtapositions of content in the layout of the journal produce the "third effect": additional meanings, at once social, cultural, and political, are evoked in readers as they consider images placed side by side in terms of information, order, and relative size.[53] When on the pages of the *Gartenlaube* editors and then liberal family readers matched articles about bourgeois life against those about monastic life, and illustrations of the factory against those of the monastery, they were thinking about who they were and what the German nation was supposed to be socially, economically, and morally. They surveyed an array of bürgerlich identities in positions of authority, leadership, and service. By means of contrast, they romantically fantasized about the stalwart banker, the dutiful civil servant, the dedicated industrialist, the levelheaded rationalist, the enlightened scientist. These were the captains of

50. "Ein Besuch im Kloster," *Gartenlaube* (1868): 203–5, quotation at 203.

51. Ibid.

52. Ibid., 205.

53. Catherine A. Lutz and Jane L. Collins, *Reading National Geographic* (Chicago: University of Chicago Press, 1993), 74.

Emil N., achtzehn Jahre alter Mikrocephale.

Figs. 14 and 15. "Emil N., achtzehn Jahre alter Mikrocephale," *Gartenlaube* (1868): 204; and *(facing page)* "Emil N. beim Anhören von Musik," *Gartenlaube* (1868): 205. Emil N., a microcephalic "ape man," was discovered at a monastery near Aachen. Emil dances to music while pointing up to the heavens. He merely "apes" his monastic masters, who live equally pathetic lives.

Emit R. beim Anhören von Musik.

progress, modern heroes meeting the challenges of industrialization and nation building. They were liberal, masculine, nationalist, and all, no doubt, Kulturkämpfer role models. For in this age of progress, the monk and the monastery could be, at best, only social and economic deadweight; a drain on capital; medieval leftovers from a bygone age of dogma, superstition, and stupidity. At worst they were treasonous ultramontane agents of the Vatican, enemies dedicated to the destruction of a unified, modern, and dynamic German nation.

The Nun in the Dungeon: Liberalism as a Convent Atrocity Story

In the summer of 1869, as the papacy prepared to convene the Vatican Council, anti-Catholicism and anticlericalism in Germany reached a crescendo. The satirical liberal *Berliner Wespen,* for example, ran an illustration depicting monks preparing for the council: "liberalism," "Lutherism," and "press" are stacked like logs on a bonfire. Under the banner "Inquisition," heretics are hanging by the neck from a scaffold.[54] It was in this context that people all over Germany were soon captivated by the grisly drama of a Catholic nun held prisoner in a convent in Cracow, capital at that time of the Province of Galicia in the Austrian Empire. According to liberal newspapers a young nun, Sister Barbara Ubryk, of a closed and "barefoot" Carmelite order had been imprisoned in the convent in a cold, dark, dank dungeon barely eight feet long by six feet wide. Here she had lived alone since 1848. For twenty-one years, she survived on rotten potatoes and water. A cesspool drained into her cell. Mud, vermin, and her own waste covered her naked, shivering body. According to her testimony given later before the Austrian state courts, Sister Barbara maintained a tenuous hold on sanity during her imprisonment only with fervent prayer and by repeatedly counting the individual strands of hair on her head one by one by one.[55]

Finally state authorities heard a rumor about Sister Barbara's imprisonment and appeared before the convent gates. Despite the denials and protests of the mother superior, the confessor of the convent, and the other nuns, the officials entered and demanded that they be taken to Sister Barbara. When they located and opened the dungeon door, they recoiled and gasped with horror. There in the dark crouched a "completely naked, wild, half-mad female." According to liberal newspapers, she was the picture of death. "She was emaciated. Her face had hardly any flesh. Her eyes were hollow. Her eyebrows and lashes had entirely fallen out. Her pupils were dull." "I'm hungry; pity me," she meekly pleaded. "Give me some meat, and I'll behave."[56] Why had Barbara been locked away down in the dungeon? She said that she had broken the vow of celibacy. Feeble though she was, Barbara then gathered what little strength she had. She threw herself

54. *Berliner Wespen*, 4 July 1869.

55. *National Zeitung*, 26 July 1869; *Vossische Zeitung*, 27 July 1869, 29 July 1869. Barbara Ubryk's own account of her captivity, allegedly, can be found in *The Convent Horror: Or The True Narrative of Barbara Ubryk, A Sister of the Carmelite Convent at Cracow, Who Has Been Walled Up in a Dungeon* (Philadelphia: C. W. Alexander, 1869). Other sensationalist accounts include S. J. Abbott, *The Empress and the Carmelite Nun, or Twenty-one Years in a Convent Dungeon* (London: Convent Enquiry Society, 1902); *The Convent Horror: The Story of Barbara Ubryk Twenty-one Years in the Dungeon Eight Feet Long, Six Feet Wide* (Aurora, Mo.: Menace, 1890); and A. Rode, *Barbara Ubryk oder die Geheimnisse des Karmeliter-Klosters in Krakau* (Munich: Neuberger und Kolb, 1869). See also Michael B. Gross, "The Strange Case of the Nun in the Dungeon, or German Liberalism as a Convent Atrocity Story," *German Studies Review* 23 (2000): 69–84.

56. *National Zeitung*, 26 July 1869, 27 July 1869; *Vossische Zeitung*, 27 July 1869, 29 July 1869.

against the other nuns screaming, "But these here are also impure; they're not angels!" And she threw herself at the confessor, shouting, "You monster!"[57] While Barbara was led from the convent to the insane asylum, the confessor and the mother superior were arrested. According to the liberal *National Zeitung,* here was an "episode from the Inquisition in the nineteenth century," a scene that "even Dante with all his powers of imagination could not depict."[58]

Reports arriving from Vienna gave detailed accounts of the reaction of the Cracow population to Barbara's brutal treatment. Not the popular mob but rather hundreds from "the better strata," the "Bürger, not of the crowd," according to the newspapers, gathered at the Carmelite convent.[59] So enraged were they that they abandoned their regard for propriety, took up battering rams, and forced their way through the gates of the Carmelite convent. They smashed the windows and destroyed the courtyard. Shouting "away with the nuns!" they stormed into the convent building and invaded the inner chambers. The police and military finally forced the rioters to retreat.[60] During the following day, however, large crowds gathered again in front of the convent. At night they were joined by a procession from the suburbs. Numbering about four thousand, the crowd repeated the attack on the convent until cavalry dispersed it with drawn sabers.[61] A mob gathered again, worked itself into a frenzy, shouted "down with the Jesuits!" and headed to the Jesuit house. Rioters smashed the windows, pressed through the gates, scaled the walls, chased and beat the Jesuits. The mob then moved on with shouts, "to the Franciscans!" and "to the other nunneries!" where the attacks were repeated.[62] In the morning, cavalry and infantry reinforcements occupied the grounds of the monasteries and closed and patrolled the streets. While municipal authorities sympathized with the bitter and "legitimate" feelings of the population about "the medieval, inhuman deed," they also made appeals for the return to peace, order, and law.[63]

Throughout the next months, this dramatic and curious story—

---

57. *Vossische Zeitung,* 27 July 1869; *National Zeitung,* 27 July 1869. The clear suggestion according to Barbara's testimony reproduced in the *Convent Horror: Or The True Narrative* is that she had been drugged, raped by the convent's confessor, and then intimidated into silence by the mother superior.

58. *National Zeitung,* 27 July 1869.

59. *National Zeitung,* 26 July 1869; *Vossische Zeitung,* 27 July 1869.

60. *National Zeitung,* 26 July 1869, 27 July 1869; *Vossische Zeitung,* 27 July 1869.

61. Abbott, *The Empress,* 10–11.

62. *National Zeitung,* 26 July 1869; *Vossische Zeitung,* 27 July 1869, 29 July 1869.

63. *Vossische Zeitung,* 29 July 1869, 30 July 1869.

what became known as the Ubryk affair—became a public obsession as it continued to unfold in liberal newspapers throughout Germany. The horror story of the barefoot Carmelites at Cracow confirmed suspicions about unregulated female behavior. Beyond the authority of men, alone and unsupervised, women in convents ultimately became the victims of their own propensity for religious fanaticism. Soon after Sister Barbara was released from her dungeon, reports in liberal papers of a room-by-room search of the convent offered a disturbing if also fascinating peek behind closed doors into female communal life. On the table in the refectory was a human skull, a constant memento mori for nuns who had forsaken the material world beyond the convent. The adjacent room was a veritable museum of tools for torture. Here, according to the newspapers, large eighty-pound crosses were carried by the sisters on their backs to atone for their sins. Heavy marble stones on long straps were used to whip their breasts. The nuns pressed crowns with thorns or large nails on their heads; they whipped each other with knotted ropes. The "torture chamber," according to the newspapers, included long belts with needles or nails that were strapped around the nuns, piercing their flesh.[64]

As news of Sister Barbara's imprisonment spread across Europe and the United States, all-too-familiar convent atrocity stories sprang up in the liberal press. According to the *Vossische Zeitung,* "Different cities are reporting that old and recent acts of barbarism have occurred in these medieval institutions of lazy daydreaming."[65] According to liberal newspapers "no more than fourteen days have passed" since a tragedy similar to that in Cracow occurred at the convent of the Sisters of Mercy near Prague. A nun was imprisoned for violating her vow of chastity. She hanged herself in despair. The mother superior insisted that the nun had been insane and had tried to flee the convent. An examination of her corpse disclosed that she had been four months pregnant.[66] Two other nuns had, according to the papers, mentally collapsed under the strain of the stringent rules of convent life and had to be removed to an insane asylum.[67] In the town of Brün a skeleton was found behind a wall in a former Dominican monastery.[68] At the same time, at a Carmelite convent in Posen skeletons had been unearthed. Several nuns, according to the report, had apparently been walled in or

64. *National Zeitung,* 3 Aug. 1869; *Vossische Zeitung,* 4 Aug. 1869.
65. *Vossische Zeitung,* 31 July 1869.
66. Ibid.; *National Zeitung,* 31 July 1869.
67. *Vossische Zeitung,* 31 Aug. 1869, 1 Sept. 1869; *National Zeitung,* 31 July 1869.
68. *Vossische Zeitung,* 3 Aug. 1869.

hurriedly buried. The story of "Sister X" that appeared in the *Garten-laube* was true to form. An emotionally vulnerable young woman, her heart broken by a breached promise of marriage, was cunningly enticed into a convent without the knowledge of her parents and then held captive.[69] Meanwhile, liberal papers reported that at a Dominican monastery in Düsseldorf a monk was accused of sexually abusing five-, six-, and seven-year-old girls.[70] In an article repeated in the *Vossische Zeitung,* the *Rheinische Zeitung* was alarmed to find nuns in charge of the education of children at a convent in Düsseldorf. Their methods of instructing and punishing the children included "incarceration in a death chamber in a convent, etc., etc."[71] It is the "etceteras" here that repay attention since they admit a measure of wry self-reflection: the convent narrative had become so formulaic and well rehearsed that its atrocities hardly needed specification.

Both exploiting and feeding the appetite for information about Sister Barbara and the secrets of female monasticism promised, no doubt, higher circulation and lucrative rewards for newspapers, journals, and independent authors. One writer in a seemingly superhuman effort managed to produce in four weeks a twelve hundred–page tome entitled *Barbara Ubryk oder die Geheimnisse des Karmeliter-Klosters in Krakau.*[72] The titillating advertisement for the book in one liberal newspaper promised that "centuries of darkness and secret crimes" were exposed "in their naked truth." "Horror will grasp the hearts of even the most hardened men."[73] Readers were not disappointed. In the book, they were treated to all the gruesome details of Barbara's misery. Included also is the verbatim official report of Barbara's physical and mental condition during her stay in the insane asylum. Before the court-appointed medical personnel, she stripped off her clothing, according to the document, and "winked quite unambiguously at the men." Sister Barbara, the physicians concluded, was a case of nymphomania, a condition of lunacy she had endured since her adolescence and ultimately attributable to her religious fanaticism. Because she had

---

69. "Hinter dem Klosterpforte," *Gartenlaube* (1870): 72–74.

70. *Vossische Zeitung,* 14 Aug. 1869.

71. *Rheinische Zeitung,* 11 Aug. 1869, reported in *Vossische Zeitung,* 19 Aug. 1869. See also *Vossische Zeitung,* 14 Aug. 1869.

72. Rode, *Barbara Ubryk,* 1213–44.

73. A two-page advertisement for the book appeared in *Vossische Zeitung,* 25 Aug. 1869. For incredulous readers who doubted that such a large book could be produced so rapidly, the publisher in the preface to the book explained that these and other chapters had already been written. Only the concluding chapter on Sister Barbara had been hurriedly written and added to the volume in order to take advantage of the moment.

been imprisoned in the convent and denied the services of a mental institution where she properly belonged, there was, sadly, no hope for her recovery.[74] The author's conclusion based on an account of convent atrocities through the ages confirmed the worst suspicions: "If only Barbara Ubryk were the only one so unfortunate to have been secretly imprisoned! But she is lucky compared to thousands of other victims in the convents. There is hardly a monastery in which monks or nuns were not buried alive and cruelly martyred. In all the state archives there are documents concerning former monasteries that record such atrocities."[75] Such stories provided evidence for antimonastic petitions to the Austrian government reproduced in the liberal German press. They argued that the atrocity at the Carmelite convent proved how inadequately present legislation protected "modern culture, bürgerlich freedom, humanity, and the Enlightenment against their irreconcilable enemies."[76] Meanwhile, at a convention in Vienna German journalists proclaimed it "a debt of honor for every thinking man to enter the lists" for the abolition of monasteries and the expulsion of the Jesuits. They expected deputies to the Prussian parliament to fulfill their obligations to do so as well.[77]

In the larger context of the convent atrocity narratives of the anti-Catholic culture of nineteenth-century Germany, the incarceration of Sister Barbara is reminiscent of the kind of legend used profitably by Jacob Burckhardt to explore the dimensions of the elite culture of Renaissance Italy. It was, as he would have argued, "one of those stories that are true and not true, everywhere and nowhere."[78] Hardly new, accounts of atrocities in convents were part of a tradition of popular anticonvent and antimonastic literature throughout the century. In lurid stories in pamphlets, books, journals, and newspapers, unsuspecting young women were lured into convents, where they were subjected to sexual exploitation that led invariably to madness, suicide, or murder. Stephan Gätschenberger's *Enthüllungen aus bayerischen Klöstern aus der neueren Zeit,* published in 1868, was at the time of the Ubryk affair only

74. Rode, *Barbara Ubryk,* 1220–34. Sister Barbara's nymphomania was reported also in *Vossische Zeitung,* 5 Aug. 1869.

75. Rode, *Barbara Ubryk,* 1238–39.

76. *Vossische Zeitung,* 5 Aug. 1869. The *Vossische Zeitung* paid rapt attention to the antimonastic petition movements in Cracow, Vienna, and Prague. See *Vossische Zeitung,* esp. 29 July 1869, 1 Aug. 1869, 5 Aug. 1869, 7 Aug. 1869, 8 Aug. 1869.

77. Kissling, *Geschichte des Kulturkampfes* 1:329; Anderson, *Windthorst,* 123.

78. Jacob Burckhardt, *Die Kultur der Renaissance in Italien* (Stuttgart: Alfred Kröner Verlag, 1976), 21–22.

the most recent example.[79] The ribald melodrama of nuns and convents belonged especially to the anticlerical satire of the Enlightenment and the French Revolution and included, for example, *Aufgefangene Briefe einer Nonne an Ihren Beichtvater,* appearing in 1781, and Joseph Richter Obermayer's *Bildergalerie klösterlicher Mißbräuche,* published in 1784.[80] Again during the Revolution of 1848, nunneries were portrayed in liberal satirical journals like the *Leuchtkugeln* as "depraved dens" of "bickering nuns" where "violent force was exerted on young nuns and candidates for the order."[81] The journal portrayed a young nun "walled in and chained, surrounded by evil nuns in the convent. Yearningly she gazes out into unattainable freedom!" Her "sad sight," a woman without any hope for love, inspired the verse:

Long live the freedom to love!
But so long as nuns are not free and happy,
There is no freedom to love![82]

Antimonastic attacks on nuns continued in the decade of reaction with the appearance of Wolfgang Menzel's novel *Furore: Geschichte eines Mönchs und einer Nonne aus dem Dreißigjährigen Kriege,* published in 1851, and then afterward with A. L. Stachelstock's *Licht und Finsterniß oder die freien Gemeinden und die Jesuiten,* appearing in 1861, which included the portrait of monks and nuns meeting in secret tunnels to exchange sexual favors.[83] Similar fanciful diatribes included R. Sommer's *Vernunft gegen Pfaffenpolitik und Nasenweisheit,* published in 1865, and *Gemälde aus dem Nonnenleben oder enthüllte Geheimnisse* in

79. Stephan Gätschenberger, *Enthüllungen aus bayerischen Klöstern aus der neueren Zeit* (Würzburg: Selbstverlag der Verfassers, 1868). See also for other examples *Klostergeschichten oder Betrügerein der Pfaffen und Mönche* (Chemnitz, 1871); *Magdalena Paumann oder die eingekerkerte Nonne im Angerkloster zu München* (Munich: J. J. Lentner'schen Buchhandlung, 1870); *Memoiren einer Nonne* (Munich, 1874); and *Memoiren der Schwester Angelika, einer entlaufenen Nonne des Klosters zu Cork* (Leipzig, 1873).

80. *Aufgefangene Briefe einer Nonne an Ihren Beichtvater* (n.p.: Sebastian Hartl, 1781); Joseph Richter Obermayer, *Bildergalerie klösterlicher Mißbräuche* (Frankfurt am Main, 1784).

81. *Leuchtkugeln,* Bd. 1, Nr. 6, 1848, quoted in Friedhelm Jürgensmeier, *Die katholische Kirche im Spiegel der Karikatur: Der deutschen satirischen Tendenzzeitschriften von 1848 bis 1900* (Trier: Verlag Neu, 1969), 112.

82. *Leuchtkugeln,* Bd. 1, Nr. 22, 1848, quoted in Jürgensmeier, *Katholische Kirche,* 112.

83. Wolfgang Menzel, *Furore: Geschichte eines Mönchs und einer Nonne aus dem Dreißigjährigen Kriege* (Leipzig: F. A. Brockhaus, 1851); Stachelstock, *Licht und Finsterniß,* 54–55.

1870.[84] *Pfaffenwesen, Mönchsscandale und Nonnenspuk: Beitrag zur Naturgeschichte des Katholizismus und der Klöster,* written by a certain Lucifer Illuminator, appeared in 1871 on the eve of the Kulturkampf.[85] In his study of religious conflict and national identity, Helmut Smith has pointed out that gendered discourse, central to the German nationalist tradition in general, was particularly important to Kulturkampf anticlerical poetry. Valiant German men typically rescue innocent young women in the confessional from the prurient intentions of their priests.[86] But the most elaborate fantasies of heroism and liberation involve nuns. In "Die Nonne" the poet Bernhardt Endrulat yearns to save a young woman, "a pale child," from "silence and death" and from "the dark madness" of the convent.[87]

On the surface, recycled stories about nuns, imprisoned in dungeons, sexually abused, walled in and left to die, or driven to insanity or suicide, provided under the guise of humanitarian outrage titillating scandals, sensational and pornographic entertainment. But these stories were hardly gratuitous artifacts of culture. They provided a disciplinary service within bourgeois society, warning young women of the punishment that awaited them if they abandoned their responsibilities as wives and mothers by entering the religious life. A full-page illustration in the liberal satirical magazine *Kladderadatsch* reveals the deep meaning at another level of the convent atrocity story (fig. 16).[88] At the height of the Ubryk affair, the classic female figure of Liberty is identified with the long-suffering nun, specifically with Sister Barbara. Wearing the liberty cap, she is imprisoned in a cell. Her arms are shackled to the table, and her ankle is chained to an iron ball. Forlorn and weary, her head heavy and held up by an arm, she gazes in a moment of melancholic self-reflection at her once proud and high hopes, "Liberté, Égalité, Fraternité," now mocking reminders of ideals defeated and forgotten. The classic female image of liberalism is now a nun in a

---

84. R. Sommer, *Vernunft gegen Pfaffenpolitik und Nasenweisheit: Erstes Referat aus dem Rubenschen Nachlass* (Leipzig: Spielmeyersche Buchhandlung, 1865); *Gemälde aus dem Nonnenleben oder enthullte Geheimnisse* (Munich, 1870).

85. Lucifer Illuminator [Daniel von Kaszony], *Pfaffenunwesen, Mönchsscandale und Nunnenspuk: Beitrag zur Naturgeschichte des Katholizismus und der Klöster* (Leipzig: Gustav Schulze, 1871).

86. Smith, *German Nationalism,* 36.

87. Bernhardt Endrulat, "Die Nonne," in *Gegen Rom: Zeitstimmen Deutscher Dichter,* ed. Ernst Scherenberg (Elberfeld: Bädeker'sche Buch- und Kunsthandlung, 1874), 21–22, quoted also in Smith, *German Nationalism,* 36.

88. *Kladderadatsch,* 8 Aug. 1869.

Fig. 16. "Nichts Neues unter der Sonne!" *Kladderadatsch,* 8 August 1869. In the illustration "Nothing New under the Sun," liberalism after the Revolution of 1848 has become a convent atrocity story. Identifying with nuns imprisoned and sexually abused, German liberals thematized their own psychological trauma in Bismarck's authoritarian state during an age of Catholic popular reaction.

dungeon. The *Oberin* (mother superior) spies unnoticed through a window on her naked body. (The figure is labeled *Oberin.*) The Oberin is unmistakably a man with a full beard and mustache and, one can imagine, about to repeat the brutal crime. She is the monstrosity, the hermaphrodite or "she-man": in liberal social-sexual ideology the woman who refuses to assume her natural role and duties as wife and mother and makes a mockery of male authority.[89] Surreal and traumatic, this is a remarkably frank and self-conscious depiction of the liberal nightmare.

89. Chapter 4 examines the image of "Männin" (she-men), in religious congregations threatening to break down the gender-specific distinction between public and private.

The image helps us understand why the convent atrocity story was such a phantasmagoric obsession for liberals. That Sister Barbara had been imprisoned in 1848, the year of the revolution, is not a mere coincidence but the entire point of her misfortune. The "Krakauer Schauferballade" (The Cracow ballad of horror) appearing in the liberal journal *Berliner Wespen* had already connected the defeat of the 1848 Revolution with Sister Barbara's imprisonment and brutal treatment.

> Forty-eight! The storm of freedom
> Rages across the world.
> In the quiet convent
> The nun is secretly put away.

> With the Carmelites
> Lives one pious, chaste and pure,
> But to claim their inheritance
> They walled the sister in.

> Her ghastly screams and whimpers
> Vainly plead for pity.
> The mother superior only snickers:
> My dear child, you're damned!

> Up above in the convent
> They live pious and happy.
> While year after year the poor girl
> Tosses in the putrid straw.

> Her hair grows gray and wild,
> Her body mere skin and bones.
> For twenty-one long years
> The girl endures the torture.

> The dungeon door is burst open,
> Oh, wicked malice!
> She stumbles out, a skeleton,
> A grisly sight of madness.

> Saved at last and secure,
> The wrong at last made right.—

Are they humans or are they devils,
Who do this "For the Glory of God"?[90]

Here freedom and the liberal aspirations of 1848 are personified as a nun—defeated at the moment of the revolution; shackled and alone, all but dead; then liberated, and recalled to life only after twenty-one years of imprisonment. The *Kladderadatsch* illustration of Liberty imprisoned repeats the identification of the nun with the defeat of the revolutions in Europe in 1848. Its caption reads: "The nun Barbara Ubryk has hardly been freed from her dungeon in Cracow, when one is already on the trail in Paris of another woman who since 1848 has been held in prison in humiliation. Furthermore other poor nuns in shackles are said still to be languishing in various other countries." The reference in the last sentence would, of course, include Germany. German liberalism was the convent atrocity story. In the liberal imagination, Sister Barbara was liberalism's body bound and raped. In the Ubryk affair, as their loathing of nuns and Catholicism expressed itself in a creative leap of fantastic transference, liberal men thematized their own deep-set psychological trauma with their defeat in the revolution. There is another point. The title "Nothing New under the Sun" indicates that the liberal identification with the nun was already familiar to readers of the *Kladderadatsch;* it had become routine mental work. Liberals who identified with the nun, therefore, consciously belied the bravado of liberalism. At the same time that they imagined a manly fight with the church that would only lead to their triumph, they created and suffered fits of anxiety and inadequacy that demolished this confidence. The nightmare scene depicts the liberals' experience of emasculation as their own hopes are dashed by "obscurantism" and "medievalism." Defeated in 1848; then suppressed by reactionary government during the 1850s; split politically during the constitutional conflict with Bismarck in 1862–66; faced now with the power of the revived Catholic Church, liberalism was still in 1869 an ideal waiting to be realized. Similar sentiments of despair had already been expressed by a cartoon in the *Berliner Wespen:* the arms of a nutcracker labeled (Vatican) "Synod" and "Council" are breaking a walnut marked "science" and "reason."[91] There is a final point. The fantasy of Sister Barbara is a marker of the liberal obsession with the relations of power between men and women. At once raped and emasculating, she depicts

90. "Krakauer Schauerballade," *Berliner Wespen,* 1 Aug. 1869.
91. *Berliner Wespen,* 26 Dec. 1869.

one way in which fears of sexual inadequacy and fears of women were deeply implicated in anti-Catholicism, a theme we can note here and develop in chapter 4.

Catholics and the Catholic Church hardly remained silent during the liberal attack on female convents. Catholic newspapers and spokesmen claimed that Sister Barbara had long suffered from mental illness and had been locked away for her own protection. Drawing on the stock of Catholic prejudices, Catholic papers assumed that the whole affair was the invention of the "democratic Jewish" and "Freemasonic press."[92] Such responses were predictable and are not in themselves particularly remarkable. More important is that the Catholic and liberal exchange during the Ubryk affair was an especially well-developed example of the way Catholics and liberals locked in a rhetorically dependent relationship, promoting each other's cultural productivity of meaning by reappropriating vocabulary, symbols, and metaphors. When liberal papers claimed that the convents and their atrocities were throwbacks to the Dark Ages, Catholic papers like the *Freiburger katholischer Zeitung* condemned the capitalist exploitation of women in the modern age of industrialized labor.

In huge industrial plants thousands of miserable women and girls suffer, yearning for salvation. From early morning until late in the evening they are forced to do hard work, pitiable heathen slaves,

---

92. References to anti-Jewish prejudice in the Catholic Church and press are found in *Berliner Wespen,* 1 Aug. 1869, and *National Zeitung,* 10 Aug. 1869. References to the slander of the "Jewish and Freemasonic press" are found in the Catholic *Freiburger katholische Kirchenblatt* reproduced in *Vossische Zeitung,* 19 July 1869. For Catholic anti-Judaism and anti-Semitism in nineteenth-century Germany, see Olaf Blaschke, *Katholizismus und Antisemitismus im deutschen Kaiserreich* (Göttingen: Vandenhoeck und Ruprecht, 1997); idem, "Wider die Herrschaft des modern-jüdischen Geistes: Der Katholizismus zwischen traditionellen Antijudaismus und modernem Antisemitismus," in *Deutscher Katholizismus im Umbruch zur Moderne,* ed. Wilfred Loth (Stuttgart: W. Kohlhammer, 1991), 236–63; Rudolf Lill, "Die deutschen Katholiken und die Juden in der Zeit von 1850 bis zur Machtübernahme Hitlers," in *Kirche und Synagoge: Handbuch zur Geschichte von Christen und Juden,* ed. Karl Heinrich Rengstorf and Siegfried von Kortzfleisch (Stuttgart: Klett, 1968–72); 2:377–94; Helmut Walser Smith, "Religion and Conflict: Protestants, Catholics, and Anti-Semitism in the State of Baden in the Era of Wilhelm II," *Central European History* 27 (1994): 283–314; idem, "Learned and the Popular Discourse of Anti-Semitism in the Catholic Milieu of the Kaiserreich," *Central European History* 27 (1994): 315–28; Uriel Tal, *Christians and Jews in Germany: Religion, Politics, and Ideology in the Second Reich, 1870–1914,* trans. Noah Jonathan Jacobs (Ithaca: Cornell University Press, 1975), 85–95; for the popular Catholic attitude toward Freemasons, see Sperber, *Popular Catholicism.*

and indeed often in an atmosphere equal to the stench of Ubryk's cell. Rude, obscene talk gushes from the mouths of many supervisors and demoralized co-workers; these defenseless women have to endure even worse. . . . The greed and the hatred for the church of many money-grubbing industrialists even force the unfortunate [women] to miss mass on Sundays and holidays. So their bodies are not only exploited for work; their souls are also condemned to eternal damnation.[93]

In the attempt to deflate liberal anticonvent allegations, the Catholic paper co-opted and pushed inside out the vision of nuns imprisoned in the convent. It offered Sister Barbara in the dungeon as now the "factory atrocity story," young women locked away in the industrial plant, part of the larger attack on an increasingly materialistic and secular German nation.[94] For liberals and progressives, the Catholic Church's opposition to female factory labor only served to confirm its image as a brake on the wheels of progress, a boulder in the path of industrial growth.

Of course, the Catholic hostility to industrial production and Sunday factory labor was nothing new. Even before the 1848 Revolution, for example, the Catholic *Allgemeine Kirchen-Zeitung* in Darmstadt reported on the Magdeburger Börde, a largely rural area experiencing industrialization in Saxony. According to the newspaper, the factory owners in that region were

veritable enemies of the human race, for their God is money, their temple is the brewery or distillery, or the factory with its incense-like smoke. Their hymn is the roaring of the boilers and the throbbing of the machine. . . . When they think they can get away with it, they frequently break the law against Sunday labor, which indeed cannot be enforced to the letter. When they are forced to conform to the law, and thus talk of their day of rest, then they often mean by this simply that they are spending one day

93. Article from *Freiburger katholische Zeitung* reprinted in *Vossische Zeitung,* 19 July 1869.

94. The paper also attempted to undercut the liberal attack on the convent by accusing of hypocrisy liberals who had drawn so much attention to Ubryk at the same time that prisoners were incarcerated during the revolution in Italy. "Compared to the Italian dungeon, Ubryk's cell is nothing. European liberalism shows no concern for these victims of the revolution who have been buried alive. It only has sympathy for mentally ill Polish people and is horrified that Ubryk's room was not sufficiently ventilated." Quoted in ibid.

indulging in even more sensual pleasures than usual. Hardly anyone talks of going to church, or communing quietly with himself, or of composing his mind in a religious sense, and rousing his feelings to the contemplation of the Deity, neither on Sunday, nor, it need hardly be said, on weekdays.[95]

Here again is the familiar argumentative topos with its mocking reversal of images. The industrial mill—the secular house of material worship with its "incenselike smoke," "hymns" offered up with thumping machinery, and "attendance" required on the Sabbath—is the reappropriation of the vision of the parish church that wedded God and community in the tranquil, premodern *Heimat.*

And then again in the liberal imaginary the church harbored its own peculiar form of industrial production: convents, female religious, congregations, and philanthropic institutions for girls all were mere fronts for factories that secretly churned out religious products for sale on the market for the profit of the Roman Church.[96] What made the factory production in the "work convents" illegitimate according to liberals was not the employment of women and girls but their employment in a commercial activity that competed with reputable, bürgerlich business. Since work convents paid lower wages to their labor, they were able to undercut market prices and shut down competition. "Work convents," liberals claimed, drove wages so low that their female workers had no other way to survive but to supplement their meager income with prostitution. Liberals could satisfy themselves with a conclusion based on the objective application of logic and deduced from the first principles that governed the free market. In accordance with the iron laws of wages and prices the convent became again the whorehouse already familiar in anticlerical discourse.

The "Moabiterklostersturm": The Nation as the Antithesis of the Monastery

According to the *National Zeitung,* the fact that the Catholics of Cracow, "a not so much pious as bigoted city that once was called Polish Rome," had attacked the Carmelite convent and the Jesuit residence

---

95. Quoted in Richard J. Evans, "Religion and Society in Modern Germany," *Rethinking German History: Nineteenth-Century Germany and the Origins of the Third Reich* (London: HarperCollins, 1987), 125–55, quotation at 143.
96. See the argument in Stachelstock, *Licht und Finsterniß,* 87–88.

could only be a significant sign of the times, irrefutable proof of the extent of monastic depravity. The attacks by angry mobs were understandable. They were not merely an expression of the bitterness toward the Carmelite convent but of the long-accumulating hostility toward religious orders and monastic life in general.[97] If in the heart of Catholic Poland monasteries were intolerable, the paper argued, they were even more so in Protestant countries like Prussia. Diatribes like those on the pages of the *Gartenlaube* for the past decade had prepared and contributed to an atmosphere of antimonastic fervor.

Amid the hysteria that was both cause and effect of the Ubryk affair, it was perhaps no surprise that on an early August Sunday in 1869 an angry crowd gathered before the newly consecrated chapel in the Moabit district of Berlin. Here four Franciscan friars had established an orphanage. They were soon joined by two Dominican monks who came to attend to the spiritual life of workers in the neighboring factories. Liberal newspapers claimed, however, that a dozen Dominican and Franciscan monks had established a "monastery" in the middle of Berlin's industrial suburb.[98] The crowd before the Dominican chapel prepared themselves for the rituals of *Katzenmusik* (cat music), the version in central Europe of charivari, the symbolic shaming in public of those who deviated from the prescribed codes of community behavior. Cat music included taunts, howls, and high-pitched screeches; its usual victims were those who had violated the norms of sexual conduct—prostitutes and women who cheated on their husbands. Within the cultural logic of symbolic action, cat music at a "monastery" indicated that monks in the anticlerical imagination were linked to feminine and deviant sexual behavior. Shorn of all facial hair at a time when beards, muttonchops, and mustaches were features of masculine fashion, monks looked emasculated and feminine, and, indeed, in antimonastic discourse monks and members of religious charitable organizations were no better than "begging women." Cartoonists in leading journals apparently could hardly help themselves: wherever there are chubby, bald monks, they invariably assume dainty, "feminine" postures: half bent, hands clasped, simpering, eyes cast upward. At the same time, sensational stories of a delinquent relationship between a Dominican priest from Düsseldorf and a young woman and in late summer allegations that another Dominican had sexually abused two female children contributed to the wildest

97. *National Zeitung,* 29 July 1869.
98. Windell, *Catholics and German Unity,* 235.

antimonastic fantasies. Monastics now in Moabit represented, therefore, a sexual taboo, a threat to the basic codes of social conduct.[99]
Soon howls and taunts escalated to stone throwing and shattered windows. Rioters pelted the monks and splattered their residence with
horse excrement off the street.[100] As was the habit with cat music, local
authorities turned a blind eye, condoning a popular rite that was integral to the maintenance of moral order.[101]

At the same time, for liberal, middle-class Berliners a Dominican
"monastery" in the middle of a productive industrial suburb of Berlin
was an absurd incongruity. Already in the 1840s and 1850s the factories of Berlin had begun to move out to Moabit and Wedding. By the
late 1860s they had become the centers of industrial pride and achievement and were to become under the empire among the most important sites for heavy production. Now, however, according to the liberal *National Zeitung,* the speech given by a priest at the consecration
of the chapel had been a public scandal, an insult to industrialization.
Moabit had been described by the Catholic clergy as a symbol of
"excess; the chase after material success; modern, steam-driven industry which knows and pursues only earthly purpose." "Was any of
this," the paper asked, "appropriate and edifying for the ears of the
factory owners present?" The priest giving the speech had spoken of a
"'Goliathian struggle' [*Goliathkampf*] that should be waged against
this symbolic place and the Zeitgeist, a Goliathian struggle led by a
few praying monks!" The speech was a provocation, claiming that on
this site of industrialization, "here in Moabit, where one is so urgently
needed," a "monastery" was to be established; "here in Jerusalem, a

99. Ross, *Failure of Bismarck's Kulturkampf,* 19, 26.

100. *Vossische Zeitung,* 11 Aug. 1869. Accounts of the rioting at the Dominican residence
include but are not limited to Heinrich Brück, *Geschichte der katholischen Kirche in Deutschland im neunzehnten Jahrhundert* (Münster: F. Kirchheim, 1905), 282–86; Thomas Lindenberger, "Berliner Unordnung zwischen den Revolutionen," in *Pöbelexzesse und Volkstumulte
in Berlin: Zur Sozialgeschichte der Straße (1830–1980),* ed. Manfred Gailus (Berlin: Verlag
Europäische Perspektive, 1984), 49–77, esp. 49–50; Ross, *Failure of Bismarck's Kulturkampf,*
26–27; Bernhard Strasiewski, "Die Dominikaner in Berlin, ein kirchengeschichtlicher
Überblick," *Wichmann Jahrbuch* 21–23 (1967–69): 30–41, esp. 35–36; Windell, *Catholics and
German Unity,* 235; and Kurt Wernicke, "Der "Moabiter Klostersturm,'" *Berlinische
Monatsschrift* 3 (1994): 3–14.

101. For the tradition of cat music in nineteenth-century Germany, see Sperber, *Rhineland
Radicals,* 86–87. See also Carola Lipp, "Katzenmusiken, Krawalle und 'Weiberrevolution':
Frauen im politischen Protest der Revolutionsjahre," in *Schimpfende Weiber und patriotische
Jungfrauen: Frauen im Vormärz und in der Revolution 1848/49,* ed. Carola Lipp und Beate
Bechtold-Comforty (Moos and Baden-Baden: Elster, 1986), 112–30.

new Rome will arise!"[102] An editorial in the *Vossische Zeitung* complained that the establishment of a monastic contemplative order—for monks devoted not to work but solely to prayer—struck a blow against the achievements of labor and industry in Moabit.

> In Moabit, the seat of thriving commercial activity, in what was one of the most inhospitable sand wastes now belonging to the most renowned representatives of industry, which produces prosperity and wealth for many thousands, where under the direction of philanthropic factory owners schools, public institutions, and savings associations thrive, in short, where work shows its most beautiful and ethical side, . . . this mere prayer industry [*Gebetsindustrie*] is now setting up a place for canting the rosary and for contemplating the five miracles of Christ.[103]

The *Berliner Wespen* picked up the characterization of the monastery as a Gebetsindustrie, producing only useless prayer with mindless puppets of the church. In a cartoon two monks are rigged to a machine that hoists them into various positions for prayer. The caption reads, "the new machine-prayer plant in Moabit has stirred up great interest everywhere. But it should be closed again."[104] In an age demanding productive labor and efficiency, the monasteries were the models of waste. The notion that useful work was antithetical to the monastery was repeated in the *Vossische Zeitung*. The paper reported that in a speech delivered at an assembly in Vienna, a speech to which, according to the paper, Berliners too should pay close attention, the goal of the state was moral and economic. "The latter is based on work; but monasteries are dedicated to futile contemplation."[105] Liberals constantly worried that the church might undermine an ethic of work with useless religious rituals. At the height of the Ubryk affair the *Vossische Zeitung* reported the view that the Jesuits sowed devotion

---

102. The speech was reprinted in the *National Zeitung*, 6 Aug. 1869. See the article "Eine seltsame Kirchenweihe," *National Zeitung*, 8 Aug. 1869; *Vossische Zeitung*, 8 Aug. 1869.

103. *Vossische Zeitung*, 8 Aug. 1869. According to the article Berlin had no less than six Roman Catholic orders and congregations; in Prussia, despite their having once been abolished, 700 monasteries with 6,000 members had spread like a "pestilence." Meanwhile the number of Jesuits in Germany, France, Austria, Belgium, and the Netherlands had doubled under Pope Pius IX and according to the article had risen during the same time from 640 to 2,190. "The rest of the world has the remaining 6,400, much too many."

104. *Berliner Wespen*, 22 Aug. 1869.

105. *Vossische Zeitung*, 12 Aug. 1869.

and destroyed production: wherever there have been Jesuits, "people have been drawn into a daily routine of devotion instead of reserving observance to the day of rest as prescribed by religion. The people have descended into misery and laziness, frittering away the time for labor with praying in the church."[106]

The monastic order, according to the liberal press, was no more than "a brotherhood of beggars." Producing nothing of value themselves, monastics only lived off the labor of others. In the industrial suburb of Berlin, according to the *Kladderadatsch,* they could be nowhere more inappropriate, nowhere more an outrage: in Moabit "where the flames of work glow, / there the beggar is thriving again!"[107] Not just a drain on the resources of society, the monastic life, according to an article that ran in the *Vossische Zeitung,* provided an embarrassing model for a destitute population that might otherwise through rehabilitation eventually contribute to the productive labor force. "We have enough beggars, and it would certainly not contribute to their decrease if the people . . . see that [monks] go begging entirely undisturbed from house to house, while the poor father of a family, exhausting himself for a little piece of bread for his starving children, is cleared out and punished by the wardens of the law."[108] The example of monks begging only sanctioned similar behavior among the poor, undermining the ethic of labor.

A "monastery" in Moabit for the Berlin public was not only an affront to industrialization and productive work. After a month of grisly articles about Sister Barbara, convent atrocity cases, and stories about "lascivious" monks and "captive" nuns, the monastery had also become a site for prurient fantasy. The press continued to offer the public stories of monks and nuns kissing and groping each other while strolling among Moabit's factories and meeting at night in monastic tunnels.[109] Berliners streamed to the site hoping to catch glimpses of "the nuns," "underground passages," and other "monastic secrets."[110] Curious crowds of several hundred pressed up to the gates of the chapel in Moabit and taunted the monks with jokes and questions.

106. *Vossische Zeitung,* 7 Aug. 1869.

107. See the "Bettelbrüderlied," *Kladderadatsch,* 15 Aug. 1869. See also *Vossische Zeitung,* 17 Aug. 1869, for monks as beggars.

108. *Vossische Zeitung,* 27 Aug. 1869.

109. *Kladderadatsch,* 15 Aug. 1869. In a cartoon in *Kladderadatsch* captioned "Pious Architecture" a nun and monk meet secretly in an underground tunnel between the monastery and the convent. *Kladderadatsch,* 22 Aug. 1869.

110. Jürgensmeier, *Katholische Kirche,* 126.

One asked if too much praying with the rosary caused calluses on the hands.[111] On Sundays the site was the destination for a family outing. Going to a "monastery" in Moabit was, as the *Kladderadatsch* self-mocked, not just for the "riffraff." It was an occasion worth dressing for.

Hurrah! We're there too.
We have to go there!
The police are indulgent,
Letting us view the thing from outside,
free but without entry!

Come, Mother, dress yourself up,
The new hat with roses.
Augusta, take the red shawl;
Little Karl, you're off to the scandal!
Quick, put on your new pants![112]

The Protestant Church leadership meanwhile believed that Dominican and Franciscan monks in the heart of the predominantly Protestant capital of Prussia were an unacceptable provocation. One Protestant pastor recommended that Berliners assemble in thousands in protest before the "monastery." Together they would sing "the old Protestant fight song," "A Mighty Fortress Is Our God." That, he believed, would be a memorable sight, "truly Evangelical and Protestant."[113] The monastery provided an attraction as a historical relic, a vestige from a distant age that both enticed and strained the bourgeois modern imagination. According to the *Vossische Zeitung*, "The busy Bürger and artisan, indeed, even the more educated man and specialist of the present age, can only with great strain transplant himself back into the dead days of the Middle Ages." An age so unlike the present, the paper explained, "it was without public schools, the Enlightenment, and the dissemination of morals." Monks had been the sad examples of that time. While one diligently studied in his cell, according to the paper, hundreds of others indulged their lavish tastes and carnal desires. From within the walls of the monastery "only the

---

111. *Vossische Zeitung*, 18 Aug. 1869. For the curiosity of the crowds, see *Vossische Zeitung*, 19 Aug. 1869; and *National Zeitung*, 17 Aug. 1869.
112. "Neuester Schwindel," *Kladderadatsch*, 22 Aug. 1969.
113. Quotations in Kissling, *Geschichte des Kulturkampfes* 1:330.

screams of women and children, only the howl of dogs, only cursing and the sound of hard drinking" could be heard.[114] The monastery was the vision of sloth and promiscuity, a medieval anachronism in the age of industry and reason.

Associations like these only fueled Berlin's antimonastic frenzy. According to a cartoon in the *Berliner Wespen,* all of Berlin would soon be in danger of being overrun by religious orders. No story or cartoon seemed too outlandish to run in the press: "A Future Scene from Berlin" depicts two monks raping a woman in front of the factories in Moabit. At the same time, "Sisters of the Good Heart" are too busy whoring on the street to take any notice. A heretic is burned at the stake in an auto-da-fé while a monk with a torch and a dagger is charging into "Jew Street." Meanwhile the courthouse has been taken over by the "Inquisition," and the Ministry of Education crumbles to the ground in neglect.[115] It was not long thereafter that, as in the case of the *Berliner Wespen,* monks were fully dehumanized, transformed into reptiles, snakes, crabs, bats, life-destroying parasitic worms, and terminal diseases. Monks were trichina, burrowing into healthy flesh, consuming the body from the inside out. They were a cancer from which one never recovered.[116] Not only dehumanizing, such nightmarish visions also exposed, despite outward bravado, the deep-seated doubt among liberals about their ability to rid themselves of the monks and monasteries infesting the German social body.

In mid-August after a barrage of antimonastic images—monks as indigents uselessly reciting the rosary, as lazy beggars siphoning off social resources and tumbling nuns, as mindless puppets of the church, or as various kinds of vermin—a crowd again gathered before the Dominican chapel. As a character in *Kladderadatsch* complained with a measure of facile irony, Berliners had become by now fully saturated with such visions: "I've had it up to my neck with nuns; monks fill me with disgust. Gondolizing through half of Germany during the last four weeks—everywhere the same story! Monastic tales, walled-in skeletons, castrated Abelards, mad Heloises."[117] The mob formed in the evening, chanting insults and hurling stones and excrement. Nightfall provided the cover for the frontal attack. The mob, armed with

114. *Vossische Zeitung,* 15 Aug. 1869.
115. *Berliner Wespen,* 15 Aug. 1869.
116. *Berliner Wespen,* 29 Aug. 1869. For monastics as vermin see *Berliner Wespen,* 12 Sept. 1869.
117. *Kladderadatsch,* 15 Aug. 1869.

crowbars, axes, and clubs, ripped down the fence, stormed into the courtyard, and smashed into the chapel. Rioters took charge of a transport loaded with stones, unleashed a hailstorm, destroyed the windows, and brought down the steeples. The monks fled for their lives, and the mob continued its work until two o'clock in the morning. The following evening authorities did not wait for several hundred men, women, and children to finish the job. Eighty mounted policemen with military reinforcements charged the rioters with drawn sabers. The streets were cleared and order restored in Moabit. Police patrolled the neighborhood. Thirty police officers (later reduced to five) were stationed in the courtyard of the chapel and remained there for eleven weeks at public expense to prevent further disorder. As an afterthought, the police president explained that there had been an unfortunate misapprehension: this was not a monastery in the strict sense of the word but a chapel and orphanage.[118]

Meanwhile, fears spread that the "monastery" in Moabit only signaled the start of more and more monasteries in Berlin and throughout Germany. According to the *Vossische Zeitung,* monks in Austria would think that in Prussia, where the Protestants were "extraordinarily tolerant," monks lived undisturbed and that Prussia would therefore be ideal for the spreading of ultramontane propaganda. "If it ever comes to this, it will be a great shame for our state."[119] The *Kladderadatsch* ran a cartoon, "A Country Outing from Austria," depicting monks arriving in Moabit. A monk and a nun are kissing but still manage to trundle a load of bricks with a mortar. They are on their way to wall her in. Other monks are boozing themselves into a stupor and hauling an assortment of tools for inquisitional torture.[120] The journal explained that the Dominicans and Franciscans had merely opened the gates to other horrors: the Capuchins, Carthusians, and Carmelite nuns were already planning to settle in the city. They were expected to be joined by Jesuits, Benedictines, Augustinians, and Cistercians, along with "fakirs" and "dervishes."[121] The *National Zeitung* blamed the invasion on the unwillingness of the Prussian government to take the steps needed to dam the flood. While in 1855 the number of monasteries in Prussia had been 69, the number in 1864 reached 243; in 1855 there had been 976 monks and nuns, but now in

118. *Vossische Zeitung,* 18 Aug. 1869, 19 Aug. 1869. See also Ross, *Failure of Bismarck's Kulturkampf,* 26–27.
119. *Vossische Zeitung,* 17 Aug. 1869.
120. *Kladderadatsch,* 15 Aug. 1869.
121. *Kladderadatsch,* 22 Aug. 1869.

1864 there were 5,259. In 1866 the number of monasteries had jumped to 481. The paper argued that the increasing number of male and female monastic institutions in Prussia was dangerous to the state (*staatsgefährlich*); the best defense was to strengthen the resolve of "free men and the Bürgertum."[122] Monasteries and the church, the paper demanded, must be countered with the manly virtues of Enlightenment liberal idealism: "If monks spread darkness and idiocy; spread light and knowledge! If the church preaches passivity and subjection; preach independence, manliness, freedom!"[123] The *Vossische Zeitung* preferred a more direct solution. Although there was nowhere a more tolerant people than those of Berlin, the paper explained, the slap delivered by the speech at the consecration of the chapel in Moabit must be met with a "balled fist."[124]

In the weeks following the "Moabiterklostersturm," as the incident became known, liberal and progressive community leaders tapped into and encouraged popular, street-level antimonasticism. They organized a series of public rallies and assemblies in order to obtain signatures for petitions demanding the abolition of monastic orders in Prussia.[125] At one such meeting, a speaker warned that the significance of the establishment of a monastery in Moabit should not be underestimated. He encouraged everyone to remember the efforts of the monks to take over the education of children. He was referring to an article in the *Berliner Wespen* that had argued that the "fat, indulgent monks," "the asses P. Francisco and P. Domino," intended with the assistance of the "Gray Sisters" to take over education in Moabit. According to the speaker, girls in particular were in danger, and he drew on the story of Sister Barbara in Cracow:

> The Gray Sisters will drill you well.
> They'll be mothers to you in the future.
> They'll flagellate themselves, pray, and then wall you in.[126]

The speaker pointed out that the monks had above all played on the hearts of women, manipulating them emotionally—and not without dire consequences.[127] Nuns who took over the position of the mother

---

122. *National Zeitung*, 25 Aug. 1869.
123. *National Zeitung*, 6 Sept. 1869.
124. *Vossische Zeitung*, 6 Sept. 1869.
125. Kissling, *Geschichte des Kulturkampfes* 1:330; Brück, *Geschichte der katholischen Kirche*, 283.
126. *Berliner Wespen*, 29 Aug. 1869.
127. *Vossische Zeitung*, 18 Aug. 1869.

and then abused her children and monks who preyed upon women undermined the authority of the father and broke apart the family. Similar antimonastic assemblies and petition drives were organized in other cities as well. At a rally of over five thousand in Dresden, for example, a resolution was passed declaring that "monastic life, because it is an obsolete and dangerously hierarchical institution, runs in every respect directly counter to the humane demands of our time." The resolution added, "medieval monasticism not only did not contribute to the individual's natural and reasonable growth . . . , it also decisively hindered it."[128] Across Germany, wherever antimonastic assemblies were held, Catholics tried their best to disrupt the proceedings. In Berlin, the public assemblies sponsored by Progressives became theaters of political combat. Catholics invented tactics that were later employed effectively against the rallies of political opponents during the Kulturkampf and then again throughout the rest of the century. Led by Missionsvikar Eduard Müller, Catholics packed the meetings, disrupted them with hisses and catcalls, and drowned out speakers with hymns. Where Catholics comprised the majority, they demanded the floor, called for a "podium election," installed their own chairman, and took charge of the meeting. At other antimonastic public assemblies where such tactics could not prevail, Catholics simply incited riots in order to force gendarmes to intervene and close down the meetings.[129]

Despite the impressive organization and effectiveness of the Catholic counterattack, liberal and progressive associations succeeded in drawing up twelve antimonastic petitions, eleven in Berlin and one in Elbing, to be sent to the Prussian parliament.[130] In the fall of 1869 these petitions recorded a new level of antimonastic hysteria at the same time that they also registered the demands for liberal modernity in Germany. Four separate petitions sponsored by the bookbinder Robert Krebs; Gustav Großmann; Röhr, May, and associates; and F. Romstädt demanded the abolition of all monasteries, ecclesiastical seminaries, and religious charitable institutions, Catholic and Protestant, without hesitation, as of 1 January 1870 and then "for all eternity." The petitions asked that no one ever again be allowed to assume the probationary position of a novitiate in preparation for monastic life. The petitions also recommended that monastic property and

128. *National Zeitung,* 22 Sept. 1869.

129. For tactics developed by Catholics to disrupt the meetings of political opponents, see Anderson, *Practicing Democracy,* 298–305.

130. The petitions are summarized and quoted in *SBHA,* Anlagen 2, 990–1007.

assets be appropriated by the state. Finally, the petitioners called for the revocation of the Prussian state's concordat with the papacy, the Circumscriptions Bull of 1821. One petition, representing a public assembly of citizens in Berlin, complained to Parliament that monasteries and nunneries had been for hundreds of years "hotbeds of superstition, sloth, and fornication" among the German people. Yet monasteries continued to exist despite the edict of 30 October 1810 prohibiting monastic orders. Despite "this century of freedom and work" they even continued to spread right under the eyes of the Kultusministerium.[131] Petitioners asserted that it was a matter of honor for all "thinking men" to work for the abolition of monasteries and the expulsion of the Jesuits by all legal means, and they expected the Prussian national deputies to do their duty.

Another set of petitions sponsored by Dr. Holthoff and associates, Ferdinand Benary and associates, master carpenter Rüthnick, Dr. Kache and associates, Schröder and associates, and Raaz and associates called upon the deputies to uphold the law according to the edict of 30 October 1810 and to forbid the establishment of any more monasteries, "not only those that are called by that name but also those that try to hide what they really are behind the names hospital, orphanage, etc."[132] The petition sponsored by Rüthnick asked Parliament to determine the legal status of monasteries within the monarchy. The petition insisted that monasteries were not independent associations but rather religious corporations not sanctioned by the edict of 30 October 1810. If Parliament determined that religious orders were not legally sanctioned according to the edict, then the "monastery" in Moabit should be closed. The petition from Elbing sponsored by Jachmann and associates argued that monasteries disturbed religious peace and unity. Further, "monasticism because of its religious views [*Anschauungen*] belongs to a bygone age no longer understandable to us. Monastic vows and monastic life are in complete contradiction with the spirit of our time, with the spirit of freedom and industriousness [*Arbeitsamkeit*]. The contemporary goal of the monasteries is to spread ultramontanism and papal authority."[133] As these petitions indicate, monasteries and monastic life provided affirmation of the tenets of modern identity. In these petitions as in the antimonastic campaign of the liberal press throughout Germany, the nation—social, economic,

131. Ibid., 990–91.
132. Ibid.
133. Ibid. 991.

and moral—was the antithesis of the monastery. Again the contrast may have been coarse, but antimonasticism was a powerful and comprehensive survey of the principles of bourgeois respectability and national character. With the monastery as the reference, a whole range of binary oppositions—sloth/industry, obsolescence/progress, fanaticism/reason, celibacy/family, prurience/propriety, subservience/freedom, medieval/modern—completed a vision of illegitimate/legitimate social and cultural order.

In the fall, these petitions were duly received by the Prussian parliament and directed in the regular manner to the Committee for Petitions. The situation was politically explosive. Catholic deputies in the Prussian parliament as well as the Catholic population in general feared the petitions would lead to a state crackdown on the independence of the church comparable to the "church reforms" in Baden. Bismarck himself appears not to have interfered in the committee's deliberations, though in 1869 he no doubt preferred to avoid a major confrontation in Parliament that would only further strain the cause of national unification.[134] The chair of the commission, Constanz von Saucken-Julienfelde, representing an electoral district in Gumbinnen, was a Progressive. The commission's vice chair and senior member, Professor Rudolf von Gneist, representing an election district in Düsseldorf, was a National Liberal. Gneist's attitude toward the whole affair and the petitions even before the committee received them was a foregone conclusion: among Catholics, he had become known as "Klosterstürmer-Gneist." A rabid anti-Catholic, he was later as a prominent Kulturkämpfer called by Adalbert Falk to the Kultusministerium and an important author of antichurch legislation. The committee was composed of twelve from liberal parties and seven from conservative parties. All deputies sitting on the committee were Protestant with the exception of Aloys Goeddertz, a Catholic and a member of the left center Freie Vereinigung, representing an election district in Cologne. As the most junior and least influential, he appears at the bottom of the list of deputy members of the committee.

The committee completed its work on 17 December 1869. Its seventeen-page double-column report offers insight into the attitude of the liberal leadership toward the monasteries and suggests its answer to the larger Catholic problem on the eve of the unification of Germany. Given the committee's predominant political and religious composition, the sentiments it expressed collectively sympathizing with the

---

134. Windell, *Catholics and German Unity,* 236–37.

petitions and condemning monasticism were no surprise.[135] The committee noted that antimonastic antipathy was principally directed not at religious philanthropic organizations but at mendicant monks and Jesuits. "The Franciscans and the Dominicans represent in any age the 'Freikorps of the papal army,' the Jesuits a 'Bodyguard.'" Even so, the committee based on a systematic account of state law evenhandedly refuted the petitions' arguments that the religious orders were not legally sanctioned. The committee confirmed current legislation, including the fundamental statute of the Catholic Church of 1821 and the constitution of 1850, that guaranteed the autonomy of Catholic religious orders in the monarchy. The report concluded that the allegation that a Franciscan and Dominican monastery had been established in Berlin was false. The monks had in fact established an orphanage for young boys. At the same time, the committee's recommendations to Parliament included the introduction of legislation proscribing the establishment of monasteries, religious orphanages, hospitals, and educational institutions in the future. Furthermore, the committee recognized "that in many ways legal regulation of the entire field of religious societies equally for all provinces seems desirable."[136] It concluded, therefore, that the government should secure the enactment of such legislation by the North German Confederation while taking measures immediately to eliminate inconsistencies in existing legislation.

On 8 February 1870, when the committee's report was placed on the agenda for debate in the Prussian parliament, the state's parliamentary spokesman, Count Bethusy-Huc, tried to table the report. He made an ardent plea that Parliament not throw the nation into endless religious turmoil. Nevertheless, on 9 February, the showdown Bismarck hoped to avoid on the floor of Parliament took place when Catholic deputies demanded that the report be addressed. Catholic deputies insisted that the report undermined the basic principles of the Prussian constitution that guaranteed the independence of the church. Hermann von Mallinckrodt, prominent leader of the Catholic deputies in Parliament, submitted a motion that the issue be placed at the top of the agenda for the session of the following day. He shouted that the report was a gauntlet thrown down at the feet of all Catholics and "we do not intend

135. For party and confessional affiliations of the Commission members see Schwarz, *MdR Biographisches Handbuch.*
136. *SBHA*, Anlagen 2, 1007.

to let it lie there."[137] Ludwig Windthorst rose and added, "In my long parliamentary life no document has ever been introduced that contained more provocative insults toward a large segment of the membership of the House and toward a large segment of the population of this country." A noisy demonstration immediately erupted on the floor. When order was restored and Windthorst could again command attention, he once more took up Mallinckrodt's warning: "We cannot permit the gauntlet that has been thrown at our feet to lie without regard."[138] Again Parliament broke into protests. After order was finally restored by the chair, Mallinckrodt's motion went down in defeat in a standing vote.

During the next few days, Catholic deputies backed off and then dropped the debate on the committee's report on the petitions relating to the Moabiterklostersturm. Much more, however, was made of the episode outside Parliament in the German Catholic political public. The antimonastic rioting in Berlin and its aftermath were among the principal reasons Catholic politicians and the religious leaders concluded that an organized political party was needed to protect Catholic interests. Within the next few months the task of reconstructing the Center Party in Prussia was taken up by Peter Reichensperger, Hermann von Mallinckrodt, Ludwig Windthorst, and others.[139] Meanwhile, in its report the Committee on Petitions had also indicated a measure of its own displeasure with the unseemly rioting against the monks and the destruction of property within Berlin, the seat of law and order in Prussia. The report in its very first sentence reproached the citizens of the city for their "uncivil excesses" associated with the opening of a Dominican "monastery" on 4 August 1869.[140] After the two decades of antimonastic hysteria that included the Ubryk affair and culminated in the violence of the Moabiterklostersturm, liberal notables recognized that they had to choose their anticlerical partners with a degree of circumspection. Dealing with the spread of convents and monasteries in Prussia—like the larger problem of Catholicism—could not be left as a matter for renegade mobs under the cover of night. Indeed, civil courts ordered the Berlin municipal authorities to compensate the Catholic Church the sum of 425 thalers for failing to

---

137. *SBHA,* 9 Feb. 1870, 2039–40.
138. Ibid., 2040–41.
139. Windell, *Catholics and German Unity,* 239.
140. *SBHA,* Anlagen 2, 1007.

sufficiently provide for the safety of the monks and their property.[141] The campaign against the church had to be orderly, led by elites, and prosecuted by appropriate legislation with the judicious application of state force. It was therefore the Moabiterklostersturm that provided the experience that served as the foundation for the liberals' partnership with the authoritarian power of the Bismarckian state in a Kulturkampf against Catholicism and the Catholic Church.

141. Ross, *Failure of Bismarck's Kulturkampf,* 27.

CHAPTER 4

The Women's Question, Anti-Catholicism, and the Kulturkampf

Historians have viewed the Kulturkampf of the 1870s not simply as an attempt to preserve the secular state from the reach of the Roman Catholic Church but alternately as a defensive campaign against the threat of political Catholicism, an attempt to rebuild the German nation after unification according to the precepts of high-cultural Protestantism, or a battle between the "modern" outlook of liberal nationalists and "backward" Catholics.[1] On the one hand, the Kulturkampf was a complex and broad enough campaign against the church to include all of these dimensions. On the other hand, these perspectives and even the composite picture they together provide exhaust neither the points of view nor the kinds of analyses needed to understand the significance of liberal anti-Catholicism in general and the origins of the Kulturkampf in particular. Several significant and interlinked issues and developments current in German society, culture, and politics in the decades after 1848 together gave the Kulturkampf its peculiar meaning and furor. These not only included the emergence of mass militant Catholicism, confessional rivalry, social and class tensions, and the political participation available to men with the new democratic franchise. They also included the liberal-bourgeois ideology of public and private, the revival of the women's movement, and the increasingly prominent and conspicuous role of women in the Catholic Church and Catholic life, all issues that have not received sufficient attention in the history of the Kulturkampf.

1. For these three arguments, see, first, Anderson, "The Kulturkampf"; idem, *Practicing Democracy;* idem, *Windthorst;* second, Smith, *German Nationalism;* and finally, Blackbourn, *Marpingen;* idem, "Progress and Piety."

Though these concurrent issues at first glance might seem unrelated, they were, in fact, so tightly interwoven in the attitude of middle-class liberals toward Catholics and Catholicism that they often became indistinguishable. The challenge is to unravel the close-knit themes and developments analytically, to explore the significance of the component strands, and then to reassemble the strands in order to appreciate the meaning and origin of the Kulturkampf in their complexity. This kind of analysis reveals that for German liberals, both progressives and nationalists, two new challenges to the bourgeois social, political, and sexual status quo—the revival of popular Catholicism during the 1850s and 1860s and the resurgence of the women's movement in the mid-1860s—were inextricably intertwined. The Catholic Church, personified as a woman, and Catholics, as they participated in the missions and practiced their faith in public, undermined the separate spheres of public and private, one reserved, according to liberal social and sexual ideology, for women in the life of the family and the other reserved for men in the world of social and political citizenship. In the estimation of liberal men, the problem of Catholicism was at the same time the problem of women in public. It followed that the Kulturkampf, the liberal attempt with the sponsorship of the state to solve the Catholic problem, was deeply enmeshed in the *Frauenfrage,* the women's question, that hotly debated issue involving the position of women in society and their access to work, public life, and ultimately politics. Roman Catholics, because they seemed irrational, dependent, and untrustworthy, were as unacceptable in the liberal vision of the modern nation as women, for the same reasons, were in the public sphere. Deeply inscribed in anti-Catholicism was, therefore, the sexism typical of the liberal middle class. To phrase it another way, for liberal Kulturkämpfer the issue with Roman Catholicism was never simply religious. It was biological, a matter of sex type, and the most ardent and dedicated among them revealed the strain of gynephobia and misogyny embedded in the anti-Catholic campaign.

In this analysis the Kulturkampf ultimately emerges as a Geschlechterkampf, a contest between men and women, for the public sphere during a period undergoing profound social and political transformation. Concentrating new light on the Kulturkampf from this angle permits a fresh evaluation of the origins of liberal anti-Catholicism in the period following the 1848 Revolution and of the meaning of the anti-Catholic campaign in the 1870s. It makes clear why liberals across the spectrum from left to right banded together with such dedication and fury with the incessant invocation of masculine bravado against the Catholic Church as a threat to middle-class social, political, and sexual hegemony. The confluence of several significant developments, including Catholic popular and political resurgence, the reemergence of the women's movement and the women's question, the democratic franchise and middle-class fears of mass culture, and finally German unification and with it fears of French revanchism, explains the timing of the Kulturkampf in the first decade of the new empire. This chapter is, therefore, the center and pivot point of our evaluation of liberal anti-Catholicism in the nineteenth century.

The Reemergence of the Women's Movement

Not only the popular Catholic revival but also the German women's movement had its origin in the decade of ideological, religious, and political fervor that culminated in the Revolution of 1848. The early German women's rights movement developed in the hundreds of dissenting separatist religious movements that emerged in both Catholic and Protestant congregations during the prerevolutionary period. The most successful of these new congregations was the movement first organized in 1845 under the leadership of an excommunicated priest, Johannes Ronge. Ronge and those who followed him called themselves *Deutschkatholiken,* German Catholics, as distinct from Roman Catholics. Initially, German Catholics mobilized to protest the popular pilgrimages encouraged by the papacy and conservative Catholic leaders in 1844 to the Holy Shroud at Trier. A half million pilgrims made the journey within the space of seven weeks to see the garment purportedly worn by Jesus on the cross, making this the largest of all similarly organized religious displays of the first half of the nineteenth century. This important watershed in the awakening of Catholic piety was regarded by German Catholics as a grotesque spectacle of humbug and stupidity. They coupled their disgust toward the Trier pilgrimages with a general resentment for the authoritarianism, ultramontanism, and anti-Enlightenment position of the Roman Catholic Church. In response German Catholics turned toward rationalism and Enlightenment principles and used them specifically to oppose clerical celibacy, the Latin mass, and auricular confession. Through their criticism of Roman Catholicism ran a current of Vormärz German patriotism. German Catholics were nationalist liberals, calling for the subordination of the Catholic Church to a unified and liberal German state.

Soon Protestants too joined the dissenting German Catholics because they were drawn by the energy of the movement and because they had become alienated from an Evangelical Church they believed had become too remote, conservative, and hierarchical. Together Catholic and Protestant dissenters broke off from the established churches and founded their own democratically run congregations. They devoted themselves to individual freedom of belief, humanist Christianity, confessional reconciliation, and the separation of church and state. The German Catholic movement grew most quickly in regions where Catholics were the minority in a mixed population or where the Roman Catholic Church failed to receive the support of secular authorities. Most of the early congregations were started in Saxony, but eventually more than half the congregations were located in Prussia. The largest German Catholic congregation was in Breslau in Prussia, where one thousand people signed a membership declaration of separation in early 1845 and over eight thousand joined the congregation by 1847. By contrast, there were only seven German-Catholic congregations in Catholic Baden by 1847. By 1848 the total membership in the German Catholic movement had grown to between one hundred thousand and one hundred fifty thousand, and it was rapidly becoming the largest protest movement of any sort in prerevolutionary Germany.[2] Everywhere dissenters enjoyed the support of many liberals who saw the dissenting movement as an opportunity to reopen political and social issues and to press forward demands for reform.

One study of the religious politics of gender in prerevolutionary Baden has argued that the feminism of the German-Catholic dissenters was not as radical as other historians have believed. Here the dissenting movement's call for women's emancipation was compromised by the politics of the private sphere and male sexual rights. In these conflicts, the dissenter's liberal male leadership continued to uphold the importance of marital union, the family, and the essential differences between men and women.[3] This should hardly come as a surprise given the prevailing social and cultural ideology of the Restoration and Vormärz. Even so, this study agrees with other work on the dissenting congregations that in several respects German Catholics experimented

2. Gould, *Origins of Liberal Dominance,* 74–75; Herzog, *Intimacy and Exclusion,* 3–4, 59–60, 85–87, 108–10.

3. Herzog, *Intimacy and Exclusion.* Compare to Sylvia Paletschek, *Frauen und Dissens: Frauen im Deutschkatholizismus und in den freien Gemeinden, 1842–1852* (Göttingen: Vandenhoeck und Ruprecht, 1990); and Catherine M. Prelinger, *Charity, Challenge, and Change: Religious Dimensions of the Mid–Nineteenth Century Women's Movement in Germany* (New York: Greenwood, 1987).

with egalitarianism.[4] In doing so, they made important contributions to the origins of the first organized women's movement in Germany. For example, dissenting congregations included full suffrage rights for women in congregational meetings, promoted the social emancipation of women, and demanded equal treatment of women before the law. Women in the German Catholic congregations also entered into public positions of prominence in fund-raising and philanthropy. The leadership exercised by German Catholic women was otherwise unheard of in mid-nineteenth-century German society. Louise Otto (later Otto-Peters), the most celebrated women's rights activist of nineteenth-century Germany and herself a member of a German Catholic congregation, believed that the prominence of women in the dissident movement constituted an invasion of the public of unprecedented importance for the emancipation of German women. In Hamburg, for example, German Catholic women organized the Hamburger Hochschule für das weibliche Geschlecht, a college that offered a secular higher education for women from all social classes and a bold, unique institution in the context of contemporary Germany.

During the 1840s the women's movement centered in the dissenting congregations shared in the enthusiasm for political and social emancipation that created the Revolution of 1848. The politicization of German society that came with the revolution only furthered the radicalization of women in the congregations. Many in fact now joined the demand for women's emancipation with the revolution's demands for political change and German unification. At the height of the revolution, new women's organizations were founded in many cities, dedicated not simply to charitable work but rather now to women's social, educational, and political rights, including the right to vote. After the defeat of the revolution and under the heel of the conservative reaction, however, the women's movement in Germany abruptly collapsed due to repression and censorship. The new Law of Association and Assembly of 1850 in Prussia forbade the participation of women in any meetings sponsored by political organizations or parties. Though in Baden, Hesse, Württemberg, the free Hansa city-states, and some of the smaller polities, association laws were not as restrictive, in other states such as Bavaria and Saxony the prohibitions against women at political clubs and assemblies at this time were even more severe. Throughout Germany, feminist newspapers folded and women's orga-

4. Paletschek, *Frauen und Dissens;* Prelinger, *Charity, Challenge, and Change.*

nizations shut down, and in Hamburg the Hochschule für das weibliche Geschlecht closed its doors.

Throughout the reactionary 1850s and into the early 1860s the organized women's movement was all but forgotten. It was not until the mid-1860s, during the breathing space offered by the New Era and the renewal of liberal pressures for political reform during the constitutional crisis with Bismarck, that the women's movement reemerged at the national level. New organizations took up and promoted demands specifically for middle-class women's rights to education and employment. The immediate impetus was the need to establish access to appropriate vocational and professional opportunities for the rising number of single bourgeois women who either could not be supported by their families or insisted now on assuming greater responsibility for themselves. In 1865 the Allgemeine Deutscher Frauenverein (ADF) or General German Women's Association was founded in Leipzig, organized and led by women who had been activists during the revolution, chief among them Louise Otto, who became the association's president. During its first years the membership of the ADF grew dramatically, and by the mid-1870s it reached eleven thousand. During the 1870s and 1880s and into the 1890s the ADF was the most important organization of the German women's movement. Soon after the founding of the ADF, the Verein zur Förderung der Erwerbsfähigkeit des weiblichen Geschlechts or the Association for the Advancement of the Employment Skills of the Female Sex was established in Berlin. For the sake of convenience it was called the Lette Association after its founder and chairman, Wilhelm Adolf Lette, a national liberal, onetime representative to the Frankfurt National Assembly, and later a deputy in the Prussian parliament. The Lette Association promoted the vocational and professional education of women and demanded the removal of all obstacles and prejudices curtailing their employment. In 1869 it helped women's organizations in Berlin, Bremen, Breslau, Brunswick, Kassel, Karlsruhe, Darmstadt, Mainz, Hamburg, and Rostock join together to found the Verband deutscher Frauenbildungs- und Erwerbsvereine, the Union of German Women's Educational and Employment Associations.[5]

In contrast to the women's organizations that had close ties to the democratic and liberal movements of 1848–49, the ADF, now under

5. Ute Frevert, *Women in German History: From Bourgeois Emancipation to Sexual Liberation,* trans. Stuart McKinnon-Evans (New York: Berg, 1989), 117.

the threat of the Law of Association and Assembly, steered clear of any affiliation with political parties and organizations. While the ADF pressed for wider social emancipation for women, it assiduously avoided a political program. The ADF leadership concluded that it was premature to press for women's suffrage, and the demand for equal political rights that had been raised by women's rights activists in 1848 was set aside at least for the time being. It accepted the notion that women had to prove themselves worthy of the vote through educational and professional progress. Here feminism was circumscribed by a liberal ideology that postulated that citizenship rights, including the franchise, were not inherent to the individual. Instead political citizenship was a responsibility that one exercised only after acquiring the characteristics of sufficient social and cultural maturity: education and independence, both manifested in the ownership of property. Leaders therefore believed that for the present it was necessary for the organization to devote itself to the improvement of women's education and to vocational and professional opportunities, especially medicine, and to charitable work directed toward working-class young women. Initially the Lette Association expressly rejected political rights for women. The first report of the association in 1866 stated that nothing could be further from its aims than the "so-called emancipation for women in the social not to mention the political sphere."[6] After the death of Adolf Lette in 1868, however, the Lette Association moved toward the position of the ADF on the issue of women's political rights. It no longer categorically rejected women's suffrage but rather argued that women should gradually and patiently move toward the right to vote after having first achieved the right to employment and education. By 1876 the ADF and the Lette Association had signed a joint declaration outlining their similar views on women's suffrage. It was not until 1894, however, that the women's organizations began to agitate for suffrage.

In other respects as well the activists who revived the women's movement broke from the feminist theory and praxis of the Vormärz and 1848. They stressed that the women's movement was not now a campaign in the service of personal, individual "emancipation" but rather of humanity and social reform. Leaders of the women's movement insisted that they neither advocated "free love" nor challenged the primacy of marriage and the family. They distanced themselves from the

6. Quoted in ibid.

caricature of the emancipated women and offered assurances that they neither dressed like men nor smoked cigars.[7] It is tempting to regard the insistence of the new women's movement on the "natural vocation" of women as mothers and wives and the reluctance of women activists to assert a full equal-rights ideology as acquiescence before the authoritarian state and as timidity toward the class to which most of them belonged.[8] Feminist goals were, however, not simply limited to the expansion of educational and professional opportunities. Many feminists of the 1860s and 1870s believed that their right to education and employment was linked ideologically to their right to join actively and productively in the public concerns of society and the nation.[9] They believed that the participation of women in social service was a duty of citizenship comparable to military service for men. These feminists, therefore, insisted on the interdependence of the family and nation, or private and public spheres; they connected motherhood in the home with their role in the nation understood as the "great social household." They argued that modern society with its industrial traumas, working-class malaise, housing shortages, mounting alcoholism, and rampant prostitution had become callous, masculine, and dehumanizing. Modern society, they therefore believed, required the emotional attendance and maternal ministering of women. Women activists believed that it was the cultural task of women to contribute their humanity to the inhuman world of men. On the other hand, however, the lone radicals Hedwig Dohm and Lily Braun refused to be bound by a movement based on women's "natural" virtues and talents and never abandoned the demand for women's equal political rights.

While the reorganized women's movement that emerged in the mid-1860s was fundamentally different from the radical feminism of the revolution, it did push what contemporaries called the women's question to the forefront of national attention.[10] The women's question unleashed an impassioned debate, and in the mid-1860s and for the rest

7. Herrad-Ulricke Bussemer, *Frauenemanzipation und Bildungsbürgertum: Sozialgeschichte der Frauenbewegung in der Reichsgründungszeit* (Weinheim and Basel: Beltz Verlag, 1985), 22.

8. Richard J. Evans, *The Feminist Movement in Germany, 1894–1933* (New Brunswick: Rutgers University Press, 1976); Bussemer, *Frauenemanzipation.*

9. Ann Taylor Allen, *Feminism and Motherhood in Germany, 1800–1914* (New Brunswick: Rutgers University Press, 1991). See also Frevert, *Women in German History,* 126.

10. For a discussion of the topologies of feminism in Germany, see Richard J. Evans, "The Concept of Feminism: Notes for Practicing Historians," in *German Women in the Eighteenth and Nineteenth Centuries: A Social and Literary History,* ed. Ruth-Ellen B. Jones and Mary Jo Maynes (Bloomington: Indiana University Press, 1986), 247–58.

of the century it was on everyone's lips. Already in 1866 Louise Otto could happily claim, "In the political doldrums in which we currently live the women's question has leaped into the foreground. It now dominates to such an extent no one earlier would have thought imaginable. No one can pick up a newspaper, no association, no meeting can take place in which the question is not discussed."[11] Within the women's movement, novelists Emma Laddey wrote *Auf eigenen Füssen* (On her own feet) and *Aus freier Wahl: Charakterbilder aus dem Frauenleben* (By free choice: Character portraits from the lives of women), and Wilhelmine von Hilleren wrote *Aus freier Kraft* (By her own means), novels that proffered, as their titles indicated, positive alternatives to the roles traditionally prescribed to women.[12] Meanwhile exasperated social critics complained:

Women's question!—women's association!!—women's emancipation!!!—Everywhere, at all social gatherings and at just about every public assembly, these themes are constantly debated with genuine passion. All the political and literary magazines are rushing to print articles about them. Women have already set up an entire series of journals dedicated to the "representation of their interests." An avalanche of books and brochures all concerning the "burning question" of "women's emancipation" has overwhelmed the literary market. They want to examine it from historical, physiological, legal, and God-only-knows-what other perspectives.

Enough, this "emancipation" is a theory as laughable as it is impractical like all the other theories of the communists and the socialists. Beyond this laughable aspect, however, "emancipation" also has a very serious and dangerous side about which we should not remain quiet particularly as it concerns women. The ultimate consequence is namely nothing less than *the abolition of marriage and the destruction of the family.* (Emphasis in the original.)[13]

---

11. Louise Otto-Peters, "Altes und Neues aus der Frauenwelt I," *Deutsches Wochenblatt,* Nr. 8, 18 Feb. 1866, 60, cited in Bussemer, *Frauenemanzipation,* 16.

12. Emma Laddey, *Auf eigenen Füssen: Erzählungen* (Stuttgart, 1870); idem, *Aus freier Wahl: Charakterbilder aus dem Frauenleben* (Stuttgart, 1874); Wilhelmine von Hilleren, *Aus eigenen Kraft,* 3 vols. (Leipzig, 1872). See Bussemer, *Frauenemanzipation,* 20.

13. Otto Glagau, "Gegen die 'Frauenemancipation' I," *Der Bazar,* Nr. 22, 8 June 1870, 181; idem, "Gegen die 'Frauenemancipation' II," *Der Bazar,* Nr. 24, 23 April 1870, 196; quoted in Bussemer, *Frauenemanzipation,* 14–15, 54.

Since middle-class women by the end of the eighteenth century were not only confined in fact to the private household but also served as the personification of domesticity, the women's question challenged traditional family order and potentially threatened to undermine gendered public and private spheres, the central ideological cornerstone of nineteenth-century bourgeois society. Women activists affirmed the "natural" role of woman as wives, but the claim that women belonged also in the public was of particular concern to bourgeois associations and liberal newspapers and journals. During the 1850s and early 1860s the liberal press had not given any attention to women's issues, but now an intense debate about women's education and work took place on its pages. The *Vossische Zeitung* continuously ran reports about the debates concerning the women's question taking place in various organizations, the establishment of the Lette Association, female vocational training and education, the women's suffrage movement in the United States, and the advantages and disadvantages of women's emancipation.

By 1869, when the attention of the nation was fixed on the intensity of the Catholic missionary campaign and then riveted on the fate of Sister Barbara in the dungeon, the women's question had become an explosive topic. In that year appeared John Stuart Mill's *On the Subjection of Women,* which was immediately made available to the German public in a translation by Jenny Hirsch, cofounder of the ADF and leader of the Lette Association. Mill made a forceful case for the full equality of women, including the right to vote, and attacked the claim that women were predetermined by nature for matrimony and motherhood. Mill even went so far as to argue that "what is now called the nature of women is an eminently artificial thing—the result of forced repression in some directions, unnatural stimulation in others."[14] Mill denied that "anyone knows, and can know, the nature of the two sexes, as long as they have only been seen in their present relation to one another."[15] His previous works on women's emancipation and women's right to vote had attracted little attention in Germany in the context of the 1850s and early 1860s, but with the reorganization of the women's movement such revolutionary views sent a shock wave through the public debate of the women's question. His message did not merely challenge men of any political disposition; it challenged lib-

14. John Stuart Mill, *On Liberty with The Subjection of Women and Chapters on Socialism,* ed. Stefan Collini (Cambridge: Cambridge University Press, 1989), 138.
15. Ibid.

erally inclined women, whose activism in comparison to Mill's views seemed to fall well short both in theory and practice.

Mill, the leading authority on liberalism across the English Channel in the home of classical liberalism, now became the point of departure for any debate concerning, in particular for feminists, the orientation of the women's movement and, in general for the larger public, the role of women in contemporary society. Across Germany, liberals were now forced to respond to Mill and to articulate their views concerning women in marriage, family, public, politics, and society. Even so, the debate remained largely one sided. Positive liberal responses were confined to the call for the improvement of vocational and professional opportunities for unwed women who might contribute their otherwise unused labor for the good of the national economy. Liberal men from the left to the right, with the exception of a notable few like Franz von Holtzendorff, cochairman of the Lette Association, overwhelmingly rejected outright the notion that women were autonomous individuals, defined not simply by marriage and the family but entitled to equal social, legal, political, and citizen rights. The well-respected liberal progressive social reformer Arwed Emminghaus, who otherwise believed that the women's question had the potential to revitalize the educational system, dismissed Mill's demands for the full social and political emancipation of women as an English problem, one that in Germany had long since been settled.[16] On the issue of women, Mill was just as easily dismissed by other German liberals on the right. Upon Mill's death in 1873, Heinrich von Treitschke callously reduced his life to two sentences: "He had an atrocious bluestocking for a wife with whom I couldn't have lived for eight days. She impressed the good-natured fellow, but then he came to the ridiculous idea that women should be equal to men."[17] Authoritative, never at a loss for an opinion, and with a particular penchant for summation, Treitschke delivered the final German liberal verdict on Mill.[18]

16. Bussemer, *Frauenemanzipation*, 69.

17. Quoted in Ute Frevert, *"Mann und Weib, und Weib und Mann": Geschlechter-Differenzen in der Moderne* (Munich: C. H. Beck, 1995), 96.

18. Joan Wallach Scott has argued in the context of the conflict between nineteenth-century liberalism and feminism that "feminist claims revealed the limits of the principles of liberty, equality, and fraternity and raised doubts about their universal applicability." Joan Wallach Scott, *Only Paradoxes to Offer: French Feminists and the Rights of Man* (Cambridge: Harvard University Press, 1996), xi. In nineteenth-century Germany, the relationships and tensions between liberalism and feminism still remain remarkably understudied topics. For an exception and important start, see Herzog, *Intimacy and Exclusion.* For a study of social and institutionalized antifeminism during the Wilhelmine period, see Ute Planert, *Antifeminismus im Kaiserreich* (Göttingen: Vandenhoeck und Ruprecht, 1998).

Kulturkämpfer, the Women's Question, and Misogyny

Numerous historians in recent years have shown that the ideology of gender difference was fundamental to nineteenth-century middle-class identity—not just in Germany but throughout the West.[19] A review of the revival of the women's movement for access to the public in Germany has, however, served to set the context in which to recognize that the link between gender and Catholicism was embedded in German liberals' social, cultural, and political self-understanding. While in Germany the connection between anti-Catholicism and fears of women in public has not been adequately identified by historians of culture and society, it is an important key to understanding the nature of liberalism and the origins of the Kulturkampf.[20] Closer inspection

19. There is a large body of literature on the public sphere as theorized by Jürgen Habermas in *Strukturwandel der Öffentlichkeit: Untersuchungen zu einer Kategorie der bürgerlichen Gesellschaft* (Neuwied: Luchterhand, 1962). An accessible introduction to his original argument is idem, "The Public Sphere," *New German Critique* 3 (1974): 49–55. For a broad theoretical and historical critique of the public space since Habermas's original conceptualization see the contributions in Craig Calhoun, ed., *Habermas and the Public Sphere* (Cambridge: MIT Press, 1992). The long tradition in Western thought of assigning men and women to public and private spheres is outlined in Jean Bethke Elshtain, *Public Man, Private Woman: Women in Social and Political Thought* (Princeton: Princeton University Press, 1981). As an example of the ideological foundation of politics and theoretical division between public and domestic, see Linda J. Nicholson, "John Locke: The Theoretical Separation of the Family and the State," in *Gender and History: The Limits of Social Theory in the Age of the Family* (New York: Columbia University Press, 1986), 133–66.

For a discussion in the German context of the division of men and women according to the alleged natural and unalterable characteristics of their sex, see Karin Hausen, "Family and Role-Division: The Polarisation of Sexual Stereotypes in the Nineteenth Century; An Aspect of the Dissociation of Work and Family Life," in *The German Family: Essays on the Social History of the Family in Nineteenth- and Twentieth-Century Germany,* ed. Richard J. Evans and W. R. Lee (Totowa, N.J.: Barnes and Noble, 1981), 51–83; and idem, "Öffentlichkeit und Privatheit: Gesellschaftspolitische Konstruktionen und die *Geschichte der Geschlechterbeziehugen,"* in *Frauengeschichte-Geschlechtergeschichte,* ed. Karin Hausen and H. Wunder (Frankfurt am Main: Campus, 1996), 81–88. See also Frevert, *"Mann und Weib."* For German middle-class male and female roles and relations, see the following in *Bürgerinnen und Bürger: Geschlechterverhältnisse im 19. Jahrhundert,* ed. Ute Frevert (Göttingen: Vandenhoeck und Ruprecht, 1988): Ute Frevert, "Bürgerliche Meisterdenker und das Geschlechterverhältnis: Konzepte, Erfahrungen, Visionen an der Wende vom 18. zum 19. Jahrhundert," 17–48; Karin Hausen, "'. . . eine Ulme für das schwankende Efeu': Ehepaare im Bildungsbürgertum; Ideale und Wirklichkeiten im späten 18. und 19. Jahrhundert," 85–117; and Yvonne Schütze, "Mütterliebe-Vaterliebe: Elternrollen in der bürgerlichen Familie des 19 Jahrhundert," 118–33.

20. For an important start and point of departure for an analysis of liberal attitudes toward Catholicism and women in Germany see the comments in Hugh McLeod, "Weibliche Frömmigkeit—männlicher Unglaube? Religion und Kirchen im bürgerlichen 19. Jahrhundert," in *Bürgerinnen und Bürger: Geschlechterverhaltnisse im 19. Jahrhundert,* ed. Ute Frevert (Göttingen: Vandenhoeck und Ruprecht, 1988), 134–56, esp. 143; and Blackbourn, *Marpingen,* 261–63.

reveals that for German liberals the women's question and the "Catholic problem" were one and the same. Their attitude toward women was necessarily an expression of their attitude toward Catholics. It was no mere coincidence, therefore, that leading liberals from the political left across to the right were as agitated by and outspoken on the topic of women in public as they were about the Catholic Church, "Jesuitism," monasticism, and ultramontanism. Prominent Kulturkämpfer like the progressive Rudolf Virchow and educational reformer Jürgen Bona Meyer and nationalist liberals like Heinrich von Sybel and Johann Bluntschli, for example, all came publicly forward in the debate on the women's question. Their positions were clear: they were ardent opponents of women's emancipation, and from the left across to the right they offered cogent and representative liberal attitudes toward the feminist movement. Taken together their views suggest what was at stake in the liberal animus toward Roman Catholicism and the Catholic Church.

Rudolf Virchow—leader of the Progressive Party in the Prussian parliament, world-renowned pathologist, and the one who later coined the term *Kulturkampf*—immediately attacked the emergence of the women's movement in 1865 with the publication of *Über die Erziehung des Weibes für seinen Beruf.* Typical of his bourgeois society, Rudolf Virchow believed it was self-evident, an axiom of nature, that men participate in the public sphere while women remain at home. He argued that it was a mistake to think that women should "enter the market of public life and actively participate in the disputes of the day."[21] Only in the home as wives and mothers could women serve the fatherland and humanity. It was the duty of the wife to preserve the home as an enclave of harmony, stability, and peace, a sanctuary to which men could return after fighting the day-to-day battles of public life. The emancipation of women from the home, Virchow argued, could lead only to the destruction of the family and to communal rearing of children. He argued that the entire future of the human race was threatened by the emancipation of women from their assigned role as caretakers of the home.

Virchow was joined from the liberal right by the historian Heinrich von Sybel, editor of the prestigious *Historische Zeitschrift,* in 1874 founder with colleagues at the University of Bonn of the anti-Catholic Deutscher Verein (German Association), and later author of *Die Begründung des Deutschen Reiches durch Wilhelm I,* the official history

21. Rudolf Virchow, *Über die Erziehung des Weibes für seinen Beruf* (Berlin: T. C. F. Enslin, 1865).

of the founding of the German Empire. Sybel was spurred to action by Mill's radicalism, and he led the liberal counterattack with the publication in 1870 of "Über die Emancipation der Frauen." Sybel explained that the belief in the equality of the sexes, the demand that women not be viewed and treated differently by law and by society, was though regrettable not surprising. It was a consequence of the democratic spirit of the age. However popular, the campaign for equal rights for women amounted to throwing sand against the wind: the separation of male and female *Lebenssphäre* (spheres of life) outside and inside the family was an immutable law of nature. The raising of children had to be a task left to the wife for the self-evident reason that "the crude hand" of the father was useless. A career for the mother outside the home would lead to the demise of her health, the destruction of the household, the ruin of her children, and the betrayal of the entire purpose of her existence. While "the mother must care for the children and the house and for nothing else," the husband attended to affairs outside the home and represented the family in public, "engaging in the battle of life with the weapons of the law."[22] If, according to Sybel, the wife was the "living soul" of the house, the husband as "the logician and dialectician" was its master. The separate spheres of life and duty were the consequence of the fact that women were sentimental, not reasonable, beings. In women nature has substituted "the methodological development of reason" with "an innately fine and quick total sentimentalism."[23] While women rely on their immediate feelings to form impressions, men make judgments based on logic and reasoned discussion in public. Bourgeois liberals relied on the general principle that the more an occupation required the capacity for reason, the less appropriate it was for women.

Sybel allowed that some women because of their talent for caretaking might contribute to medical and religious charitable work. But the woman who attempted the professions of philosophy, law, politics, economics, industry, literature, or journalism was a hermaphrodite, the image of the woman, dressed in man's clothing and smoking a cigar, an embarrassment to the family, to the public, and to the state. According to Sybel, a professional woman was a *Männin,* a she-man who was "worth precisely as much to the world as the *weiblicher Mann*

22. Heinrich von Sybel, "Über die Emancipation der Frauen," in *Vorträge und Aufsätze* (Berlin: A. Hoffmann, 1874), 59–79, quotations at 67 and 69.
23. Ibid., 70.

[effeminate man]."[24] Since the husband represented the wife, whose interests were supposed to be identical, and women were unfit for public responsibility, it followed that granting women political rights was both redundant and harmful to the state. Sybel despised democratic systems that presumed "mere birth" as the qualification for the vote. In 1867, as a member of the parliament of the North German Confederation, he had voted against the universal, direct, equal male franchise. The error of the suffrage of the North German Confederation was that it now compelled one to concede on principle that a right granted to "the most stupid cobbler's helper and crudest Negro" could not be denied to an educated woman.[25] Johann Bluntschli echoed the argument that suffrage for women would be both "dangerous for the state and ruinous for women."[26] Liberal men could not imagine the politicization without the defeminization of women. In the shock following the introduction of universal male suffrage in 1867, Robert von Mohl, the liberal professor of civil law, also warned against the tendency to go to extremes and tear down all the dams that experience and reason had erected. If nothing could be done to prevent universal male suffrage, he argued, one could at least prevent even more damage by preventing the vote for women.[27]

Jürgen Bona Meyer, the respected proponent of progessive educational reform, also took up the women's question in the series Frauengeist und Frauenbildung, which appeared in the liberal literary journal *Gegenwart* in 1872.[28] In contrast to Sybel, Meyer argued that women did not lack the capacity for logical reasoning. It was rather, he explained, their incapacity to discipline their excessive emotions that

24. Ibid., 73.

25. Ibid., 74. Suggesting that "even less-democratic liberals recognized feminism's link with liberal ideology," Amy Hackett not only conflates democratic and liberal ideology but on this point also seriously misjudges Heinrich von Sybel, who she argues was "torn between his liberal premises and his prejudices about women and the overwhelming majority of liberals during the 1870s and 80s." Amy Hackett, "Feminism and Liberalism in Wilhelmine Germany, 1890–1918," in *Liberating Women's History: Theoretical and Critical Essays,* ed. Berenice A. Carroll (Urbana: University of Illinois Press, 1976), 127–36, see 129.

26. Johann Caspar Bluntschli, ed., *Deutsches Staatswörterbuch* (Stuttgart: Expedition des Staatswörterbuch, 1857–70), 11:130.

27. Robert von Mohl, *Politik* (Tübingen: H. Laupp, 1869), 2:20. For liberal opposition to women's political rights, see Frevert, "*Mann und Weib,*" 109–25.

28. Jürgen Bona Meyer, Frauengeist und Frauenbildung, *Gegenwart* 1 (1872): 182–84, 323–25; 2 (1872): 85–87, 101–2. Meyer was also the author of *Zum Bildungskampf unserer Zeit* (Bonn: Adolf Marcus, 1875) and *Der Wunderschwindel in unserer Zeit* (Bonn: Max Cohen und Sohn, 1878).

made them unsuitable for participation in public life. Suggesting a considerable amount about the bourgeois persona in public, Meyer explained, "Given the pressures of bürgerlich and state professions . . . it is often necessary that the will, without feelings, even in opposition to feelings, do what cold duty or naked necessity requires."[29] Unlike men, who are able to check their emotions, he argued, women have more irritable nervous systems and more excitable passions, which impair their capacity for clear and sustained thought. The strict separation of male and female *Arbeitsgebiete* (spheres of work) was required to quarantine within the household the inability of women to master their emotions. The work of the state, of science, of law and art, liberal men like Meyer agreed, required decisions based on rational disputation. In opposition to women's rights activists, who argued that the nation, "the great social household," urgently needed an infusion of feminine virtues, Meyer believed that the progress of civilization, culture, and the nation depended on a public life without the distraction of both unseemly and debilitating feminine sentiment. Only in the home could the woman as mother and wife profitably contribute her natural sense of harmony and beauty. The predisposition of women for sentiment and emotion also meant that they were by nature more inclined to religion than men, who, due to their even temper, remained for the most part religiously indifferent.

What is interesting for our purposes is not the ideology of separate spheres itself, which has already sustained an entire generation of research on nineteenth-century society and, in fact, is now so well established in historical literature that it has become an integral part of the master narrative of the West, but more specifically the coupling of this ideology with anti-Catholicism in Germany. As prominent Kulturkämpfer defended the ideology of separate spheres against the radicalism of the women's movement, they made sense of the state and the church in terms of gender and the relationship between genders. For example, in a set of widely read essays in the *Gegenwart,* Johann Bluntschli, dedicated anti-Catholic and fanatical Jesuit hater, argued that in the Catholic feudal ages the church was understood as the soul and the state as the body of one being, a notion, he believed, still propagated among the people by the Jesuits. In the modern period, however, the church and the state had separated and become two separate bodies. Just as all human beings were by nature either male or female, it followed that the state and church were two different sexes. What

29. Meyer, Frauengeist und Frauenbildung, Gegenwart I (1872): 323–25.

science had only belatedly discovered in the modern period, Bluntschli patiently explained, language had long ago recognized: in the languages of modern Europe the state is gendered masculine (e.g., *der Staat, l'état, el estádo, il stato*) and the church feminine (e.g., *die Kirche, l'église, la iglesia, la cheisa*).[30] Like other liberal men, Bluntschli believed the state was "defined by an inherently masculine will" and endowed with "the self-confident, masculine *Volksgeist*."[31] Conservatives agreed that of course the state was male: political offices of authority could only be occupied and administered by men.

As liberals coded public life and the state as masculine, they coded the domestic sphere and Catholicism as feminine. The church just like a woman was inclined toward revelation and sentiment rather than knowledge and thinking.[32] In the war with the Catholic Church and the forces of militant ultramontanism, the enemies of all modern culture, science, Bildung, liberalism, and progress, Bluntschli warned that the state must remember that the church uses her feminine wiles to exploit the weaknesses of her opponent to her advantage.[33] If the state is a man, he argued, then the church is like a woman, or more precisely a vamp, who gives the appearance of innocence yet knows full well how to sway a man now one way with her charms, now another way with her tears. She may no longer have enough power to launch a holy crusade as she did in the Middle Ages, but she has become "a very fashionable lady" who can still whip up confusion within the state.[34] Liberals like Bluntschli liked therefore to think about the relationship between the state and the church as a dyad, a man and a woman, locked in a dysfunctional and tension-ridden competition, a condition they believed surely not the fault of the man. It was impossible for liberals to think about the relationship at least under the circumstances as a healthy and supportive marriage between equals or as a relationship between a brother and a sister, naturally bound by mutual respect if not affection.

30. Johann Caspar Bluntschli, "Deutsche Briefe über das Verhältniss von Staat und Kirche: Der Dualismus von Staat und Kirche," *Gegenwart* 1 (1872): 81–82; idem, "Deutsche Briefe über Staat und Kirche: Der Staat als Geisteswesen," *Gegenwart* 1 (1872): 97–98. See also idem, *Über den Unterschied der mittelalterlichen und der modernen Staatsidee* (Munich: Literarisch-artistische Anstalt, 1855), 15–16.

31. Bluntschli, "Über das Verhältniss des modernen Staates zur Religion," in *Gesammelte Kleine Schriften* (Nördlingen: C. H. Beck, 1881), 2:148–80, quotation at 154.

32. Bluntschli, "Deutsche Briefe über der Verhältniss von Staat und Kirche." See also idem, "Über das Verhältniss des modernen Staates zur Religion," 174.

33. Bluntschli, *Charakter und Geist der politischen Parteien* (Nördlingen: C. H. Beck, 1869), 50.

34. Ibid.

At the same time, if the Catholic Church was an aging lady, then liberalism was a young man, assertive and in the prime of life. The model was again offered by Bluntschli, who argued in his widely read *Charakter und Geist der politischen Parteien* that liberalism was "a young man, who has his formal education behind him and steps forward into life fully aware of his strength and self-confidence."[35] He has abandoned speculation and fantasies for logical discourse: he tests the ground on which he stands and upon which he plans to build with scientific criticism and precision. He is equally mature, seasoned by experience. Liberalism, Bluntschli explains, is no revolutionary. He has no desire to tear things down or to be contrary. He is interested, rather, foremost in the pursuit of truth. According to Bluntschli, the liberal man lives his life energetically organizing, testing, evaluating, improving, or discarding. Liberalism is tireless, looks carefully, and then moves incessantly forward, and unlike reckless radicalism he patiently prepares the present for the future. While he supports legitimate and necessary authority, blind obedience to absolute authority is incompatible with his character. If he must choose revolt for the sake of progress as a final resort, he will restore social and political order based on law as quickly as possible. For Protestant national liberals like Bluntschli, Luther in his battle against the pope and against the hierarchy of the bishops was the best model of liberalism that ultimately had been driven to revolt against the tyrannical authority of the pope. Indeed, in the face of the condemnation of modern liberalism by Pope Pius IX in the Syllabus of Errors, Bluntschli was sure that Christ himself, when he came again to save the world and pronounce the final judgment, would be a liberal.

Above all, liberalism was distinguished by his strength of character and his desire for independence and freedom properly understood. For true liberalism freedom was not some abstract notion, a "mathematical equality" espoused by the radicals of the French Revolution. Freedom was organically rooted in the personality of the individual. Even so, the liberal is not merely given his freedom as a gift. He earns his freedom through the experience of life and through his dedication to Bildung. Liberalism loathes the notion that "a mindless mass of humanity ruled by superstitions" could ever be as free as "a manly *Volk* exercising thought and will."[36] Bluntschli admitted that in public life liberals were still at the beginning of their development, but no one could deny the progress of liberalism within the respective liberal par-

---

35. Ibid., 119.
36. Ibid., 128.

ties. The experience of defeat in 1848 had only deepened and broadened liberalism. The settlement and alliance with Bismarck in 1867 following the constitutional crisis and the first wars of unification against Denmark and then against Austria had proven the mature development of liberal practice and theory since the revolution. It was the hard lessons of Realpolitik and the association with Bismarck that had strengthened liberal politics for the better, conditioned it into greater exertions of masculinity: "the spirit and character of the liberal parties became more manly."[37]

At the center of liberal anti-Catholicism was, therefore, not religion but biology, not mere religious intolerance but a more fundamental sexism. Due to their incapacity for sustained, disciplined thought, women were seen as more susceptible than men to the irrationalism, excessive emotion, and superstitious nonsense of Roman Catholicism and the Catholic Church. Stories endlessly circulated about the influence that the clergy was able to exert on unsuspecting and innocent young women. Such fears were only confirmed by Prussian state authorities, who were particularly concerned about the Jesuits' alleged control over Catholic women. At Aachen, Police President Hirsch reported to District Governor Friedrich Kühlwetter that in the congregational assemblies of the parish churches, Jesuits were competing against the local clergy for the loyalty of the women. Jesuits, he reported, were "applying all their oratorical skill to win over the members for themselves. . . . They are especially training their attention on the women in the congregation."[38]

If Jesuits thought that there was little hope of winning over the husband, liberals and state authorities believed they turned to the "weaker sex" as the back door to the family. In 1848 liberals had fought the monarchy in the streets and on the barricades; now in the battle with the church, according to the liberal journal *Grenzboten,* "the woman is the barricade behind which the priest takes cover if he cannot reach the husband directly."[39] According to liberal newspapers, journals, books, and pamphlets, Jesuits coaxed women in the confessional into revealing the secrets of the family and then used their confidence and intimacy to sever the bonds of loyalty between wives and husbands and daughters and families. Women were then recruited as the church's

37. Ibid., 132.

38. LHAK, Best. 403, Nr. 7511, PP Hirsch, Aachen, to RP Köhlwetter, Aachen, 10 Oct. 1865. Also HSTAD, Best. RA, P, Nr. 1239, PP, Aachen, to RP Kühlwetter, Aachen, 10 Oct. 1865.

39. *Grenzboten* 1 (1875): 72.

"spies within the family." It was, therefore, not merely the zealous proselytizing of the Jesuits that made them such hated enemies but their "crude exploitation of the weakness of the female sex" and their "peace-destroying interference in the life of the family," the foundation of bourgeois order.[40] "Woe to the man to whom the Jesuits are not well disposed; it is a matter that concerns the peace of his house."[41] The woman who shared his bed might be an agent of the Jesuits, and her husband might imagine he was literally sleeping with the enemy, a sexual anxiety peculiar to liberal Jesuitphobia. The *Vossische Zeitung* reported as a warning: "Wherever the Jesuits showed up, they sowed discord within the family circle; society was thrown off the track of progress and Bildung declined."[42]

As an example of the malicious influence of Jesuits on impressionable young women and of their ability to turn daughters against fathers, one writer related the story of a merchant's daughter who attended confession at a Jesuit mission. The eternal damnation with which the confessor had threatened her had, according to the account, a deep and destructive impact on her psyche. Her anxiety only increased with each visit. Worried about the condition of his daughter, the father pleaded with her not to go to the mission so often. "You're Satan. Stay away from me!" she screamed. Her mental derangement led her to the insane asylum. Several days later she threw herself out of the window to her death.[43] The paterfamilias believed he not only had to do battle in the professional and civic contests of daily public life; he also had to safeguard his family and private life against the Jesuits who threatened to destroy it from the inside out. Destroying the family was, according to liberals, only the means to the end. The real goal of the Jesuits was the usurpation of the state. An example is again Johann Bluntschli's belief that "the indirect influence of many confessors and court priests on administration and policy is still prevalent in many states. If they do not manage to win over the heads of state themselves, they often know how to stir the female heart and to use women to rule over men."[44]

From the perspective of the gendered discourse of Catholicism and liberalism, the war between liberals and the Catholic Church takes on

40. Stachelstock, *Licht und Finsterniß,* 36.
41. Ibid., 69.
42. *Vossische Zeitung,* 7 Aug. 1869.
43. Stachelstock, *Licht und Finsterniß,* 78–79.
44. Bluntschli, "Über das Verhältniss des modernen Staates zur Religion," 155.

the dimensions of a more fundamental conflict between men and women for access to the public and the defense of the private. The historian of nineteenth-century German liberalism Dieter Langewiesche has pointed out that according to liberals, women were not among those in the population who could become, either now or in the future, emancipated and independent members of bourgeois society, and their thinking on this did not change until late in the century.[45] It was, therefore, not simply that liberalism was closed to women due to the 1850 Law of Association and Assembly in Prussia prohibiting women from joining political associations and parties. The Law of Association was instead only a codification of the prevailing liberal ideology concerning character, maturity, independence, and the respective positions of women in the home and men in society.[46] Public meetings and voluntary associations promoted the emergence of civil society in Germany and served as the institutional foundations crucial for the ideological development and social inculcation of liberalism. But liberals like those in Leipzig also saw public voluntary associations as a means to cultivate Bildung, independence, *Selbststätigkeit* (self-reliance), and *Gemeinsinn* (civic sense), all the characteristics ultimately of manliness.[47]

If practicing Catholicism was feminine and subservient, standing up to the power of the church required exertions of masculinity, public character, and independence. For example, consider the response already mentioned in the previous chapter in the liberal press during the Moabiterklostersturm of 1869: the *National Zeitung* argued that the resolve of "free men and the Bürgertum" offered the best defense against the rising number of monks and monasteries in Germany.[48] The paper urged its readers to practice "independence, manliness, and freedom" against monastic "darkness and idiocy," "passivity and subjection."[49] In 1873 a liberal political manifesto in the *Crefelder Zeitung* demanded the election of a candidate who was a "man" who, in the face of the ultramontane opposition, wanted "political freedom and

---

45. Langewiesche, "Nature of German Liberalism," 101.

46. Blackbourn, *Marpingen,* 261.

47. Páll Björnsson, "Liberalism and the Making of the 'New Man': The Case of the Gymnasts in Leipzig, 1845–1871," in *Saxony in German History: Culture, Society, and Politics, 1830–1933,* ed. James Retallack (Ann Arbor: University of Michigan Press, 2000), 151–65.

48. *National Zeitung,* 25 Aug. 1869.

49. *National Zeitung,* 6 Sept. 1869.

independence based on sound, intellectual Bildung."[50] The president of
the Reichstag from 1874 to 1879, Max von Forckenbeck, a liberal
nationalist and himself a Catholic, called upon his colleagues to offer a
"manly defense" of their parliamentary accomplishments. Heinrich
Kruse of the liberal *Kölnische Zeitung* was congratulated for the
paper's "firm, manly role" in the campaign against clericalism. Heinrich von Sybel as president of the anticlerical Deutscher Verein of the
Rhine Province was applauded by its executive committee for his
"manly demeanor" in the face of unjustified opposition.[51] At the level
of intragroup dynamics, chest-thumping displays of bravura rallied
liberal men in the homosocial fight against the Catholic opponent. At
the level of social-sexual ideology, the incessant invocation of masculinity in the face of Catholicism served to define and to defend the
public space against women.

In liberal psychology the other side of the militant Catholic revival
was, therefore, always the woman in public, or, to carry the point to its
conclusion, when liberals feminized Catholicism, the consequent anti-
Catholicism was misogyny. For example, consider again Johann
Bluntschli, for whom nothing produced as much candid disgust as the
coupling of Catholicism and women. As he traveled through the
Rhineland in the late 1860s, he observed women praying in the convent
at Aachen "with the expression of idiocy and boundless, pathetic stupidity."[52] For Bluntschli, his gynephobic and misogynistic anti-
Catholicism could have traumatic repercussions. As he simultaneously
waged war against women's emancipation and the Catholic Church, he
relentlessly tortured himself with visions of impotence and castration
at the hands of the Jesuits and ultramontane clergy. His entire corpus
of anticlerical literature since the middle of the 1860s and the rise of the
women's movement is fraught with these nightmares. In 1868, in "Über
das Verhältniss des modernen Staates zur Religion" he argued that in
ultramontane Catholicism medieval romanticism and the drive for
power within its hierarchy had been mixed into a poison. Princes and
peoples who imbibe too much of the toxic brew lose their capacity to
govern the modern state. "Their political character is emasculated."[53]
According to *Charakter und Geist der politischen Parteien,* published in

50. HSTAD, RD, Nr. 2619, "Die Anordnung der Schulpfleger bzw. Kreisschulinspektoren (kath.) und Förderung des Schulwesens durch die Geistlichen," Bd. 1, 1872–73, newspaper clipping from *Crefelder Zeitung,* 23 Oct. 1873.

51. Forckenbeck, Kruse, and Sybel quoted in Blackbourn, *Marpingen,* 261.

52. Ernst Walter Zeeden, "Die katholische Kirche in der Sichte deutschen Protestantismus
im 19. Jahrhundert," *Historisches Jahrbuch* 72 (1953): 433–56, quotation at 448.

53. Bluntschli, "Über das Verhältniss des modernen Staates zur Religion," 156.

1869, Bluntschli believed that wherever the power of ultramontanism reaches, not only are economic progress curtailed, industrial production hampered, the Bildung of the upper classes ruined, and science enslaved by the church. "The state is castrated and devalued."[54] His *Wider die Jesuiten* (1872) argues that a nation or any part of a nation under the sway of the Jesuits becomes not just superstitious, ignorant, spiritually crippled, and blind. Jesuits "castrate" a nation's character. The proof he cited was southern Europe.[55] "Römische Weltherrschaft und deutsche Freiheit," written for his collection of essays in *Rom und die Deutschen* (1872) argues, "The rule of priests always means the castration of the people." If the papacy had succeeded in establishing absolute authority during the Middle Ages, "the European people would have had to sacrifice their masculinity."[56] In Bluntschli's view, priests, Jesuits, and the Catholic Church were incessant, merciless attacks on manhood. It is tempting to dismiss his traumatic visions as, to be sure, an interesting but after all extraordinary case of anti-Catholic paranoia. But Bluntschli was exceptional only to the extent that he was always particularly candid and eager to give expression to the liberal dysphoria.

In the anti-Catholic imagination it was the confessional, seemingly dark and mysterious, that was the site for particularly concentrated and creative work.[57] It therefore provides especially illuminating examples of misogynistic anticlericalism. Here in the dark and quiet church, alone, close, and in whispers, confessors, liberals imagined, used their power to undo and then entrance women.[58] An illustration in the *Gartenlaube* depicts a young woman on her knees, hands outstretched and raised in emphatic submission at the feet of her confessor. "Enough, Oh, woman! Stop humiliating yourself!" is the journal's apostrophe (fig. 17). The poem "Am Beichtstuhl" (The confessional) by Ernst Scherenberg that accompanies the article was subsequently published separately with a volume of other anti-Catholic verse.[59] It

---

54. Bluntschli, *Charakter und Geist,* 37.

55. Bluntschli, *Wider die Jesuiten* (Eberfeld: Verlag von R. L. Friederichs, 1872), 16–17.

56. Bluntschli, *Rom und die Deutschen,* part 1, *Römische Weltherrschaft und deutsche Freiheit* (Berlin, 1872), 15.

57. On the topic of Catholic women and their confessors, see Edith Saurer, "Frauen und Priester: Beichtgespräche im frühen 19. Jahrhundert," in *Arbeit, Frömmigkeit und Eigensinn: Studien zu historischer Kulturforschung,* ed. Richard van Dülmen (Frankfurt am Main: Fischer Verlag, 1990), 141–70.

58. See Geoffry Cubbitt, *The Jesuit Myth: Conspiracy Theory and Politics in Nineteenth-Century France* (Oxford: Oxford University Press, 1993), 234–41.

59. Ernst Scherenberg, "Am Beichstuhl," in *Gegen Rom! Zeitstimmen Deutscher Dichter,* ed. Ernst Scherenberg (Elberfeld: Bädeker'sche Buch- und Kunsthandlung, 1874), 79.

Fig. 17. "Am Beichtstuhl," *Gartenlaube* (1874): 151. An illustration in the *Gartenlaube* depicts a young woman, on her knees in emphatic submission to her confessor. "Enough, oh, woman! Stop humiliating yourself!" is the caption.

immediately became the favorite in the substantial repertoire of Kulturkampf poetry and reads in part:

You too, my Volk, have knelt in the dust
For a hundred years before the Roman tyranny;
The church has robbed you of your best part—
Rid yourself now of her yoke![60]

60. *Gartenlaube* (1874): 150–51.

The "best part" of the Volk could only have been its manly independence and character or, not to put too fine a point on it, for gynephobic liberals like Bluntschli, the male genitalia.

As the power of the confessional reduced the nation to feminine subservience, it also represented anxieties of sexual rivalry with priests. In another illustration in the same journal a young woman, "beautiful despite sorrow and distress," dutifully awaits the summons of the priest to enter his dark confessional. His one-eyed peek from behind his curtain and wide, tight simper indicate that he is going to enjoy himself.[61] If women's religious fanaticism was nymphomania, current too as we have seen in the convent atrocity story, such psychological pathologies immediately explained why women so eagerly went to confession or entered the religious life. In an illustration in the *Berliner Wespen,* exuberant, giggling nuns line up before the confessional. "Confessor: Pious sisters, do you want to endure the utmost for the church and carry on until the last man? All: With pleasure!"[62] Liberal men recognized and enjoyed hyperbole, no doubt, but if taken seriously such images provide insight into the liberal psychology that coupled anti-Catholicism and antifeminism during the reemergence of the women's question. The image of Catholic women disarming men of their masculine faculties of reason with their disingenuous tears and charms, and the nightmare of the church and Jesuits as women castrating men, revealed the deepseated misogynistic strain running through liberal anticlericalism. If for liberal men the war against Catholicism required the exertion of manhood, it was manhood itself that was at stake.

Kulturkampf and Geschlechterkampf

The liberal ideology of the sexes in society reflected the shifting patterns of faith and worship within Roman Catholicism in Germany. Since the late eighteenth century women had been playing an increasingly prominent and visible role in the Catholic Church and in the popular practice of Catholicism.[63] Historians have argued that this consti-

61. *Gartenlaube* (1874): 398–99.
62. *Berliner Wespen,* 23 April 1875.
63. The discussion concerning the more prominent role of women in both Catholicism and Protestantism in the nineteenth century has become substantial. It includes but is not limited to McLeod, "Weibliche Frömmigkeit"; Rebekka Habermas, "Weibliche Religiosität—oder Von der Fragilität bürgerlicher Identitäten," in *Wege zur Geschichte des Bürgertums: Vierzehn Beiträge,* ed. Klaus Tenfelde and Hans-Ulrich Wehler (Göttingen: Vandenhoeck und Ruprecht, 1994), 125–48; Norbert Bush, "Die Feminisierung der ultramontanen Fröm-

tuted a feminization of the church, a transformation occurring not just in the German states but also in England, France, and the United States throughout the nineteenth century.[64] To liberal observers and critics of the growth of Catholicism like Johann von Schulte and Paul Hinschius, however, the role of women in Catholicism seemed especially critical in the German states after the 1848 Revolution.[65]

Nowhere was this more evident than in the growth of female religious orders and congregations. Prior to the revolution, there were in Germany only a few Ursuline, Dominican, and Carmelite female orders and a handful of female religious congregations. According to statistics compiled by the Prussian parliament in 1869, however, there were now in Prussia thirty different female orders and congregations. Table 4 indicates that according to the state compilation the number of women belonging to six different female orders with forty-one convents totaled 924 including nuns, novices, and lay sisters. Table 5 indicates that by 1869 there were fourteen different open congregations with 690 convents or residential institutions. The number of women in

migkeit," in *Wunderbare Erscheinungen: Frauen und katholische Frömmigkeit in 19. und 20. Jahrhundert,* ed. Irmtraud Götz von Olenhausen (Paderborn: F. Schöningh, 1995), 203–20; and Meiwes, *"Arbeiterinnen des Herrn."* For indications that the church was becoming more feminine, see also Lucian Hölscher, "Moglichkeiten und Grenzen der statistischen Erfaßung kirchlicher Bindungen," in *Seelsorge und Diakonie in Berlin: Beiträge zum Verhältnis von Kirche und Großstadt im 19. Jahrhundert und beginnenden 20. Jahrhundert,* ed. Kaspar Elm and Hans-Dietrich Loock (Berlin: W. de Gruyter, 1990), 39–62. For a critical appraisal of the feminization of religion, see Caroline Ford, "Religion and Popular Culture in Modern Europe," *Journal of Modern History* 65 (1993): 152–75; and for the German case, see the objections by Margaret Lavinia Anderson, "The Limits of Secularization: On the Problem of the Catholic Revival in Nineteenth-Century Germany," *Historical Journal* 38 (1995): 647–70, esp. 654.

64. For France, see Ralph Gibson, *A Social History of French Catholicism, 1789–1914* (London: Routledge, 1989); and Claude Langlois, *La Catholicisme au féminin: Les congrégations français à supérieure générale au XIX siècle* (Paris: Cerf, 1984). For the United States, see Richard D. Shiels, "The Feminisation of American Congregationalism, 1730–1835," *American Quarterly* 33 (1983): 46–62; and Barbara Welter, "The Feminization of American Religion, 1800–1860," in *Clio's Consciousness Raised: New Perspectives in the History of Women,* ed. Mary Hartmann and Lois Banner (New York: Harper and Row, 1976), 136–57. See also Mary Ewens, *The Role of the Nun in Nineteenth-Century America* (New York: Arno Press, 1978). To make a comparison to the Roman Catholic female religious orders and congregations in England, see Susan O'Brien, *"Terra Incognita:* The Nun in Nineteenth-Century England," *Past and Present,* 121 (1988): 110–40; and idem, "French Nuns in Nineteenth-Century England," *Past and Present,* 161 (1997): 142–80. There is no study of the images of nuns in Germany comparable to Susan Casteras's study of English nuns, "Virgin Vows: The Early Victorian Artists' Portrayal of Nuns and Novices," *Victorian Studies* 24 (1981): 157–84.

65. Schulte, *Die neueren katholischen Orden und Congregationen;* Hinschius, *Die Orden und Kongregationen der katholischen Kirche.*

TABLE 4. Female Religious Orders in Prussia in 1869

Order	Convents	Nuns	Novices or Lay Sisters
Ursuline	24	368	214
Women of the Good Shepherd	6	83	45
Benedictine	4	60	31
Carmelite	3	36	8
Elizabethan	2	33	3
Clarissen	2	32	11
Total	41	612	312

Source: "Übersicht der in Preußen vorhandenen Stationen geistlicher Orden," 1000–1002.

TABLE 5. Female Religious Congregations in Prussia in 1869

Congregation	Convents	Sisters	Novices or Lay Sisters	Service
Sisters of Mercy	521	2,986	626	care for the sick
School Sisters	63	299	84	education
Our Dear Lady	31	235	0	education
Sisters of the Poor Child of Jesus	23	480	11	education
Our Holy Catherine	19	137	17	education
Sisters of Christian Charity	15	133	13	education
Recollects	6	37	13	education
Salesians	4	77	40	education
Sisters of the Sacred Heart of Jesus	2	39	36	education
English Fräuleins	2	17	15	education
Sisters of St. Gertrude	1	16	0	education
Sisters of St. Salvator	1	15	0	education
Sisters of St. Michael	1	15	12	education
Association for the Improvement of Female Servants	1	11	0	moral improvement
Total	690	4,497	867	

Source: "Übersicht der in Preußen vorhandenen Stationen geistlicher Orden," 1000–1002.

these congregations totaled 5,364 including sisters, novices, and lay sisters. The number of women in religious orders and congregations in Germany now dramatically surpassed the number of men in religious orders. In 1865, according to Schulte, the ratio of men to women religious in Prussia was 1 to 3.3 and in Bavaria 1 to 3.25. In Hesse the ratio had risen to 1 to 8, and in the other German states there were no male orders at all. In Austria, by contrast, there were 500 more men than women in closed religious orders and open congregations.[66] The Catholic Church did not compile its own statistics, but the disproportionate number of women in the service of the church was readily understood by Catholics. When in May 1872 during the intense debate on the controversial anti-Jesuit bill in the Reichtag the rabid Jesuit hater Rudolf von Gneist alleged the "head count today is already more than 20,000," he did nothing to make it clear whether he meant the number of priests across Germany or Jesuits everywhere in the world. Center Party deputies immediately shouted out "Nuns! Nuns!"[67]

Schulte explained that there were several reasons for the dramatic growth of female congregations since 1848. He believed it was becoming increasingly difficult for women, especially in the midsized cities, to find a partner for marriage. Contemporaries also agreed that bourgeois families were apparently no longer able to provide financially for their unmarried adult daughters. At the same time, Schulte argued that housing was becoming scarce and food more and more expensive. In general, therefore, women were finding it increasingly difficult to earn sufficient wages to support themselves on their own. Since many women could no longer rely on marriage as a strategy for material security, many from the "better strata" were now turning to the convents. Besides providing security, life in the convent also offered an escape from the life of a housewife, a life that young women knew required working all day, staying up nights to care for sick children, and attending the whimsical moods of a husband. Meanwhile, in the convent young women, he believed, soon adjusted to getting up early at the appointed hours and to praying throughout the day. Everything—eating, sleeping, praying—was determined by the clock. For

66. Schulte, *Die neueren katholischen Orden und Congregationen,* 36. According to Relinde Meiwes the number of women in religious orders and congregations in Prussia jumped from 579 in 1855 to 8,011 by 1873. The number of male monastics lagged behind, increasing from 397 to 1,037 in the same period of time. Meiwes, *"Arbeiterinnen des Herrn,"* 77. Meiwes's statistical tabulations should be weighed against mine. In any case at issue here is the liberal perception of the dramatic increase in female orders and congregations and that increase relative to male orders.

67. Anderson, "Limits of Secularization," 653–54 n. 26.

young women all this seemed to ensure a life of peace, harmony, punctuality, prayer, and the labor of love. "Not bad," Schulte thought. "Why wouldn't many girls prefer being a nun to enduring a life full of pain and misery as a maid, seamstress, washer, the wife of a petty bureaucrat, artisan, or worker?"[68]

Schulte, clearly, had little real appreciation for the realities of a life dedicated to work in the female religious congregations. Female religious who belonged to nursing orders would have disagreed with his rosy portrait. The so-called Gray Sisters, for example, were required to work 250 day shifts and 180 night shifts in hospitals and infirmaries staffed by the order. Under the physical and emotional strain the health of the nuns rapidly broke down. Most died from overexertion before they were fifty years old.[69] Yet liberal men echoed Schulte's attitudes. They argued again and again that the nunneries drained the pool of women available for marriage, undermining the woman's role ordained by nature as wife and mother, the "living soul" of the private sphere. Since convents, Sybel explained, had not the least relationship to the household and the family, they lent nothing to the education of girls for their true duties.[70] Virchow argued that female congregations divested the family of girls and young women and then subjected them to dogmatic religious indoctrination. The convents offered little instruction of practical worth and even less of intellectual value, and they did nothing to prepare young women for their roles as housewives.[71] He believed that female congregations served neither the family nor the state but only the interests of the church. They broke apart the natural unity of the family and depleted German society of wives and mothers.

Schulte connected the dramatic proliferation of female congregations to the new demands for access to the social and political public, the rising tide of democracy, and the reemergence of feminism. Religious convents and orders were viewed as small social republics within the state, pockets of communism and the women's movement. "Their increase during our time is explained in part by the socialist current and by the pressure of women for emancipation." Female congregations, he continued, were also part of the larger attempt to "Christianize capital," to place industry, factories, and craft work under the authority of priests and nuns. Schulte concluded, "If this were done,

68. Schulte, *Die neueren katholischen Orden und Congregationen,* 40.
69. Ross, *Failure of Bismarck's Kulturkampf,* 87 n. 52.
70. Sybel, "Über die Emancipation der Frauen," 78.
71. Virchow, *Über die Erziehung des Weibes,* 21–22.

clerics would rule the world."[72] The new congregations were also French enclaves within Prussia. They were often controlled, according to Schulte, by French mother superiors who imported French forms of Catholicism. Possession of French prayer books, for example, was a sign of devotion, and French words were used to designate religious offices and religious congregations. Schulte echoed the common opinion among liberals that the new congregations, especially the teaching institutions, were laced through with ultramontane militancy, spreading hatred of Prussia. Female religious congregations and orders were also sites for concentrated concern about unsupervised female association. The story current in the summer of 1869 of Sister Barbara, imprisoned for twenty-one years by the nuns of a barefoot Carmelite order in Cracow, seemed to provide the proof that without paternal discipline, women would degenerate into religious fanaticism, barbarity, and nymphomania.[73]

The distrust of and hostility toward Catholic women increased with the threat of French revanchism and with the church-state battle of the 1870s. The article "Die katholische Frau als Werkzeug der Feinde Deutschlands" in the *Grenzboten* argued, for example, that Catholic girls confined within the walls of the convent were molded into submissive, single-minded agents of the church.[74] In the convent schools they heard almost nothing about the fatherland and its history. The girls learned just as little about the German poets; in the convent schools they promised not to read Goethe and Schiller. They were taught, according to the article, from an early age not to marry Protestants and that tolerance for other religions was a sinful act of indifference. Every day their heads were filled with stories about miracles and devils. After women left the convent, they preferred "the most miserable novels from the lending libraries, French above all." "They remain forever submissive daughters of their church and diligently go to confession. They believe it is a mortal sin to question the sanctity of their priests and the power of the church alone for salvation." Most women, according to the article, never recovered from the indoctrination that took place in the convents. "They are that for which they were raised: blind tools of the church."[75] When such articles were allegedly

72. Schulte, *Die neueren katholischen Orden und Congregationen,* 42.

73. The story of Sister Barbara's incarceration and its meaning are explored in detail in chapter 3.

74. "Die katholische Frau als Werkzeug der Feinde Deutschlands," *Grenzboten* 1 (1874): 234–37.

75. Ibid., quotations at 235, 235–36.

written by Catholic clerics or laity, as in the case of the article in the *Grenzboten,* which included the byline "a Catholic woman," there was an added air of authenticity.

The form of religious life that especially flourished among Catholic women after 1848 was the active congregation devoted to public philanthropy. This too was part of the feminization of the church. But the point is just as much that the new female religious congregations were part of the movement by women to gain access to the public. The growth of the religious congregations was part of the revival of women's demands for independence, emancipation, and larger social relevance. For many Catholic women the new religious congregations offered opportunities for women to take their fate into their own hands. Many women joined these congregations not because they were religious fanatics or because they believed (or their families believed) their prospects for marriage were bleak. They joined because they realized that they could combine as sisters in orders a religious life with their own aspirations for a professional life. They found rewarding work in public as teachers, nurses, welfare workers, and administrative personnel in Catholic schools, hospitals, orphanages, asylums, women's shelters, and reformatories for young women. In religious congregations, women pursued an associational life outside the home and filled valuable roles in public service to the sick and poor.[76]

Liberals immediately recognized the significance of the new, more influential, visible role that women were now playing in society through the philanthropic work of the congregations. Schulte explained, "In the old orders women are completely dead to the outside world. But in the new congregations they often have a far-reaching influence. The new congregations pursue mostly social work, including education and instruction, caring for the poor and the sick."[77] Liberals repeatedly argued that the charitable agencies established by female religious orders only served to extend the reach and

76. This is the refreshing argument offered by Relinde Meiwes, "Religiosität und Arbeit als Lebensform für katholische Frauen: Kongregationen im 19. Jahrhundert," in *Frauen unter dem Patriarchat der Kirchen: Katholikinnen und Protestantinnen im 19. und 20. Jahrhundert,* ed. Anselm Doering-Manteuffel, Martin Greschat, Jochen-Christoph Kaiser, Wilfried Loth, and Kurt Nowak (Stuttgart: W. Kohlhammer, 1995), 69–88; and idem, *"Arbeiterinnen des Herrn,"* which argues that the Catholic female religious congregations represented one important component of the larger women's movement. Meiwes makes important arguments about the spread of female congregations, the character of conventual life and philanthropic activity, and the "feminization" of church personnel, and my arguments here should be weighed against her study.

77. Schulte, *Die neueren katholischen Orden und Congregationen,* 8.

promote the power of the church. Behind the cloak of humanitarianism, nuns allegedly took advantage of the vulnerable condition of the poor and invalid to indoctrinate them with dogma and convert Protestants to Catholicism. Eduard Zeller's influential liberal treatise systematically outlining the right of the state to supervise and restrict church affairs argued that care for the sick and the poor was the proper and exclusive responsibility of the secular state. Catholic philanthropic institutions should be taken over, he explained, because they could not be trusted as the state could be trusted with the competent administration of social health and welfare.[78] Zeller's complaint at least seemed measured, but the hysterical violence directed toward charitable institutions was indicated by a liberal academic in the journal *Im Neuen Reich:* they were the same as "phylloxera, Colorado beetle and other enemies of the empire."[79]

At the same time, for critics the Catholic missions taking place all over Germany were disgusting displays of women in public at their worst. Women, kneeling or prostrate at the feet of the missionaries, apparently mentally and emotionally unhinged, not only flooded the public with irrationalism.[80] Social observers also warned that mothers at the missions threatened to destroy the family. If mothers had surrendered themselves to fanaticism, it was the children who suffered most. According to one critic, with the break of dawn large numbers of women from all social strata were fleeing from their duties at home and streaming to the sermons at the Jesuit missions. Caring for the household and for the children was left to the men or otherwise simply abandoned. "You very often see children hungry and freezing in the streets. They wander around unattended, crying in front of the doorways and calling for their mothers. 'The mother? And where is the mother?'— 'At the mission! At the mission!' sob the poor orphans."[81] In another story, a mother locked her two small children in her home and left for the mission. Unsupervised, one child fell into the fire and was burned to death; meanwhile "the mother was practicing pious exercises with her Jesuit confessor."[82]

Since the missions were extraordinary events, there was, of course,

78. Eduard Zeller, *Staat und Kirche* (Leipzig: Fues's Verlag, 1873), 248.
79. Kissling, *Geschichte des Kulturkampfes* 3:58. Cited also in Blackbourn, *Marpingen,* 257; and idem, "Progress and Piety," 149.
80. *Allgemeine Zeitung,* Nr. 316, 1852, *Aktenstücke,* 174.
81. Stachelstock, *Licht und Finsterniß,* 76–77.
82. Ibid., 77.

considerable truth to the accusation that they disrupted the normal routines of family life and community affairs. When the Franciscan mission came to Dahl in 1857 even the parish priest admitted in a report to the bishop of Paderborn that "all the grownups streamed to the church, and many houses were just left to the children."[83] Another priest reported that families ate only cold food during the weeks of the missions so that mothers would be free to attend the sermons.[84] Women who flocked to the missions and religious associations, joined the pilgrimages, and attended church events were, therefore, not simply a public nuisance. They betrayed their responsibilities as mothers and caretakers of the home. But in another sense as well women who brought their Catholicism out into the open represented a breakdown of the distinction between public and private: if Catholicism was a woman, "irrational" and "fanatical," it belonged, if anywhere, at home.

Women not only joined the new religious congregations and participated in the missions in large numbers. Women also assumed more prominent and conspicuous roles in Catholic communities and in the popular practice of Catholicism. The promulgation of the Immaculate Conception of the Virgin by the Vatican in 1854 and the new forms of Marian devotion, including hymns, prayers, and liturgical practices, all encouraged by the missionary associations, were part of the growing predominance of women in the lay popular practice of Catholicism.[85] It was Mary who in the Catholic life of prayer served as the intermediary for her son Christ, and it was Mary who according to the church instructed Saint Dominic to distribute and teach the rosary, the prayer cycle that included the Hail Mary. For Catholic women, veneration of the Virgin may have sanctified virginity, motherhood, and other "female virtues" including humility, forbearance, and graceful suffering, but the Mother of Jesus also offered an image of feminine power, grace, and authority. In the world of Catholic women, the presence of the Virgin Mother of Jesus and with her the model for feminine behavior were constant. It was inculcated through the recitation of the Hail Mary; in the endless pins and pictures that bore Mary's image;

83. Pf. Sachs an Bischof Conrad Martin, Dahl, 3 April 1857, *Volksmissionen der norddeutschen Franziskaner*, 46–47.

84. Ibid., 12.

85. Michael N. Ebertz, "Maria in der Massenreligiosität: Zum Wandel des popularen Katholizismus in Deutschland," in *Volksfrömmigkeit in Europa: Beiträge zur Soziologie popularer Religiosität aus 14 Ländern*, ed. Michael N. Ebertz and Franz Schultheiss (Munich: Chr. Kaiser Verlag, 1986), 65–84. On Marian devotion encouraged by the missions, see Gatz, *Rheinische Volksmission*, 126.

and with the thousands of women who bore her name, the most common name in the Catholic population, if not in all of Germany.

At the same time, women were drawn to the Catholic Church because it offered one of the few social and public spaces available to them outside the workplace. Following a visit by missionaries to their communities, women established their own religious organizations. For wives and mothers, the religious associations offered friendship circles in which they could share and discuss their problems and the rare opportunity, if only for a short while, to flee from the responsibilities of the home and the family. At the same time, religious organizations were attractive to women because they offered a measure of independence from male supervision, even if the priest, of course, remained.[86] Most important, joining the new religious associations set up by the missionaries was one of the new opportunities for women to play more important roles in Catholic communities and in the popular practice of Catholicism. Women eagerly pursued the chance to assume organizational and leadership positions otherwise denied to them by men and did so with the assurance that it was a religious duty. For all these reasons, the new female religious organizations became so popular and successful that among the laity, women often dominated the religious life of the parish. Schulte complained that communities in many Catholic regions had become "mere ladies' societies."[87] Meanwhile, liberal newspapers like the *Vossische Zeitung* did not fail to notice the large attendance of women at the public assembly of the Catholic Association in Düsseldorf in 1869.[88] Even despite the legal ban on female participation in political clubs and gatherings, in predominantly Catholic cities hundreds of women participated in "lecture evenings" dedicated to clear political questions like state supervision of schools.[89] The dominance of women in the new religious associations, assemblies, and meetings was only one part of their expanding role in the church. Women helped organize pilgrimages, too, and their participants, liberals complained, were mostly female.

The missionary crusade, the new religious congregations, charitable

86. See McLeod, "Weibliche Frömmigkeit," 145. See also Sperber, "The Transformation of Catholic Associations." For France, see Martine Segalen, *Mari et femme dans la société paysanne* (Paris: Flammarion, 1980), 156–58. For England, see L. Davidoff and C. Hall, "The Architecture of Public and Private Life: English Middle-Class Society in a Provincial Town, 1780 to 1850," in *The Pursuit of Urban History,* ed. Derek Fraser and Anthony Sutcliffe (London: E. Arnold, 1983), 327–45.

87. Schulte, *Die neueren katholischen Orden und Congregationen,* 41.

88. *Vossische Zeitung,* 11 Sept. 1869.

89. Anderson, *Practicing Democracy,* 127.

societies, church associations, pilgrimages, and shifting devotional patterns were dramatically changing the lives of Catholic women. All introduced women to public life. Obviously, the church fathers were decidedly no more feminist than they were democratic. Indeed, they continued to see women as large children requiring supervision, morally weak vessels prone to sin, sexually dangerous and untrustworthy—a deep-seated Catholic conviction that tarred the feminine as far back biblically as Eve in Eden. The church's teachings circumscribed women in the home and upheld matrimony, procreation, and motherhood as the paramount responsibilities of women. To be sure, the new opportunities for women within the church were also confined and qualified. On the subject of women, the Catholic Church leadership and liberals shared views rather more than either could recognize or would admit. But all this should not blind us to the opportunities opened up by the Catholic revival that had been previously unavailable to young women and mothers in German society. At the very time that liberal critics complained that the Roman Church was "antimodern" and "backward," exploiting "naive" women to enhance the power of the church, Catholic women found within the church opportunities to organize together, enter professional life, expand their roles within their communities, and exercise authority. By comparison, it would only be much later and then only rarely that the German labor movement would be able to mobilize and employ so many women. It was not the case, therefore, that Catholic women were lagging behind middle-class secular and Protestant women in their demand for access to public space. Already in the 1850s and early 1860s, even while the bourgeois women's movement had disappeared and well before the founding of the Allgemeine Deutscher Frauenverein in 1865, Catholic women were coupling religious life with public life in open religious congregations, associations, assemblies, and the missions in ways generally not available to women or not desired by women at the same time in Protestant bourgeois culture.

Protestant middle-class women had, of course, engaged in public philanthropic work, charitable activities, and poor relief initiatives since the early decades of the century, in, for example, national organizations like the Vaterländischer Frauenverein (Patriotic Women's Association), a nursing sisterhood established in 1866 after the Austro-Prussian War, and through various local and municipal societies. The participation of Catholic women in public was, however, both quantitatively and qualitatively different than that of their Protestant social counterparts. The flood of Catholic women in the years after 1848

entering the public through female congregations, church organizations, parish life, and religious devotion was faster, more dramatic, and
therefore more conspicuous than the engagement of Protestant
women. To contemporaries the influx of Catholic women in public
looked like a sudden expansion, a virtual explosion relative to the
number of Protestant women who remained committed to philanthropic work and church affairs. The engagement of Catholic women
was more impressive precisely because it was new and, more important, because it was coupled with the power of the missions and the
revival of popular Catholicism. Women of the Protestant middle class
may have joined in public work through secular organizations like the
Vaterländischer Frauenverein, with a membership in 1873 of some
thirty thousand, in the spirit of nationalist service and through other
municipal charities in the spirit of civic volunteerism. But Catholic
women joined in philanthropic work as a consciously pious act of
Catholic faith. Their work in hospitals, asylums, schools, orphanages,
shelters for women, and correctional homes for wayward women was,
like their religious worship, suffused with and empowered by female
forms of religious devotion such as the Marianism specific to Roman
Catholicism.

It was this in part that provoked a backlash from critics convinced
that Catholic sisters in public work could not be trusted to provide
without prejudice for those in their care. *Schwester Adolphe, oder die
Geheimnisse der inneren Verwaltung des bürgerlichen Invalidenhauses in
Mainz,* published anonymously in 1863, was meant to expose a case in
point.[90] It gives a detailed account of the Sisters of Mercy, who
included among their nursing duties at the St. Rochus Hospital in
Mainz subjecting their invalid "inmates," physically dependent and
emotionally susceptible, to a daily regime of incessant prayer. In one
instance among others, an eighty-year-old invalid, Adam Hattemer by
name, former saddler by trade, was ordered by the sisters to attend
church every day, twice a day, in the cold despite his frail condition.
Two weeks after making a complaint he was a corpse.[91] According to
the account, the Sisters of Mercy were clearly doing more harm than
good. All this meant that Catholic middle-class women were entering
the public sphere in quite different ways, with greater attention and
with more controversy, than Protestant women. It was Catholic
women in every aspect of their religious life, whether in their charitable
activities or attending the missions, not Protestant women, who

90. *Schwester Adolphe, oder die Geheimnisse der inneren Verwaltung des bürgerlichen
Invalidenhauses in Mainz* (Frankfurt am Main: Druck von R. Baist, 1863).
91. Ibid., 40–41.

seemed to critics to be doing the demonstrable damage to the traditional separation of public and private.

Meanwhile, most Catholic men did not directly contest the participation and relative autonomy of Catholic women in the religious associations and activities. Instead bürgerlich Catholic men preferred their own separate and secular associational life, joining the numerous political and social organizations closed to women. This was only typical of the gendered attitude middle-class men held toward religious practice. They were for the most part not pious themselves, and they particularly resented the priests' claim to authority over them. Nonetheless, they valued the power of religion to inculcate moral behavior among people, that is to say other people, and believed a certain piety in their wives and daughters, their presence at church and in religious associations, to be respectable and entirely appropriate to their sex. At the same time, Catholic workers retreated in large numbers to the tavern, that other refuge of male fellowship. It was here that they developed together anticlerical and secular attitudes.[92] Many of them felt betrayed by their priests, who in reply to their complaints about oppressive working conditions and starvation wages counseled only prayer, forbearance, and obedience. One well-known example was the clay miner Nikolaus Osterroth from the Bavarian Palatinate, who has left eloquent testimony not only of his physically crippling work but of the indifference of his parish priests to it. In the taverns after church in the company of co-workers he learned to curse the parish priests (mere "Center Party men," he called them) along with the mine owners.

How did the priest use his influence? Instead of defending the rights of the oppressed, whose leadership he regarded as his monopoly, he preached submission and patience to the workers. He sat at the table of the rich and accepted their gifts that they had wrung from the poor, instead of reminding them that their actions were hardhearted and unchristian. Instead of saying to the mine owners, "Thou shalt love thy neighbor as thyself," he said to the exploited and raped workers, "You are servants, and servants you must remain; God wills it for your salvation."[93]

---

92. For the tavern as a center of male anticlericalism and hostility to the missions, see Sperber, *Popular Catholicism,* 62–63.

93. Nikolas Osterroth, "Nikolaus Osterroth, Clay Miner," in *The German Worker: Working Class Autobiographies from the Age of Industrialization,* ed. Alfred Kelly (Berkeley: University of California Press, 1987), 160–87, quotation at 169.

Finally Osterroth abandoned his faith. In his case apostasy culminated in his political conversion from the Center Party to social democracy.

Liberal men hoped Catholic men would sooner or later turn their backs on Catholicism not because their priests were too often blind to the reality of their lives but because the religion itself was, they claimed, ridiculous. Catholic women were hopelessly lost to Catholicism, liberals concluded, but Catholic men, after all, were endowed with the faculty of reason and might finally use it to shed the feminine veil of Catholicism. By 1868 even Bluntschli thought there were some grounds for hope. He believed that the majority of educated Catholic men no longer accepted the teachings of the church; they had left it, he presumably thought, to women and the ignorant.[94] One historian of religion and secularization in the nineteenth century has concluded that Catholicism not just in Germany but also in England, France, and the United States became feminized both because more women joined the church and because men fled from it, a process that accelerated with the increasing size of the industrial working class in the course of the nineteenth century.[95]

The larger measure of piety among Catholic women, their participation in religious associational life, and their part in the public activities of the church helped prepare them to play another role as public protesters during the Kulturkampf. The antichurch campaign immediately generated a determined popular Catholic resistance, and state authorities found they were unprepared to meet the open defiance of Catholics. State officials mistakenly assumed that resistance to the Kulturkampf would emanate from a finite number of readily identifiable pockets within the Catholic population: the clergy, the Catholic lay leadership, and a few Catholic associations like the Mainzverein (Mainz Association).[96] Instead the response of the Catholic population was widespread and spontaneous. So dramatic in fact was the agitation of the Catholic population that it was not until the outright revolution of 1918 that imperial Germany would again see such levels of collective action against state authority. It was, however, the predominant role of women in the passive and active resistance to the Kulturkampf that was especially surprising to liberals and state authorities alike. Catholic women from the upper, middle, and lower classes across Prussia in cities and rural areas organized themselves, attended rallies, flooded cathedral squares in demonstrations, collected

94. Bluntschli, "Über das Verhältniss des modernen Staates zur Religion," 166.
95. McLeod, "Weibliche Frömmigkeit," 134–56.
96. Ross, *Failure of Bismarck's Kulturkampf,* 132.

signatures for statements of solidarity, wrote newspaper editorials, and marched in support of their church leadership. A good example was the over one thousand Catholic aristocratic women in Cologne, including the wives of local Landräte and judicial officials, who publicly expressed their support for the bishop. Again during the summer of 1874, thirty-five women of the Westphalian aristocracy created a public scandal when they were arrested and put on trial for lending their support to the bishop of Münster who in an address had allegedly insulted the majesty of the law. Such episodes were repeated across Prussia in almost all episcopal centers, where long processions of women paid tribute to their bishops as an act of piety.[97]

Behind the scenes, the prominent women of parishes orchestrated other forms of passive resistance to the state. They arranged the social ostracization of so-called state pastors or May priests, clerics who agreed to the state's demand that they take an oath of allegiance in accordance with the antichurch May Laws of 1873 and 1874. Women of the parish organized the boycotts of shops and businesses of Kulturkampf sympathizers and informers, and they also took direct action against the state. Frequently they demanded the participation of their husbands; often they simply acted by themselves. When state authorities auctioned off the furniture of the bishop at Freiburg, a bevy of Catholic women came armed with umbrellas. They threatened to thrash anyone who might try to bid against the Catholic community's designated buyer, whose job was to purchase the furniture and then return it to the bishop.[98] At a school in a town in Upper Silesia the intervention of the army was required to break up a group of women who had assembled to guard religion classes held by priests not authorized by the state. At another town close by the army was called in again to put down women rioting against a school where classes were conducted by an Old Catholic.[99] Catholic women paid the price for their defiance of police proscriptions against public demonstrations and scenes of support for the church leadership: they were arrested, charged fines, and sent to jail. Girls too had their own particular kind of public role to play, infused with the symbolism of, at once, youthful innocence and feminine defiance, in scenes that infuriated Kulturkampf supporters. When in 1874 the young priest Julius Büsch returned to his hometown after nineteen days of internment at Koblenz for refusing to abide by the terms of the May Laws, he was

97. Ibid., 133 n. 45.
98. Anderson, *Windthorst*, 174.
99. Anderson, *Practicing Democracy*, 126.

met by a cheering crowd of about a thousand parishioners on the bank of the Moselle River. In a ritual reenacted in villages, towns, and cities across Germany whenever interned priests returned to their congregations, girls dressed in white formed a circle around the priest, and one stepped forward to hand him a bouquet.[100]

Policemen and gendarmes, soldiers, mayors, municipal officers and commissioners, civil servants, deputies, and other authorities who tried to implement Kulturkampf legislation and the will of the state repeatedly found themselves pitted against Catholic women protesters who mocked, heckled, jeered, and beat them with umbrellas. Officials often coupled the scandal of Catholic women demonstrators with that other form of disreputable female presence in public. In a typical incident, a representative of the state squared off against a crowd of angry women and declared them "all a bunch of prostitutes." This was the standard rhetorical assassination of the reputation of women outside normal social conventions and male control, and the official made clear that he meant "especially those of you who go to wretched masses and those who help that theater of apes." He also railed against "the uselessness of husbands who are stupid enough to go along just to show their spunk."[101] Liberals assumed that Catholic men demonstrated not because they believed in the cause but either because they were mere ruffians or because they were forced to do so by their wives. Liberals routinely branded particular kinds of popular resistance and mass demonstrations that had to be contained with policemen as "female" even if those participating in the agitation were actually men.[102] This was the case, for example, with the crushing crowds that so emotionally greeted bishops released from imprisonment that they had to be held back by the gendarmes. Liberals believed these and other demonstrations were "female" despite the fact that they were clearly organized by prominent Catholic men and led by priests.

Meanwhile, the Catholic confessional and political leadership inculcated the image of the Catholic community in its time of crisis as inspired at its best by the feminine virtues of stamina and common sense. Catholic deputies on the floor of the Prussian parliament and in the Reichstag and Catholic journal and newspaper editors in their columns invented the "Catholic woman" who gave a levelheaded voice to Catholics collectively in the face of the liberals' extravagant accusa-

100. Ross, *Failure of Bismarck's Kulturkampf,* 142.
101. McLeod, "Weibliche Frömmigkeit," 143.
102. Blackbourn, "Progress and Piety," 150.

tions against the church.[103] The feminine character of Catholic agitation against the Kulturkampf inculcated by both liberals and Catholics became so prominent that it even colored the attitude of those at the highest level of state government. At a dinner party in January 1875 Bismarck during a season of especially heated combat with Ludwig Windthorst expressed particular concern about those "feminine influences" that complicated the campaign against the Catholic Church.[104] Bismarck's confession that evening that he hated Windthorst as much as he loved his wife was a remarkably telling instance of the sexed dynamics and tension-ridden conflation that laced relationships in the discourse of the Kulturkampf.

Kulturkampf altercations, therefore, took on more and more the appearance of a Geschlechterkampf, a running battle between men and women for access to the public, between men charged with public authority on the one side and wives, mothers, young women, and even girls on the other. This was the element of the ordeal, distorted and exaggerated, that repeatedly focused the attention of Kulturkämpfer and state authorities. Everywhere, Catholic women on the loose attending the missions, joining assemblies and associations, participating in pilgrimages, and organizing anti-Kulturkampf protests were not just a nuisance. For liberal men, these were women who literally did not know their place. Their open defiance was a formidable challenge to the state at the same time that the state's exertion of physical force against the "weaker sex" was a public embarrassment to its authority. Their loyalty to the Roman Church with acts of religious faith and state resistance and more fundamentally Catholicism itself gendered as a woman defied the strictures of society organized according to public or private.

Class, Democratization, and Anti-Catholicism

Not only the women's question, the women's movement, and the ideology of separate spheres but also social class were enmeshed in liberal anticlericalism and anti-Catholicism. Liberals routinely argued that Catholicism was practiced only by aristocrats, useless leftovers from the feudal ages, on one end of the social scale and by the allegedly backward working and rural peasant class on the other end. The liberal

---

103. Anderson, *Practicing Democracy*, 127.
104. Pflanze, *Bismarck and the Development of Germany*, 2:241.

National Zeitung, therefore, merely repeated the well-worn stereotype when it stated that Catholicism was "a religion of the uneducated. At its top it has priests, a few princes and nobles, behind it a following of speechmakers, sophists, and miracle-workers: the great part of its members are workers and peasants."[105] Liberals, self-professed middle-class heroes of culture, science, industry, and progress, did nothing to veil their contempt for the Catholic peasants, whom they considered dirty, ignorant, and submissive. Bluntschli and Virchow, who were on opposite ends of the liberal political spectrum, held interchangeable opinions on the topic. Bluntschli argued that "ultramontanism plays on the uneducated, the natural need for authority, and the traditional and acquired beliefs of the masses."[106] As early as 1849, when Virchow visited Silesia during a typhoid epidemic, he reported that the rural population, submissive as it was to the clergy, was "lazy, unclean, dog-like in its devotion, and inflexibly averse to any physical or mental exertion."[107] "The people," he explained, "are physically and morally weak and need some kind of tutelary guidance."[108] Later, in the 1870s, in an age that he believed should have been enlightened, rational, and scientific, Virchow attacked the Catholic population's obsession with miracles and observed that "the regions along the Rhine are completely dazzled by them."[109] In 1854 the eminent liberal historian Johann Gustav Droysen wrote to Heinrich von Sybel that the new veneration of the Virgin Mary was a form of "idolatry" suitable only to the "mob."[110]

Meanwhile, not just liberals but Protestants and social democrats too tirelessly bemoaned the Bildungsdefizit, the backward educational status and lackluster academic performance of the Catholic population, in every possible venue, including in books and newspaper and journal articles, at public meetings, and on the floor of the Prussian parliament and the Reichstag. According to critics, the problem in general seemed to be due to a deep-seated Catholic indifference to if not

---

105. Quoted in Blackbourn, "Progress and Piety," 149.

106. Johann Caspar Bluntschli, "Zwei Feinde unsres Staats und unsrer Cultur," *Gegenwart* 3 (1872): 310–11, quotation at 310.

107. Blackbourn, *Marpingen,* 290.

108. Blackbourn, "Progress and Piety," 149.

109. Rudolf Virchow, *Über Wunder: Rede gehalten in der ersten allgemeinen Sitzung der 47. Versammlung deutscher Naturforscher und Ärzte zu Breslau am 18. September, 1874* (Breslau, 1874), 3.

110. Johann Gustav Droysen to Heinrich von Sybel, 12 Dec. 1854, in Hübner, *Johann Gustav Droysen Briefwechsel,* 2:300.

disdain for knowledge and learning since Catholic religious culture appeared to value only faith and obedience. This evaluation was bigoted, but work on Catholic reading habits suggests that it was not until the 1890s that Catholics became interested in becoming intellectually cultivated according to the dominant culture's standards of taste and sensibility as a way to emerge from their social "ghetto" and redraw the boundaries of national participation.[111] Sybel himself believed that, in the Rhineland at least, the problem was more specifically the dismal failure of the Catholic Gymnasia. A quarter of the students could not, he complained, write grammatically correct German; as many as three-quarters could barely read an easy Latin or Greek text.[112] Sybel's disgust for the apparently hopeless intellectual inferiority of Rhenish Catholics was so intense that it was literally palpable: in the Prussian parliament in 1879 he explained that he always broke out with "goose bumps" whenever a student from the Rhineland enrolled for his courses at the University of Bonn. He was delighted whenever a gentleman from the eastern provinces signed up.[113]

Critics of Catholic culture ultimately blamed priests for the intellectual inferiority of Catholics. Liberals endlessly complained that Catholic priests were just peasants themselves and, therefore, as unwashed, ignorant, and blind as those they led. Liberal papers recycled story after story about the embarrassing social inferiority of priests. The *Vossische Zeitung,* for example, explained to its readers that "the Catholic priest is with few exceptions a peasant's son. He is kept away from the university, . . . from association with educated circles, especially from educated ladies. He therefore remains a peasant and retains the manners, the ways of thinking, of the under classes." It followed that the Catholic priest was in the best position to understand and influence "the crude masses." In contrast to the rustic and socially disreputable Catholic priest, the paper argued, the Protestant pastor was either the son of a pastor or a Bürger. He attended the university and naturally associated with those in the educated circles. The Protestant pastor could, therefore, never be popular among the masses.[114]

Though Catholics understandably objected to such self-serving and

---

111. Jeffrey T. Zalar, "The Process of Confessional Inculturation: Catholic Reading in the 'Long Nineteenth Century,'" in *Protestants, Catholics, and Jews in Germany, 1800–1914,* ed. Helmut Walser Smith (Oxford: Berg, 2001), 121–52.

112. Heinrich von Sybel, *Klerikale Politik im neunzehnten Jahrhundert* (Bonn: M. Cohen und Sohn, 1874), 95–96.

113. Anderson and Barkin, "The Myth of the Puttkamer Purge," 679.

114. *Vossische Zeitung,* 26 Aug. 1869.

prejudiced characterizations, the *Vossische Zeitung* was in point of fact not far off the mark. While most priests in Germany at the beginning of the century had been recruited into the Catholic Church mainly from the urban classes, later in the century priests came from overwhelmingly rural backgrounds. Irmtraud Götz von Olenhusen in her research on the Catholic clergy in Baden demonstrates that Catholic priests, in fact, were routinely drawn from the lowest level of the rural social scale. The German priesthood largely came from outside the processes of urban and industrial growth under way throughout the country.[115] It does not follow that this was another indication that the Catholic Church was a recalcitrant anachronism out of touch with the "modern" spirit of the age. Like nineteenth-century liberals, some recent historians of Catholicism in Germany have not recognized that the ultramontane revival, however conservative, was with its mass organization, mobilization, and commercialization, and reliance on communication and transportation as much part of the age as urbanization and industrialization.[116] Here, however, was precisely the paradox. The church was quite ready and able to embrace modern means in its fight against the capitalism, materialism, rationalism, and science that threatened to corrode the foundations of faith.[117]

The *Vossische Zeitung* was also by and large not mistaken when it argued that Protestant pastors failed to wield the same religious, social, and political influence on their congregations as Catholic priests.

115. Götz von Olenhusen, "Klerus und Ultramontanismus."

116. For examples of work that have argued that antimodernism was fundamental to the ultramontane movement and the church's ideological and political response to modernity, see, in addition to Götz von Olenhusen, "Klerus und Ultramontanismus"; also idem, "Ultramontanisierung des Klerus"; Christoph Weber, "Ultramontanismus als katholischer Fundamentalismus," in *Deutscher Katholizismus im Umbruch zur Moderne,* ed. Wilfried Loth (Stuttgart: W. Kohlhammer), 20–45. See also the critical comments by Anderson, "Limits of Secularization," 661; and David Blackbourn, "The Catholic Church in Europe since the French Revolution: A Review," *Comparative Studies in Society and History* 33 (1991): 778–90. Zalar argues that his work on Catholic reading habits suggests that research has overemphasized the success of the clergy in creating a reactionary subculture against modern influences. There is an interesting and not yet resolved debate concerning the significance of popular Catholic reading habits in the nineteenth century. In contrast to Helmut Walser Smith's analysis of Catholic reading material, Zalar argues Catholic reading shows that the boundaries separating official German intellectual and aesthetic culture from the Catholic milieu have been drawn too sharply. See Zalar, "Process of Confessional Inculturation"; and Smith, *German Nationalism,* 20–37, 80–86.

117. See Altermatt, "Katholizismus: Antimodernismus mit modernen Mitteln?"; Michael Klöcker, *Katholisch—von der Weige bis zur Bahre: Eine Lebensmacht im Zerfall?* (Munich: Kösel-Verlag, 1991), 23–27; and Thomas Nipperdey, *Deutsche Geschichte 1800–1866: Bürgerwelt und starker Staat* (Munich: C. H. Beck, 1983), 412–13.

Catholic priests remained formidable and for the most part uncontested voices at the center of Catholic communities, particularly in small towns and the villages of the countryside. Protestant pastors by contrast were socially removed from the experience of the Mittelstand and working-class members of their churches. In addition they were usually merely one voice to be heard among other educated, socially established, professionally respected, and politically elite authorities in Protestant society.

Liberals and authorities believed the ignorance and social inferiority of priests and their flocks were important explanations for the level of violence in the anti-Kulturkampf protests. The open rebellion by the population of Essen in 1872 against authorities who had tried to close the local Jesuit residence and chapel was one of the first indications that Catholics when provoked could turn into a violent mob. Catholics openly battled the police in the streets for several days, and the riots culminated in an attack on the home of a suspected liberal Freemason. Battalions of infantry were required to restore order.[118] In 1874, state officials were disturbed by the sight of "strange people, most with blank, stupid faces" who flooded into Cologne in large numbers from the countryside to join in anti-Kulturkampf agitation. The *Magdeburgische Zeitung* claimed that the Catholic mob got drunk, roamed the streets in a stupor, and looked for trouble. The paper warned that if the Catholic ruffian element "ever got power into its hands, one could expect the very worst." Officials in east Prussia worried that they would have to battle Catholic Poles of "the poorest and least educated classes."[119]

When exasperated state authorities met Catholic crowds with the use of force, they justified it in terms of Catholic recalcitrance. In 1875 reports of the appearance of the Virgin Mary in the village of Marpingen in the Saarland attracted thousands of pilgrims from all over Germany. District officials called up a company of infantry to disperse the pilgrims in a futile and misguided effort to crush ignorance with outright brutality.[120] At the same time liberal circles were hardly surprised

---

118. *Essener Zeitung,* 25 Aug. 1872; *Vossische Zeitung,* 7 Sept. 1872; HSTAD, RD, Nr. 20111, "Jesuiten oder Orden der Gesellschaft Jesu und verwandte Orden," Bd. 1, 1870–72, newspaper clipping from *Berliner Börsen Zeitung,* n.d.; HSTAD, RD, Nr. 20112, "Jesuiten oder Orden der Gesellschaft Jesu und verwandte Orden," Bd. 2, 1872–73, newspaper clipping from *Spenersche Zeitung,* 6 Sept. 1872; HSTAD, RA, Nr. 10699, "Orden der Gesellschaft Jesu bzw. die Ausführung des Gesetzes vom 4 Juli 1872," PP and LR to Regierung, Abtheilung des Innern, Aachen, 4 Dec. 1872, Bl. 88–89.

119. These examples and quotations in Ross, *Failure of Bismarck's Kulturkampf,* 133.

120. Blackbourn, *Marpingen,* 263–67, 271–74.

that the whole affair was due to the rumors started by three peasant girls. An article entitled "Moderne Krankheitssymptome" appearing in the liberal literary journal *Grenzboten* argued that religious apparitions were attributable to the overexcitement of the imagination, vanity, and "tendentious consciousness" of girls.[121] In these cases the face of bourgeois class prejudice is again unmistakable, but the impression that anti-Kulturkampf violence seemed to be the work of the Catholic lower classes often incited by women or girls and led by clerics was not wholly inaccurate. Middle-class Catholics as a whole shied away from anti-Kulturkampf violent agitation. As members of the Bürgertum they were reluctant to participate in demonstrations against authority and alarmed by disorderly conduct that damaged private property.[122] Indeed, they were often proponents of the Kulturkampf themselves.

The issue was not simply that the "crude" and "dangerous" Catholic masses were intellectually inept, socially contemptible, and given to violence. Just as important, "ignorant" and "unruly" Catholics in the age of democratic suffrage posed a political problem. Following the victory against Austria in 1866, Bismarck called to life direct, equal, male suffrage with the founding of the short-lived North German Confederation. Then when King Wilhelm of Prussia was hailed as German Kaiser at Versailles in 1871 during the war against France, the new empire inherited the most progressive franchise in Europe. Germany's leap into a new age of democratic suffrage threatened to overthrow the status quo and challenged the liberal concept of politics. Liberals in the new political order pointed to the proclamation of infallibility by Pope Pius IX in 1870 as the root of the problem. The new papal proclamation might have pertained only to matters of dogma, but it seemed to make the Roman Church's positions, including those regarding the ballot box, matters of absolute obedience. If so, voting Catholics now expressed the will of a foreign power in domestic politics. According to liberals, the new Catholic voters were not autonomous individuals free to cast their ballots as they saw fit but a voting bloc. In point of fact, critics said that liberal candidates addressed their constituencies as fellow "citizens," but the new Center Party called its supporters "the Catholic people" or the Catholic "flock."[123] Opponents of the Center

121. Moderne Krankheitssymptome, 1: "Der religiöse Mädchenspuk," *Grenzboten* 3 (1876), 21–26.

122. Ross, *Failure of Bismarck's Kulturkampf*, 134 n. 48.

123. Blackbourn, "Catholics and Politics in Imperial Germany," 200.

referred to Catholic political practice as "ballot Catholicism."[124] Liberals then looked on with disgust when on the morning of the first elections in the new empire in March 1871 priests instructed their congregations how they should vote. After mass, priests took their parishioners to the polling stations.[125] For Bluntschli as for many others this was simply unbearable.

> The same class of people that considers it intolerable that the state approves legislation without its representation, that takes part independently in the state's administration of justice as jurymen and aldermen, that constantly limits the entire political and economic administration of the state with its control, and that elects its own mayors and district magistrates is also the class that submits itself to the unqualified authority of the pope and [Vatican] Council, the bishops and their ecclesiastical seats.[126]

Bluntschli thought it was hypocrisy that Catholics on the one hand offered themselves like children to the despotism of the Roman Church yet on the other hand insisted that they exercise the public and political responsibilities of citizenship in the nation. Sybel echoed the concerns about the lack of maturity and independence among Catholic voters and the growing power of the Center Party, which seemed to enjoy the unqualified obedience of its constituency. He feared that the tight-knit organization of the Center Party would eventually overwhelm liberal voters, who, in contrast to Catholics, valued their personal freedom more highly than their discipline.

> The more democratic the current of the times becomes, the more power is going to be exercised by a party that can control more than a million and a half voters with military command. Though liberals may still be numerically superior to [the Center Party], it compensates for this with the force of its discipline. Its voters and deputies in Parliament vote like one man according to the orders of their leader. By contrast, on the liberal side it is precisely personal independence and loyalty to one's own convictions that are

124. Anderson, *Practicing Democracy,* 133.
125. For an example, see Margaret Lavinia Anderson, "Voter, Junker, *Landrat,* Priest: The Old Authorities and the New Franchise in Imperial Germany," *American Historical Review* 98 (1993): 1448–74, esp. 1451–52.
126. Bluntschli, *Charakter und Geist,* 54–55.

highly valued. These may be high virtues, but they are not always tempered with moderation, and they often degenerate into righteousness and factiousness.[127]

There is the hint here of envy. Liberals immediately recognized the advantages of reliable voters delivering ballots en masse and the vulnerability of parties constituted by Honoratioren who jealously guarded their idealism and independence in a new age of democracy determined ultimately by large bloc votes. The impact of the democratic franchise, the role of the Center Party, the influence of clerical electioneering, and the consequences of the Catholic population "practicing democracy" reshaped German political culture.[128] The first elections in the empire, which included an aggressive Catholic turnout for the Center, looked like a disaster according to liberals. Immediately following the elections, Heinrich von Treitschke complained in 1871 that universal male suffrage was "an invaluable weapon of the Jesuits, which grants an unfair advantage to the powers of tradition and stupidity."[129] In a democratic age that gave the Catholic "masses" the vote, when political decisions were not determined by the reasoned argument of independent gentlemen but by the brute power of voting blocs, the liberal virtue of independence seemed now a liability, an irony that lay at the center of the liberal fear of and enmity toward the Center Party. The alleged femininity of Catholics coupled with their subservience to a despotic authority beyond the empire, therefore, made them not only unfit for political responsibility but also a threat to liberal politics, liberal political hegemony, and the independence of the state. Over and over liberals warned that with the Catholic voting bloc at its disposal, the Catholic Church was not simply a "private society" but a public power against which the state had to defend itself.[130]

In the Rhineland, the Deutscher Verein was organized to coordinate and mobilize liberal opposition against the rising tide of political Catholicism. Sybel heralded the association as an attempt at "intensive personal engagement with the masses of the Volk" though there is at the same time an indication here of the continuing attachment to an

127. Sybel, *Klerikale Politik,* 116–17.
128. Anderson, *Practicing Democracy.*
129. Heinrich von Treitschke, "Parteien und Fractionen (1871)," in *Historische und politische Aufsätze,* 7th ed. (Leipzig: S. Hirzel, 1915), 3:608.
130. See, for example, Zeller, *Staat und Kirche,* 63–64, 97. For Zeller's considerable influence on prominent liberals see Keith Anderton, "The Limits of Science: A Social, Political, and Moral Agenda for Epistemology in Nineteenth-Century Germany" (Ph.D. diss., Harvard University, 1993), 308–12.

individual, face-to-face mode of political persuasion.[131] The claim of Pope Pius IX in a letter to Kaiser Wilhelm I in August 1873, first published by the *Staatsanzeiger* in October 1873, that everyone who had been baptized Christian belonged to the pope only confirmed liberal fears.[132] According to the *National Zeitung,* the letter was nothing less than a declaration "that the war, which is already under way, is supposed to be carried through by the curia until the German Empire is destroyed." "The Jesuits through the mouth of the pope," the paper continued, "have spurred on the German priests and Catholics to the most fierce battle against the fatherland."[133]

So similar were the problems with women and the masses that they were ultimately conflated in liberal anti-Catholicism. Liberals believed that their own masculine independence, civic spirit, and Bildung were as uncharacteristic of the lower classes as they were of women. Priests seemed to be able to sway and manipulate the lower-class masses in the same way and for the same reason that they were able to control and use women. Like women, the masses were irrational, prone to excitement, and predisposed to religious fanaticism and were, therefore, easily manipulated by the clergy. To cite Bluntschli once again, the Jesuit order "worked sometimes secretly through 'pious women' on weak men, sometimes openly through the stirred-up masses."[134] Just as liberals conceived of Catholicism as a mob, the nineteenth-century bourgeoisie, not just in Germany but throughout Europe, thought of the masses and mass culture as a woman; authentic culture belonged alone to men.[135] Theories of mass behavior such as those developed by French social psychologists, including Hippolyte Taine, Gabriel Tarde, and particularly Gustave Le Bon in his enormously popular *Psychologie des foules* (appearing in English as *The Crowd*), represented the belief already current in the latter half of the century that mobs, impulsive, irrational, and prone to violence, were distinguished by their "feminine" (as well as mentally ill, alcoholic, and savage) char-

131. Quoted in Sheehan, *German Liberalism,* 150.

132. Letter of Pope Pius IX to Kaiser Wilhelm I, 7 Aug. 1873, in *The Age of Bismarck: Documents and Interpretations,* ed. Theodore S. Hamerow (New York: Harper and Row, 1973), 163. For a liberal reaction see Johann Caspar Bluntschli, *Die rechtliche Unverantwortlichkeit und Veranwortlichkeit des römischen Papstes: Eine völker- und staatsrechtliche Studie* (Nördlingen: C. H. Beck, 1876), 8.

133. Quotations in Theodor Wacker, *Friede zwischen Berlin und Rom? Geschichtliche Erinnerungen aus der Blüthezeit des Kulturkampfes* (Freiburg im Breisgen, 1879), 11–12.

134. Bluntschli, *Charakter und Geist,* 36.

135. Andreas Huyssen, "Mass Culture as Woman: Modernism's Other," in *After the Great Divide: Modernism, Mass Culture, Postmodernism* (Bloomington and Indianapolis: Indiana University Press, 1986), 44–62. See also Sidonia Blätter, *Der Pöbel die Frauen, etc.: Die Massen in der politischen Philosophie des 19. Jahrhunderts* (Berlin: Akademie Verlag, 1995).

acteristics.[136] According to Le Bon, "The simplicity and exaggeration of the sentiments of crowds have the result that a throng knows neither doubt nor uncertainty. Like a woman, it goes at once to extremes. . . . A commencement of antipathy or disapprobation, which in the case of an isolated individual would not gain strength, becomes at once furious hatred in the case of an individual in a crowd."[137] Le Bon argued that crowds upon closer examination also exhibited a peculiar religious sentiment, necessarily accompanied by intolerance and fanaticism, and religions, he believed, were founded on crowds that sought happiness in worship and obedience.

But the confounding of women, religious fanaticism, and the masses is only half the point. In the liberal imagination Catholicism as a feminine and stupid mob threatening to overwhelm and disorient the public was intertwined with other enemies inside and outside German borders. The *Gartenlaube* argued that Catholicism, especially monasticism, was also a form of communism. The journal claimed that the possessions of the church were the common property of all its members.[138] To cite Bluntschli once again, he argued in "Zwei Feinde unsres Staats und unsrer Cultur" that ultramontanism and communism were two enemies of the state and culture that despite their differences shared many characteristics. Communists and the Catholic clergy might despise each other's beliefs, but they were joined in their mutual desire to destroy the authority of the state. Jesuits and ultramontanes might represent the past and the communists might claim to represent the future, but both shared an aversion to the present. Both fed on the lower classes, and both were international movements. Both played on the irrationalism of the masses and directed mob violence against the state and society. Bluntschli argued that the present age distinguished itself from the age of the Enlightenment by the democratic dissemination of rights among the "Volksclassen" and the "terroristic tendency" of the present age to erupt into violence in the form of ultramontanism and communism. The state, he therefore warned, must arm and ready itself now for the inevitable war against both ultramontanes and communists.[139]

136. Susanna Barrows, *Distorting Mirrors: Visions of the Crowd in Late Nineteenth-Century France* (New Haven and London: Yale University Press, 1981). This is the point made in Blackbourn, "Progress and Piety," 149–50.

137. Quoted in Huyssen, "Mass Culture as Woman," 53.

138. See, for example, "Aus dem österreichischen Klosterleben," *Gartenlaube* (1874), 483–85, 616–18.

139. Bluntschli, "Zwei Feinde."

Bluntschli's fears were repeated over and over by other prominent liberals. Emil Friedberg, member of the Evangelischer Oberkirchenrat and a prominent architect of Kulturkampf legislation, believed in an ultramontane-socialist alliance. Both ultramontanes and socialists, Friedberg explained, "deny the right of the state [to exist] and try to root it out; both ultimately suffer from notions of property that lack legal precision, even if the ultramontanes demand the property of their neighbors . . . for the Roman pope and, therefore, only indirectly for themselves while the socialists demand it for their own direct use."[140] For Friedberg it was only logical to assume that the "socialist-international" would join the "ultramontane-international" in a war to reduce the German Empire to rubble and to declare victory over its separate states. This was a war from which Germans should not flinch; indeed, it would be welcomed: "violence will be beaten down to the ground with violence, and the strength of our people is too great to be crippled by the ultramontane-socialist league. In order to lay holy steel on the body of the state, perhaps it is just as well if the social boil breaks open."[141] Heinrich von Treitschke too warned that priests, instead of preaching peace and reconciliation to the masses, were "allying themselves with the apostles of communism and glorifying revolt against the law as a battle of light against darkness."[142]

In 1872, in a catalog of the mistakes in the recent history of France that Germany should endeavor to avoid, Sybel freely mixed his fear of French radicalism with anticlerical hysteria. The horror of the Paris Commune of 1871—which included the arrest of thirty-eight thousand, execution of twenty-eight thousand, and deportation of seventy-five hundred Communards—was, he argued, the inevitable consequence of the hierarchical establishment of the French Catholic Church. "If Germany has the desire to see the situation in Paris repeated on its own soil, it only needs to establish its ecclesiastical life along the principles of the French Church: unqualified submission of the laity to the priests, the priests to the bishops, the bishops to the pope. Then we would experience the Communes in Germany too."[143] And according to Sybel it was again the French Catholic clergy that had whipped up

140. Quoted in Birke, "Zur Entwicklung und politischen Funktion des bürgerlichen Kulturkampfverständnisses," 272.

141. Emil Friedberg, *Das deutsche Reich und die katholische Kirche* (Leipzig: Duncker und Humblot, 1872), 40–41.

142. Heinrich von Treitschke, "Die Maigesetze und ihre Folgen," in *Zehn Jahre deutscher Kämpfe: Schriften zur Tagespolitik* (Berlin: G. Reimer, 1879), 432–44, quotation at 438.

143. Heinrich von Sybel, "Was Wir von Frankreich Lernen Können," in *Vorträge und Aufsätze* (Berlin: A Hoffmann, 1874), 336–47, quotation at 342. The pamphlet was first published in 1872.

the hatred against Prussia that had brought war in 1871. Those who were neither members of the "black" nor the "red" international movements, according to Sybel, should therefore be thankful that Germany had prevailed.[144] Writing shortly after the Franco-Prussian War and the founding of the empire and with reference to the protection offered the papacy in Rome by Napoleon I during the campaign for Italian unification, Emil Friedberg warned, "If Napoleon I openly confessed that he has achieved political goals through the *Französirung* [Frenchification] of the papacy and wants to win political supremacy over the Catholics, how much greater is the threat today." Now the population had been organized into a fanatical army of Catholic associations. "Today the bishop of all the German dioceses sits in Rome and places himself under the tutelage of the French government."[145] Liberal newspapers and journals joined in the hysterical conspiracy theory, and no accusations seemed too outlandish. The *National Zeitung* argued that the pope had formed an alliance with the French in order to destroy the German Empire.[146] When Catholics protested Sedan Day, the anniversary of the Prussian triumphant battle against the French army, by flying the papal flag, liberal nationalists took this as an indication of pro-French sentiment.

As the Kulturkampf gathered momentum, the liberal election campaign of 1874 was more vigorous and harsher than it had been three years before. In Baden, National Liberals now called Center Party deputies not just *Reichsfeinde,* enemies of the empire, but also *Franzosenvertreter,* representatives of the French.[147] In that same year, on the fifth anniversary of the victory at Sedan, the executive committee of the Deutscher Verein distributed election leaflets reminding citizens of the Rhineland that France had been allied with the Jesuits against Germany.[148] Such associations were politically marketable to be sure. But the connection between socialists, the French, Jesuits, and the rabble was so deeply ingrained in anticlerical discourse that it was featured in Wilhelm Busch's best-selling allegory *Pater Filucius,* a combination of cartoon and malicious verse. "Pater Luzi looking ominous secretly sneaks about the house" plotting to stir up some mischief. He teams up

144. Heinrich von Sybel, "Das neue deutsche Reich," in *Vorträge und Aufsätze* (Berlin: A. Hoffman, 1874), 305–30. The article originally appeared in 1871.

145. Friedberg, *Das deutsche Reich und die katholische Kirche,* quotations at 26–27.

146. See quotation from the *National Zeitung* in Wacker, *Friede zwischen Berlin und Rom?* 12.

147. Sperber, *Kaiser's Voters,* 166.

148. HSTAD, Best. RK, Nr. 2723, "Die Enthebung der katholischen Geistlichen von der lokalen Schulaufsicht und deren Nachfolger, 1874–1875," Bl. 8.

with a ragamuffin socialist, "an Inter-Nazi," and with a Frenchman, Jean Lecaq. The trio is easily outwitted by the master of the house. They are roundly thrashed, and a swift defenestration lands them where they belong: in a pool of filth.[149]

By the early 1870s all the various threats in this age of militant Catholicism *and* the women's movement *and* democratization *and* nascent socialism *and* French revanchism could no longer be managed separately in the liberal imaginary. The burden of such a formidable array of enemies meant that they were collapsed into a single meta-enemy. This had the advantage of psychological efficiency: a blow, imaginary or actual, delivered against the Jesuits, Catholics, feminists, French revanchists, or communists seemed to be a blow delivered against them all. There was also little incentive among liberals to separate out their various enemies, since each by mere association with the others was all the more discreditable. To cite once more Sybel as an example, when he referred to the clerical party as the "enemy," threatening the empire from the inside just as France threatened the empire from the outside, he consciously gendered the word feminine (*Feindin*). "Whoever promotes the wishes of the clerics in important matters," he added, "also opens the borders to the foreign enemy of the empire."[150] That these enemies were collapsed together in the liberal imagination is illustrated by a cartoon in the *Berliner Wespen* in 1873 (fig. 18). In "The Political Concert Hall" the "European Ladies Orchestra" is rehearsing. A woman is reading from a music score marked "Commune." She is blowing over the neck of a bottle labeled "petrol," a reference that would have conjured the memory of the ruthless *pétroleuses*—Communard women who according to legend in their desperation set the French capital ablaze in the final week of senseless self-destruction. Another woman whips up French hatred for Germany, clanging together cymbals while pounding on a bass drum labeled "revanchism." And another plays the trombone, following the score of the communist "International." A fourth woman, wearing the unmistakable broad black hat with curled rim of the Jesuits, plucks the strings of a double bass marked "*Germania,* Majunke." The leading Catholic newspaper and its priest-editor and Center Party deputy Paul Majunke are the puppets of the Jesuits. Another woman plays a bassoon to the

---

149. Wilhelm Busch, "Pater Filucius" in *Wilhelm Busch: Historisch-Kritische Gesamtausgabe,* ed. Friedrich Bohne (Wiesbaden: Vollmer Verlag, 1960), 2:347–80. See also Healy, "Anti-Jesuitism in Imperial Germany," 165. The connection between Jesuits, socialists, and the French is made in Gross, "Kulturkampf und Unification," 564–66.

150. Sybel, *Klerikale Politik,* 119.

Fig. 18. "Aus dem politischen Concertsaal," *Berliner Wespen,* 10 October 1873. A range of liberal enemies—Jesuits, the Catholic press, women in public, French revanchism, and Communards—are brought together in the "political concert hall." The "European Ladies Orchestra" is conducted by a female pope.

tune of financial ruin. Conducting the "orchestra" from behind is, finally, a woman who wears, of course, the papal crown.[151] The cacophonic ensemble looked laughable, to be sure, but it provided only a moment's comic relief from the fears that otherwise incessantly haunted German liberals.

Women in public; French revanchists in Alsace and Lorraine; Catholics everywhere; Jesuit missionaries roaming across Germany; priests, monks, and nuns; the Center Party and its press organs; communard arsonists; the democratic rabble, all were enemies allied within and against the new empire. Liberals believed their influence had to be met with the full force of the state, destroyed in a campaign that required an effort no less than war. What has emerged in an exploration of liberal gender ideology and the women's question is a complex array of imperatives that shaped the campaign against the Catholic Church and Catholicism in the 1870s. The Kulturkampf unleashed following the founding of the empire should be understood not as it has so often been portrayed as simply an attack on the Roman Church for the sake of the autonomy of the state, a political campaign against the introduction of universal male suffrage, an assault on

151. "Aus dem politischen Concertsaal," *Berliner Wespen,* 10 Oct. 1873.

"backward" Catholicism, or an effort to impose Protestant culture on the German nation. To be sure, the Kulturkampf was in part all of these. In themselves, however, they do not ultimately account for the deep-seated fury of the Kulturkampf, a campaign whose origins were seated in the 1850s and 1860s during the Catholic popular revival and the reemergence of the women's movement. From this perspective, the Kulturkampf was a complex attempt during a period of dramatic pressures for change to orient and preserve liberal modernism, an entire political, social, and sexual order that rested ultimately on the distinction between public and private life.

CHAPTER 5

Kulturkampf, Unification, and
the War against Catholicism

In July 1870 in a coincidence of history, the French government declared war on the North German Confederation within a day of the Vatican Council's proclamation of papal infallibility. The third of the wars of German unification had begun. Soon the French army was forced to retreat and then was pinned down and humiliated at the battle of Sedan. Paris was taken, France defeated, and the German states were reconstituted in a united empire under the aegis of the Prussian monarchy. For many nationalist liberals, France laid low *and* Germany unified, two dreams realized at once and with the same stroke, proved almost too much to bear. Shortly after the new Kaiser's proclamation of the German Empire in the Hall of Mirrors at Versailles on 18 January 1871, Heinrich von Sybel voiced in a letter to his colleague Hermann Baumgarten the general feeling so euphoric that there seemed practically nothing more worth living for. "How have we deserved God's grace to be permitted to experience such great and mighty things? And for what shall one live hereafter? That which has been for twenty years the object of all our wishes and efforts has now been achieved in such a bounteous, magnificent way. Where shall I at my age find a new purpose for living?"[1] This was a question for which Sybel and other liberals who felt like him soon found an answer. In the heady years following the triumph over France, with the nation united and the external borders of the new empire fixed, liberals found

---

1. Letter from Heinrich von Sybel to Hermann Baumgarten, 27 Jan. 1871, in *Deutscher Liberalismus im Zeitalter Bismarcks: Eine politische Briefsammlung,* ed. Julius Heydorff and Paul Wentzcke (Osnabrück: Biblio Verlag, 1967), 2:494. See also Pflanze, *Bismarck and the Development of Germany,* 2:172.

another cause worth their wholehearted dedication. They committed themselves now to a war against the Roman Catholic Church and with it the consolidation within Germany of modern society, culture, and morality.[2]

Liberals recognized that this would be no less a challenge than the war against France had been. They believed that realizing the ideals of the Enlightenment, unifying the empire, and cultivating German spirit had, ironically, been made all the more difficult by the spoils of victory. The annexation of Alsace-Lorraine as a *Reichsland* (imperial province) on the southwestern periphery was doubly problematic. Its conquered inhabitants were not only French; they were also overwhelmingly Catholic. In this new territory the Protestant population of 250,000 was outnumbered by 1,200,000 Catholics. The Catholic demographic density of Alsace-Lorraine was among the highest in Germany, and the population was well supplied with priests. Nationalist liberal journals like the *Preußische Jahrbücher, Grenzboten,* and *Im Neuen Reich* repeatedly complained that the French Catholic Church continued to exert a powerful hold on the population.[3] There were reasons to believe their fears were well grounded. According to one stipulation of the Frankfurt Treaty, French bishops retained at least provisional authority over dioceses in Alsace and Lorraine. At the same time, Catholic priests in the Reichsland, where the Prussian attack on Catholic Austria in 1866 was still in recent memory, equated Germany with Prussia and Prussia with Protestantism. A Catholic priest, writing to the bishop of Strasbourg in March 1871, explained that the Prussians were universally despised in Alsace-Lorraine. The bishop of Angers warned King Wilhelm of Prussia, the new Kaiser of Germany, that Alsace

2. On the problem of the social and cultural consolidation of imperial Germany, see Eley, "State Formation, Nationalism, and Political Culture," 277–301, and especially for the role of the Kulturkampf following unification, 284, 290. For the Kulturkampf as "simply the next stage of unification," see idem, "Bismarckian Germany," 20–25. See also James J. Sheehan, "What Is German History? Reflections on the Role of the Nation in German History and Historiography," *Journal of Modern History* 53 (1981): 1–23. For the concept of the German Empire as an "unfinished nation" see Theodor Schieder, *Das deutsche Kaiserreich von 1871 als Nationalstaat* (Cologne: Westdeutscher Verlag, 1961).

3. See "Zur Statistik des Klosterwesensin Elsaß-Lothringen," *Gegenwart* 3 (1873): 17–20; "Deutsche Aufgaben in Elaß-Lothringen," *Grenzboten* 2 (1871): 565–76, 621–32, 657–68, 747–56; "Der Staat und die Bischofswahlen in Elsaß-Lothringen," *Grenzboten* 2 (1874): 227–35; "Zur innern Wiedergewinnung Elsaß-Lothringens," *Grenzboten* 3 (1874): 106–13; "Der innere Situation des Reichslandes," *Im Neuen Reich* 3 (1873): 507–12, where Alsacian Catholics are the "submissive tools of the clergy"; "Ultramontane Umtriebe im Elsaß," *Im Neuen Reich* 3 (1873): 527–36; "Staat und Kirche in Elsaß-Lothringen," *Im Neuen Reich* 9 (1879): 131–43; "Die katholische Kirche im Elsaß und in Preußen," *Preußische Jahrbücher* 27 (1871): 716–39.

would never belong to a Prussian monarch.[4] The annexation of the population of the Reichsland seemed to compound the problem of the Catholic Polish-speaking population in the east already suspected of unreliable loyalty to the Kaiser and empire. The acquisition of Alsace-Lorraine only made the need to "Germanize" the empire by destroying Roman Catholic clerical power all the more apparent.[5]

Now that liberals believed they were at the height of their power, with the nation united and no need to fear that a move against the church might prevent the acceptance of unification in the largely Catholic southern states, there seemed no reason to delay the attack against the enemy within.[6] The final provocation had already come in the form of the Vatican Council's proclamation of papal infallibility. In this age of modern science and progress and at the moment of nationalist pride in the modern state, the Vatican declaration was for liberal Germans not only a grotesque aberration but also an assault on the independence of the state. Papal infallibility seemed to require the allegiance of German Catholics not to the Kaiser but to the pope and the subordination of the sovereignty of Berlin to the rule of Rome. In his paradigmatically liberal attack on papal infallibility, *Die päpstliche Unfehlbarkeit und das vatikanische Koncil*, the prominent National Liberal deputy Paul Hinschius argued that the Vatican's proclamation was nothing less than a "death sentence" passed against the modern state.[7] Though an extravagant assertion, this was an opinion widely shared among liberals. When in February 1872, little more than a year after the founding of the empire, the liberal *National Zeitung* argued that Germans could now no longer accept suppression at the hands of the Catholic Church, it merely echoed the predominant liberal point of view. The German, the paper explained,

will not tolerate a spirit that comes from Rome either among his people or in any of his churches. He does not want clerical rule

---

4. Dan Silverman, *Reluctant Union: Alsace-Lorraine and Imperial Germany, 1871–1918* (University Park: Pennsylvania State University Press, 1972), 91.

5. Ibid.

6. Evans, *German Center Party*, 48.

7. Paul Hinschius, *Die päpstliche Unfehlbarkeit und das vatikanische Koncil* (Kiel: Universitäts-Buchhandlung, 1871). See also idem, *Die Stellung der deutschen Staatregierung gegenüber den Beschlüssen des vatikanischen Koncils* (Berlin: J. Gutentag, 1871). Hinschius was a major architect of Kulturkampf legislation. For a similar systematic refutation of papal infallibility, see Johann Caspar Bluntschli, *Die rechtliche Unverantwortlichkeit und Verantwortlichkeit des römischen Papstes.*

and the people reduced to stupidity. He wants, rather, enlightenment, an honest conscience, and work. Attaining a new, as yet
never achieved, level of moral freedom, a national morality that is
shared by Germany's churches and confessions, that is the task
for this founding period of the new empire.[8]

For liberals and progressives a campaign against the power of the
Catholic Church had become an urgent matter. It was not only necessary to secure national unity. It was also required to preserve the very
existence of the new empire. Catholic leaders read the mood now
prominent among liberals. According to the Catholic *Badische
Beobachter,* "The liberal leaders declare that the war is now just really
starting; we have made peace with France; with Rome, we will never
make peace."[9] The campaign that was launched against the church in
the name of German unity, the modern state, science, progress, Bildung, and freedom became known as the Kulturkampf, a "cultural
struggle" or a "battle for culture," legislated by liberal elites and
enforced with the power of the state. In the dramatic formulation of
one historian, however, it was no less than a *Vernichtungskrieg,* a war
to exterminate the Roman Catholic Church as a spiritual-religious and
political power.[10] This war against the church was waged with legislation enacted primarily in Prussia with concurrent campaigns in Baden
and Hesse and occasional legislation enacted at the imperial level.

The predominant interpretations of German liberalism in the Kulturkampf during roughly the first decade of the new empire have
argued that liberals compromised their own principles in their attack
against the Catholic Church. On this reading, by sponsoring illiberal
legislation and by allying themselves with the Bismarckian authoritarian state in the antichurch campaign, German liberals betrayed their
fundamental belief in individual rights, freedom, and toleration.
Indeed, the view that the Kulturkampf represented the liberals' aban-

8. *National Zeitung,* 25 Feb. 1872.
9. Quoted in Sperber, *Kaiser's Voters,* 167.
10. Herbert Lepper, "Widerstand gegen die Staatsgewalt: Die Auseinandersetzung der
Generaloberin der Franziskanerinnen Elisabeth Koch zu Eupen mit den Staatsbehörden um
die Ausführung des 'Klostergesetzes' vom 31. Mai 1875," in *Lebensraum Bistum Aachen: Tradition—Aktualität—Zukunft,* ed. Philipp Boonen (Aachen: Einhard Verlag, 1982), 98–139,
esp. 124. Excellent recent works on the Kulturkampf include Blackbourn, *Marpingen;* Ross,
Failure of Bismarck's Kulturkampf; and Smith, "The Kulturkampf and German National
Identity," chap. 1 in *German Nationalism.*

donment of liberalism has sustained a large body of research that has become the authoritative narrative.[11] In one especially pointed formulation, the liberals "prostituted their principles" by waging the Kulturkampf. By the end of the Kulturkampf, before the party finally split in 1878, the National Liberal Party, according to this argument, had betrayed nearly every principle that liberalism once stood for. Indeed, in this estimation it was the Center Party, not the National Liberal or Progressive Party, that served as the equivalent of a liberal political party in imperial Germany. Center delegates behaved as liberals, supporting the interests of ethnic and religious minorities.[12] One account has carried this transposition of political and ideological identities a step further, arguing that while Catholicism pursued liberal goals, liberalism became a conservative force during the Kulturkampf.[13] The Kulturkampf has been understood, therefore, as an episode of misdirected passion, a moment of apparent absentmindedness during which liberals forgot who they were and what they were supposed to stand for.

Other work on the Kulturkampf has, however, questioned this almost axiomatic account. Recent attempts to evaluate the church-state conflict suggest that the Kulturkampf in Germany, like the attack on the Roman Catholic Church elsewhere in continental Europe, was

---

11. Heinrich Bornkamm has argued, "During the Kulturkampf all of liberalism had to put up with the fact that its practical politics contradicted the basic foundations of its teaching. Viewed from the fundamental idea of freedom, it was twice on the wrong front: during the development of the campaign it voted for blatantly coercive legislation; during the dismantling [of the legislation] it voted against peace and the granting of new freedoms." Bornkamm, *Staatsidee im Kulturkampf*, 18. Gordon Craig with reference to Bismarck's anti-Catholic policy argues that liberals were not coerced by the state into the antichurch campaign but, "in a kind of doctrinaire besottedness, went their own way eagerly, and with scant regard for their principles." Liberals, he has argued, "placed their party, which pretended to maintain the cause of the individual against arbitrary authority, squarely behind a state that recognized no limits to its power. Even if Bismarck had not abandoned and broken them in 1879, it is doubtful whether they could have survived this betrayal of their own philosophy." Craig, *Germany*, 77–78. Similarly, Hajo Holborn has argued that the measures exerted against the Catholic Church "constituted shocking violations of liberal principles. German liberalism showed no loyalty to the ideas of lawful procedure or of political and cultural freedom which had formerly been its lifeblood." Holborn, *Modern Germany*, 2:264. Other works also indicate how well the view that liberals betrayed themselves during the Kulturkampf has been embedded in the historiography: Lill, "Kulturkampf in Preußen," 38; Pflanze, *Bismarck and the Development of Germany*, 2:178; Schmidt, "Die Nationalliberalen," 214. David Blackbourn argues that left liberals ultimately "swallowed their doubts when it came to the Kulturkampf." *Marpingen*, 266.

12. Anderson, *Windthorst*, 290, 192, 402.

13. Tal, *Christians and Jews in Germany*, 119.

"a strategic rather than accidental commitment."[14] Accordingly the Kulturkampf was the logical next stage of unification, a struggle to free German society from the superstitions and archaic institutions of the church. Reexamination has also suggested that the attack on the Catholic Church was not a contradiction of but consonant with liberal beliefs. Contemporary German liberals, whether they stood on the right as Protestant nationalists like Heinrich von Treitschke or on the left as secular progressives like Rudolf Virchow, did not believe that they were contradicting the precepts of liberalism as they called upon the power of the state in the campaign against Catholicism.[15]

Surprisingly, the motives behind the antichurch legislation passed by liberal nationalist and progressive deputies in the Reichstag and in the Prussian parliament have not been rigorously evaluated by historians. Two seminal debates in the course of the Kulturkampf, those involving the *Kirchenfrage,* the question of church-state relations, and the Jesuit law, convey the liberals' own understanding of their role and what they hoped to accomplish in the attack on the Catholic Church. Though it has hardly attracted the attention of historians, the Kirchenfrage under closer examination indicates that German liberals did not believe that the invocation of state force was inconsistent with their attitude toward the issue of the separation of Roman Church and nation-state. During the debate on the Kirchenfrage, leading liberal Kulturkämpfer either rejected the principle of separation or believed that the principle did not prohibit a role for the modern state in church affairs. The overwhelming majority of liberals on both the left and the right argued that liberal ideals of freedom and progress demanded subordination of the church to the authority of the state, a subordination that required under the circumstances the application of force. In doing so, they established the ideological rationale behind the liberal and state-sponsored legislation abrogating the autonomy that the Catholic Church in Prussia had enjoyed since the constitution of 1850.

14. Eley, "Bismarckian Germany," 21; and similar comments in idem, "State Formation." See also Eley's review of *Windthorst: A Political Biography,* by Margaret Lavinia Anderson, *New German Critique* 32 (1984): 189–96. Adolf M. Birke with recourse to the notion of German "exceptionalism" has argued that only those who have become accustomed to understanding German liberalism as sharing the same precepts as its "Western counterpart" will find in the Kulturkampf liberal self-betrayal. Birke, "Zur Entwicklung und politischen Funktion des bürgerlichen Kulturkampfverständnisses," 275. See also the account of the Kulturkampf and of liberal attitudes toward Catholicism in Langewiesche, *Liberalismus in Deutschland,* 68–69, 180–86.

15. Smith, *German Nationalism,* 37–41.

During the hysterical debate between liberals and Catholics on the Jesuit law that closed the Society of Jesus and suspended the right of residence of German citizens, liberals insisted that they were upholding the principles of freedom and progress. Democrats may have defended the rights of citizenship, opposing the Jesuit law; liberals, however, believed that freedom and progress as well as their commitment to science, Bildung, the modern state, and German unity required them to wage a war against the Catholic Church. The Kulturkampf in liberal political discourse was the continuation within the empire interior of the war that had been waged against France. In this sense, the Kulturkampf was meant to be literally another and final war of German unification, waged if not with artillery and sabers then with the weapons of legislation and the authority of the state.

The Kirchenfrage, State Power, and Freedom

Constantin Rößler at the beginning of perhaps the best known piece of Kulturkampf literature, *Das deutsche Reich und die kirchliche Frage,* argued in 1876 that the struggle between the church and the state was the greatest contest that the nation and indeed the world had yet faced. "The struggle in which the German Empire is engaged with the Roman pope is indisputably the greatest affair of the political world of our day. More than the military success of the last war, more than the work of legislation in the realm of state institutions and social movements, this contest draws the attention of foreign nations and especially thoughtful foreign politicians to Germany."[16] Hyperbole, perhaps, but these were sentiments taken seriously and shared by leading liberal social and legal theorists, who, following the promulgation of papal infallibility in 1870, passionately devoted themselves to the question of the relationship between the Catholic Church and the Prussian state. One of the foremost liberal thinkers on the issue, equal in stature to Rößler, was the historian of philosophy Eduard Zeller of the University of Berlin. In his exhaustive and highly influential examination of the Kirchenfrage, *Staat und Kirche,* published in 1873, Zeller argued, "Of the many and important questions that currently occupy the attention of our people and our statesmen, there is none whose solution is more imperative and of more sweeping significance for our entire state and cultural life than this."[17] Such

16. Constantin Rößler, *Das deutsche Reich und die kirchliche Frage* (Leipzig: Fr. Wilh. Grunow, 1876), 1.

17. Zeller, *Staat und Kirche,* 1.

words help us retrieve the urgency and passion with which the Kirchenfrage, in retrospect perhaps seemingly dry and uninspiring, was regarded by contemporary politicians, theologians, and social theorists. For them, nothing less than the life of the new empire, founded in the crucible of war with France and the final fulfillment of the dream for unification, was at stake.

Staat und Kirche offered in comprehensive detail a new foundation for the relationship between church and state and a systematic refutation of the independence of the church. Here and in other essays such as "Preußen und die Bischöfe" published in 1871, Zeller outlined both the nature of the threat posed by the Catholic "state within the state" and the legislative force liberals needed and demanded in order to ensure and to promote the principles of freedom and progress.[18] He called upon the state "to secure itself from its irreconcilable enemy and thereby perform an immortal service for our entire national and cultural life."[19] In accordance with the modern age and in contrast to the medieval period, the state must provide for its own secular independence.

> We should take from the hand of the clergy what it has garnered for itself in government functions and in control over civil life, the family, and the schools. Without damaging any of its rights, we should remove from it the privileges that it has always used to the detriment of the freedom of the people, the independence of government life, confessional peace, and the progress of all human cultivation.[20]

Zeller, therefore, allowed that there might be some rights appropriate to the church, as long as they were understood as strictly religious rights. He did not, however, subscribe to the concurrent liberal American model of the separation of church and state; on the contrary, Zeller argued that under current conditions direct intervention in the

---

18. Zeller, "Preußen und die Bischöfe," in *Eduard Zellers Kleine Schriften,* ed. Otto Leuze (Berlin: Georg Reimer, 1911), 3:402–7. The article originally appeared in *Preußischer Jahrbücher* 28 (1871): 205–9. For Zeller's liberal credentials and for his influence on leading liberals and anti-Catholic scientists such as Emil Du Bois-Reymond, Hermann Helmholtz, and Rudolf Virchow, see also Anderton, "The Limits of Science," 308–12.

19. Zeller, "Preußen und die Bischöfe," 407.

20. Ibid., 405.

affairs of the church was required to preserve freedom and independence. Separation of church and state would be possible only if and
when the church did not represent a threat to the state and to the individual. In Germany, Zeller argued, the "power of the Catholic Church
becomes all the greater the more the people in the state are allowed to
participate in legislation and state administration. The Roman Church
by controlling the people will attain a far-reaching, perhaps even irre-
sistible, influence on the state."[21] Zeller believed that the doctrine of
papal infallibility clearly indicated that Catholics were subjects of Pope
Pius IX and, as such, owed their first allegiance to a foreign monarch.
Catholics were, therefore, a foreign power within the state. According
to Zeller, the church threatened the most basic freedom of conscience
and independence of the individual—an individual who as a citizen
had the right to vote and to serve on juries. It was the purpose of the
state to protect the freedom of its citizens, a freedom that as "a general
and inalienable human right" one held as "an unconditional moral
obligation."[22] These were rights and duties, inalienable, that even the
individual himself had neither the power nor the freedom to abrogate.

Zeller did not hesitate to invoke the use of state force to preserve the
right of citizens to make their own political decisions and to declare
their loyalty to the state. Since the pope was undermining the German
state through antiliberal teaching and since Catholic dogma not only
prevented independent thought but also required obedience to a dangerous foreign authority, the state had the right "to make the promulgation of these teachings punishable, or, given a church that did not
respect the sovereignty [of the state] and organized itself as a conquer-
ing enemy power, to abrogate the recognition and rights it had condi-
tionally granted."[23] Zeller's catalog of the abuses of the Roman
Church was exhaustive: the church inculcated in the population the
belief in miracles in order to swindle money out of the gullible; pilgrimages and processions were only invitations to mischief, public dis-
turbance, and violence; pulpits and confessionals were platforms for
political indoctrination. Monks exerted influence not only on religious
but also on political, economic, and cultural life, in ways that endangered public peace, education, and the integrity of the state. In the
Jesuit order and the monastic religious orders that demanded the vows

21. Zeller, *Staat und Kirche*, 63.
22. Ibid., 92.
23. Ibid., 97.

of poverty, chastity, and obedience, members surrendered the very rights that the state by definition was bound to preserve: property, family, and independence. Religious orders that required the unqualified obedience of their members were, according to Zeller, no better than institutions of slavery; the vow of obedience served only to create a terrified and obedient army. In the hands of the church, schools turned large sections of the population into *Werkzeugen* (tools); religious welfare organizations existed in order to convert to Catholicism the sick and destitute in their vulnerable moments of despair. For this reason, the state was bound by duty to prohibit religious orders from teaching in schools and to abolish religious welfare organizations. Since the state existed to protect the rights of its citizens and the welfare of the nation, the state should, according to Zeller, "do everything in its power" within the bounds of legality to defeat the Catholic Church.[24]

Zeller's *Staat und Kirche* appeared at the same time as Adolf Zeising's *Religion und Wissenschaft, Staat und Kirche*. Zeising, a liberal philosopher and respected authority on the matter of church and state at the University of Munich, propounded an even more categorical affirmation of state power and refutation of the principle of the separation of church and state.[25] According to Zeising, granting the Roman Church the autonomy it desired by protecting the church from the interference of the state would be precisely the wrong conclusion to draw from the principles of liberalism. Indeed, separation of the church from the state would only lead to the ruin of the very virtues for which liberalism stood: freedom, progress, Bildung, and science. Such a policy would be, Zeising insisted, "the most dangerous and destructive nonsense that one could conclude from the liberal standpoint."[26] It was, he averred, as much a mistake to believe that separation of church and state followed from liberal principles as it was to believe that liberalism demanded the same tolerance of idiocy and lies as it did of freedom and truth. Like Zeller, Zeising argued that the state had both the

24. Ibid., 107.
25. Adolf Zeising, *Religion und Wissenschaft, Staat und Kirche: Eine Gott- und Weltanschauung auf erfahrungs- und zeitmäßiger Grundlage* (Vienna: Wilhelm Braumüller, 1873). For further on Zeising's book as a liberal attack on the church, see Kissling, *Geschichte des Kulturkampfes*, 2:275–76.
26. Zeising, *Religion und Wissenschaft*, 451–52. Here is spirited refutation of Hajo Holborn's argument that in the Kulturkampf "only those laws that separated state and church could be defended from a liberal point of view." Holborn, *History of Modern Germany*, 2:264.

right and the duty to regulate the affairs of the church. Indeed, since only the state was capable of realizing the highest moral, artistic, and scientific ideals and attaining the greatest endeavors of humanity, it had to be "within its borders totally autonomous and omnipotent."[27] Accordingly, no person or institutional body within the territory of the nation had the right to conduct its affairs independent of the state, and the state granted legally only those freedoms that it deemed appropriate. In religious matters, he insisted, the conduct of the minority had to submit to the demands of the majority. Zeising counseled that those in the Catholic minority find some consolation in the fact that in matters of inner conviction they were free to contemplate whatever they wished.

On the issue of authority, according to Zeising, in the struggle between the state and the church no compromise was possible. The conflict between the two could end only in the complete subordination of the one to the other. For the state to meet the challenge of the Roman Church with less than absolute resolution, therefore, would be to affix its "signature to its own death warrant."[28] Tolerating the church would lead not only to the destruction of the power of the state but also to the violent suppression of all freedom, Bildung, culture, and civilization. In fact, with the declaration of the Syllabus of Errors in 1864 condemning progress, liberalism, and modern civilization; the proclamation of papal infallibility; and the campaign of the ultramontane press against liberalism, Zeising argued, the modern state was already in the middle of a war with the church. Bishops and priests, "slaves of the Roman curia," and the Catholic population, "in contradiction to its political and national duty," were the instruments of the enemy power.[29] In order to ensure that the Catholic population could not destroy the state, Zeising recommended that the following paragraph be inserted directly into the constitution of the empire:

Only those who swear full, unconditional obedience to the laws and the constitutional authority of the state and who recognize no other authority over their actions have a claim to the full enjoyment of the rights of state citizenship. These include the ability to

---

27. Zeising, *Religion und Wissenschaft,* 451, quotation at 448.
28. Ibid., 429.
29. Ibid., 431.

hold public office and titles, as well as to vote in public affairs, to elect or be elected, or to exercise other political rights. Whoever, by invoking another authority, be it secular or spiritual, refuses this declaration or acts contrary to it forfeits the claim to these rights.[30]

Rejection of the separation of the church and state and the invocation of state power in the name of freedom, progress, and the autonomy of the modern state were views widely shared among the leading National Liberal Kulturkämpfer. According to Heinrich von Sybel, for whom the sad state of affairs in foreign countries so often served as the counterexample for Germany, the situation in Ireland and North America was a daily reminder that the policy of the separation of church and state would lead to the "gradual growth of clerical power and the inevitable subjugation of the state in the future."[31] For the Catholic clergy, according to Sybel, the policy of separation was meaningless, amounting to no more than the indifference of the state. Meanwhile, like a "militarily organized corporation," the church in Germany had enrolled over thirty thousand agents sworn to strict obedience. With unqualified omnipotence, he argued, the clergy taught young people blindly to revere the church and to turn their backs on the fatherland. According to Sybel, only the positive intervention of the state could match the threats posed by the church. Where the "clerical system" had established its despotic rule, the state had to establish independence and enforce legal protection. For Sybel the campaign against the church could only have been as frustrating as it was urgent. He chastised "naive liberals" who believed that "lasting clerical rule is impossible in our enlightened nineteenth century." "Our exciting century has certainly had many great pages," he explained, "but in religious matters it ranks, as all the facts have indicated, not among the enlightened, but among the reactionary ages."[32]

In 1874, entering the height of the Kulturkampf, Sybel had no patience left for those who disagreed with the policy directed against the church. For them he had a ready answer: "For those who are uncomfortable with the idea that a nation forms its legal affairs according to its own discretion and demands the obedience of every

---

30. Ibid., 457.
31. Sybel, *Klerikale Politik,* 114.
32. Ibid., quotations at 116.

inhabitant of the country, one can only suggest that they leave the territory they find so unsatisfying."[33] Zeising had already concluded that it must ultimately come to this, arguing that every German Catholic now had to make a final choice: "Either he must, in order to live up to his duties to the state, reject his religious conviction, or he must, in order to abide by this, break his sworn oath to the state."[34] The exclusion and coercion registered deeply within the Catholic community. Even conservative Catholic monarchists recognized that their loyalty to the crown and dedication to the state would remain forever in doubt and that their status as citizens was tenuous. The Catholic dilemma was clearly expressed by Joseph von Radowitz, a general of the Prussian army and a Catholic, who wrote in his memoirs:

> Those who are at once members of the Catholic Church and citizens of Prussia, both with deep conviction and total sincerity, will not find it easy to face the world. If it is the lot of such a man . . . to be called upon in moments of consequence, he will be exposed at every corner to suspicion, misinterpretation, and vilification. Not even the strictest of consciences or the most careful exercise of caution will protect him: rather it will increase the distrust with which he is regarded and propagate it more widely. The Catholic "party" will accuse every Prussian Catholic of sacrificing the interests of the church to the glory and grandeur of Prussia. . . . The Prussian "party" will suspect that same Prussian Catholic of neglecting the advantage of his state in favor of the glorification of his church.[35]

In 1873, following the first round of the so-called May Laws, which among other measures provided for the state examination of clerics and state approval of all clerical appointments, Heinrich von Treitschke enthusiastically advocated the use of state force. He worried not about its justification but only about the state's resolve.[36] He argued that in the war against the ultramontanes, the executive power had nothing to fear but its own lack of conviction (not the lack of liberal endorsement). A single step back and the war would be lost, he

33. Ibid., 115.
34. Zeising, *Religion und Wissenschaft,* 431.
35. Quoted in Hyde, "Roman Catholicism and the Prussian State," 121.
36. See, for example, Treitschke, "Die Maigesetze und ihre Folgen."

warned, and he urged the state to stay the course and press on to the end. As concerns education, for example, the state realized that the younger generation belonged to the Volk as a whole and that a certain measure of humanistic Bildung was required of each of its members. It was the purpose of the state to ensure, therefore, that the religious fanaticism of adults did not lead to popular stupidity. "The German state forces parents to educate their children," he argued; "it does not give them the right to their Catholic idiocy."[37] The separation of church and state as practiced in the American system, Treitscke explained, had no place in Germany. Here the state was not as in America a force "that must be constrained, so that the pleasure of the individual remains undisturbed, but a cultural power [*Culturmacht*] from which we require a positive influence on all realms of national life."[38] The refutation of the separation of church and state and the call for the exertion of state force were shared by principal liberal architects of anti-Catholic legislation like Paul Hinschius and Emil Friedberg, both members of the Evangelischer Oberkirchenrat. Friedberg did not flinch when it came to the use of state power against the Catholic Church; on the contrary he was an enthusiastic advocate. As concerned the Catholic Church after the Vatican Council, it was Friedberg who insisted that it was the duty of the state "to suppress it, to destroy it, to crush it with violence," an attitude that he was no doubt happy to bring to his work as a member of the government's committee drafting the May Laws.[39]

Progressives might have taken different positions on the issue of separation more often than liberal nationalists, but they too believed that freedom was coupled with the exertion of state power. Indeed, it was a left liberal, Rudolf Virchow, who in a speech to the Prussian parliament in 1873 introduced the concept of a literal Kulturkampf, a battle

37. Ibid., 437.
38. Ibid., 439–40.
39. Friedberg, *Deutsche Reich und die katholische Kirche*, 27. For Friedberg's exhausting legalistic and historical delineation of the relationship between state and church, see idem, *Die Gränzen zwischen Staat und Kirche und die Garantieen gegen deren Verletzung* (Tübingen: H. Laupp'sche Buchhandlung, 1872). Other influential works by Friedberg include idem, *Die Genesis des Kirchenpolitischen Conflicts* (Leipzig, 1875); idem, *Der Staat und die Bischofswahlen in Deutschland: Ein Beitrag zur Geschichte der katholischen Kirche und ihres Verhältnisses zum Staat* (Leipzig, 1874); idem, *Der Staat und die katholische Kirche im Grossherzogthum Baden seit dem Jahre 1860* (Leipzig, 1874). For Hinschius's attack on the Catholic Church and papal infallibility see n. 7 in this chapter.

cry that was then immediately echoed in every corner of the empire.[40] In a subsequent speech he outlined the twofold aim of the Kulturkampf: first, to free religion from the domination of the church and to free secular life from the domination of religion and, second, to compel the state to recognize its duty to achieve this emancipation and to impose it upon the nation as a whole. Here Virchow claimed the Kulturkampf as a liberal and secular—neither state nor Protestant—crusade. It was not Chancellor Bismarck who had to coax liberals into the campaign against the church, as has so often been the impression given by historians; on the contrary, leading liberals believed they had to remind the Bismarckian state of its responsibility to use its power for the sake of the state and society. In fact, it was Virchow who went so far as to claim that the success of the Kulturkampf and the assurance of freedom might require "a dictatorship of ministers."[41] His fellow Progressive Eugen Richter, even as he stood with the Center leader Ludwig Windthorst defending free speech by opposing legislation regulating what clerics could say in the pulpit, believed that freedom for the individual as well as independence for the state ultimately required the employment of state power. "It was not possible," he argued, "for the state to liberate itself from clerical domination without interfering in the course of events."[42]

Nationalist and progressive liberals agreed, therefore, that individual freedom was not achieved despite but because of state force. For Johann Caspar Bluntschli, the Protestant nationalist, the conflict with the church reduced itself to a "conflict between Roman clerical rule and German freedom." With a vivid and arresting image characteristic of his anti-Catholic fanaticism, Bluntschli argued that the Jesuits "rip out the love of freedom from the hearts of the young." Not the particular states, but only the empire, he argued, "is spiritually and on account of its power equal to the huge task of saving humanity from the false authority of the church without destroying the church and of defending freedom without destroying religion."[43] The employment of the power of the state in the service of freedom was a theme repeated at

40. Rudolf Virchow, in *SBHA* (Berlin: W. Moeser, 1873), session 28, 17 Jan. 1873, 631. For examples of Virchow's condemnation of Catholicism based on empirical, hard science see Rudolf Virchow, *Über die nationale Entwickelung und Bedeutung der Naturwissenschaften* (Berlin, 1865); and idem, *Über Wunder.*

41. Tal, *Christians and Jews,* 82.

42. Quoted in ibid., 83.

43. Johann Caspar Bluntschli, "Die Debatte über die Jesuiten im deutschen Reichstage," *Gegenwart* 1 (1872): quotations at 305 and 305–6.

the same time by the National Liberal Rudolf Gneist. In his theory of the *Rechtsstaat*, a state based on the rule of law as opposed to arbitrary authority, he included the argument that "society can find the personal freedom, the moral and spiritual development of the individual only in permanent subordination to a higher, constant authority."[44] The *Klosterstürmer* of the summer of 1869 knew full well that the war on behalf of freedom against the Catholic Church would take more than the "weapons of spirit and truth"; it required the strong arm of the state.[45] For Gneist, as it was for other Kulturkämpfer from the liberal right to left, the Kulturkampf was the final phase in the Hegelian teleology of the state, "a momentous turning point in which the German state . . . attained self-knowledge, that is, its full freedom."[46] When liberals attacked the Catholic Church, they did so with the solemn assurance that it was a matter of duty in the cause of freedom.

Historians disagree about precisely when liberals and the state embarked on the Kulturkampf. Some date it starting already in July 1871, when Bismarck dissolved the Catholic section of the Ministry of Educational and Ecclesiastical Affairs in Prussia. The first piece of antichurch legislation brought before the Reichstag and overwhelmingly supported by liberals was, however, the "pulpit paragraph."[47] Issued in December 1871, the law made public discussion of matters of state by clerics "in a manner endangering public peace" a criminal offense (and this remained so, in the statute books at least, until 1953). In 1872 two seminal pieces of legislation critical for liberal plans for the modern, independent, and secular state went into effect. First, in March, in the Prussian parliament, supervision of the schools by the churches was abolished. Clerics who served as school inspectors no longer did so by virtue of their religious office but at the discretion of the state. In principle the legislation allowed the removal of both Catholic priests and Protestant ministers. In practice the law was, at least in the Rhineland, aimed exclusively at Catholic clerical inspectors. Catholic clerical supervisors at the district level were replaced by

44. Rudolf Gneist, *Der Rechtsstaat* (Berlin: J. Springer, 1872), 12. For an example of the reception of Gneist's *Der Rechtsstaat*, see the review, not in every respect favorable, in the liberal *Preußische Jahrbücher* 31 (1873): 217–20.

45. See Gneist's speech in the Reichstag demanding the Jesuit law in *Für und Wider die Jesuiten*, part 3, *Stenographische Berichte der Reichstagsverhandlungen über das Gesetz betreffend der Orden der Gesellschaft Jesu*, session 48, 19 June 1872 (Berlin: Verlags der Reichs-Gesetze, 1872), 126–32.

46. Quoted in Tal, *Christians and Jews*, 84.

47. Among the Progressives only Eugen Richter and among the National Liberals only Eduard Lasker voted against the "pulpit paragraph" and supported freedom of speech.

lay supervisors, many of whom were liberal Old Catholics.[48] While local clerical school inspectors were supposed to be replaced by lay professional inspectors, due to the scarcity of qualified lay replacements Bürgermeister more often than not either used the opportunity or were given the opportunity by default to assume control of the local school inspectorships. In doing so, the Bürgermeister consolidated his local authority, freeing himself of a priest who, as the school inspector, could be a real or potential challenge to his voice in the community. In fact, the Bürgermeister often himself denounced the clerical inspector as incompetent, *staatsfeindlich,* or alcoholic to the state authorities. In the same breath, he often recommended his own services to the state as the replacement. A second law passed in July, soon after the school supervision law, banned the Society of Jesus as well as the Redemptorist order and Lazarist order on German soil. The law provided for the expulsion of foreign Jesuits and the relocation of German Jesuits within the empire.

In May 1873 the first of the so-called May Laws in Prussia revised Articles 15 and 18 of the constitution that since 1850 had granted to the churches the right to manage their own affairs independently. Henceforth all aspiring clergymen were required to attend German universities and to pass state examinations in German philosophy, history, and literature as prerequisites to their appointments to parishes as priests. At the same time, Protestant Church authorities were assured sotto voce that the law did not apply to them. A Court of Ecclesiastical

48. This conclusion and the following are based on materials in HSTAD, Best. RK, Nr. 2724, "Die Enthebung der katholischen Geistlichen von den lokalen Schulaufsicht und deren Nachfolger, 1875"; HSTAD, Best. Kr. Bonn, "Verzeichniss derjenigen Pfarrer beider Confessionen, welche zur Zeit als Lokal Schulinspektoren fungiren (26 July 1875)"; HSTAD, Best. RD, PB, Nr. 1308, "Schulangelegenheiten betr. alle Schulreform, Bd. 5, 1870–75"; HSTAD, Best. RD, Nr. 2619, "Die Anordnung der Schulpfleger bzw. Kreisschulinspektoren (kath.) und Förderung der Schulwesens durch die Geistlichen," Bd. 1, 1872–73, and Bd. 2, 1874; HSTAD, Best. RD, Nr. 2722, "Die Enthebung der katholischen Geistlichen von der lokalen Schulaufsicht und deren Nachfolger, 1872–1874"; HSTAD, Best. RD, Nr. 2723, "Die Enthebung der katholischen Geistlichen von der lokalen Schulaufsicht und deren Nachfolger, 1874–1875"; HSTAD, Best. RD, Nr. 2725, "Die Enthebung der katholischen Geistlichen von den lokalen Schulaufsicht und deren Nachfolger, 1875"; HSTAD, Best. RA, Nr. 17587, "Kreisschul-Inspektoren, 1876–1878"; LHAK, Best. OPR, Nr. 10412, "Die Kreisschulinspectoren Bezirke und die Kreisschulinspectoren"; LHAK, Best. OPR, Nr. 15196, "Die Kreisschuinspectoren in Regierungsbezirk Düsseldorf"; LHAK, Best. OPR, Nr. 10412, "Die Kreisschulinspections Bezirke und die Kreisschulinspectoren." For further on the implementation of the school supervision law, see Lamberti, "State, Church, and the Politics of School Reform"; and idem, *State, Society, and the Elementary School in Imperial Germany* (Oxford: Oxford University Press, 1989).

Affairs was established that abolished the authority of the pope over the Catholic Church in Prussia and claimed final jurisdiction on all matters of internal church discipline. The laws also facilitated withdrawal of members from the church. In 1874 another round of May Laws more punitive in nature was enacted. In the Expatriation Act, the government had the power to confine or banish recalcitrant priests who continued to carry out their clerical functions in defiance of state injunctions. Another provision provided for the state administration of dioceses left vacant by the church. A final law further defined and extended the terms for the education of clergy.

In April 1875, at the height of the Kulturkampf, the Prussian state responded to a papal encyclical declaring invalid all ecclesiastical legislation in Prussia with the so-called Breadbasket Law (*Brotkorbgesetz*). The statute suspended most of the state's annual subsidy to Catholic dioceses and clerics until their bishops pledged in writing to abide by Kulturkampf legislation. Soon afterward the state abolished Article 16 of the constitution, which granted to the Catholic Church the right to communicate with the Vatican. Then in May the capstone of all Kulturkampf legislation, the Congregations Law, banned all remaining religious orders except those devoted to hospital work and teaching. The law affected several thousand clerics and nuns and according to one estimate closed 189 monasteries and cloisters within the next two years.[49] The property was appropriated by the state. Within the first four months of 1875, the Hohenzollern state in the course of its attack on the Catholic Church had fined or arrested 241 priests, 136 newspaper and journal editors, and 210 other Catholics; in addition, 20 newspapers were confiscated, 74 houses searched, 103 individuals expelled or incarcerated, and 55 public meetings closed down.[50] Over 900 parishes were without priests. Of the 12 Prussian dioceses, 5 were without bishops due to judicial removal, and 4 others were vacant where

---

49. Like the Breadbasket Law, the Congregations Law proved to be less effective than anticipated by state authorities. Two-thirds of the more than 900 religious orders and congregations in Prussia provided charitable and educational services that the state could not itself afford to replace. By the end of the Kulturkampf only 340 monasteries and cloisters had been shut down. Ronald J. Ross, "Enforcing the Kulturkampf in the Bismarckian State and the Limits of the Coercion in Imperial Germany," *Journal of Modern History* 56 (1984): 456–82. For a study of the fate of monastic orders and congregations after their expulsion from Prussia, see Rita Müllejans-Dickmann, *Klöster im Kulturkampf: Die Ansiedlung katholischer Orden und Kongregationen aus dem Rheinland und ihre Klosterneubauten in belgisch-niederländischen Grenzraum infolge des preußischen Kulturkampfes* (Aachen: Einhard, 1992).

50. Anderson, *Windthorst*, 178.

the bishops had died and not been replaced.[51] A year later, across Prussia 1,400 parishes, a third of those that existed, did not have incumbent priests.[52]

Liberals, Jews, Democrats, and the Jesuit Law

When in 1872 liberal deputies introduced a bill in the first session of the new Reichstag calling for the closing of the Society of Jesus and other religious orders they did so according to Article 23 of the constitution, which allowed the Reichstag to suggest legislation and forward petitions to the Bundesrat (Federal Council) and chancellor. The bill called for the abolition of the order, the expulsion of foreign Jesuits from German soil, and the relocation of individual German Jesuits. It also set off an explosion of public debate that included all levels of German society and politics. There may have been only about two hundred Jesuits within the empire, but the intense hatred among liberals and Protestants and the equally intense loyalty among Catholics toward the Jesuits were in no proportion to their modest number. During the first half of 1872, petition campaigns against or in support of the Jesuits swept the entire length and breadth of the empire.[53] The controversy ripped the nation along the political-confessional divide as liberal and Protestant associations held protest meetings while the Center Party and Catholic associations held even more numerous rallies in support of the Jesuits.

The most prominent National Liberal deputies led the attack against the Jesuits in the Reichstag, foremost among them Rudolf Gneist, who along with his liberal colleagues had garnered the lessons of the Moabiterklostersturm. But it was Eduard Windthorst, an Old Catholic Progressive deputy from Berlin, who laid out the liberal position in a lengthy speech on the floor. Eduard Windthorst argued that "the burning hate with which the German Empire persecutes Jesuitism" was entirely justified: "Germany is the land of the Reformation, the land of free science, the land of tolerance and enlightenment."[54] Voting for the

---

51. Evans, *German Center Party,* 76.

52. Craig, *Germany,* 75.

53. Petitions that were sent to the Reichstag can be found in *Für und Wider die Jesuiten,* part 2, *VI und XIV. Bericht der Kommission für Petitionen, betreffend die Petitionen für und wider ein allgemeines Verbot des Jesuiten-Ordens in Deutschland.* See also the collection of materials in Moufang, *Aktenstücke.*

54. *Für und Wider die Jesuiten,* part 1, *Stenographische Berichte der Reichstagsverhandlungen über Besetzung des Botschafter-Postens in Rom und die Petitionen für und wider die Jesuiten,* session 21, 14 May 1872, 79.

abolition of the Jesuit order, he believed, was a duty that outweighed any obligations he had to Catholicism, political or religious.[55] Indeed, he took it upon himself as a liberal to instruct Center deputies on the liberal principle of freedom and rights of association. The pleas of deputies of the Center "to us, the liberals" to abide by the principle of freedom, he argued, were premised on a false concept of freedom. Catholic deputies, he explained, understood freedom to mean the freedom to suppress the freedom of the people. He argued that liberals vindicated the right of every person and every citizen to enjoy his civil rights but in contrast to Catholics, and here was the heart of the matter, "only after withdrawal of those [civil rights] that must be sacrificed for the good of the totality and of the state." For Eduard Windthorst it made no sense on principle to tolerate that which negates the principle in the first place. "Freedom," he explained, "protects everything except unfreedom, and tolerance endures everything except intolerance."[56] Eduard Windthorst outlined the paradigmatically liberal definition of freedom, a definition, he believed, that was wholly consonant with a law that abolished the Society of Jesus, expelled foreign Jesuits, and suspended the residence rights of German citizens. As a liberal and an Old Catholic—a Progressive and the nephew of the leader of the Center no less—Eduard Windthorst could only have based his motives on the liberal principle of freedom. When it came to the Jesuits, therefore, he like other German liberals believed himself fully justified in invoking the immortal words of Voltaire, that quintessential figure of the Enlightenment: "Ecrasez l'infâme!"[57] The Old Catholic Eduard Windthorst was joined by Catholic liberal deputies in the Liberale Reichspartei, by the Catholic National Liberals Friedrich von Schauss of Oberfranken and Paul Tritscheller of Baden, and by the Catholic Progressive Anton Allnoch of Breslau, all of whom voted in favor of the anti-Jesuit bill.

Historians of German liberalism and politics have traditionally cited the National Liberal deputies Eduard Lasker and Ludwig Bamberger as examples of liberals who, standing alone in the Reichstag against the pressure of their colleagues, refused to participate in the betrayal of liberalism.[58] Historians have argued that the Jesuit law was a notoriously

55. Eduard Windthorst is listed as *altkatholisch* in Mann, *Biographisches Handbuch für das preußische Abgeordnetenhaus*, 419. He voted for the anti-Jesuit bill on the second vote and was on vacation during the final vote.

56. *Für und Wider die Jesuiten*, part I, session 21, 14 May 1872, quotations at 93.

57. Ibid., 94.

58. As an example, see Craig, *Germany*, 77.

illiberal piece of legislation but was recognized as such only by a hand-ful of liberal and progressive deputies. Following this logic, it was not Lasker and Bamberger but rather the other 122 National Liberal deputies *not* voting against the bill who turned their backs on their lib-eral convictions.[59] Despite or perhaps given the wide acceptance of this interpretation, the anti-Jesuit bill, its debate, and the votes cast by the deputies have remained surprisingly unexamined. But a careful appraisal of positions on the anti-Jesuit bill offers the opportunity to better understand not only the Kulturkampf but also liberalism, polit-ical Catholicism, and Jewish political attitudes toward the church-state conflict in the second half of the nineteenth century. More thorough analysis reveals that opposition to the bill was shaped not just by polit-ical ideology but also by religious identity. Taking into account the confessional composition of the deputies' respective constituencies suggests that opposition to the bill was shaped in the new age of the democratic franchise. Specifically, Lasker and Bamberger discovered that the anti-Catholic exceptional legislation was in conflict with their religious identity. At the same time, Catholic liberal deputies more true to liberalism than they were to the church at least politically paid the price: they were voted out by their political constituencies in the subse-quent election.

Lasker, a deputy from Saxony, shared the anti-Catholicism of liber-als. Like other liberals he believed that the Catholic Church was incompatible with economic growth, scientific progress, educational reform, and German unification. He did stand against the "pulpit paragraph" legislation as a violation of civic rights, but in subsequent anti-Catholic May Laws in Prussia, Lasker supported the measures along with his colleagues.[60] Bamberger, deputy from Hesse, also voted

59. There is considerable confusion among historians about the liberal voting record on the anti-Jesuit bill in the Reichstag: Blackbourn inadvertently states that Rudolf von Ben-nigsen was one of only two National Liberals to vote against the expulsion of the Jesuits. Blackbourn, *Marpingen,* 449 n. 88. Bennigsen voted for the bill, and Otto Bähr, also a National Liberal, voted along with Lasker and Bamberger against the bill. For further on Bähr see n. 80 in this chapter. Rudolf Lill states that the National Liberal Johannes von Miquel also voted with Lasker and Bamberger. Lill, "Der Kulturkampf in Preußen," 38. Miquel, in fact, failed to vote on both readings of the bill. The total number of National Lib-eral deputies is recorded as 125 in *Statistisches Jahrbuch für das deutsche Reich* (Berlin: Puttkammer und Mühlbrecht, 1880), 1:140–41. This count includes 119 deputies of the National Liberal Party and 6 "outside the National Liberals and the Progressives" aligned politically with the National Liberals. For the voting record on the anti-Jesuit bill see *Für und Wider die Jesuiten,* part 3, session 45, 17 June 1872, 96–97, and session 48, 19 June 1872, 140–41.

60. See James F. Harris, *A Study in the Theory and Practice of German Liberalism: Eduard Lasker, 1829–1884* (Lanham, Md.: University Press of America, 1984), 49.

for other anti-Catholic legislation. He, in fact, was always an enthusiastic Kulturkämpfer. Already in November 1871 he referred to the fight against the Catholic Church as the "signature of the empire." "I myself am busy with the affair in the most intimate circles," he wrote. "It will not end for a long time."[61] As the Kulturkampf in Prussia intensified, Bamberger's enthusiasm only grew. Indeed, according to his own account, he was beside himself with delight about its success: "I am truly intoxicated to observe how this development so correctly takes the course which my best expectations had demanded of it."[62] On legislation connected to the Kulturkampf, only on the prohibition of the Jesuit order did Bamberger break from his National Liberal colleagues.

Given the small minority within which Lasker and Bamberger found themselves in the Reichstag and given that in every other respect they shared the hostility of their liberal colleagues toward the Catholic Church, both felt compelled to clarify the reasons for their votes in opposition to the anti-Jesuit bill on the second reading on 17 June and again on the final reading on 19 June. Speaking before the Reichstag, Lasker addressed his comments foremost to his party colleagues. He assured them that he represented a very small group that preferred to be hand in hand with "Kampf-Genossen" (comrades-in-arms). Lasker agreed with his colleagues that the conflict with the church should be resolved with all the assistance that law and the authority of the state could provide. On the anti-Jesuit bill, however, he was bound to place himself in opposition. He justified his position by emphasizing that the purpose of the struggle with the Catholic Church should be, as he said, "to reconcile feelings," not to force the suppression of opposing views. He attacked the abrogation of the residence rights of German citizens by means of the suspension of normal juridical procedure.[63] Defending such rights was a matter of moral duty and liberal principle, he insisted. From a pragmatic point of view, there was the added problem that it would be simply too difficult for authorities to determine who was a member of the Society of Jesus.

Lasker was clearly unhappy with his own position relative to his liberal colleagues and must have recognized that his points of view expressed here may not have seemed consistent with his earlier position

61. Quoted in Stanley Zucker, *Ludwig Bamberger: German Liberal Politician and Social Critic, 1823–1899* (Pittsburgh: University of Pittsburgh Press, 1975), 95.

62. Quoted in ibid.

63. For Lasker's speech see *Für und Wider die Jesuiten*, part 3, session 45, 17 June 1872, 101–6.

regarding matters of church and state. Always on other occasions a fiery and effective speaker, he came across at the end of his speech unmistakably embarrassed. It was, he admitted, a matter of "great pain" not to be able to be on the side of his esteemed friends. Lasker asked for a reconciliation and hoped that the future would bring liberals together again. Though Lasker was in the decided minority, entirely isolated, his comments were nonetheless at once a significant withdrawal of support and an indication of his unrepentant conduct within his own party and toward the state government. His outspoken independence on this occasion once again fueled the anger directed against him by both liberals and Bismarck. Here was another case of what the liberal nationalist circle grouped around Heinrich von Treitschke and Wilhelm Wehrenpfennig called "Laskerei." Lasker represented treachery on the left side of the National Liberals that threatened to split the party as it had threatened repeatedly since 1866 and would so again during the heated intraparty conflict during the crisis over the military Septennat budget of 1874. At the same time, it was only confirmation that Lasker had reached the height of his prestige and power in the Reichstag that Bismarck openly admitted he now hated Lasker as much as he did Ludwig Windthorst.

Meanwhile Bamberger simply sat silently in his seat throughout the entire debate in the Reichstag. Three days after the final vote on the anti-Jesuit bill, with the matter an accomplished fact, he finally offered an account for his opposition on the pages of the *Gegenwart*. Bamberger claimed that the bill had been too hastily submitted and not based on a rational response to the Jesuit problem. He argued that the deputies and the government had been too eager to agree on the bill; they were, as he put it, "not there to exchange compliments." (The bill had been initially introduced in the Reichstag by the imperial government, withdrawn, and then reintroduced by the liberal leadership.) The proposed Jesuit law, Bamberger further argued, was also insufficient since by focusing only on the Jesuits, it did not address the larger problem of the entire Catholic Church. In addition, Bamberger rejected the argument that deputies were compelled to support the bill since, if they had done otherwise, they would have discouraged the "similar efforts" of the government. The government, he insisted, had already been assured on previous occasions of the Reichstag's cooperation on such matters. Only at the very end did Bamberger indicate that the law was not only ineffectual but, perhaps, also an unsavory display of state coercion. "Nothing," he argued, "had proven itself more useless in the last half century as the attempt to fight against the currents of public spirit whether good or bad with police repression," a comment that colleagues would have recognized as a reference not only to the enthusiastic support of the Jesuits by the Catholic population but, in fact, also to previous state attacks on their own liberal activism.[64] In several respects Bamberger's remarks were a striking contrast to Lasker's argument and, indeed, next to Lasker's logical and personalized testimony, curiously circuitous and halfhearted. The two were clearly not in step and had done little, if anything, to coordinate their opposition. Indeed, Bamberger had done nothing constructive to resist the anti-Jesuit bill, merely offering a defense to his colleagues for his vote after the fact.

The tenor and substance of Lasker's and Bamberger's respective statements hint that the reasons articulated for their opposition were only a partial account. In order to appreciate the significance of Lasker's and Bamberger's exceptions to the anti-Jesuit bill, it is necessary to identify what remained in the background, present but passed over in silence. In addition to their opposition, what distinguished Lasker and Bamberger from other liberal deputies voting in support of the bill was an identity they shared. Lasker and Bamberger were Jews.[65] They stood almost entirely alone among liberals against the Jesuit law because they recognized that as Jews they were an even smaller, more vulnerable, minority within the empire than Catholics.[66] At the time of the founding of the empire, Jews comprised under 1 percent of the total German population. Heinrich Berhard Oppenheim, himself Jewish and liberal, readily recognized how difficult, even embarrassing, it must have been for his coreligionists to compromise one identity for the sake of the other. But as a friend he suggested in a

---

64. Ludwig Bamberger, "Die Motive der liberalen Opposition gegen das Jesuitengesetz," *Gegenwart* 1 (1872): 337–38. See also Marie-Lise Weber, *Ludwig Bamberger: Ideologie statt Realpolitik* (Stuttgart: F. Steiner Verlag, 1987), 168; Zucker, *Bamberger,* 96.

65. Both Lasker and Bamberger were secular Jews who remained bound to their Jewish identities even as they distanced themselves from the religious practice of Judaism. For Lasker's and Bamberger's relationships to Judaism, their relationship to the German Jewish community, and their positions on Jewish issues, see James F. Harris, "Edward Lasker: The Jew as National German Politician," *Leo Baeck Institute Yearbook* 20 (1975): 151–77; and Stanley Zucker, "Ludwig Bamberger and the Rise of Anti-Semitism in Germany, 1848–1893," *Central European History* 3 (1970): 332–52.

66. Lasker and Bamberger were joined on the final vote by one other National Liberal and by twelve Progressives.

letter to Lasker that his speech had been "almost too temperate, although not as timid as Bamberger's article."[67]

Lasker's and Bamberger's conflicted opposition to the Jesuit law, however, represented the dilemma shared by the leadership of the German Jewish population in general in its relationship to the Kulturkampf. As the historian of German Jewish-Christian relations in the nineteenth century Uriel Tal, has shown, Jewish communities followed the early years of the Kulturkampf with great interest.[68] The Kulturkampf was a serious matter in public debates and private discussion in the Jewish community. It was a familiar topic of humor and satire in Jewish regional and local newspapers and a subject critically examined by the Jewish community councils. The views of most Jewish leaders, educated Jews, and the Jewish population, insofar as they were publicly expressed by rabbis in their sermons, teachers in the classroom, and editorialists in the press, welcomed the early phase of the Kulturkampf. For the most part, the Jewish public supported the "pulpit paragraph" adopted by the Reichstag in March 1871, prohibiting the use of religious sermons for political purposes, since the law seemed to ensure the separation of church and state. By and large educated Jews saw the anti-Catholic campaign in general as a defense of liberalism, nationalism, and scientific progress, and Jewish economists in particular asserted that the "ultramontanists" advocated an economic policy contrary to free trade and free competition, favored protectionism, and sought to preserve preindustrial society. More important, Jews believed their own emancipation within German society was dependent on the realization of liberal, humanistic, and rational values and, therefore, they looked forward to the victory of the liberals. Other recent research concludes that liberals regarded Jewish emancipation as an integral part of their political program, and Jews relied on liberals as the staunchest, indeed the only, allies of Jews in their struggle for emancipation and equal rights.[69]

67. Letter of Heinrich Bernhard Oppenheim to Eduard Lasker, 4 July 1872, in Heydorff and Wentzcke, *Deutscher Liberalismus im Zeitalter Bismarcks,* 2:55–56. Oppenheim continued, "The Progressive Party took a good position in such conflicts, and if our close friends had done the same, the National Liberal Party would be morally stronger and more influential." Oppenheim, again, was Jewish.

68. This and the following are based on Tal, *Christians and Jews,* 81–120.

69. Werner E. Mosse, "Introduction: German Jewry and Liberalism," in *Das deutsche Judentum und der Liberalismus,* ed. Friedrich-Nauman-Stiftung (Sankt Augustin: Comdok-Verlagsabteilung, 1986), 15–27. Earlier work had noted instances of liberal ambivalence or prejudice toward Jews. See Reihard Rürup, "German Liberalism and the Emancipation of

Conspicuously absent from the examination of the Jewish relationship to liberalism and the anti-Catholic campaign in particular, however, is the significance of the Jesuit law. Yet an examination of the larger debate concerning the Jesuit law indicates not only a sea change in the Jewish attitude toward the Kulturkampf but also the development of deep suspicions among Jews about liberals and liberalism. With the introduction of the law, leading Jews became profoundly ambivalent about their relationship toward the progress of the Kulturkampf. German Jews had good reason to be concerned that the Jesuit law as an *Ausnahmegesetz* (exceptional law not part of the normal juridical process) would establish a legal precedent that could be turned against any other religious or social group labeled "staatsfeindlich." It was therefore with the passage of the Jesuit law that leaders of the Deutsch-Israelitischer Gemeindebund (Union of German Jewish Communities), Jewish students, rabbis, teachers, and readers of the *Allgemeine Zeitung des Judenthums,* the principal organ of German Reform Judaism, began a more critical evaluation of the antichurch campaign. Increasingly the Kulturkampf evoked Jewish concerns about excessive state coercion in the spheres of society and religion, and it ultimately shook Jewish confidence in liberal policy itself. The *Allgemeine Zeitung,* for example, now expressed doubts about liberalism's willingness to tolerate Judaism as a cultural and religious identity. If German liberalism was unable to tolerate Jewish "individuality," the paper threatened, "there is nothing we can do except express our disapproval, deplore its shortsightedness, and refrain from following in its footsteps."[70] In the same year, the *Allgemeine Zeitung* extended its criticism to Rudolf Virchow's "scientific liberalism" and to Ernst Haeckel's and Louis Büchner's "scientific materialism." If not resisted, the newspaper argued, liberal science would undermine the spiritual life of the nation and lead to intellectual regimentation. By the mid-1870s, Jewish leaders were complaining that the policy pursued by liberal-nationalistic Kulturkämpfer would lead not to the emancipation of the state but instead to the spiritual and cultural conformity of religious and social minorities in the empire.[71]

---

the Jews," *Leo Baeck Institute Yearbook* 20 (1975): 59–68; and Eleonore Sterling, *Judenhaß: Die Anfänge des politischen Antisemitismus in Deutschland, 1815–1850* (Frankfurt am Main: Europäische Verlagsanstalt, 1969). See also Herzog, *Intimacy and Exclusion,* 53–84.

70. Tal, *Christians and Jews,* 109.

71. Ibid.; and Tal, *The Kulturkampf and the Jews of Germany* (Jerusalem: International Center for University Teaching of Jewish Civilization, 1980), 19–23.

Though the meaning of Lasker's and Bamberger's votes against the anti-Jesuit bill has been largely missed by subsequent historians, it was not lost on contemporaries.[72] Moritz Schulz, Bismarck's confidant, for example, believed he understood the significance of Lasker's and Bamberger's opposition. He scornfully noted that outside the Center only Jewish deputies voted against the bill because they feared that at some point in the future the population would be aroused enough against Jews to demand an exceptional law.[73] When it came to a vote to abolish the Jesuit order with an exceptional law, just as Catholic liberal deputies in the Liberale Reichspartei, Catholic National Liberals like Schauss and Tritscheller, and the Catholic Progressive Allnoch had to choose between loyalty to the Catholic Church or the Kulturkampf, so did Lasker and Bamberger have to choose between their identity as Jews and their identity as liberals. Interestingly enough, among the National Liberals it was not Catholics but Jews who broke the ranks of the party when faced with the choice. In fact, the issue was important enough for Bamberger to risk the liberal support he needed in his electoral district to retain his seat in the Reichstag.[74] (He was, ironically, replaced in that seat by a Center deputy in the election of 1874.) This argument is also made compelling by the case of the only deputy, Isaac Wolffson of Hamburg, who abstained on the second reading of the bill. A National Liberal, he too was Jewish. Unwilling to choose one identity at the expense of the other, he abstained again on the final reading of the anti-Jesuit bill.[75]

The case of the aging Saxon "Forty-Eighter" historian and National Liberal Karl Biedermann is also instructive. In private correspondence he confided to Lasker that he intended to vote against the anti-Jesuit bill. He objected to the law not for reasons of legal compunction or liberal idealism but because of the heavy-handed manner in which it was

72. One exception is Helmut Walser Smith, who mentions that Eduard Lasker "resisted anti-Catholic legislation" and suggests "it seems more likely that a figure like Lasker assumed a reserved attitude towards the Kulturkampf, not because he was a liberal, but because he was Jewish." Helmut Walser Smith, "Nationalism and Religious Conflict in Germany, 1887–1914," (Ph.D. diss., Yale University, 1991), 47–48 n. 53. But the issue for Lasker at least was not the Kulturkampf itself and its attack on the Catholic Church but rather exceptional legislation and its implications. As noted, only on the "pulpit paragraph" and the Jesuit law did Lasker take exception to Kulturkampf legislation.

73. Cited in Zucker, *Bamberger,* 96.

74. Ibid., 96.

75. The only other deputy besides Wolffson to abstain on the final vote was also a National Liberal.

negotiated between the Reichstag and the imperial executive. He would do so even though among his voters, when it came to the Jesuits, "the most angry is not angry enough."[76] When it came to the actual vote, he apparently succumbed to the intense pressures he alluded to in his letter to Lasker, since on both the second and final readings of the bill, he failed to vote. Finally, concerning National Liberals, historians have repeatedly stated that only Lasker and Bamberger voted against the Jesuit bill.[77] As a matter of record, however, a review of the votes indicates that one other, Otto Bähr, the National Liberal deputy from Kassel and a Protestant, voted against the bill. Unfortunately, his motives remain unknown since he did not speak publicly to the bill either in the Reichstag or subsequent to the debate.[78]

Those historians who have trained their attention on the anti-Jesuit bill have not only missed the meaning but have also been confused about the vote count itself, recording conflicting counts of Progressive votes for and against the bill.[79] Clarity therefore about the facts is, first of all, necessary: as tables 6 and 7 indicate, sixteen Progressives voted for and sixteen voted against the bill on the second reading and/or on the final reading. All Progressive votes in support of the bill were cast by deputies from predominantly Protestant constituencies. Among those Progressive deputies voting against the bill, three—Joseph Gerstner, Carl Herz, and Franz Wigard—represented districts with

---

76. Letter of Karl Biedermann to Eduard Lasker, 12 June 1872, in Heydorff and Wentzcke, *Deutscher Liberalismus in Zeitalter Bismarcks,* 2:53–54; see also Harris, *Study in the Theory and Practice of German Liberalism,* 49.

77. As an example, see Zucker, *Ludwig Bamberger,* 96.

78. I have assumed that the "Dr. Bähr" listed in the voting record as reproduced in *Für und Wider* is Dr. Otto Baehr, National Liberal, representing Wahlkreis 2, Kassel, member of the Reichstag from 1867 to 1880. All information concerning the party affiliations, religions, and electoral districts of the deputies, unless otherwise indicated, is based on Schwarz, *MdR Biographisches Handbuch,* a source admittedly not without some discrepancies. Where I have found inaccuracies I have tried to correct them. No discrepancy that I have found alters this analysis.

79. Here are indications of the extent of the confusion: Anderson states that eight Progressives voted against the bill and that the Progressives Hermann Schulze-Delitzsch and Eugen Richter led those Progressives who refused their support. Anderson, *Windthorst,* 166. Schulze-Delitzsch, in fact, voted for the bill on both readings, and Richter failed to vote. Bornkamm states that twelve Progressives voted against the bill. Bornkamm, *Staatsidee,* 19 n. 1. Evans states that nine Progressives voted for and eleven voted against the bill and fifteen abstained. Evans, *German Center Party,* 61. Lill states that the majority of the Progressives voted against the bill. Lill, "Der Kulturkampf in Preußen," 38. For the voting record on the anti-Jesuit bill see the verbatim reproduction of the stenographic report of the Reichstag debates and votes in *Für und Wider die Jesuiten,* part 3, session 45, 17 June 1872, 96–97; session 48, 19 June 1872, 140–41.

TABLE 6.   Progressive Reichstag Deputies Voting in Favor of the Anti-Jesuit Bill, 17 and 19 June 1872

Name	Religion	Electoral District	Predominant Religion
Allnoch, Anton	Catholic	Wahlkreis 4, Breslau	Protestant
Becker, Hermann	Protestant	Wahlkreis 6, Arnsberg	Protestant
Böhme, Emil	Protestant	Wahlkreis 21, Saxony	Protestant
Emden, Louis	Protestant	Wahlkreis 7, Potsdam	Protestant
Franke, Wilhelm	Protestant	Wahlkreis 2, Gumbinnen	Protestant
Harkort, Friedrich	Protestant	Wahlkreis 4, Arnsberg	Protestant
Knapp, Johann	Protestant	Wahlkreis 4, Wiesbaden	Protestant
Lorentzen, Wilhelm	Protestant	Wahlkreis 5, Schleswig-Holstein	Protestant
Löwe, Wilhelm	Protestant	Wahlkreis 5, Arnsberg	Protestant
Oehmichen, Wilhelm	Protestant	Wahlkreis 10, Saxony	Protestant
Rohland, Otto	Protestant	Wahlkreis 8, Merseburg	Protestant
Runge, Heinrich	Protestant	Wahlkreis 4, Berlin	Protestant
Schmidt, Theodor Carl	Protestant	Wahlkreis 4, Stettin	Protestant
Schulze-Delitzsch, Hermann	Protestant	Wahlkreis 6, Berlin	Protestant
Seelig, Wilhelm	Protestant	Wahlkreis 9, Schleswig-Holstein	Protestant
Windthorst, Eduard	Old Catholic	Wahlkreis 3, Berlin	Protestant

Source: Schwarz, *MdR Biographisches Handbuch; Für und Wider die Jesuiten,* part 3, session 45, 17 June 1872, 96–97; session 48, 19 June 1872, 140–41; Ritter and Niehuss, *Wahlgeschichtlichtliches Arbeitsbuch;* 49–53, 60–61.

TABLE 7.   Progressive Reichstag Deputies Voting in Opposition to the Anti-Jesuit Bill, 17 and 19 June 1872

Name	Religion	Electoral District	Predominant Religion
Banks, Edward	Protestant	Wahlkreis 2, Hamburg	Protestant
Dickert, Julius	Protestant	Wahlkreis 3, Königsberg	Protestant
Duncker, Franz	Protestant	Wahlkreis 5, Berlin	Protestant
Erhard, Otto	Protestant	Wahlkreis 5, Mittelfranken	Protestant
Gerstner, Joseph	Catholic	Wahlkreis 6, Unterfranken	Catholic
Hagen, Adolf	Protestant	Wahlkreis 1, Berlin	Protestant
Hausmann, August	Protestant	Wahlkreis 8, Potsdam	Protestant
Herz, Carl	Catholic	Wahlkreis 4, Mittelfranken	Catholic
Hoverbeck, Leopold von	Protestant	Wahlkreis 7, Gumbinnen	Protestant
Kirchmann, Julius	Protestant	Wahlkreis 6, Breslau	Protestant
Klotz, Moritz	Protestant	Wahlkreis 2, Berlin	Protestant
Müller, Louis	Protestant	Wahlkreis 9, Liegnitz	Protestant
Schaffrath, Wilhelm	Protestant	Wahlkreis 9, Saxony	Protestant
Wigard, Franz	—	Wahlkreis 5, Baden	Catholic
Wiggers, Moritz	Protestant	Wahlkreis 3, Mecklenburg-Schwerin	Protestant
Ziegler, Frantz	Protestant	Wahlkreis 7, Breslau	Protestant

Sources: Schwarz, *MdR Biographisches Handbuch; Für und Wider die Jesuiten,* part 3, session 45, 17 June 1872, 96–97; and session 48, 19 June 1872, 140–41; Ritter and Niehuss, *Wahlgeschichtlichtliches Arbeitsbuch,* 49–53, 60–61.

Catholic constituencies. At least the first two of these deputies were Catholic. (The religion of the third is not known.) According to one historical account, fifteen Progressives, that is, the plurality, abstained, but the vote record indicates, in fact, that no Progressives abstained.[80] As table 8 indicates, twelve Progressives were listed as either "on vacation" or "failing to vote" on both ballots, categories distinct from the category for abstention and with different implications. The number "on vacation" or "failing to vote" was not more than the number of Progressives voting on the bill.

Because of the Progressive deputies' split on the anti-Jesuit bill, it is more difficult to evaluate the meaning of their votes. Some were perhaps torn between liberal anticlerical convictions and reservations about enacting an exceptional law. In any case, not all Progressives who opposed the bill did so necessarily because they objected in principle to the suspension of the civil right of residence of German citizens. On the contrary, many Progressives apparently believed the bill as it was proposed did not carry the attack on the Catholic Church far enough. Though Progressives who voted against the bill may have found themselves temporarily standing with the Center, Hermann

TABLE 8.   **Progressive Reichstag Deputies Not Voting on the Anti-Jesuit Bill, 17 and 19 June 1872**

Name	Religion	Electoral District	Predominant Religion
On Vacation			
Klotz, Jakob	Protestant	Wk. 1, Wiesbaden	Catholic
Köchly, Hermann	Protestant	Wk. 14, Saxony	Protestant
Failed to Vote			
Crämer, Karl	Protestant	Wahlkreis 1, Mittelfranken	Protestant
Eysold, Arthur	Protestant	Wahlkreis 8, Saxony	Protestant
Forchhammer, Wilhelm	Protestant	Wahlkreis 4, Schleswig-Holstein	Protestant
Hänel, Albert	Protestant	Wahlkreis 7, Schleswig-Holstein	Protestant
Hausmann, Franz	Protestant	Wahlkreis Lippe-Detmold	Protestant
Kraussold, Max	Protestant	Wahlkreis 2, Oberfranken	Protestant
Ludwig, Richard	Protestant	Wahlkreis 16, Saxony	Protestant
Minckwitz, Heinrich	Protestant	Wahlkreis 19, Saxony	Protestant
Muellauer, Robert	Protestant	Wahlkreis 3, Gumbinnen	Protestant
Richter, Eugen	Protestant	Wahlkreis Schwarzburg-Rudolstadt	Protestant

Source: Schwarz, *MdR Biographisches Handbuch; Für und Wider die Jesuiten,* Part 3, Session 45, 17 June 1872, 96–97; and session 48, 19 June 1872, 140–41; Ritter and Niehuss, *Wahlgeschichtlichtliches Arbeitsbuch,* 49–53, 60–61.

80. Evans states that fifteen Progressives abstained. Evans, *German Center Party,* 61.

Schulze-Delitzsch, the Progressive deputy from Berlin, was quick to point out that there was a critical distinction between Center deputies and Progressives who objected to the anti-Jesuit bill.

> Gentlemen! There is a very important difference, indeed a diametrical opposition, between the opponents of this proposed law. The esteemed speaker whom you first heard speak against the bill [the Center Party deputy Hermann von Mallinckrodt] opposes it because he wants no measures taken against the Jesuits at all. He wants nothing to be done to them. I myself and a large number of my political friends are against the proposed law because we think it is *too weak* in every respect. We think it is inadequate to attain the goal for which it is clearly intended. (Emphasis added.)[81]

The anti-Jesuit bill as it was proposed, he argued, was merely a limp gesture in the struggle against the Roman Church. Schulze-Delitzsch and others had become impatient with mere words about the government's power and the significance of the Kulturkampf: "Where are the actions, gentlemen? Words should find their expression in real, practical measures. Otherwise they are merely empty phrases about the alleged strength of the government, since up to now we have not seen any really decisive intervention."[82] While others wasted time exchanging phrases and slogans about the Jesuit problem, Schulze-Delitzsch believed at issue was no less than an "Existenzfrage" (a question of survival): "the existence of our young German state on the one side and the existence of the Jesuit order on the other." He announced that consequently he and his colleagues would vote not for but against the bill. They wanted another, more punitive, anti-Jesuit bill with a "really decisive measure" against the church.[83]

Many Progressives, therefore, disapproved of the anti-Jesuit bill, and some possibly even voted against it because they preferred to see a more draconian bill introduced later in the individual state parliaments. Schulze-Delitzsche's pugnacious challenge came as a surprise to no one, least of all fellow Progressives. He accepted and let it be known without compunction the belief that the campaign against ultramontanism entailed a "ruthless struggle," and he and Progressives like him were ready for the sake of progress to take up Bismarck's call to wage

81. *Für und Wider die Jesuiten,* part 3, session 43, 14 June 1872, 17.
82. Ibid.
83. Ibid., 18.

"proxy wars."[84] But, in the end, Schulze-Delitzsch himself decided to vote for the anti-Jesuit bill in the Reichstag, apparently believing there might not be the opportunity later to introduce a more forceful bill in either the Reichstag or in state parliaments. The willingness among Progressives to suspend civil liberties is not surprising if we recall that it was precisely a Progressive, Eduard Windthorst, who had on the basis of avowedly liberal precepts demanded the restriction of citizens' rights. Finally, it is worth noting that even the champion of individual civic rights, the Progressive Eugen Richter, erroneously cited by some historians as one of the few liberals unequivocally opposed to the Kulturkampf, did not stand in the way of the anti-Jesuit bill.[85] He did not oppose the bill with his vote. He did not abstain. He was not on vacation. Voting at neither the second nor final reading of the bill, Richter simply did nothing.

Of the Progressive deputies who voted against the bill at either the second and/or final reading, only a Catholic, Joseph Gerstner, voiced reasons for doing so. Gerstner explained he was as a liberal an advocate of German Bildung, morals, and freedom and an enemy of the Jesuits. But he objected to the exceptional law because it was reactionary. Gerstner pointed out that this bill introduced and supported by nationalist liberals ironically evoked memories of the Karlsbad Decrees enacted in 1819 against liberal nationalists during the Restoration earlier in the century. The Jesuits, he insisted, must be defeated not with the police-state tactics of reaction but with "the force of ideas and conviction and the power of Bildung and freedom."[86] These were words no doubt calculated to strike deep into liberal consciousness. Just as important, however, Gerstner also recognized that the legislation would be construed by the Catholic population not simply as an attack on the Jesuits but also as an attack on the entire Catholic Church. Even those few Catholics not favorably disposed to the Jesuits, he argued, would resent the law and come to the defense of the order.[87] There are two points to make here. First, this admonition may have revealed Gerstner's own sentiments. As a Catholic he resented the damage the law would do to the Catholic Church. Second, he was no doubt aware that according to the political reality of the new age of democracy, deputies were answerable to their electorate. If the Jesuit

84. Blackbourn, "Progress and Piety," 157.

85. See ibid., 160; Blackbourn, *Marpingen,* 266; and Anderson, *Windthorst,* 166.

86. For Gerstner's speech, see *Für und Wider die Jesuiten,* part 3, session 45, 17 June 1872, 56–63, quotation at 61.

87. Ibid., 59. Gerstner repeated this point at 94.

law was going to be unpopular with Catholics, then this was a bill that Gerstner, representing the overwhelmingly Catholic constituency of Unterfranken in Bavaria, would do well not to support. He was in the end talking about his own political career.

If Progressives did not offer a united front against the bill, unqualified opposition came further to the political left, from the democrats Karl Gravenhorst and Leopold Sonnemann. As democrats they demarcate the fault line of German liberalism in the Kulturkampf.[88] Gravenhorst, an independent not formally affiliated with a party in the Reichstag, represented a Protestant district in Hanover. Though certainly no friend of the Jesuits, Gravenhorst rejected the Jesuit bill because it, like the "pulpit paragraph," was an exceptional law.[89] Gravenhorst proudly asserted that from his "democratic standpoint" he could not do otherwise. He claimed it as a democratic responsibility to reject the bill because it "entailed harm to personal freedom and an infringement on the most important political rights."[90] He drove home the distance between liberals and democrats when he further warned liberals that the time might come when the Prussian state would sue for peace with the Catholic Church and the Center Party. Gravenhorst saw what liberals would not: the Jesuit law would provide Bismarck with an opportunity he could put to use against them. The state, he pointed out, would exploit precisely the liberals' insistence on the exceptional law in order to broker an alliance with the Center against the liberal party—an appraisal as prescient as it was astute.

Leopold Sonnemann was Frankfurt's most prominent democrat. He was a founding member of the German People's Party in 1867 and the only member of that party in the Reichstag from 1871 through 1874. (By 1875 he had become the unofficial leader of the small group of democratic deputies in the Reichstag.) Like Lasker, Bamberger, and Wolffson, Sonnemann was also Jewish. With Sonnemann the pattern is complete: all Jewish deputies in the Reichstag refused to vote for the bill, either voting against it or abstaining. The fact that Sonnemann

88. For Sonnemann's democratic credentials see Klaus Gerteis, *Leopold Sonnemann: Ein Beitrag zur Geschichte des demokratischen Nationalstaatsgedenkens in Deutschland* (Frankfurt am Main: Kramer, 1970). Gravenhorst proudly proclaimed himself a democrat distinct from the liberals in his speech on the anti-Jesuit bill. *Für und Wider die Jesuiten,* part 1, session 23, 15 May 1872, 112. At the time of the vote, neither Sonnemann nor Gravenhorst was formally a member of a party in the Reichstag.

89. For Gravenhorst's speech, see ibid., 112–18.

90. Ibid., 112.

was a democrat and secular Jew explains why the *Frankfurter Zeitung,* the newspaper he owned and edited, opposed from the beginning the exceptional law and the repressive measures of the Kulturkampf. The *Frankfurter Zeitung,* the largest and most important democratic newspaper south of the Main, denounced the repressive legislation not as illiberal but as undemocratic. The Jesuit law, the paper argued, was a violation of the principle of the separation of church and state. Such anti-Jesuit repression, furthermore, would be useless in the campaign against the church. The day before the final vote on the anti-Jesuit bill, the paper stated, "Ultramontanism will not be affected. The prohibition is not going to curtail its opposition to freedom but will merely bestow the mantle of martyrdom upon it."[91] Prussian state authorities may have been annoyed by the position of the newspaper, but they were hardly surprised. Frankfurt was itself a remarkable hotbed of Jewish democratic activism, so much so that as far as state officials were concerned Frankfurt Jews and Democrats were synonymous.[92]

Specifying the position of the *Frankfurter Zeitung* is important since even some of the best historians of nineteenth-century society and liberalism have assumed that the newspaper was liberal and have repeatedly cited the paper as an example of liberal opposition to anti-Catholic legislation.[93] By doing so, they have obscured the boundaries and the character of the antichurch campaign. The *Frankfurter Zeitung,* in fact, stood up like a flag demarcating the religious and political-ideological contours of the Kulturkampf. Since Sonnemann openly despised the Jesuits and ultramontanism, it was only on democratic principle that during the following years he and his newspaper opposed the antichurch campaign. Unlike Lasker and Bamberger, who, as noted, after the anti-Jesuit bill voted for other antichurch leg-

---

91. For the democratic credentials of the *Frankfurter Zeitung,* its opposition to the Kulturkampf, and the quotation, see *Geschichte der Frankfurter Zeitung, 1856 bis 1906* (Frankfurt am Main: Verlag der Frankfurter Zeitung, 1906), 227.

92. Palmowski, *Urban Liberalism,* 107.

93. Jan Palmowski: "The *Frankfurter Zeitung* was, perhaps, the most important liberal newspaper which spoke out for Roman Catholics during that period." Palmowski, *Urban Liberalism,* 107. In an otherwise careful study, Palmowski too easily elides democrats, left liberals, and national liberals, and democratic and liberal ideology. David Blackbourn: "The liberal *Frankfurter Zeitung,* which anxiously monitored the record of custodial sentences meted out to Catholics, remarked on one occasion that Germany resembled 'one great prison.'" Blackbourn, "Progress and Piety," 156–57. See other examples at 251, 258, 266. Kissling identified the *Frankfurter Zeitung* as democratic and argues that the *Frankfurter Zeitung* protested the Jesuit law "surely not for love of religion but because it considered the law undemocratic." Kissling, *Geschichte des Kulturkampfes,* 2:292.

islation with their liberal colleagues, Sonnemann aggressively attacked these measures as well. In addition, starting in 1875 the *Frankfurter Zeitung* ran a fortnightly Kulturkampf Calendar documenting the state's repressive measures against Catholics and the church. These included the banning of Catholic organizations and the searching of Catholic homes by state authorities. Far from being liberal, the paper was attacked by liberals for standing in opposition to the state's prosecution of the Kulturkampf. The liberal *Grenzboten* disparagingly branded the editors of the paper "radical democratic."[94] It was clear for all Roman Catholics who cared to notice that the undivided refusal of Jewish deputies and the *Frankfurter Zeitung,* not to mention the *Allgemeine Zeitung des Judenthums,* to give their support to the Jesuit bill exposed as a lie the popular Catholic canard that "Jews" were responsible for the Kulturkampf.

During the debate on the anti-Jesuit bill, Sonnenmann and Gravenhorst introduced a bill calling for the separation of church and state that was defeated. Since the individual votes on the bill were not recorded, it unfortunately is not possible to correlate votes on the anti-Jesuit bill with positions on the issue of separation. As noted earlier in this chapter, however, the principle of separation was not characteristic of German liberalism. The demand for separation was, rather, characteristic of democrats. Protestant liberals on the right rejected separation of church and state because they feared that separation would weaken the Protestant Church. This included Paul Hinschius, member of the Evangelischer Oberkirchenrat, who opposed separation and voted in favor of the anti-Jesuit bill. At the same time, liberals from left to right, including the Old Catholic Progressive Eduard Windthorst, the Protestant National Liberal Friedrich Kiefer, and the Catholic Liberale Reichspartei deputy Ludwig Fischer, believed there was no contradiction between separation and the Jesuit law. For Eduard Windthorst as for Kiefer and Fischer, the principle meant simply the full secularization of state affairs, above all the schools, not that the state had no right to regulate the affairs of the church in order to ensure its independence.[95] Meanwhile, the Progressive Joseph Gerstner explicitly dismissed "the slogan separation of church and state" when he spoke and voted against the Jesuit bill.[96] Neither National Liberals

94. "Die Frankfurter Zeitung und der 'Culturkampf,'" *Grenzboten* 3 (1875): 356–59.

95. For Kiefer's position on separation of church and state, see *Für und Wider die Jesuiten,* part 1, session 23, 16 May 1872, 105–7; for Eduard Windthorst's position, ibid., session 22, 15 May 1872, 93; for Fischer's position, ibid., session 23, 16 May 1872, 148–57.

96. *Für und Wider die Jesuiten,* part 3, session 45, 17 June 1872, 56.

nor Progressives considered separation of church and state a principle that should determine their votes on the anti-Jesuit bill.

The debate and the vote count on the Jesuit law of 1872 indicate, therefore, that among liberals the reasons for voting in opposition to the bill were varying and complex. Liberal deputies voted against the bill because they were Jewish, because the bill was ineffectual or too weak, or because the bill was repressive. Other liberal deputies voting against the bill objected to the manner in which the bill had been negotiated between the state government and the Reichstag or among the Reichstag deputies themselves. Still other deputies feared (with good reason) that the bill would be interpreted by the Catholic population as a wider attack on their church and religion. Some were themselves Catholic, sympathetic perhaps to the church and/or worried they might alienate their Catholic constituencies if they supported the bill. Meanwhile, democratic deputies unequivocally claimed that it was a democratic responsibility to oppose the legislation and defend the civil rights of German citizens, even those of the Jesuits whom they despised.

The Jesuit law was the most heated issue on which the Reichstag voted during its first session from 1871 to the next election in 1874. The issue mobilized the population into petition campaigns that swept the entire length and breadth of the empire against or in support of the Jesuits.[97] Liberals and Protestants held protest rallies, and Catholic associations held even more numerous counterrallies. Both because elections to the Reichstag were direct and equal and because the Jesuit law was by far the most important and popularly debated issue decided by Reichstag deputies, the election returns of 1874 allow us to register an impression of the popular reaction to that seminal piece of legislation abolishing the Jesuit order. Voting on the Jesuit bill brought with it hard lessons about the nature of the new democratic franchise.[98] Though Gerstner voted against the bill, he found that this was not enough to save his seat in Catholic Unterfranken. In the next Reichstag elections of 1874 he was replaced by a Center deputy. Catholic members of the Liberale Reichspartei who had voted in favor of the Jesuit law while representing electoral districts with predominantly Catholic constituencies lost their seats: a deputy from Aachen, two deputies from Schwaben, two from Oberbayern, a deputy from

97. Petitions that were sent to the Reichstag can be found in *Für und Wider die Jesuiten,* part 2, 3–52. See also the collection of materials in Moufang, *Aktenstücke betreffend die Jesuiten.*

98. For the significance and the meaning of the franchise for the political culture of the empire, see Anderson, *Practicing Democracy;* and idem, "Voter, Junker, *Landrat,* Priest."

Niederbayern, and one from Unterfranken were all replaced by Catholic Center deputies.[99] Their careers in the Reichstag were over.[100] Of the four remaining Catholics of the Liberale Reichspartei who voted for the bill, one from a predominantly Catholic yet traditionally liberal district in Baden and one from a predominantly Protestant electoral district in Mittelfranken were replaced by National Liberals.[101] Another moved to the ranks of the National Liberals and was reelected in the heavily Catholic district Schwaben-Immenstadt.[102] Prince Hohenlohe-Schillingsfürst became for a brief stint an independent before moving to the conservative German Reich Party in a predominantly Protestant voting district in Oberbayern. The Liberale Reichspartei, therefore, disappeared as a party that politically reconciled liberalism and Catholicism.

Among Progressives, Eduard Windthorst lost his voting district. He must have found it ironic that his overwhelmingly Protestant district in Berlin chose none other than Carl Herz, the Catholic Progressive who had voted against the Jesuit law.[103] Herz was fortunate since he no longer had a future in his original, predominantly Catholic voting district in Mittelfranken, which now elected a Center candidate. The Catholic Progressive Anton Allnoch of the predominantly Protestant voting district in Breslau and the only two Catholic National Liberals, Schauss of a Protestant district in Oberfranken and Tritscheller of the predominantly Catholic but urban and traditionally liberal district of

99. The deputies were, respectively, Richard Hasenclever; Ludwig Fischer and Wilhelm Behringer; Wilhelm von Kastner and Emeran Kottmöller; Ludwig von Lottner; and Winfried Härmann. Politically the Liberale Reichspartei lay with the National Liberal Party on the liberal right. The only Catholic independent ("bei keiner Fraktion"), Ignatz Bürgers of Cologne, was also replaced by a Center Party deputy. The religious compositions of each imperial voting district (*Reichswahlkreis*) are given in Gerhard A. Ritter and Merith Niehuss, *Wahlgeschichtliches Arbeitsbuch: Materialen zur Statistik des Kaiserreichs 1871–1918* (Munich: Beck, 1980), 60–61. The religious compositions of the electoral districts are based on this source unless otherwise indicated.

100. None was ever reelected to the Reichstag, at least not until the Kulturkampf was over. Fischer was elected again in 1884.

101. The deputies were Franz Roggenbach and Marquard Barth, respectively. The district in Baden, Wahlkreis 4, Baden-Lörrach, voted for either National Liberals or left liberals up to 1918 with the one exception of 1890, when it voted Center.

102. The deputy was Joseph Völk. The electoral district continued to hold on to Völk until it went to the Center in 1881.

103. The district was Wahlkreis 3, Berlin, which had a Protestant constituency of over 80 percent and voted consistently for Progressive deputies. Eduard Windthorst, although never again a member of the Reichstag, did hold a seat subsequent to the vote on the anti-Jesuit bill in the Prussian parliament from 1873 to 1879 as a member of the left-liberal Deutsche freisinnige Partei from a Protestant voting district in Minden.

Baden-Freiburg, all voted for the Jesuit law with impunity.[104] Of the sixteen Protestant Progressive deputies who voted in favor of the anti-Jesuit bill, nine from the predominantly Protestant districts Gumbinnen, Wiesbaden, Arnsberg, Schleswig-Holstein, Saxony, Stettin, and Merseburg retained their seats in 1874, and four passed their seats to Progressive candidates. Of those thirteen Protestant deputies from Protestant districts who voted against the anti-Jesuit bill, ten representing Protestant districts in Berlin, Potsdam, Königsberg, Breslau, Liegnitz, Mittelfranken, and Mecklenburg-Schwerin retained their seats. Of the twelve who did not register a vote, six from Protestant electoral districts in Schleswig-Holstein, Saxony, Lippe-Detmold, Mittelfranken, Schwarzburg, and Gumbinnen also either retained their seats or passed them to another Progressive. Three seats were replaced in a predominantly Catholic district in Wiesbaden and in predominantly Protestant districts in Oberfranken and Schleswig-Holstein by National Liberals. Two seats in Saxony now moved to the Social Democrats. The conclusion is that, unlike liberal deputies in the Liberale Reichspartei from Catholic constituencies, Protestant Progressive deputies could vote in support of or in opposition to the bill without losing their Protestant constituencies or at least their constituencies to another party. The fate of the Jesuits was less important to the majority of Protestant Progressive voters.

Catholic electoral districts that had voted for Catholic liberals were now voting for Catholic Center deputies. For most Catholics, especially for rural peasant or artisan Catholics, there were now to be no ambiguities. The line was drawn. In the wake of the passage of the Jesuit law and under the force of the Kulturkampf, most of the Catholic voting population decided that it was impossible now to be both Catholic and liberal.[105] The attack on the Jesuit order had consequences that went beyond the elimination of liberal Catholic political representation at the national level. The dumping of liberal Catholic deputies in favor of Center candidates by unforgiving Catholic electoral districts was accompanied by the replacement of Catholic conservative deputies from the nobility by Center deputies. In the rural and eastern state of Oppeln alone, three prominent Junker who had been absent during the vote were ousted by Center deputies. Though they themselves were also lords of large estates, a taste of things to come

---

104. Baden-Freiburg also eventually went to the Center in 1878. Catholic deputies of the conservative Deutsche Reichspartei who voted for the Jesuit law and retained their seats included Robert (Ferdinand) Lucius of Erfurt and Carl Schmid of Württemberg.

105. For the elections during the Kulturkampf see also Sperber, *Kaiser's Voters,* 160–79.

was offered by the case of Baron Schenk von Stauffenberg, who as a Catholic National Liberal from Munich's first voting district did not cast a ballot at either vote on the anti-Jesuit bill. In 1874 he retained his seat while he watched Munich's second voting district align itself with the Center, replacing a Catholic Liberale Reichspartei deputy who had voted for the bill. In the subsequent election the baron was himself replaced by a Center candidate and a commoner. He found a future in the Reichstag only as a deputy from a predominantly Protestant district in Braunschweig.

One of the most significant consequences of the Jesuit law and the attack on the Catholic Church was the activation and reorientation of the Catholic electorate. Exercising the vote under the pressures of the Kulturkampf, Catholics signaled the shift from the old "politics of notables"—deference to those qualified for office by virtue of social status—to a new "politics of identity"—support for those representing identical social and cultural experience.[106] But the new political alignments involved not just votes for specific persons: they also included a more abstract identification with confessional (or class or ethnic minority) interests. This entailed a transition from an experience of local politics rooted in parishes, villages, and small towns to imagining a level of national politics and competition. Thinking in terms of a national "imagined community" did not mean that voters would exercise their civic rights with a greater measure of individual freedom.[107] At the polls, large-estate landlords who ordered their tenants to vote

106. Anderson, *Practicing Democracy;* idem, "The Kulturkampf and the Course of German History"; and idem, "Voter, Junker, *Landrat,* Priest." In the elections of 1874 the Center Party jumped from 63 to 91 seats. Meanwhile, the National Liberals also moved from 125 to 155 seats, and the Progressive Party increased slightly from 46 to 49 seats. It was the two conservative parties, reduced from a combined 94 to 55 seats, and the Liberale Reichspartei, reduced from 30 to 3 seats, that suffered as the result of the electorate's move toward the National Liberal and Center Parties. The combined total seats of the remaining parties—the SPD, Polish, Danish, Alsatian, Guelph (Hanoverian particularist), Volkspartei, and Protest Party—remained relatively stable, moving from 24 to 34 with gains of 7 and 5 seats for the SPD and Protest Party, respectively. *Statistisches Jahrbuch,* 140–41. The fact that, while voter participation in the Reichstag election in 1871 had been 51.0 percent, by 1874 it had made an impressive jump to 61.2 percent, and specifically the fact that those voting for the Center had jumped from 18.6 percent in 1871 to 27.9 percent in 1874, were also indications of the political mobilization unleashed by the first years of the Kulturkampf. See Langewiesche, *Liberalismus in Deutschland,* 308–9. Meanwhile, support among eligible Catholic voters for the Center in constituencies with Center candidates leaped from 34.0 percent in 1871 to 59.0 percent in 1874. Of Catholics voting during the Kulturkampf, four-fifths voted for the Center Party. Blackbourn, "Catholics and Politics in Imperial Germany," 189, 206.

107. The phrase is from Benedict Anderson's path-opening *Imagined Communities: Reflections on the Origin and Spread of Nationalism* (London: Verso, 1983).

Conservative or face beatings and eviction, industrialists who demanded that their workers vote National Liberal or face dismissal and blacklisting, parish priests who instructed their congregations to vote Center or face the wrath of God, all these were indications that Germany was entering an age of modern, democratic politics.[108]

Kulturkampf legislation strictly speaking was not a direct attack against Catholic belief or worship. Instead, legislation attacked the leadership and placed controls on the administration of the church. Before the Kulturkampf was over, Prussia's twelve bishops had been imprisoned or forced to flee in order to avoid arrest or imprisonment. Religious orders, monasteries, and convents were closed in accordance with the Congregations Law of 1875. Lower clergy were fined or jailed in thousands of cases for their defiance of Kulturkampf laws. But as the electoral response in the Reichstag elections of 1874 indicated, Catholics rejected any notion that there was or could be a distinction between the attack on the church leadership and an attack on Catholic life. Claims by liberals and by state authorities that they were opposed to the power of the priests, the Jesuits, ultramontanism, and Rome but not opposed to the Catholic religion struck Catholics as disingenuous. Catholics had listened for years to the barrage of liberal and state prejudice against "backward" Catholicism and "stupid" and "un-German" Catholics.

Catholics were also deeply loyal and personally attached to their religious leadership. Many priests were raised in the very communities they later served, tied to their congregations through personal and familial relationships. For those of the parish laity the priest therefore was not simply the official representative of the church; he was often one of their very own. We need not subscribe to a simple top-down, intentionalist model of local secular priests as "milieu managers" to recognize that the priest was in Catholic communities both the "father of the community" and the "spiritual father."[109] The priest organized the numerous religious associations for men, women, girls, and boys; he administered the artisan and peasant credit banks, journeymen organizations, and miners' sodalities.[110] Priests provided leadership for the coordination of social and civic events, and as local and regional school inspectors, priests oversaw the administration of education.

---

108. Anderson, *Practicing Democracy.*

109. Olaf Blaschke, "Die Kolonisierung der Laienwelt: Priester als Milieumanager und die Kanäle klerikaler Kuratel," in *Religion im Kaiserreich,* ed. Olaf Blaschke and Frank-Michael Kuhlemann (Gütersloh: Chr. Kaiser, 1996), 93–135. See the critical comments by Smith and Clark, "The Fate of Nathan," 10.

110. Blackbourn, "Progress and Piety," 153.

During elections it was the priest who organized local support for Center deputies. When not attending to such organizational tasks, priests gave lectures to their communities on hygiene, health, practical living, husbandry and economic improvement, appropriate reading habits, and the correct way to honor feast days. More important, Catholic communities depended on their priests for religious instruction, pastoral care, and administering the sacraments of baptism, confirmation, the Eucharist, matrimony, penance, and extreme unction, the life cycle of spiritual milestones that imparted meaning to individuals, families, and communities.[111] Ultimately it was the presence and ministrations of the priest as the intermediary to God in the community that made possible the salvation of souls. The priest stood at the very center of the social, political, and spiritual life of Catholic communities. Catholics recognized immediately therefore that the Kulturkampf as an attack on their leadership was a war against their entire way of life.

The War against Catholicism

The Jesuit law specified that within six months of the enactment of the legislation the Society of Jesus was to be closed in the empire and all foreign Jesuits deported. Resolutions appended to the anti-Jesuit bill by the Bundesrat also prohibited Jesuits from hearing confessions, giving sermons, holding mass, and teaching in schools.[112] Jesuits were expelled from their districts, their residences and churches were locked, and the keys were handed over to government district authorities.[113] The Catholic Church and individual Jesuits railed against the oppression of the state and argued in the Catholic press that members of the Society of Jesus stood under the exclusive authority of their leadership in Rome.[114] Far from striking a blow whose impact was confined to the ˙

111. Michael Klöcker's *Katholisch—von der Weige bis zur Bahre* provides an anthropological, alltäglich history of each of the sacraments as a means of understanding the events that define Catholic culture generally.

112. A copy of the order from the Ministry of the Interior and the Ministry of Educational and Ecclesiastical Affairs, Berlin, to the provincial governor of the Rhineland and materials documenting the implementation of the law can be found in LHAK, Best. 403, OPR, Nr. 7512, "Der Orden der Gesellschaft Jesu und die mit ihm verwandten Orden und Congregationen: Ausführung des Reichs-Gesetz vom 4.7.72, 1872–1875."

113. A detailed account of the closing of the missions in the dioceses is given in August Sträter, *Die Vertreibung der Jesuiten aus Deutschland im Jahre 1872* (Freiburg im Breisgau: Herder, 1914).

114. HSTAD, RD, Nr. 20111, Bd. 1, 1870–72, newspaper clipping from *Essener Zeitung,* a reprint of an article appearing in the *Kölnische Zeitung,* 18 Aug. 1872.

Jesuit order, the law led the Catholic laity to identify even more closely with their church under attack. The liberal *Kölnische Zeitung* happily told its readers that the law ripped through the Catholic population like "a bolt of lightning" but failed to appreciate that in doing so the law had also electrified the Catholic population.[115]

When in the summer of 1872, for example, police authorities in Essen emptied and locked up the local Jesuit residence, the Catholic population went to the streets and erupted in rebellion. Gendarmes and Catholics met in pitched battles. Catholic rioters tried to reopen the Jesuit chapel by force.[116] They demolished the home of a local Freemason, the natural target of Catholics who believed that Freemasonry, liberalism, and hatred of Jesuits were synonymous. The Oberbürgermeister and the editors of the *Essener Blätter* powerlessly pleaded with Catholic workers to desist and return to work. Two full battalions of fusiliers from the Seventh Army Corps, Fourteenth Division, were finally required to quash the rebellion.[117] The Catholic *Duisberger Zeitung* told its readers that the riots proved that "you can't always answer deeds with mere words"; the liberal *Spenersche Zeitung* recognized that the "Essen rebellion" was only a taste of things to come.[118] The Essen riots forced state authorities momentarily to retreat. Fearful of inciting more Catholic rebellions, they slowed the pace of the closing of the Jesuit missions and houses.[119] At the same time, the Jesuit law and the explosion of the Catholic population now moved the Kulturkampf into more dangerous and contested terrain, one in which the new German Empire looked increasingly like a theater of war.

So it was a pleasure for the prominent leader of the National Liberals Rudolf von Bennigsen to write in a letter to his wife in 1875 that a recent piece of Kulturkampf legislation would "go off like a bomb

---

115. HSTAD, RD, Nr. 20111, Bd. 1, newspaper clipping, 6 Aug. 1872. See also in this file the newspaper clipping from *Neue Preußische Zeitung,* 6 Aug. 1872.

116. HSTAD, RD, Nr. 20111, Bd. 1, report of BM Gustav Adolf Waldthausen, Essen, 14 Aug. 1872; report of Abtheilung des Innern, 19 Aug. 1872; report of the police inspector, Essen, 24 Aug. 1872; newspaper clipping from *Essener Zeitung,* 25 Aug. 1872.

117. *Vossische Zeitung,* 7 Sept. 1872; HSTAD, RD, Bd. 1, Nr. 20111, newspaper clipping from *Essener Blätter,* 25 Aug. 1872; Commander, Seventh Army Corps, Fourteenth Division, to RP von Ende, Düsseldorf, 26 Aug, 1872.

118. HSTAD, RD, Nr. 20111, Bd. 1, newspaper clipping from *Berliner Börsen Zeitung,* n.d.; HSTAD, RD, Nr. 20112, Bd. 2, newspaper clipping from *Spenersche Zeitung,* 6 Sept. 1872.

119. See HSTAD, RA, Nr. 10699, "Orden der Gesellschaft Jesu bzw. die Ausführung des Gesetzes vom 4 July 1872," PP and LR to Regierung, Abtheilung des Innern, Aachen, 4 Dec. 1872, Bl. 88–89.

under the clericals."[120] Metaphors for anti-Catholic legislation as explosives or swords or lances—legal weapons of discipline or coercion—came naturally to Kulturkämpfer. As social and political elites they thought of themselves as officers leading the charge against Vatican armies or knights laying low the church. The *Kladderadatsch* envisioned Kulturkämpfer as a *Ritterschaft* (league of knights) protecting Germany under the banner "Gegen Rom und Pfaffentrutz!" (Against Rome and clerical defiance!).[121] Liberals and liberal journals repeatedly stated they were at war or in a "Kriegszustand," a state of war with the Roman enemy. The *Kladderadatsch* was typical in this respect. Already in November 1870, following the victory over France, the journal issued a call "for the local militia against the black invasion."[122] The year 1871 was no time for peace: "Where there was darkness, there must be light. This year we still have to finish off the black army." "Reichstag-Uhlans" were implored to take up their lances against the reactionary ultramontanes.[123] In the ballads "Im jungen Reich" (In the young empire) and "Zum letzten Kampf!" (To the final battle!) Germans protect freedom against black myrmidons with mighty slashes of the sword.[124] In June 1872, immediately following the debate on the Jesuit law, the journal joyfully proclaimed that the "War, War with Rome!" had finally come, a war that would unite all Germans despite regional differences against the common enemy.

> You Saxons, Franconians, Bavarians, Alemanians,
> All Germans, forward into war!
> Lorrainers, Alsacians, send your men too,
> That part that's up for the fight!
>
> War, war with Rome! Do you hear Delbrück calling?
> Do you see the banners flapping in the wind?
> This is no fight with words and slogans—
> The terrible battle has begun!
>
> Already I see the armies engaging—
> Forward now, loyal guard on the Rhine!
> Infantry, attack! Bold uhlans,
> Take up your lances!

120. Quoted in Blackbourn, *Marpingen*, 264.
121. *Kladderadatsch*, 3 Aug. 1873.
122. *Kladderadatsch*, 27 Nov. 1870.
123. *Kladderadatsch*, 12 March 1871.
124. *Kladderadatsch*, 19 Nov. 1871.

On to Rome! I can see it already,
The Vatican captured by our army.
Shudder Pius! Here come the Teutons!
Give up your ridiculous delusions![125]

This was, however, no ordinary war waged on traditional fields of battle, across borders and with clear fronts. Jesuits like partisans roamed through the country. They were invisible, toxic gases, known only by their stench. The *Kladderadatsch* provided the "Kampfgesang der Jesuiten" (Battle song of the Jesuits), which included the following verse:

We are elusive like the air,
Quietly floating through the night,
Like vapors rising from a bog
Or shrub or poisoned goblet.
When you think you've grabbed us,
We have already disappeared,
Slipping away into a hidden lair;
You can sooner fumigate pests,
Than us, the Jesuits![126]

Such images help explain the frustration liberals felt in their combat with the Jesuits and why even the exceptional law could never be enough to rid them of their enemy: Kulturkämpfer wanted like a serried phalanx of hussars to meet their opponent squarely as men on the field of battle. Jesuits, however, seemed to be ghosts, slipping through their ranks.

Kulturkämpfer continuously tried to imagine a conventional military campaign like the recent war against France when defeats and victories had been measured by the amount of terrain won or lost. The liberal *Berliner Wespen* ran a series entitled Despatches from the Clerical Theater of War. While, according to the newspaper, this war had not begun as auspiciously as that against France, the nation was following its movements and results with no less attention. The population, the paper claimed, awaited with feverish anticipation reports returning from the "front"—Koblenz, Cologne, Breslau, and Wupperthal ("Enemy almost entirely pressed back in this position"). From "Headquarters Berlin" announcements were regularly issued concerning the progress of the campaign and levels of clerical resistance.[127] The paper

125. *Kladderadatsch*, 23 June 1872; see also 20 Oct. 1872. Rudolf von Delbrück was president of the Imperial Chancellor's Office during the Kulturkampf until his resignation in 1876.
126. *Kladderadatsch*, 1 Oct. 1871.
127. *Berliner Wespen*, 14 June 1872.

pictured Ludwig Windthorst on horseback, saber drawn high, leading a charge of armed Jesuits into battle.[128] In a local liberal election manifesto in the *Crefelder Zeitung* in 1873, veterans of the war of 1870 were reminded that a more dangerous enemy than France now threatened the nation. "To your weapons, *Kriegskameraden* (comrades-in-arms), against clerical rule, against Roman rule!"[129] According to the *National Zeitung,* the letter of Pope Pius IX to Kaiser Wilhelm I in 1873 claiming all baptized Christians as his own proved "that the curia intends to continue the war, which is already under way, until the German Empire is destroyed."[130]

In the crusade against the black ranks, Bismarck was the knight in shining armor. "Now, chancellor, show us that you are a knight, without fear or reproach." "Now, chancellor," called the *Berliner Wespen,* "swing your mighty sword." Bismarck is a mighty champion, driving his spear through the dragon (fig. 19). At his feet is the monster with three heads labeled "Reichensperger," "Windthorst," and "Mallinckrodt," the leadership of the Center, "part worm, part newt, and part dragon, procreating in a pool of slime."[131] Liberals promised to support the state, unification, and the empire if Bismarck in exchange would only kill the political power of Catholicism, an arrangement they eagerly proffered since it entailed no challenge to their convictions in the first place. On the contrary, it was all too agreeable in every respect. "Strike, strike! Plunge your blade with gallant courage!"[132] Here is the voice of liberals that belies the suggestion that it was they who had to be lured by Bismarck into the attack on the Catholic Church. Liberals pleaded with Bismarck, the very personification of state power, to lead the war against the church. By 1875, at the height of the Kulturkampf, with the abolition of the monasteries and closing of religious orders, Bismarck and Minister of Educational and Ecclesiastical Affairs Adalbert Falk of Prussia appear as victorious Teutonic knights. Behind them, a monastery has been sacked and lies in ruins. Bismarck before his soldiers raises high his sword in triumph. The caption announces that they will not rest until this den of thieves is laid waste and only the black flag is left flapping above a pile of rubble.[133]

128. *Berliner Wespen,* 28 June 1872.
129. HSTAD, RD, Nr. 2619, newspaper clipping from *Crefelder Zeitung,* 23 Oct. 1873.
130. Quotation in Wacker, *Friede zwischen Berlin und Rom?* 11–12.
131. "Der Kampf mit dem Drachen," *Berliner Wespen,* 16 Feb. 1872.
132. Ibid.
133. *Berliner Wespen,* 30 April 1875.

Fig. 19.   "Der Kampf mit dem Drachen," *Berliner Wespen,* 16 February 1872. In 1872, as the Kulturkampf gathered momentum, Bismarck appeared as the liberals' champion in the contest with the dragon whose three heads were Reichensperger, Windthorst, and Mallinckrodt, the leadership of the Catholic Center Party.

These were not merely examples of journalistic sensationalism. Such visions were an accurate reflection of the war fever of Kulturkampf legislators. During the debate on the Jesuit law, here again is Eduard Windthorst: "We cannot advance further until we have leveled the battlefield, until we have cleared away the greatest obstacles in our path. The greatest impediment now is the polluting and suffocating spirit of Jesuitism that unfortunately has already completely penetrated into large districts of our fatherland."[134] Eduard Lasker and Ludwig Bamberger were no exceptions. As the Catholic Fraktion organized itself in

134. *Für und Wider die Jesuiten,* part 1, session 22, 15 May 1872, 94.

the first Reichstag into the Center Party, Lasker believed that liberals no longer had any doubts that an ultramontane "war party" was emerging opposed to the German nation and the modern state and in support of the "worldwide rule of the pope."[135] Bamberger believed that the Kulturkampf was nothing short of a "guerre à outrance." With his characteristic fanaticism, he argued that if no free exchange of arguments was possible, one was obliged "to equip oneself with the greatest possible cold-bloodedness."[136] Catholic leaders also quickly adopted for rhetorical advantage the image of the church at war, a war the church, they believed, had done nothing to instigate. Center deputies like August Reichensperger argued that the closing of the Jesuit order and the campaign against the church were no less than a "war against Catholicism."[137] Ludwig Windthorst exclaimed to liberals in defiance, "You wanted a war, you shall have it."[138] The Catholic *Sonntagsblatt Eucharius* for the Diocese of Trier announced in 1874 that the "Kampf against the Holy Church" was even a "world war."[139]

At the time of the debate on the Jesuit law, Johann Bluntschli in an article appearing in *Gegenwart* argued that the Jesuits constituted the general staff of a new military campaign that the Vatican had directed against the modern state and modern civilization. "It draws up the plans, it instructs the leaders, it arms the masses, it selects the goals and directs the operations."[140] Just as the liberal literary journal *Grenzboten* argued that the Jesuit order was a company of soldiers that had become an army, divided into battalions and regiments, National Liberal deputies like Heinrich von Sybel believed the Jesuits were a "regiment of infantry, only stronger."[141] Friedrich Kiefer absurdly argued on the floor of the Reichstag that the Jesuits in Austria and Germany numbered at least sixty thousand. "Isn't that an army?" he asked. Jesuits, he believed, were busy starting small and large wars in society and a "war against the foundations and most important interests of morality"; the Catholic Church was pursuing "war against the present and future of the German Empire."[142] Richard Dove believed the

135. Quoted in Langewiesche, *Liberalismus in Deutschland*, 182.

136. Quoted in Weber, *Ludwig Bamberger*, 171.

137. *Für und Wider die Jesuiten*, part 3, session 48, 19 June 1872, 115.

138. *Berliner Wespen*, 28 June 1872.

139. Olaf Blaschke, "Das 19. Jahrhundert: Ein Zweites Konfessionelles Zeitalter?" *Geschichte und Gesellschaft* 26 (2000): 38–75, quotation at 51.

140. Bluntschli, "Debatte über die Jesuiten."

141. *Grenzboten* 2 (1872): 468; Sybel, *Klerikale Politik*, 113–14.

142. See Kiefer's speech in *Für und Wider die Jesuiten*, part 1, session 23, 16 May 1872, 97–111, quotations at 108, 106, and 100, respectively.

Jesuits were engaged in "a war with the German Empire," a war he considered more difficult than that with France. Nonetheless, he predicted the war against Rome would bring a victory like the triumph over Paris.[143] Meanwhile academic Kulturkämpfer like Eduard Zeller argued that the religious orders bound by the vow of obedience were a "terrible, fully disciplined army."[144] Adolf Zeising believed that the worldwide clergy were an "extraordinarily well organized and disciplined army" and that since the promulgation of the doctrine of papal infallibility the nation was in a "state of war."[145] As proof, Kulturkämpfer pointed to Catholic missionaries and priests who told their congregations to think of themselves as soldiers in an army commanded by officers and generals of the church.

Leaflets distributed by the executive committee of the liberal Protestant Deutscher Verein and addressed to all "Rhinelanders" leave no doubt that the attack on the Catholic Church was for Kulturkämpfer a continuation of the wars for unification. On the occasion of the fourth anniversary of the victory over France at the battle of Sedan, the committee announced that "at that time German unity was externally founded by warfare, after which it was established internally by the excitement of the entire people." "But," the leaflet asked, "do we still have complete German unity in the interior?" While the exterior enemy France had been defeated, the inner enemy, "which was allied with Napoleon at that time," had only become more powerful. The Jesuit and ultramontane party was "now burrowing into the heart of Germany against German unification." "A nation that had strongly defended its freedom against the outside will not tolerate in the interior the tyranny of an exploitive hierarchy." The committee insisted that the attack on the church was "a matter of completing what was begun at Sedan with ongoing work, with continuous unity, with uninterrupted struggle against the enemies of the fatherland."[146] For liberals the war against the Catholic Church was the final phase of the campaign for German unification begun with the war against France.

In this domestic war, Kulturkämpfer envisioned themselves locked in combat not only with Catholicism but with socialism and women and French revanchism, enemies that liberals conflated with one

---

143. *Für und Wider die Jesuiten,* part 3, 106–12.
144. Zeller, *Staat und Kirchen,* 153.
145. Zeising, *Religion und Wissenschaft,* quotations at 15, 440, respectively.
146. HSTAD, RK, Nr. 2723, "Die Enthebung der katholischen Geistlichen von der lokalen Schulaufsicht und deren Nachfolger, 1874–1875," Bl. 8.

another.[147] The Kulturkampf therefore became a war directed against several enemies at once on a broad front. In 1874 the conflict with the Catholic Church was only the first score to be settled in the "chivalrous" crusade of the Kulturkampf. In the *Kladderadatsch* a herald bears the banner "May Laws" in the illustration "Das schwarz-rothe Turnier des neunzehnten Jahrhunderts" (The black-red tournament of the nineteenth century). A mounted knight with lance charges a bishop. A social democrat waiting in the wing recognizes his days are numbered: "When this match is over, I'm next!"[148] Four years later, the promulgation of a second exceptional law dissolved all social democratic, socialist, and communist associations; closed social democratic meetings and publications; and banned socialist agitators from specified towns and districts. For liberal Kulturkämpfer the victory over France had outlined and fixed the boundaries of the empire. This was a momentous achievement, but only one, and not the last war needed to unify the nation. Another campaign, this time waged inside the empire against the Catholic Church and its doppelgänger, was required to complete the moral, social, and cultural unification of Germany, to secure the empire and the blessings of the Enlightenment. It required an effort, liberals imagined, not short of war, and while it may have been bloodless it was no less momentous not only for Germany, but for the world.

Liberals were ultimately disappointed. Despite their unflagging commitment to the successive rounds of Kulturkampf legislation, the war against Catholicism went poorly. By the middle of the 1870s, liberals and the state found they were not able to successfully prosecute the campaign against a well-led, well-organized, recalcitrant, and politicized Catholic population.[149] At the end of the decade, with the state bogged down in an apparently interminable fight, Bismarck decided to pursue other political options. Liberals had been warned that Bismarck might ultimately use the anti-Jesuit legislation to broker a deal with the Center against the liberal parties. As Bismarck hoped, the National Liberal Party split with the introduction of protectionist tariff reform, and he meanwhile negotiated with Center leaders for a parliamentary majority, settled with the new pope, Leo XIII, and aban-

---

147. The conflation of Catholics, women, socialism, and French revanchism is discussed in chapter 4.

148. *Kladderadatsch,* 29 March 1874.

149. Ross, *Failure of Bismarck's Kulturkampf;* idem, "Enforcing the Kulturkampf"; idem, "The Kulturkampf and the Limitations of Power in Bismarck's Germany," *Journal of Ecclesiastical History* 46 (1995): 669–88; idem, "The Kulturkampf: Restrictions on Controls on the Practice of Religion in Bismarck's Germany," in *Freedom and Religion in the Nineteenth Century,* ed. Richard Helmstadter (Stanford: Stanford University Press, 1997), 173–95.

doned state support of the Kulturkampf. After a tumultuous series of events including assassination attempts on the life of the chancellor, the dissolution of the Reichstag, and new elections, the state now directed its energies against the socialist movement with another round of exceptional laws approved by the Reichstag in October 1878. It seemed only recently that Bismarck had exclaimed in the Reichstag in May 1872, "Nach Canossa gehen wir nicht!" (We shall not go to Canossa!), indicating that the new German empire would never yield to the Vatican as Kaiser Heinrich IV had done during the Investiture Contest of the eleventh century. Anti-Catholics intended to hold Bismarck to his promise, so much so that they believed it should be literally carved in stone. On a monument erected at Bad Harzburg, formerly the seat of Heinrich IV, they inscribed the chancellor's words as a reminder for all time.[150] Now everywhere in Germany, liberal deputies, newspapers, and journals either sarcastically or mournfully repeated the pledge as proof of his betrayal.

Historians variously date the end of the Kulturkampf, some as late as 1887. The end, however, was clearly apparent to contemporary liberals, at least, who bitterly recognized the betrayal and acknowledged their own defeat by 1879. Leading liberal periodicals like the *Berliner Wespen* and the *Kladderadatsch,* which once depicted Bismarck as a knight leading the charge against the Roman enemy, throughout 1879 now showed Bismarck embracing the Jesuits and the leaders of the Center Party.[151] In the *Berliner Wespen* the Catholic political leadership had emasculated Bismarck: Ludwig Windthorst is depicted as Delilah shearing off Bismarck's hair.[152] Liberals, who had found their identity and their purpose in anti-Catholicism, had been abandoned by the state. With the Kulturkampf collapsing, they could only doubt the future for liberalism and modern culture and society in Germany. The liberal journal *Ulk* announced the return to the age of reaction and showed a feudal knight and a monk ripping through the "Liberal Constitution."[153] The *Berliner Wespen* showed a black winged dragon holding the banner "Reaction" in one hand and a whip in the other. The mighty warrior, once himself the dragon slayer, is now slain and delivered on top of his shield labeled "Liberalism."[154] By 1880, in an illus-

150. Ross, *Failure of Bismarck's Kulturkampf,* 24–25; Erich Eyck, *Bismarck: Leben und Werk* (Erlenbach and Zurich: Eugen Rentsch, 1944), 3:102.

151. Examples include *Berliner Wespen,* 23 May 1879, 6 June 1879, 27 June 1879, 11 July 1879; *Kladderadatsch,* 12 Sept. 1880.

152. *Berliner Wespen,* 5 Sept. 1879.

153. *Ulk,* 29 May 1879, 31 July 1879.

154. *Berliner Wespen,* 17 Oct. 1879.

tration titled "Des Culturkampfes Ende" (The end of the Kulturkampf), the *Berliner Wespen* indicated that the war against Catholicism was lost and the betrayal complete. The pope and his bishops are storming through a breach in the fortress wall labeled "May Laws." Bismarck behind a cannon has blown a hole in the wall from within: "The commander blasts a breach from inside the fortress wall in order to ease the storming and invasion for the enemy," reads the caption.[155] In the illustration "Vom Kulturkampfschauplatz" (The Kulturkampf theater of war), Bismarck sits on rubble marked "May Laws" and "Breadbasket Law." In the background the pope is beaming with delight.[156] By the mid-1880s most of the legislation of the Kulturkampf had been dismantled or had lapsed into disuse.

Given the liberals' identification of self and duty with the Kulturkampf, fanatical determination, and force of conviction in the 1870s, it was no less than astounding even to contemporaries how quickly they shed that mantle. In January 1882 one bewildered Progressive deputy, Albert Hänel, himself a die-hard Kulturkämpfer and still faithful to the anti-Catholic war, stood up among his colleagues in the Reichstag. He wondered out loud what had become of the Kulturkampf.

> At that time [in the 1870s] . . . it was considered necessary, correct and patriotic, yes, even a condition of being acceptable in higher society, that a person "kulturkampfed" (laughter); . . . Gentlemen, what is it like now? Now . . . I am continually asking myself, for heaven's sake, just who really were the Kulturkämpfer at that time? Now all of a sudden no one wants to have been one (laughter). And if you ask somebody, "Didn't you make Kulturkampf speeches at that time?" he says, "that's true, but privately I always said nothing can come of the Kulturkampf" (much laughter).[157]

By this time most liberals had abandoned the war against the Catholic Church, and it seemed in retrospect, as Hänel indicated, to have been in the end a useless gesture or perhaps, after all, an illusion. The Kulturkampf had become, even to its most ardent liberal and progressive prosecutors, no more than a vague, even comic, episode. Ludwig Bamberger, who once celebrated the Kulturkampf as the most important

155. *Berliner Wespen*, 23 April 1880. See also "Des Culturkampfes Ende," *Berliner Wespen*, 9 April 1880.
156. *Berliner Wespen*, 2 July 1880.
157. Quoted in Evans, *German Center Party*, 84.

work of the new empire, work that he had been proud to organize and lead, later described it as a mistake. With an abrupt about-face, he disavowed liberal responsibility for the campaign and now accused Bismarck of having initiated it as a "necessary evil to preserve the state."[158] It would be difficult to judge whether this transparent attempt to evade and transfer responsibility was due to a greater measure of political opportunism or self-delusion. In any case, Bamberger and other liberals had already lost their once commanding position in the Reichstag and Prussian parliament and now faced unprecedented political challenges on the right and the left. Nonetheless, they continued to hold on to prominent positions of authority at the regional, city, and local levels, where they continued to shape German society, culture, and politics as they continued to reshape German liberalism. Liberals moved to and grappled with other priorities: tariff protectionism, antisocialism, social welfare, a new phase of even more vibrant industrial expansion, and imperialism overseas. Anti-Catholicism certainly continued through to the end of the century and beyond, but liberals never again gave the campaign against the Catholic Church and Catholicism the paramount attention they had given it in the decade following the founding of the empire.[159]

158. Quoted in Langewiesche, *Liberalismus in Deutschland,* 184.
159. For the continuation of anti-Catholicism well after the Kulturkampf, see Ross, *Beleaguered Tower,* esp. 18–32; and Smith, *German Nationalism.*

Conclusion

From the Revolution of 1848 through the Kulturkampf to the "second founding" of the empire in 1878–79, two antithetical movements, liberalism and Catholicism, together profoundly reshaped Germany, culturally, socially, economically, and politically. With the Revolution of 1848 and then afterward,[the Roman Catholic Church organized and unleashed a campaign to roll back both the indifference that had undermined religious authority and the liberal and democratic ideologies that had threatened to topple the monarchical order.]With fervent ultramontanism, a dramatic missionary crusade, new lay associations and expressions of piety, popular mass pilgrimages to religious sites, and the proliferation of monastic orders and female religious congregations, the Catholic Church underwent a remarkable revival. For twenty-four years Catholic religious orders, the Jesuits, Redemptorists, Franciscans, and Dominicans, feverishly worked across Germany holding missions to reawaken Catholic piety and religious practice. All over Germany hundreds and thousands of Catholics streamed to the missions and pledged themselves there to a new life of religious faith and loyalty to the Roman Church. In the wake of the missions, the establishment of new Catholic societies and fraternities became the foundation for the kind of associational life that sustained in the following decades the popular Catholicism without which the ultramontanist reorientation of the church was scarcely imaginable.

A fresh appraisal of the missions based on a wide range of source material particularly in the Rhineland reveals aspects of the revival overlooked in other accounts. While church authorities, bishops, and priests, eager to put the best face on the missions, reported that the missionary campaign was a harmonious affair, other sources indicate that the heavy-handed conduct and new ultramontanism of the missionaries in the face of the relative inertia of the secular parish clergy led to frictions within the church. It makes sense to consider the repietization of the Catholic population, however successful in the long run, as not necessarily a smooth and relentless process everywhere. It encountered pockets of recalcitrance within the Catholic laity and, perhaps surprisingly, both met and contributed to resentments among the secular parish clergy. Often the older secular clergy resented the diminution of their authority in their own congregations, and they resented the younger, zealous, ultramontane regular (monastic) clergy who reoriented the laity to the authority of Rome. A reexamination of the missions also indicates that the missionaries relentlessly threatened their audiences with graphic depictions of hell and the promise of eternal torture by fire for those who remained unreconciled to the church. Congregations wailing, sobbing, and fainting; the long lines before the confessional; and the number of those who took the Eucharist for the first time in decades were the measures of success of the hellfire sermons. The popular revival of Catholic faith depended to a considerable extent, therefore, on the psychological terror used so effectively by the church in the Middle Ages and during the Counter-Reformation. At the same time, the success of the missionaries' efforts to reform popular morality was more qualified than was indicated by their own reports and the reports of parish priests and diocesan bishops. Despite the church's best efforts to inculcate moral sobriety, a wider reading of sources indicates in contrast to other accounts of the missions that, at least in the Rhineland, many of the principal features of popular culture, especially those of recreational culture, including sexual behavior, remained remarkably resilient. Peasants found that they could easily bring new religious faith into their lives without significant modification of alltäglich patterns of conduct and moral behavior, and this, in fact, was one of the reasons for the remarkable success of the Catholic revival.

At the same time, we are blind in one eye to the importance of the Catholic missions if we focus only on their more obvious role within the Catholic Church and their impact on the Catholic population. Equally significant, the missions wherever they went also drew, however unintentionally and surprisingly, large audiences from other confessions. Protestants too attended the missions. They had no desire to leave their own faith and convert to Catholicism but rather used the experience of the missionary sermons, with their fervent but general Christian messages of repentance, faith, and devotion, to undergo a confessional revival of their own. Passed over by historians of religion and society who have assumed that if secularization was not continuous during the century among the Catholic population then it was at least constant among Protestants, the Protestant revival after midcentury is largely terra incognita. Questions remain about the nature of the popular Protestant revival, its relative impact regionally, and its meaning in terms of class and gender, before it gave way to the processes of secularization toward the end of the century, but the indications of a dramatic and widespread Protestant reawakening in Germany after midcentury are clear.

Just as important, the Catholic missions created a hitherto unparalleled public space that mixed Catholics, Protestants, and Jews; men, women, and children; and aristocrats, middle-class professionals, artisans, workers, and peasants. Never before had so many different people in such large numbers crossed the boundaries between ethnic groups (Jews and Christians, Poles and Germans), genders, and classes, and the result was a dramatic recomposition of the public, aroused, volatile, and created by the Catholic Church. This is what provoked the concern of liberals and the state together, a common problem of social order that would foster their antimissionary, anti-Jesuit, and anticlerical alliance. Alarmed by the appeal of the missions to Protestants, the Protestant religious leadership worked feverishly to inculcate and preserve Protestant identity. They did so from the pulpit and with a deluge of anti-Catholic lectures, articles, pamphlets, and books. In their backlash against the Catholic revival, Protestant pastors and theologians drew a sharp line between Protestant and Catholic morality and culture and defined the two religions as irreconcilable, now locked in a titanic struggle for the future of Germany.

The religious revivals, both Catholic and Protestant, are especially important to identify because they provided, as I have argued, the context without which the reorientation of liberalism after midcentury; the resurgence of popular anti-Catholic sentiment; and ultimately the Kulturkampf itself, the elite liberal anti-Catholic campaign of the 1870s, cannot be adequately understood. Historians of Germany have made various cases for the transformation of liberalism at different periods and events during the course of the second half of the nineteenth century. I have argued that viewed from the perspective of religious revival and the concomitant anti-Catholic hysteria, liberalism underwent a sea change during the 1850s and 1860s. Following the defeat of liberals in the 1848 Revolution and the initial period of exhaustion and disarray during the conservative reaction, liberals found anticlericalism and anti-Catholicism powerful means to rehabilitate and reorient their vision for German society. Jesuits, monks, nuns, priests, and Catholics were according to liberals the agents of dogma, superstition, stupidity, subservience, intolerance, and irrationalism. In an age that should have been, liberals believed, modern and progressive, Catholicism was a medieval aberration, all that had to be left behind as the German nation moved forward into the future. By means of a specific anti-Catholic cognitive style of contrast, liberals asserted a bourgeois ideology for hegemony in German society that included industrialization, capitalist free-market economics, individualism, the autonomous state, Honoratiorenpolitik, gendered public and private spheres, rationalism, and freedom. In their effort to revive liberalism and to give it new meaning in the postrevolutionary period, leading liberals readily relied on the Protestant revival and broad Protestant anti-Catholicism to bolster and legitimize rhetorically the liberal social, cultural, and political program for reform. As liberals therefore placed anti-Catholicism at the core of their identity and at the center of their prescription for the modern nation, they were both repelled by and intertwined with the revival of Catholicism. It was the paradox of the postrevolutionary period, with Catholicism and the Catholic Church and all that they allegedly stood for as the points of reference, that liberals depended for their social, cultural, and political identity upon that which they dedicated themselves to living without.

The anti-Catholicism of liberals was so prominent in the nineteenth century that historians of modern Germany for the most part have taken it for granted, and the motives behind the liberal animus toward the Catholic Church have seemed largely self-evident. This includes the Kulturkampf, the culmination of anti-Jesuit hysteria, antimonasticism, anticlericalism, and anti-Catholicism in Germany in the nineteenth century. Historians who have focused specifically on the years of the Kulturkampf itself have argued that the liberal and state-sponsored attack on the church was an attempt to establish the autonomy of the modern nation-state or to thwart the power of mass political Catholicism. One historian has argued that the term *Kulturkampf* should be taken at "face value" as a "struggle of civilizations," a clash between the self-avowed modern outlook of liberal nationalism and the imputed backwardness of German Catholics.[1] The Kulturkampf was in some measure all of these, as I have argued, but we miss important dimensions of the Kulturkampf if we simply accept it as a straightforward response to the political, confessional, and religious power of the Roman Catholic Church. This study has therefore tried to look

---

1. Blackbourn, "Progress and Piety," 148. See also idem, *Marpingen,* 250.

beyond the surface of anti-Catholicism in order to examine more closely liberal identity and the liberal imperatives, social, cultural, and moral, that culminated in the Kulturkampf.

What has emerged is a more complex evaluation of liberalism and anti-Catholicism and of the origins and meaning of the Kulturkampf than has been recognized before. On the one hand, Roman Catholicism and Roman Catholics represented for liberals material that they could use to think creatively and constructively about who they were and what they stood for. For example, in literature, newspapers, and journals, liberals established against the image of the rotund, simpering, and effeminate monk an array of new heroic and secular personalities devoted to nation building and national prowess: the industrialist, the entrepreneur, the banker, the scientist, and the civil servant. In contrast to the monastery, a useless artifact from the Middle Ages, they fashioned visions of the robust and modern German nation dedicated to industrial expansion, capitalist economics, and bourgeois propriety even as the romanticized image of the monastery also provided a momentary escape from the new age of bureaucratic sobriety and enlightened rationalism. Liberals were unwilling or unable to recognize the modern character of the Catholic revival with its mass transportation, communication, organization, and politics; they could image Catholicism only as a "medieval" aberration in the modern age. The power of the Catholic revival and the loyalty of the Catholic population to the church and its dedication to a Roman Catholic way of life therefore gave liberals reason to doubt that relentless progress according to the laws of historical evolution was inevitable, that the religious fanaticism of the Middle Ages had been left behind for a new age of science, rationalism, capitalism, and freedom.

On the other hand, and this is no less significant, the liberal anti-Catholic cognitive style often entailed unintended and surprising consequences for liberalism and liberal identity. Derisive and comic tales of sexual intrigue in the monasteries and convents were part of the long legacy of Enlightenment anticlericalism, and they continued to serve as prurient and sensationalist entertainment throughout the nineteenth century. After 1848, however, liberals hated and attacked female religious orders not least because they were incessant reminders of their own failure. Indeed, in convent atrocity narratives, liberals followed the creative capacity of their anti-Catholicism to a startling conclusion. Their hopes for reform and freedom defeated in the revolution and continually frustrated in their subsequent efforts by the authoritarian state, liberals identified with the grisly story of young nuns hidden away in dark dungeons and raped. Beneath the liberals' outward bravura, the convent atrocity story revealed a deeply traumatized self-image. At the same time, liberals claimed a masculine identity. If liberalism was a public persona of rationalism, independence, and civic sense, then Catholicism once again by contrast exhibited all the attributes, Kulturkämpfer believed, of the feminine sex: irrationalism, fanaticism, subservience, and the ability to manipulate men emotionally. If in liberal discourse Catholicism was a woman, then it followed logically enough that anti-Catholicism was misogyny. Liberals thought about the relationship between liberalism and Catholicism as fundamentally a relationship between men and women, perhaps unavoidable, at best distrustful, at worst hostile. For some liberal men the consequence could be traumatic paranoia: priests and Jesuits became women castrating men and emasculating the population in their effort to exert the rule of Rome over Germany. Beneath the more apparent struggle to rid Germany of the deadweight of Catholicism in the modern age, therefore, were complex anxieties concerning sexual humiliation and fears of insufficient masculinity in the confrontation with the Catholic revival that shaped the Kulturkampf of the 1870s.

At another level too the Kulturkampf represented a campaign beyond the attempt to preserve the autonomy of the state or to break the cultural, political, and religious influence of Catholicism. Precisely during the reemergence of the Frauenfrage or women's question in the 1860s, the hotly debated question concerning the role of women in society and their access to education, professional opportunities, and ultimately politics, anti-Catholicism became inextricably intertwined in the liberal imagination with the threat that women posed to the traditional public. From the perspective that includes the reemergence of the women's movement, the Kulturkampf represented a campaign to preserve the distinction between gendered public and private, the very foundation of bourgeois social, political, sexual, and moral order. The practice of Catholicism, by definition feminine, at the missions, on pilgrimages, and at religious associations seemed in itself, according to liberals, to undermine the integrity of the public sphere. At the same time, the popular practice of Catholicism seemed increasingly dominated by women. Women constituted the most devout and loyal laity, and women joined the new religious congregations in dramatic numbers. Catholic women also brought the practice of their faith out of the home and church as they pursued professional opportunities as members of religious congregations committed to philanthropic work in public as educators, administrators, and nurses.

During the Kulturkampf Catholic women employed the organizational skills they had acquired as members of the new religious associations established with the missionary campaign. They organized and participated in the antistate demonstrations, accepting state censure, arrest, and fines, so much so that the counter-Kulturkampf campaign in public according to state officials and liberals looked feminine. The Catholic ecclesiastical and political leadership itself inculcated in the Catholic lay population the image of resistance to the Kulturkampf as a strong-willed, defiant woman. The Catholic revival seemed to liberals to augur a new age simultaneously of feminist recalcitrance and mass political democratization, an age indifferent or hostile to Bildung, independence, civic character, and Honoratiorenpolitik. The struggle against the power of Catholicism in an age that should have been, liberals believed, rational, scientific, and enlightened required above all greater exertions of masculinity. As Kulturkämpfer, they invoked and applauded again and again their own masculine virtues in the effort to cultivate a common anticlerical élan. Liberal men rallied together in the campaign against the church as a "manly" fight to defend the integrity of the public. Ultimately, therefore, the Catholic revival looked like one dimension of the larger women's movement for access to the public, and the Kulturkampf between liberalism and Catholicism itself took on the aspect of a *Geschlechterkampf,* a contest between men and women. Enmeshed in the women's question and in the midst of dramatic pressures for change, the Kulturkampf was an attempt to preserve the gender status quo of nineteenth-century German society.

Not just literally a "cultural struggle" or "struggle of civilizations," the Kulturkampf was, as liberals tirelessly reminded everyone, a war. Taking liberals at their word helps us understand why they devoted themselves with such fervor and devotion to the pursuit of victory. Inspired by the triumph over France, Kulturkämpfer led the domestic attack against Catholicism for the sake of state autonomy, the integrity of the public sphere, industry, progress, freedom, and unity. For liberals the war was bloodless to be sure but also vivid and elaborate. Kulturkämpfer saw themselves as armored knights or a column of uhlans, and they saw Germany as a theater of war with liberal and clerical armies advancing and retreating with victories and defeats. In the liberal imagination this was a war waged on several fronts against mass democratization, French revanchism, nascent socialism, and women in public and, as I have argued, always all at once against Catholicism. Liberals believed they were engaged in a war against the church as urgent and fateful as that against France, and they therefore believed the use of force against the domestic enemies was no less justified than the force that had been used against the external enemy. Bismarck hardly needed to coax or manipulate the liberal parties into an alliance against the Roman Church. If the victories against Denmark, Austria, and France had been Bismarck's work, liberals claimed the Kulturkampf as their contribution to the wars for German unity. It was precisely with the "cultural struggle" as the last war for unification that liberals sought to define in their own image the nation, socially, culturally, and morally.

Closer evaluation of the roots of the Kulturkampf indicates, then, that anti-Jesuitism, antimonasticism, and anti-Catholicism were not mere derivative expressions of liberalism. After 1848 anticlericalism and anti-Catholicism were integral to liberal identity and to the formation of liberal social, cultural, and economic ideology. Liberals therefore believed intolerance of Roman Catholicism and of the Roman Catholic Church was a duty, and they believed they were bound by duty to invoke the force of the state to preserve the independence of the state. For liberals, who believed the very raison d'être of the modern nation-state was to guarantee freedom and progress, the threat of "Jesuitism," monasticism, clericalism, and the authority of the church and pope required a war sponsored by the state against the domestic enemy. The weapons of war were coercive anti-Catholic laws, including anti-Jesuit legislation, an exceptional law abrogating the rights of German citizenship. Indeed, the abrogation of the citizen rights of the Catholic population of the nation was, during debate on the Kirchenfrage and as leading liberal theorists of church and state argued, not out of the question.

Though historians of liberalism and the Kulturkampf have traditionally argued that the liberals' support of anti-Catholic legislation was a betrayal of fundamental liberal principles, the argument of this book in its entirety has been, therefore, that the Kulturkampf was hardly a liberal "mistake," a moment during which liberals abandoned what they were supposed to stand for.[2] German liberals based in decades of anti-Catholic identity were high-minded, principled, and idealistic. Only Jewish liberal nationalist deputies otherwise committed to the Kulturkampf believed that the Jesuit law, an exceptional law that might serve as a precedent for further discriminatory legislation against other minorities, including Jews, went too far. It was with the

---

2. Even Dagmar Herzog's reevaluation of German liberalism concludes that liberals got "caught in the near-fatal alliance with the Prussian authoritarian state," leaving the impression that the liberals' involvement in the Kulturkampf was not based on an accurate appreciation of their own interests or intentions. Herzog, *Intimacy and Exclusion,* 168.

exceptional law of the Kulturkampf that a rift developed in the long-standing alliance between Jews and liberalism. Rejection of the Kulturkampf on the basis of principle was the position claimed by democrats, themselves no friends of clerical power and the conservative and reactionary authority of Catholicism. Nor was the Kulturkampf an isolated glitch, an epiphenomenon that historians have passed over as they trace the course of modern German liberalism.[3] To the contrary, the Kulturkampf was the culmination of a social and cultural program that was deeply rooted in the rehabilitation of liberalism in the face of the Catholic revival following the 1848 Revolution.

[For the history of liberalism in Germany, the Kulturkampf is significant not because it represented how far liberals had strayed from liberalism but, on the contrary, because it was founded on the intolerance inherent to liberalism itself.]The Kulturkampf demonstrates that liberals were not among those who advocated in theory a civil society based on unqualified tolerance and universal rights, the kind of society that historians often argued was fostered and protected by German liberals if not always as a matter of practice then at least on principle. Can we avoid, then, the conclusion that in Germany liberalism, for all its virtues yet intolerant and committed when deemed necessary to the use of state force against internal enemies, made its own contribution to a social and political tradition of intolerance and state-sponsored domestic wars against *Staatsfeinde,* a tradition that later when joined with and reshaped by genocidal racism could have devastating consequences?

If not, the question becomes whether liberal anti-Catholicism and the Kulturkampf indicate an insufficient inculcation of Enlightenment ideals and therefore ultimately a German *Sonderweg,* a special path that veered from the development of equal rights and respect for difference often assumed to be the hallmarks of Germany's Western counterparts. It might perhaps be gratifying to answer that intolerance belonged to a peculiar liberalism in Germany, thereby preserving the notion that the principle of tolerance was characteristic of European liberalism more generally[I would argue, however, that in the light of recent scholarship the liberal style of thinking about modern identity and modern society by means of apparent oppositions and the intolerance that style necessarily entailed were common to the liberal modernism of west European countries.]In his sociological study of modernity, Zygmunt Bauman has argued that the construction and

---

3. For example, Sheehan's *German Liberalism* devotes about one and a half pages to the Kulturkampf. See 135–37. A more recent and even discussion is given in Langewiesche, *Liberalismus in Deutschland,* 180–86.

arrangement of dichotomies are crucial for the practice and vision of social order. "The second member is but *the other* of the first, the opposite (degraded, suppressed, exiled) side of the first and its creation," according to Bauman. "Both sides depend on each other, but the dependence is not symmetrical. The second side depends on the first for its contrived and enforced isolation. The first depends on the second for its self-assertion."[4] Anti-Catholicism in Germany was a specific example of the intolerance that is, as Bauman argues, the inherent inclination of liberal modernism.

While the Kulturkampf pitted liberals against Catholics, it also created other deep fissures within the new German empire. The anti-Catholic policy sponsored by liberals and executed by the state divided Protestants, however much as a whole they might have shared anti-Catholic sentiments. Conservative Protestants who had joined with Bismarck in an alliance of throne and altar now when hard pressed found they feared secularization more than they hated Roman Catholicism. They saw the Kulturkampf as an attack on religion and the autonomous affairs of religious institutions, and they therefore quickly turned against liberal Protestants and the state government. With the exceptional legislation of the Jesuit law Jews once wedded to liberalism doubted, with good reason, liberalism's commitment to the inviolability of minority civil and citizenship rights. Jews, a far smaller and more vulnerable population than Catholics within Germany, worried now that such legislation might extend eventually to other undesired ethnic and religious groups, including their own. Viewed overwhelmingly by Catholic workers and peasants as an arrogant middle-class campaign and understood by liberal elitists themselves as an effort to rid the nation of the irrationalism and ignorance associated with the masses, the Kulturkampf contributed to class antagonisms.

The Kulturkampf with its emphasis on progress and rationalism and all that these implied (science, education, and development) seemed also to represent to many a fundamental conflict between two kinds of habitation, urban and rural ways of life. Increasingly it looked like a contest between urbane metropolitans and common country folk. At the same time, the Kulturkampf, deeply embedded as it was in the women's question, pitted men against women in a contest for access to the public. The Kulturkampf rallied Roman Catholics in defense of their church and forced most Catholics into a pariah community opposed to liberalism and to the state. The Kulturkampf contributed to the mass mobilization of the Catholic electorate in support of the

---

4. Bauman, *Modernity and Ambivalence,* 14 (emphasis in original).

Center Party, and it exacerbated the conflict between Catholics and Protestants as old as the Reformation. In the end, the Kulturkampf divided middle-class Catholic men and women and ripped through middle-class Catholic friendships and families, as friends and relatives turned against one another either to join the liberal campaign or to defend the church. Though a campaign meant to be the final war waged domestically for the sake of unification, the Kulturkampf, ironically, divided Germans along the lines of culture, class, gender, confession, and politics, and merely made German unity more elusive.

Bibliography

Archival Sources

Hauptstaatsarchiv Düsseldorf

Bestand Regierung Düsseldorf, Präsidialbüro (Reg. d. Präs.)
1233 Geistliche u. Kirchenangelegenheiten, Ent. u.a. Angebliche demokratische Umtriebe von kath. Geistlichen und Jesuiten (1851), Bd. 7, 1845–64.
1234 Geistliche u. Kirchenangelegenheiten, Ent. u.a. Angebliche demokratische Umtriebe von kath. Geistlichen und Jesuiten (1851), Bd. 8, 1864–79.
1250 Einfluß des kath. Klerus auf die Landtagswahlen, 1852–58.
1252 Katholische Orden und Missionen. Betr. vor allem Niederlassungen und Missionsveranstaltungen des Jesuitenordens, Bd. 1, 1852–87.
1308 Schulangelegenheiten betr. alle Schulreform, Bd. 5, 1870–75.
1309 Schulangelegenheiten betr. alle Schulreform, Bd. 6, 1874–79.
1613 Sekretande betreffend die katholischen ultramontanen Landräte, 1873.

Bestand Regierung Düsseldorf
1308 Schulsachen, 1871–75.
1317 Reorganisation des Volksschulwesens res die Einführung von Simultanschulen, 1876–82.
2596 Stat. übersichten res Verwaltungsberichte über das Schulwesen. Gen., Bd. 4, 1870–73.
2619 Die Anordnung der Schulpflegen bzw. Kreisschulinspektoren (kath.) und Förderung des Schulwesens durch die Geistlichen, Bd. 1, 1872–73.
2620 Die Anordnung der Schulpflegen bzw. Kreisschulinspektoren (kath.) und Förderung des Schulwesens durch die Geistlichen, Bd. 2, 1874.
2621 Die Anordnung der Schulpflegen bzw. Kreisschulinspektoren (kath.) und Förderung des Schulwesens durch die Geistlichen, Bd. 3, 1875–77.
3228 Jahresberichte über das Schulwesen (Krefeld), Bd. 5, 1867–72.
3229 Jahresberichte über das Schulwesen (Krefeld), Bd. 6, 1872–73.
8801 Staatsgefährdende Predigten katholischer Geistlicher.
20111 Jesuiten oder Orden der Gesellschaft Jesu und verwandte Orden, Bd. 1, 1870–72.

20112 Jesuiten oder Orden der Gesellschaft Jesu und verwandte Orden, Bd. 2, 1872–73.

20113 Ordensniederlassungen (Gesetz vom 31.5.1875), Bd. 4, 1878–87.

20180 Seelsorge der Ordensgeistlichen, 1873–74.

29314 Jesuiten, Bd. 3, 1874–1913.

29315 Klöster Bd 1, 1874.

29317 Ordensniederlassungen (Gesetz vom 31.5.1875), Bd. 1, 1875.

29318 Ordensniederlassungen (Gesetz vom 31.5.1875), Bd. 2, Sept. 1875–Juli 1876.

29319 Ordensniederlassungen (Gesetz vom 31.5.1875), Bd. 3, 1876–77.

29393 Franziskanerpatres und das Franziskanerkloster zu Düsseldorf, 1863 –1913.

29394 Dominikankloster, Düsseldorf, 1872–1913.

29410 Niederlassung der Genossenschaft der Armen Dienstmägde Jesu Christi zu Düsseldorf (Südstrasse Josephinenstift).

29418 Ursulinenkloster zu Düsseldorf.

29420 Kloster der Barmherzigen Schwestern, 1841–83.

29421 Niederlassung der Genossenschaft der Töchter vom hl. Kreuz in Düsseldorf (Altestadt).

29425 Niederlassung der Genossenschaft der Töchter vom hl. Kreuz in Düsseldorf.

29432 Niederlassung der Genossenschaft der Armen Dienstmägde Jesu Christi aus Dernbach in Benrath.

29432 Niederlassung der Genossenschaft der Töchter vom hl. Kreuz in Düsseldorf (Friedrichstr.–höhere Töcherschule).

30428 Auflössung öffentlicher Versammlungen durch die Polizei, 1874–89.

Bestand Regierung Aachen, Präsidialbüro

BR-1040–119 Orden der Gesellschaft Jesu bzw. die Ausführung des Gesetzes vom 4. Juli 1872, 1872.

753 Verwaltungsberichte in Schulangelegenheiten, 1863–82.

1211 Beschwerde gegen die Geistlichen, 1814–62.

1239 Missionare, Jesuiten Lazaristen. Ordenstätigkeit derselben in Kirche und Schule, 1835–1916.

1283 Ausführung des Gesetzes vom 31. Mai 1875 über die geistlichen Orden und ordensähnliche Congregationen der katholischen Kirche, 1875–1917.

Bestand Regierung Aachen

2122 Jahresberichte der kath. Schulinspektoren, 1871–75.

2123 Jahresberichte der kath. Schulinspektoren, 1875–80.

2450 Genossenschaft der Armen Schwestern zum Heiligen Franziskus in Aachen, 1852–94.

8918 Bericht über geistliche Orden, 1876–78.

8935 Franziskaneranstalt, 1859–90.

10508 Franziskaner, 1862–63.

10699 Orden der Gesellschaft Jesu bzw. die Ausführung des Gesetzes vom 4. Juli 1872, 1872–83.

10709 Bericht über geistliche Orden, 1875–76.

10897 Nicht aufgehobene Stifte, Klöster Bd. 2, 1840–62.

10954 Nicht aufgehobene Stifte, Klöster Bd. 3, 1862–71.
15585 Orden des Heiligen Franziskus von Assisi, Bd. 1, 1861–1921.
17530 Ortsschulvorstände und Lokalschul-Inspektoren, Allgemeines, 1876–78.
17583 Kreisschulinspektion, Allgemeines, 1879–83.
17587 Kreisschul-Inspektoren, 1876–78.

Bestand Regierung Köln
44 Die Enthebung der katholischen Geistlichen von der lokalen Schulaufsicht und deren Nachfolger, 1872–74.
45 Die Enthebung der katholischen Geistlichen von der lokalen Schulaufsicht und deren Nachfolger, 1874–75.
46 Die Enthebung der katholischen Geistlichen von der lokalen Schulaufsicht und deren Nachfolger, 1875.
47 Die Enthebung der katholischen Geistlichen von der lokalen Schulaufsicht und deren Nachfolger, 1875.
50 Die Ernennung der lokalen- und Stadtschulinspektoren, 1872–76.
51 Die Ernennung der lokalen- und Stadtschulinspektoren, 1876–79.
93 Ausführung der Kirchengesetze (1873) und Anstellung von Geistlichen, 1873–74.
143 Das Elementarschulwesen im Kreis Bonn, 1859–78.
281 Das Elementarschulwesen in Köln, 1860–75.

Stadtarchiv Düsseldorf

Bestand II.
987 Franziskaner.

Bestand III.
4698 Die Geistlichen, 1873–1900.
4725 Franziskanerkloster, 1863–1914.

Bestand XII. (Benrath)
248 Katholische Kirchenangelegenheiten.

Bestand XVI. (Kaiserwerth)
842 Aufsicht des Staates über Kirchen, Kirchendiener, Klöster und sonstige kirchliche Institutionen.

Landeshauptarchiv Koblenz

Bestand 403, Oberpräsidium der Rheinprovinz
1146 Beschwerden gegen die katholische Geistlichkeit, 1833–71.
1343 Kontroverspredigten von Geistlichen, 1840–89.
1451 Die Aufsicht auf Proselytmacherei.
3680 Die Ausführung der vier preuß. Gesetze über kirchliche Angelegenheiten vom 11., 12., 13., u. 14. Mai 1873.

6694 Die Teilnahme der Lehrer u. Beamten an Vereinen deren Tendenzen als staatsgefährlich erkannt werden (Verein deutscher Katholiken, Verein zum geheiligten Herzen Jesu), 1872–76.

7148 Beaufsichtigung der Presse, 1874–84.

7511 Die Jesuiten, 1855–65.

7512 Der Orden der Gesellschaft Jesu und die ihm verwandten Orden und Kongregationen; Ausführung des Reichs v. 4.7.1872, 1872–75.

7531 Die Auseinandersetzung des Staates mit der Kirche, 1848–53.

7532 Die Auseinandersetzung des Staates mit der Kirche, 1855–63.

7558 Die Ausführung des Reichgesetzes vom 4. Mai 1874; Unbefugte Ausübung von Kirchenämtern; Orts-Ausweisungen von Geistlichen; u.s.w., 1874–75, 1874–83.

7559 Die Ausführung des Gesetzes von 21. Mai 1874. Die Beschlagnahme und Vermögensverwaltung vakanter geistlicher Stellen, 1874–84.

7564 Ausführung des Gesetzes von 22.4.1875 bezüglich der Einstellung der Leistungen aus Staatsmitteln für die römischen katholischen Bistümer und Geistlichen, 1874–95.

8806 Verhalten von Geistlichen, Lehrer usw. bei den Wahlen, 1852–1911.

9694–9697 Die Orden und ordensähnlichen Kongregationen der katholische Kirche Gesetz v. 31.5.1875, Bd. 1, 1875, Bd. 2, 1876, Bd. 3, 1877–78, Bd. 4, 1878–80.

9909 Zeitungsberichte der Regierung zu Köln, 1871–83.

10400–10403 Die Ausführung der vier preuß. Gesetze über kirchliche Angelegenheiten vom 11., 12., 13., u. 14. Mai 1873, Bd. 2, 1873–74.

10404–10407 Die Ausführung der vier preuß. Gesetze über kirchliche Angelegenheiten vom 11., 12., 13., u. 14. Mai 1873, Bd. 6, 1875.

10412 Kreisschulinspektion-Bezirke und die Kreisschul-inspektoren, 1873–75.

10447 Katholische Bruderschaften und Vereine, 1826–95.

10524 Die Ertheilung des Schulplanmässigen Religionsunterricht.

10611–12 Die Kirchlichen und Pfarrverhältnisse in den Kreisen: St. Wendel, 1838–73, 1874–91.

10841 Nachrichten über Geistliche mit Rücksicht auf Paragraph 16 des Gesetzes vom 11. Mai 1873, 1873–77.

10851–10859 Die Ausführung des Gesetzes vom 21 Mai 1874 über Beschlagnahme und Vermögensverwaltung vakanter geistlicher Stellen: Bd. 1, 1874–75, Bd. 2, 1875, Bd. 3, 1875, Bd. 4, 1875, Bd. 5, 1875–76, Bd. 6, 1876, Bd. 7, 1876, Bd. 8, 1876, Bd. 9, 1877–81.

10860 Die Kreisschulinspektoren im Regierungsbezirk Trier, 1874–93.

10869 Ausführung des Gesetzes von 22.4.1875 bezüglich der Einstellung der Leistungen aus Staatsmitteln für die römisch-katholischen Bistümer und Geistlichen, 1875–78.

13676 Beschwerden über kath. Geistliche in gemischten Ehe-Angelegenheiten, 1849–1910.

13680 Die Ausführung der vier preuß. Gesetze über kirchliche Angelegenheiten vom 11., 12., 13., u. 14. Mai 1873.

15196 Kreisschulinspektoren im Regierungsbezirk Düsseldorf, 1873–1910.

15715 Verzeichnis derjeniger Geistlichen, welche auf Grund Art. 23, Abs. 2 des Gesetzes vom 11.5.1873 zur gerichtlichen Untersuchung gezogen und verurteilt sind.

15716 Verzeichnis derjeniger Geistlichen, welche auf Grund Art. 23, Abs. 2 des Gesetzes vom 11.5.1873 zur gerichtlichen Untersuchung gezogen und verurteilt sind. Diözese Trier.

15720 Nachrichten über Geistliche mit Rücksicht auf Par. 16 des Gesetzes vom 11.5.1873, 1878–96.

15722 Die Ausführung des Reichsgesetzes vom 4. Mai 1874; Unbefugte Ausübung von Kirchenämtern; Orts-Ausweisungen Geistlichen; usw, 1874–83.

16688 Verzeichnis der Geistlichen, deren Vermögen eingezogen war, 1873–79.

16689 Verurteilte Geistliche.

16730 Angelegenheiten von Geistlichen, insbes. Gesuche bei Stellensetzungen, politische Spannung mit der kath. Geistlichkeit im Bistum Trier, 1848–50.

Abt. 441, Regierungsbezirk Koblenz
26204 Berufung weltlicher Kreisschulinspectoren an Stelle der bisherigen katholischen Schulinspectoren.

Bestand 442, Bezirksregierung Trier
1033 Revisionsberichte der Kreisschulinspectoren, 1876–77.

3963 Wirken und Verhalten der kath. Missionen und der Jesuiten 1850–1900.

6383 Die im Rigierungsbezirk Trier bestehenden (katholischen) Vereine sowie das Vereinswesen im Allgemeinen, 1849–95.

6438 Sammlungen zur Unterstützung des Papstes; Adressen an denselben; kath. Vereine, 1861–89.

6442 Das Abhalten von öffentlichen Prozessionen und Wallfahrten. Mutter-Gottes-Erscheinungen in Marpingen, Münchweis, Berschweiler.

6660 Das Verhalten der Beamten und der Geistlichekeit bei den Wahlen zum Abgeordnetenhaus und überhaupt in politischer Hinsicht, 1866–88.

7853–54 Die politischen, kirchlichen und religiösen Vereine, 1845–74, 1874–87.

10419 Ausweisungen kath. Geistlicher, 1874–84.

10420 Verzeichnisse der in Strafanstalten inhaftierten kath. Geistlichen, 1874–78.

Newspapers

Allgemeine Evangelische Kirchenzeitung
Allgemeine Zeitung des Judenthums
Crefelder Zeitung
Deutsche Allgemeine Zeitung
Essener Zeitung
Germania
Kölnische Volkszeitung
Kölnische Zeitung
National Zeitung
Neue Preußische Zeitung (Kreuz-Zeitung)

Spenersche Zeitung
Vossische Zeitung

Journals

Berliner Wespen
Deutsch-Evangelisch Blätter
Evangelische Kirchenzeitung
Die Gartenlaube
Die Gegenwart
Grenzboten
Historisch-politische Blätter für das Katholische Deutschland
Historische Zeitschrift
Historisches Jahrbuch
Im Neuen Reich
Kladderadatsch
Preußische Jahrbücher
Stimmen aus Maria Laach
Ulk

Statistical and Reference Works and Official Publications

Allgemeine deutsche Biographie. Berlin: Duncker und Humblot, 1969.

Kalkoff, Hermann, ed. *Nationalliberale Parlamentarier 1867–1917 des Reichstages und der Einzeltage.* Berlin: Schriftenvertriebstelle der nationalliberalen Partei Deutschlands Hermann Kalkoff, 1917.

Kuhne, Thomas, ed. *Handbuch der Wahlen zum preußischen Abgeordnetenhaus, 1867–1914: Wahlergebnisse, Wahlbündnisse und Wahlkandidaten.* Düsseldorf: Droste Verlag, 1994.

Mann, Bernhard, ed. *Biographisches Handbuch für das preußische Abgeordnetenhaus, 1867–1918.* Düsseldorf: Droste Verlag, 1988.

Ritter, Gerhard A., and Merith Niehuss, eds. *Wahlgeschichtliches Arbeitsbuch: Materialen zur Geschichte zur Statistik des Kaiserreichs, 1871–1918.* Munich: C. H. Beck, 1980.

Schwarz, Max, ed. *MdR Biographisches Handbuch des Reichstages.* Hanover: Verlag für Literatur und Zeitgeschehen, 1965.

Statistisches Handbuch für den preußischen Staat. Berlin: Das Bureau, 1888 et seq.

Statistisches Jahrbuch für das deutsche Reich. Berlin: Puttkammer und Mühlbrecht, 1880 et seq.

Stenographische Berichte über die Verhandlungen des deutschen Reichstages. Berlin: Verlag der Buchdruckerei der Norddeutschen Allgemeinen Zeitung, 1871 et seq.

Stenographische Berichte über die Verhandlungen des preußichen Landtags: Haus der Abgeordneten. Berlin: W. Moeser, 1850 et seq.

Printed Primary Sources

Abbott, S. J. *The Empress and the Carmelite Nun, or Twenty-One Years in a Convent Dungeon.* London: Convent Enquiry Society, 1902.

Alt, Robert, et al., eds. *Sämtliche Werke*. Berlin: Volkseigener Verlag, 1976.

Andreae, O. *Die verderbliche Moral der Jesuiten in Auszügen aus ihren Schriften.* Ruhrort: Andreae, 1865.

————. *"Der Zweck heiligt das Mittel" als ein Moralgrundsatz der Jesuiten dargethan.* Gütersloh, 1865.

Arsac, Joanni. *Die Jesuiten: Ihre Lehre, ihr Unterrichtswesen, ihr Apostolat.* Vienna: Sartori, 1867.

Auer, Adelheid. *Die barmherzige Schwester*. Schwerin, 1870.

Aufgefangene Briefe einer Nonne an Ihren Beichtvater. N.p.: Sebastian Hartl, 1781.

Bachem, Julius. *Die Sünden des Liberalismus im ersten Jahre des neuen Deutschen Reiches: Von einem Rheinpreußischen Jurist.* Leipzig, 1872.

————. *Das Zentrum im Landtag und im Reichstag.* Cologne: Bachem, 1874.

Baumgarten, Hermann. *Wie Wir wieder ein Volk geworden sind.* Leipzig: S. Hirzel, 1870.

Baumgarten, M[ichael]. *Auf dem Wege nach Kanossa: Eine christliche Ansprache an das deutsche Gewissen.* Berlin, 1881.

————. *Der deutsche Protestantenverein, ein heiliges Panier im neuen deutschen Reich.* Berlin: Verlag von F. Henschel, 1871.

————. *Protestantische Antwort an Herrn Peter Reichensperger.* Berlin: Carl Heymann's Verlag, 1876.

————. *Der Protestantismus als politisches Princip im deutschen Reich.* Berlin: T. G. Lüderitz'sche Verlagsbuchhandlung, 1872.

Baumstark, Chr., ed. *Das Verhältnis zw. Kirche und Staat nach den Bedürfnissen der Gegenwart.* Heidelberg: J. C. B. Mohr, 1873.

Bergmann, H. A. *Die geheimen Instructionen für die Gesellschaft Jesu. Oder: Die Staat und Kirche bedrohenden Pläne des Jesuitenordens.* Erfurt: Hennings und Hopf, 1853.

————. *Die Jesuitenpest.* 1st ed. Berlin: Gebauer'sche Buchhandlung, 1852; 2d ed., 1856.

Beta, Ottoman. *Darwin, Deutschland und die Juden. Oder der Juda-Jesuitismus.* Berlin, 1876.

Bluntschli, Johann Caspar. *Charakter und Geist der politischen Parteien.* Nördlingen: C. H. Beck, 1869.

————. *Freiheit und Kirchenregiment: Meinungsstreit zwischen W.E. Ketteler Bischof von Mainz und Geheimrat J.C. Bluntschli.* Heidelberg: Verlagsbuchhandlung von Fr. Bafferman, 1871.

————. *Geschichte des Rechts und der religiösen Bekenntnisfreiheit.* Elberfeld: R. L. Friederichs, 1867.

————. *Die nationale Bedeutung des Protestanten-Vereins für Deutschland.* Berlin: Franz Lobeck, 1868.

————. *Die nationale Staatsbildung und der moderne deutsche Staat.* Berlin: C. G. Lüdertiz, 1870.

————. *Die rechtliche Unverantwortlichkeit und Verantwortlichkeit des römischen Papstes: Eine völker- und staatsrechtliche Studie.* Nördlingen: C. H. Beck, 1876.

————. *Rom und die Deutschen,* 2 parts. Part 1, *Römische Weltherrschaft und deutsche Freiheit.* Part 2, *Der Jesuitenorden und das deutsche Reich.* Berlin: C. G. Lüderitz'sche Verlagsbuchhanlung Carl Habel, 1872.

———. "Über das Verhältniss des modernen Staates zur Religion." In *Gesammelte Kleine Schriften*, 2:148–80. Nördlingen: C. H. Beck, 1881.

———. *Über den Unterschied der mittelalterlichen und der modernen Staatsidee.* Munich: Literarisch-artistische Anstalt, 1855.

———. *Wider die Jesuiten.*: Eberfeld: R. L. Friederichs, 1872.

———, ed. *Deutsches Staatswörterbuch.* Stuttgart: Expedition des Staatswörterbuch, 1857–70.

Bongartz, Arn. *Die Klöster in Preußen und ihre Zerstörung, oder Was kostet der Kulturkampf dem preußischen Volke?* Berlin: Verlag der Germania, 1880.

Braun von Brauthal, Carl Johann [Charles Jean]. *Der Jesuit im Frack: Culturgeschichtlicher Roman aus den Zeiten der Kaiserin Maria Theresia.* Vienna: Verlag der ty-liter.-artischen Anstalt, 1872.

Buchmann, F. *Über und Gegen den Jesuitismus.* Breslau, 1872.

Bunsen, Christian Carl Josias. *Signs of the Times: Letters to Ernst Moritz Arndt on the Dangers to Religious Liberty in the Present State of the World.* Trans. Susanna Winkworth. London, 1856.

———. *Die Zeichen der Zeit: Briefe an Freunde über die Gewissenfreiheit und das Recht der christlichen Gemeinde.* 2 vols. Leipzig: F. A. Brockhaus, 1855.

Busch, Wilhelm. "Pater Filucius." In *Wilhelm Busch: Historisch-Kritische Gesamtausgabe,* ed. Friedrich Bohne, 2:347–80. Wiesbaden: Volmer Verlag, 1960.

Buß, Franz Joseph. *Die Gesellschaft Jesu, ihr Zweck, ihre Satzungen, Geschichte, Aufgabe und Stellung in der Gegenwart.* Mainz: Kunze, 1853.

———. *Die Volksmissionen: Ein Bedürfnis unserer Zeit.* Schaffhausen: Hurter, 1850.

Chiniqui, Charles. *Der Priester, die Frau, und die Ohrenbeichte.* Barmen: D. B. Wiemann, 1901.

Clasen, Ludwig. *Protestantische Jesuiten.* Halle: J. Fricke, 1872.

Concile und Jesuitismus: Brennende Fragen zur Orientierung für das deutsche Volk. Stuttgart: Vogler und Beinhauer, 1870.

Constabel, Adelheid, ed. *Die Vorgeschichte des Kulturkampfes: Quellen aus dem Deutschen Zeutralarchiv.* Berlin: Rütten und Loening, 1956.

The Convent Horror: Or The True Narrative of Barbara Ubryk, A Sister of the Carmelite Convent at Cracow, Who Has Been Walled Up in a Dungeon. Philadelphia: C. W. Alexander, 1869.

The Convent Horror: The Story of Barbara Ubryk Twenty-one Years in the Dungeon Eight Feet Long, Six Feet Wide. Aurora, Mo.: Menace, 1890.

Corvin, Otto. *Paffenspiegel: Historische Denkmale des Fanatismus in der römisch-katholischen Kirche.* Stuttgart: Vogler und Beinhauer, 1870.

Dautzenberg, Leonhard. *Geschichte der Kongregationen der Mission in der deutschen Provinz.* Graz, 1911.

Deutschlands Erb- und Erzfeind: Mahnruf an das deutschen Volk von einem altem Patrioten. Coburg: F. Streit's Verlagsbuchhandlung, 1862.

Deym, Fanz Xaver. *Beiträge zur Aufklärung über die Gemeinschädlichkeit des Jesuitenordens.* Leipzig, 1872.

Dicke, C. L. *Populäre Symbolik: Aus den Quellen geschöpfte Darstellung der Über-*

einstimmung und des Unterschiedes in der Lehre der beiden abendländischen Hauptkirchen. Leipzig: G. E. Schulze, 1854.

Diegel, Gustav. *Die katholische Kirche als geschichtliche Macht und die politische Unfähigkeit der protestantischen Richtungen in Deutschland: Ein Wort zu den "Zeichen der Zeit."* Göttingen, 1856.

Diesterweg, Adolf. "Bischof und Pädagog." In *Sämtliche Werke,* ed. Robert Alt, Hans Ahrbeck, et al., 347–85. Berlin: Volkseigener Verlag, 1976. Originally published in *Pädagogisches Jahrbuch für Lehrer und Schulfreunde* 9 (1859): 89–156.

———. *Pädagogisches Wollen und Sollen: Dargestellt für Leute, die noch nicht fertig sind, aber eben darum Lust haben, nachzudenken.* Leipzig, 1857.

Dietlein, W. O. *Die katholischen Briefe, ausgelegt.* Berlin: Verlag von Wilhelm Schultze, 1851.

Dove, Richard Wilhelm. *Lehrbuch des katholischen und evangelischen Kirchenrechts mit besonderer Rücksicht auf deutsche Zustände.* Leipzig: B. Tauchnitz, 1874.

Dreves, Lebrecht. *Geschichte der katholischen Gemeinden zu Hamburg und Altona.* Schaffhausen, 1866.

Duhr, Bernhard. *Die Stellung der Jesuiten in den deutschen Hexenprozessen.* Cologne: J. Bachem, 1900.

———, ed. *Aktenstücke zur Geschichte der Jesuiten-Missionen in Deutschland, 1848–1872.* Freiburg im Breisgau: Herdersche Verlagshandlung, 1903.

Duller, Eduard. *Die Jesuiten, Wie Sie Waren, und Wie Sie Sind.* Brandenburg, 1866.

Eichler, J. S. *Kein wohlgeordneter Staat kann die römisch-katholische Kirche frei nach ihren Gesetzen leben lassen!* Darmstadt: Verlag von C.W. Leske, 1854.

Endrulat, Bernhardt. "Die Nonne." In *Gegen Rom: Zeitstimmen Deutscher Dichter,* ed. Ernst Scherenberg, 21–22. Elberfeld: Bädeker'sche Buch und Kunsthandlung, 1874.

Enthüllungen der neuesten Umtriebe der Jesuiten in Deutschland gegen Fürsten und Völker: Nebst einem Abriß der Gesellschaft des Jesuitenordens. Leipzig: Christian Ernst Kollmann, 1851.

Errinerungen eines ehemaligen Jesuitenzöglings. Leipzig, 1862.

Evangelisch oder Katholisch? Ein Gespräch über den gegenwärtigen Kirchenstreit. Rathenow, 1875.

Ewald, Heinrich. *Zweites Wort von 1862 über die heutigen Jesuiten und alles was mit ihnen zusammenhängt.* Göttingen: Dieterichsche Buchhandlung, 1862.

Fabri, Friedrich. *Staat und Kirche: Betrachtungen zur Lage Deutschlands in der Gegenwart.* Gotha, 1872.

———. *Wie Weiter? Kirchenpolitische Betrachtungen zum Ende des Kulturkampfes.* N.p., 1887.

Fetzer, Johann Jacob. *Antiromanus, das Papsttum im Widerspruch mit Vernunft, Moral und Christentum nachgewiesen.* Stuttgart, 1873.

Fiedeley, Stephan. *Die Jesuitenhetze in Bremen.* Bremen: Selbstverlag des Verfassers, 1863.

Franz, Constantin. *Die Religion des Nationalliberalismus.* Leipzig: Der Rossberg'schen Buchhandlung, 1872.

Freimut, Wahrlieb. *Allgemeine Rückblicke auf den Kulturkampf in seinen verschiedenen Phasen vom religiös-politischen Standpunkte: Eine Widmung für das deutsche Volk zur Erinnerung an das Lutherjubiläum.* Barmen, 1883.

Freimuth, Philalethes. *Das moderne deutsche Kaiserreich und die Katholiken.* Luxembourg, 1872.

————. *Das moderne Recht und die Katholiken.* Luxembourg, 1872.

Friedberg, Emil. *Das deutsche Reich und die katholische Kirche.* Leipzig: Duncker und Humblot, 1872.

————. *Die Genesis des Kirchenpolitischen Conflicts.* Leipzig, 1875.

————. *Die Gränzen zwischen Staat und Kirche und die Garantieen gegen deren Verletzung.* Tübingen: H. Laupp'sche Buchhandlung, 1872.

————. *Der Staat und die Bischofswahlen in Deutschland: Ein Beitrag zur Geschichte der katholischen Kirche und ihres Verhältnisses zum Staat.* Leipzig, 1874.

————. *Der Staat und die katholische Kirche im Grossherzogthum Baden seit dem Jahre 1860.* Leipzig, 1874.

Friedlieb, L. *Die sociale Bedeutung der Klöster in der Gegenwart.* Würzburg: Leo Woerl'sche Buch- und kirchliche Kunstverlagshandlung, 1877.

Frohschammer, J. *Über die religiösen und kirchenpolitischen Fragen der Gegenwart.* Elberfeld: Eduard Loss Verlagsbuchhandlung, 1875.

Für und Wider die Jesuiten. 3 parts. Part 1, *Stenographische Berichte der Reichstagsverhandlungen über Besetzung des Botschafter-Postens in Rom und die Petitionen für und wider die Jesuiten.* Part 2, *VI und XIV. Bericht der Kommission für Petitionen, betreffend die Petitionen für und wider ein allegemeines Verbot des Jesuiten-ordens in Deutschland.* Part 3, *Stenographische Berichte der Reichstagsverhandlungen über das Gesetz betreffend der Orden der Gesellschaft Jesu.* Berlin: Verlag der Reichs-Gesetze, 1872.

Gätschenberger, Stephan. *Enthüllungen aus bayerischen Klöstern aus der neueren Zeit.* Würzburg: Selbstverlag des Verfassers, 1868.

Geffcken, F. Heinrich. *Staat und Kirche in ihrem Verhältniß geschichtlich Entwickelt.* Berlin, 1875.

Geffcken, Johannes. *Über die sogenannte Geschichte der Katholischen Gemeinden in Hamburg und Altona.* Hamburg, 1851.

Die geheimen Pläne der Jesuiten der Neuzeit: Von einem Jesuiten (Vincenzo Gioberti, italienische Priester). Leipzig, 1848.

Geifers. *Geheime Verordnung der Gesellschaft Jesu: Ein Schanddenkmal, welche die Feinde der Jesuiten sich selbst wiederholt errichtet haben.* N.p., 1853.

Gerlach, Ernst Ludwig von. *Kaiser und Papst.* Berlin: G. van Muyden, 1872.

————. *Das neue Deutsche Reich.* Berlin: G. van Muyden, 1871.

Gerlach, Hermann. *Das Verhältnis des preußischen Staates zu der katholischen Kirche auf kirchenrechtlichem Gebiete nach den preußischen Gesetzen.* Paderborn: F. Schöningh, 1862.

Geschichte der Frankfurter Zeitung. Frankfurt am Main: Verlag der Frankfurter Zeitung, 1906.

Glagau, Otto. *Des Reiches Noth und der neues Kulturkampf.* N.p., 1879.

Gneist, Rudolf. *Der Rechtsstaat.* Berlin: J. Springer, 1872.

Griesinger, Theod. *Die Jesuiten: Vollständige Geschichte ihrer offenen und geheimen Wirksamkeit von der Stiftung des Ordens bis jetzt.* Stuttgart: A. Kröner, 1866.

Gruber, H., S. J. [Society of Jesus]. In *Kirchenlexicon oder Enzyklopädie der katholischen Theologie und ihrer Hilfswissenschaften,* ed. Weltzer and Welte, 7:1912f. Freiburg, 1891.

Hager. *Spricht die Bibel für den Katholizismus oder den Protestantismus?* N.p., 1876.

Hahn, Ludwig, ed. *Geschichte des "Kulturkämpfes" in Preußen in Aktenstücken dargestellt.* Berlin: W. Hertz, 1881.

Hase, Karl. *Handbuch der protestantischen Polemik gegen die römisch-katholische Kirche.* Leipzig: Breitkopf und Härtel, 1862.

Heppe, Heinrich. *Katholicismus und Protestantismus im Hinblick auf die Vaticanischen Concilbeschlüsse betrachtet.* Bremen: C. Ed. Müller, 1871.

Hermann, Joseph von Fugger-Glötz. *Die Staatgefährlichkeit der römisch-katholischen Kirche.* Regensburg, 1874.

Heydorff, Julius, and Paul Wentzcke, ed. *Deutscher Liberalismus im Zeitalter Bismarcks: Eine politische Briefsammlung.* 2 vols. Osnabrück: Biblio Verlag, 1967.

Hillebrand, Joseph. *Missionsvorträge.* 2 vols. Paderborn: F. Schöningh, 1870.

Hilleren, Wilhelmine von. *Aus eigenen Kraft.* 3 vols. Leipzig, 1872.

Hinschius, Paul. *Die Jahre 1874 und 1875 nebst dem Reichsgesetze vom 4. Mai 1874.* Berlin, 1875.

———. *Das Kirchenrecht der Katholiken und Protestanten in Deutschland, 1869–97.* 6 vols. Graz: Akademische Druck-U. Verlagsanstalt, 1959.

———. *Die Orden und Kongregationen der katholischen Kirche in Preußen: Ihre Verbreitung, ihre Organisation, und ihre Zwecke.* Berlin: Verlag von I. Guttentag, 1874.

———. *Die päpstliche Unfehlbarkeit und das vatikanische Koncil.* Kiel: Universitäts-Buchhandlung, 1871.

———. *Die Stellung der deutschen Staatsregierung gegenüber den Beschlüssen des vatikanischen Koncils.* Berlin: J. Guttentag, 1871.

———, ed. *Die preußischen Kirchengesetze der Jahres 1873: Mit Einleitung und Kommentar.* Berlin, 1873.

———, ed. *Die preußischer Kirchengesetze des Jahres 1874 und 1875.* Berlin, 1875.

Hofmann, Friedrich, ed. *Vollständiges Generalregister der Gartenlaube.* Leipzig, 1882.

Hoffmann, Paul E. F. *Die Jesuiten: Geschichte und System des Jesuiten Ordens.* Mannheim, 1870.

Horn, Uffo. *Die Wiedereinführung der Jesuiten in Böhmen.* Leipzig, 1850.

Huber, Franz. *Lob und Schimpf des Jesuiten-Ordens, im Interesse der bürgerlichen Wohlfahrt.* Bern, 1870.

Huber, Johannes. *Der Jesuiten-Orden nach seiner Verfassung und Doctrin, Wirksamkeit und Geschichte.* Berlin: C. G. Luderitz, 1873.

Hübner, Rudolf, ed. *Johann Gustav Droysen Briefwechsel.* Stuttgart: Biblio-Verlag, 1967.

Illuminator, Lucifer [Daniel von Kaszony]. *Pfaffenunwesen, Mönchsscandale und*

Nonnenspuk: Beitrag zur Naturgeschichte des Katholizimus und der Klöster. Leipzig: Gustav Schulze, 1871.

Isenkern, Ph. *Priesterthum und Cölibat.* Braunschweig: G. Westermann, 1872.

Jacobi, J. L. *Die Jesuiten.* Halle, 1862.

Jeinecke, Ferdinand. *Der Jesuitenpater Roh in Hannover.* Hanover, 1860.

Die Jesuiten! Ein Ruf der Warnung und Erweckung an alle Freunde der Wahrheit und des Friedens. Darmstadt: Jonghaus, 1845.

Die Jesuiten: Erinnerungen an ihre Wirksamkeit besonders in der Pfalz. Heidelberg: Akademische Anstalt für Litteratur und Kunst, 1851.

Die Jesuiten in ihrer wahren Gestalt oder: Ihre Entstehung, Verbreitung, Verjagung. N.p., 1862.

Die Jesuiten in Tirol und ihre Gegner: Offenes Schreiben an einen der Letzteren. Freiburg im Breisgau, 1869.

Die Jesuiten nach dem Urtheile grosser Männer oder: Was ist von dem Jesuiten zu halten? Paderborn: F. Schöningh, 1852.

Die Jesuiten und der Jesuitismus: Oder Geschichte, Verfassung der Gesellschaft Jesu in Bezug auf die Bestrebungen des Ultramontanismus in unserer Zeit. Nordhausen, 1845.

Die Jesuiten und ihre Moral. Danzig, 1852.

Jesuiten und Jesuitereien: Wirkliche Begebenheiten und geschichtliche Thatsachen nebst Gründen der Erfahrung. Berlin: Verlag der Vereins-Buchhandlung, 1853.

Die Jesuitenansiedlung in Westfalen und das Westfälische Junkerthum: Beiträge zur Geschichte der Volksverdummerung in Preußen. Bremen: A. D. Giesler, 1850.

Jesuitenbüchlein. Leipzig, 1845.

Jesuitendemuth und Pharisäerstolz: Offenes Sendschreiben an den Verfasser der "Jesuitenhetze in Bremen." Bremen: A. D. Geisler, 1863.

Die Jesuitenkirche zur Trier und das preußische Government. Trier, 1850.

Die Jesuitenmission in Hildesheim und damit Zusammenhängendes: Worte der Belehrung und Mahnung an den protestantischen Bürger und Landmann. Hanover: Hermann Heuer, n.d.

Die Jesuitenorden und seine Unverträglichkeit mit den deutschen Verhältnißen. Stuttgart, 1846.

Jesuiten-Statistik der Gegenwart. Grimna: Verlag des Verlags-Comptoirs, 1846.

Jesuitismus und Protestantismus: Die Realisation der geheimen Pläne der Jesuiten. Leipzig, 1852.

Jocham, Magnus. *Die sittliche Verpestung des Volkes durch die Jesuiten.* Mainz: F. Kirchheim, 1866.

Johnsen, Wilhelm. *Der Weg zum Kirchlichen Frieden: Eine kritische Studie zum preußisch-römischen Kirchenstreit nebst Stipulationen zu einer neuen Friedensbasis.* Eberswalde, 1883.

Julius, G. *Die Jesuiten: Geschichte der Gründung, Ausbreitung und Entwicklung, Verfassung, und Wirksamkeit der Gesellschaft Jesu.* Leipzig: J. Meissner, 1854.

Kallee, Richard. *Die Ausbreitung des römisch-katholischen Ordenswesens durch die Frauen-Klöster in Württemberg, 1864–1896.* Leipzig, 1896.

Kaszony, Daniel von. *Der Teufel in Beichtstuhl. Oder: Jesuitenschliche.* Leipzig, 1872.

Der Katholicismus und der moderne Staat: Andeutungen zur richtigen Würdigung ihres gegenseitigen Verhältnisses, namentlich in Deutschland und Italien. Berlin: G. Reimer, 1873.

Die katholische Religionsübung in Mecklenburg-Schwerin. Jena: Friedrich Frommann, 1852.

Katholisches Rituale. Bonn, 1875.

Ketteler, Wilhelm Emmanuel von. *Deutschland nach dem Kriege von 1866.* Mainz: F. Kirchheim, 1867.

———. *Die Katholiken im neuen Reich: Entwurf zu einem politischen Programm.* Mainz, 1873.

———. *Liberalismus, Sozialismus, und Christentum.* Mainz, 1871.

———. *Die moderne Tendenz-Wissenschaft: Beleuchtet am Exempel des Hn. Professor Dr. Emil Friedberg.* Mainz, 1873.

———. *Zur Charakteristik der Jesuiten und ihrer Gegner: Eine offene Erklärung.* Mainz: F. Kirchheim, 1866.

Kirchmann, Julius Hermann von. *Der Culturkampf in Preußen und seine Bedenken.* Leipzig: E. Bidder, 1875.

Kliefoth, Th[eodor]. *Der preußische Staat und die Kirchen.* Schwerin, 1873.

———. *Wider Rom! Ein Zeugniß in Predigten.* Schwerin: Stiller'schen Hofbuchhandlung, 1852.

Klostergeschichten oder Betrügerein der Pfaffen und Mönche. Chemnitz, 1871.

Köhler, Joseph Eduard. *Erinnerungen eines ehemaligen Jesuitenzöglings.* Leipzig: F. A. Brockhaus, 1862.

Kohlheim, F. *Enthüllung der verdammungswürdigen Lehr und Grund Sätze der Jesuiten.* Berlin, 1861.

Krabbe, C. F. *Wem steht das Eigentum der vormaligen Jesuiten Güter?* Münster: Druch und Verlag der Theissing'schen Buchhandlung, 1855.

Krüger, Albert Peter Johann. *Der Jesuit und sein Zögling: Erzählung.* Altona, 1873.

Laakman, T. K. *Auf! Zum Streite! Ermunterung an das katholische Volk zum muthigen männlichen Kampfe für seinen heiligen Glauben und für die religiöse Freiheit.* Paderborn: F. Schöningh, 1871.

Laddey, Emma. *Auf eigenen Füssen: Erzählungen.* Stuttgart, 1870.

———. *Aus freier Wahl: Charakterbilder aus dem Frauenleben.* Stuttgart, 1874.

Laicus, P. *Evangelium der liberalen Toleranz.* Mainz, 1873.

———. *Liberale Phasen.* Mainz, 1871.

———. *Wohin mit diesem Kulturkampf?* Mainz, 1875.

Langen, J. *Das Vaticanische Dogma: Von dem Universal-Episcopat und der Unfehlbarkeit des Papstes in seinem Verhältniß zum Neuen Testament und der patristischen Exegese.* Bonn: Eduard Weber, 1871.

Die Lehren der Jesuiten in Bezug auf innere Einrichtung der Gesellschaft und ihr Verhältnis zur Familie und zum Staate: Aus den Ordensgesetzen wörtlich ausgezogen. Berlin, 1874.

Leibbrand, K. A. *Die Missionen der Jesuiten und Redemptoristen in Deutschland und die evangelische Wahrheit und Kirche.* Stuttgart: E. Schweizerbart'sche Verlagshandlung, 1851.

Lernt Rom Kennen! Ein Werkruf an das deutsche Volk. Gotha: Friedrich Andreas Perthes, 1874.

Leuze, Otto, ed. *Eduard Zellers Kleine Schriften.* Berlin: Georg Reimer, 1911.

Die liberale Tagespresse Berlins im Sommer 1866: Von einem Preußischen Patrioten. Leipzig, 1866.

Die liberalen Parteien angesichts der Zukunft Preußens. Berlin, 1862.

Liskenne, Charles. *Jesuiten und Fürstenmörder: Eine Enthüllung.* Schwäbisch Hall, n.d.

Liutz, C. W. *Das Handbuch der theologischen Moral des Jesuiten Gury und die christliche Ethik: Ein Beitrag zur Kenntniß der Jesuiten Orden und des Jesuitismus unserer Tage.* Friedberg: Verlag von Bindernagel und Schimpff, 1869.

Luther oder Papst? Eine Zeitschrift für Mitglieder der evangelischen Kirche. 1851.

Magdalena Paumann oder die eingekerkerte Nonne im Angerkloster zu München. Munich: J. J. Lentner'schen Buchhandlung, 1870.

Ein Mahnwort an Deutschlands Katholiken: Von einem katholischen Reichstags-Abgeordneten. Berlin, 1872.

Majunke, Paul. *Das evangelische Kaiserthum: Zur Geschicht des preußisches Culturkampfes.* Berlin and Leipzig, 1881.

Maurer, Karl Conrad Ludwig. *Neuer Jesuitenspiegel.* Mannheim: T. Löffler, 1868.

Meissner, Alfred. *Zur Ehre Gottes: Eine Jesuiten-Geschichte.* Leipzig, 1852.

Memoiren der Schwester Angelika, einer entlaufenen Nonne des Klosters zu Cork. Leipzig, 1873.

Memoiren einer Nonne. Munich, 1874.

Menzel, Wolfgang. *Furore: Geschichte eines Mönchs und einer Nonne aus dem Dreißigjährigen Kriege.* Leipzig: F. A. Brockhaus, 1851.

———. *Geschichte der neuesten Jesuitenumtriebe in Deutschland (1870–1872).* Stuttgart, 1873.

Meyer, Ferdinand. *Die Lehre von der Unfehlbarkeit des römischen Papstes in ihrem Zusammenhange mit dem katholischen Traditionsprincipe.* Alfeld, 1872.

Meyer, Jürgen Bona. *Der Wunderschwindel in unserer Zeit.* Bonn: Max Cohen und Sohn, 1878.

———. *Zum Bildungskampf unserer Zeit.* Bonn: Adolf Marcus, 1875.

Meyer, Otto. *Um Was Streiten Wir mit den Ultramontanismus.* Hamburg, 1875.

———. *Das Veto deutscher protestantischer Staatsregierungen gegen katholische Bischofswahlen.* Rostock: Stiller, 1866.

———. *Zur Naturgeschichte des Centrums: Socialpolitische Betrachtungen.* Freiburg im Breisgau and Tübingen: J. C. B. Mohr, 1882.

Mill, John Stuart. *On Liberty with The Subjection of Women and Chapters on Socialism.* Ed. Stefan Collini. Cambridge: Cambridge University Press, 1989.

Mohl, Robert von. *Politik.* 2 vols. Tübingen: H. Laupp, 1869.

Molitor, Wilhelm. *Über kanonisches Gerichtsverfahren gegen Kleriker: Ein rechtsgeschichtl. Versuch zur Lösung der praktischen Frage der Gegenwart.* Mainz, 1856.

Moufang, Christoph, ed. *Aktenstücke betreffend die Jesuiten in Deutschland.* Mainz: F. Kirchheim, 1872.

Mücke, A. *Der kirchenpolitische Kampf und der Sieg des Staates in Preußen und im deutschen Reich.* Brandenburg a.d.H.: J. Wiesike's Buchhandlung, 1878.

Mühler, Heinrich von. *Der Krypto-Katholicismus in den Grundlinien einer Rechtsphilosophie der Staats- und Rechtslehre nach evangelischen Prinzipien.* Leipzig: Verlag von Johann Ambrosius Barth, 1873.

Mühlfeld, Julius. *Die Gesellschaft Jesu: Geschichtliches Lehr- und Warnbuch für das Volk.* Königsberg, 1872.

Müller, Hermann Alexander. *Die Ruinen des Klosters Hude im Grossh[erzogthum] Oldenburg.* Bremen: C. Ed. Müller, 1867.

Mundt, Clara [Louise Mühlbach]. *Protestantsiche Jesuiten: Historischer Roman.* Leipzig, 1874.

Mundweiler, Johannes. *P. Georg von Waldburg-Ziel: Ein Volksmissionär des 19. Jahrhunderts.* Freiburg im Breisgau: Herdersche Verlagshandlung, 1906.

Naumann, Viktor. *Der Jesuitismus: Würdigung der Grundsätze, Verfassung, und geistigen Entwicklung der Gesellschaft Jesu mit besonderer Beziehung auf die wissenschaftlichen Kämpfe und auf die Darstellung von antijesuitischer Seite.* Munich, 1905.

Neander, Aug[ust]. *Katholicismus und Protestantismus in Theologischen Vorlesungen.* Berlin, 1863.

Neueste und vollstände Geschichte der Jesuiten. Leipzig, 1845.

Nikolaus, Siegfried, ed. *Actenstücke betreffend den preußischen Kulturkampf nebst einer geschichtlichen Einleitung.* Freiburg im Breisgau: Herder, 1882.

Niller, Erich. *Grundzüge der Geschichte und der Unterscheidungslehren der evangelisch-protestantischen und römisch-katholischen Kirche.* Hamburg, 1855.

Nippold, Friedrich. *Der Jesuiten-Orden von seiner Wiederhelstellung bis auf die Gegenwart.* Mannheim, 1867.

———. *Welche Wege führen nach Rom? Geschichtliche Beleuchtung der römischen Illusionen über die Erfolge der Propaganda.* Heidelberg: Fr. Bassermann, 1869.

Nolte, C. J. *Öffentliche Disputation zwischen einem katholischen und protestantischen Geistlichen.* Heiligenstadt: B. Dunkelberg, 1864.

Obermayer, Joseph Richter. *Bildergalerie klösterlicher Mißbräuche.* Frankfurt, 1784.

Orelli, Heinrich von. *Das Wesen des Jesuiten-Ordens.* Leipzig: Stuhr'sche Buchhandlung, 1850.

Osterroth, Nikolaus. "Nikolaus Osterroth, Clay Miner." In *The German Worker: Working Class Autobiographies from the Age of Industrialization,* ed. Alfred Kelly, 160–87. Berkeley: University of California Press, 1987.

Pfaffenschwänke. Berlin: Verlag von E. Neuenhahn [1850].

Poschinger, Heinrich von. *Das Eigenthum am Kirchenvermögen mit Einschluß der heiligen und geweihten Sachen: Dargestellt auf Grund der Geschichte des Kirchenguts und des katholischen und protestantischen Kirchenrechts.* Munich: R. Oldenbourg, 1871.

Rathewitz, Joseph von. *Die Opfer der Jesuiten: Roman aus dem Leben und Treiben der Gesellschaft Jesu.* Hamburg, 1874.

Reichensperger, August. *Phrasen und Schlagwörter: Ein Noth- und Hülfsbüchlein für Zeitungsleser.* 5th ed. Paderborn: F. Schöningh, 1872.

———. *Phrasen und Schlagwörter. Ein unentbehrliches Noth- und Hülfsbüchlein für Zeitungsleser.* Paderborn: F. Schöningh, 1862.

Reichensperger, Peter. *Kulturkampf oder Friede in Staat und Kirche.* Berlin: J. Springer, 1876.

―――. *Über das Verhältniß des Staates zur Kirche im Hinblick auf die Jesuitendebatte im deutschen Reichstage.* Berlin, 1872.

Rein, Wilhelm. *Thuringia sacra: Urkundenbuch, Geschichte, und Beschreibung der Thüringischen Klöster.* 2 vols. Weimar, 1863.

Reinkens, Joseph Hubert. *Über die angebliche Verfolgung der katholischen Kirche in Deutschland besonders in Preußen.* Cologne, 1873.

Reuter, Hermann. *Über die Eigenthümlichkeit der sittlichen Tendenz des Protestantismus im Verhältniß zum Katholicismus.* Greiswald: König. Univ.-Buchdruckerei, 1859.

Riffel, Caspar. *Die Aufhebung des Jesuiten-Ordens: Eine Beleuchtung der alten und neuen Anklagen wider denselben.* Mainz: F. Kirchheim, 1855.

Ritter, H. *Deutsche Wacht wider Rom: Ein geschichtliches Gesammtbild des Culturkampfes von 1870–1875.* Potsdam, 1876.

Rode, A. *Barbara Ubryk oder die Geheimnisse des Karmeliter-Klosters in Krakau.* Munich: Neuburger und Kolb, 1869.

Rößler, Constantin. *Das deutsche Reich und die kirchliche Frage.* Leipzig: Fr. Wilh. Grunow, 1876.

Sander, I. F. *Der Beruf der Protestanten, Rom gegenüber, in dieser Zeit: Sendschreiben an die evangelischen Gemeinden.* Leipzig: Gebhardt und Reisland, 1853.

Schenkel, Daniel. *Der christliche Staat und die bischöflichen Denkschriften.* Heidelberg, 1852.

―――. *Der deutsche Protestantenverein und seine Bedeutung in der Gegenwart nach den Akten dargestellt.* Wiesbaden: C. W. Kreidel, 1868.

―――. *Deutschlands Erb- und Erzfeind: Mahnruf an das deutsche Volk.* Coburg: F. Streit's Verlagsbuchhandlung, 1862.

―――. *Das gegenwärtige aggressive Verfahren der römisch-katholischen Kirche in ihrem Verhältnisse zum Protestantismus.* Darmstadt: C. W. Lescke's Separat-Conto, 1857.

―――. *Gespräche über Protestantismus und Katholicismus: Einfach besprochen von einem katholischen Dorfpfarrer in der Nähe Heidelbergs.* Heidelberg: Akademische Anstalt für Literatur und Kunst (Karl Groos), 1852.

―――. *Die kirchliche Frage und ihre protestantische Lösung im Zusammenhange mit den nationalen Bestrebungen und mit besonderer Beziehung auf die neuesten Schriften von Döllinger und Bischof von Kettelers.* Elberfeld: R. L. Friederichs, 1862.

Scherenberg, Ernst, ed. *Gegen Rom! Zeitstimmen Deutscher Dichter.* Elberfeld: Bädeker'sche Buch- und Kunsthandlung, 1874.

Schmid, Jospeh Anton. *Die niederen Schulen der Jesuiten.* Regensburg: G. J. Manz, 1852.

Schneemann, Gerhard. *Der Jesuitenorden: Seine Gesetze, Werke, und Geheimnisse.* Regensburg: Friedrich Puffet, 1872.

Schröter, G. von. *Die katholische Religionsübung in Mecklenburg-Schwerin.* Jena, 1852.

Schulte, Franz Xaver, ed. *Geschichte des Kulturkampfes in Preußen.* Essen: Frede-beul und Koenen, 1882.

———. *Der Kampf um die Schule seit Ausbruch des preußische Kulturkampfes.* Essen, 1879.

———. *Lesebuch und Schule: Ein Wort der Mahnung an die Katholiken Westfalens.* Essen, 1875.

Schulte, Johann Friedrich von. *Kirchenpolitische Aufsätze aus den Jahren 1874–1886.* Gießen: E. Roth, 1909.

———. *Die Macht der römischen Päpste über Fürsten, Lander, Völker, Individuen nach ihren Lehren und Handlungen seit Gregor VII: Zur Würdigung ihrer Unfehlbarkeit beleuchtet.* Prague: F. Tempsky, 1871.

———. *Die neueren katholischen Orden und Congregationen besonders in Deutsch-land.* Berlin: C. G. Lüderitz'sche Verlagsbuchhandlung, 1872.

———. *Über Kirchenstrafen.* Berlin, 1872.

Schulze, F. W. *Über romanisirende Tendenzen: Ein Wort zum Frieden.* Berlin, 1870.

Schulze, Gustav. *Der Unterschied zwischen der katholischen und evangelischen Sittlichkeit.* N.p.: E. Strien, 1888.

Schuselka, Franz. *Der Jesuitenkrieg gegen Österreich und Deutschland.* Leipzig, 1845.

Schwarz, F. W. S. *Deutsche Ziele für die evangelische Kirche Preußens.* Berlin, 1875.

Schwester Adolphe, oder die Geheimnisse der inneren Verwaltung des bürgerlichen Invalidenhauses in Mainz. Frankfurt am Main: Druck von R. Baist, 1863.

Semisch, Carl. *Der Protestantismus und der Jesuiten-Orden.* Berlin, 1870.

Severinus, Adalbert. *Was Wir Wollen: Ein Wort zum preußichen Kulturkampf.* Leipzig, 1886.

Siegfried, Nikolaus. *Actenstücke betreffend den preußischen Kulturkampf nebst einer geschichtlichen Einleitung.* Freiburg im Breisgau, 1882.

Sommer, R. *Vernunft gegen Pfaffenpolitik und Nasenweisheit: Erstes Referat aus dem Rubenschen Nachlass.* Leipzig: Spielmeyersche Buchhandlung, 1865.

Speigel, Bernhard. *Der Jesuitismus und dessen Moral.* Osnabrück, 1879.

Spörlein, I. *Die geistliche Gesellschaftsordnung und die neue Zeit.* Nordleigen, 1866.

Stachelstock, A. L. *Licht und Finsterniß oder die freien Gemeinden und die Jesuiten.* Altona: Verlagsbureau, 1861.

Stahl, Friedrich Julius. *Die katholischen Widerlegungen: Eine Begleitungsschrift zur 4. Aufl. meiner Vorträge über den Protestantismus als politisches Princip.* Berlin: Verlag von Wilhelm Schultze, 1854.

Stählin, Leonhard. *Katholicismus und Protestantismus: Dartstellung u. Erläuterung der kirchengeschicht.* Augsburg, 1873.

Steitz, Georg Eduard. *Wie beweisen die Jesuiten die Nothwendigkeit der Ohren-beichte?* Frankfurt am Main: Karl Theodor Völcker, 1853.

Stiller, Erich. *Grundzüge der Geschichte und der Unterscheidungslehren der evange-lisch-protestantischen und römisch-katholischen Kirche.* Hamburg: Robert Kitt-ler, 1855.

Stöber, Adolf. *Evangelische Abwehr, katholische Angriffe.* Strasbourg: J. Kräuter, 1859.

Stolz, Alban. *Bedenkliches für die deutschen Katholiken.* Freiburg, 1873.

————. *Die Hexenangst der aufgeklärten Welt: Unversiegelter Brief an Herrn Bluntschli und Gebrüder.* Freiburg im Breisgau, 1872.

Sträter, August. *Die Vertreibung der Jesuiten aus Deutschland im Jahre 1872.* Freiburg im Breisgau: Herder, 1914.

Struhnnek, F. W. *Herrschaft und Priesterthum: Geschichtsphilosophische Skizzen.* Berlin, 1871.

Sybel, Heinrich von. *Klerikale Politik im neunzehnten Jahrhundert.* Bonn: Max Cohen und Sohn, 1874.

————. "Das neue deutsche Reich." In *Vorträge und Aufsätze,* 305–30. Berlin: A. Hoffman, 1874.

————. *Preußen und Rheinland.* Bonn: Max Cohen und Sohn, 1865.

————. *Rede des Ehrenpräsidenten des Deutschen Vereins, Abgeordneten H.V. Sybel gehalten auf der Generalversammlung des Deutschen Vereins.* Bonn, 1876.

————. "Über die Emancipation der Frauen." In *Vorträge und Aufsätze,* 59–79. Berlin: A. Hoffmann, 1874.

————. "Was Wir von Frankreich Lernen Können." In *Vorträge und Aufsätze,* 336–47. Berlin: A. Hoffman, 1874.

Theile, Heinrich. *Rom als Mittelpunkt der katholischen Christenheit.* Halle, 1861.

Thelemann, Otto. *Der Jesuitenorden nach seiner Geschichte und seinen Grundsätzen.* Detmold, 1873.

Thicke, H. *Kaiser und Papst: Ein zeitgeschichtliche Studie.* Leipzig, 1874.

Treitschke, Heinrich von. *Aufsätzen, Reden und Brief.* 5 vols. Ed. Karl Martin Schiller. Merrsburg: F. W. Hendel, 1929.

————. *Historische und politische Aufsätze.* Leipzig: S. Hirzel, 1915.

————. "Das Maigesetze und ihre Folgen." In *Zehn Jahre Deutsche Kämpfe: Schriften zur Tagespolitik,* 432–44. Berlin: G. Reimer, 1879.

Über die von Missions-Priestern aus dem Orden der Gesellschaft Jesu in Danzig gehaltenen Missionen. Paderborn: F. Schöningh, 1852.

"Übersicht der in Preußen vorhandenen Stationen geistlicher Orden und Genossenschaften." In *Stenographische Berichte über die Verhandlungen des preußischen Landtags: Haus der Abgeordneten.* Berlin: W. Moeser, 1870. 10. Legis. Per. 3 Session, 1869–70, Anlagen 2, Aktenstück no. 221, 17 Dec. 1869, 1000–1002.

Die Unfehlbarkeit des Papstes und die Schwäche der kirchlichen Opposition in Deutschland. Munich, 1871.

Das Verhältnis der Conservativen zu den Katholiken im Anschluß an Herrn von Gerlachs Schrift: "Kaiser und Papst." Berlin: G. van Muyden, 1873.

Die Verleumder der Jesuiten in Deutschland. Cologne: J. B. Bechem, 1853.

"Verzeichniß der Zahl der Klöster und klösterlichen Anstalten in Preußen." In *Stenographische Berichte über die Verhandlungen des preußichen Landtags: Haus der Abgeordneten.* Berlin: W. Moeser, 1870. 10. Legis. Per. 3 Session, 1869–70, Anlagen 2, Aktenstück no. 221, 17 Dec. 1869, 995–97.

Vilmar, A. F. C. *Kirche und Welt oder die Aufgaben des geistlichen Amtes in unsrer Zeit: Gesammelte pastoral-theologische Aufsätze.* Gütersloh: C. Bertelsmann, 1872.

Vintzelberg, G. *Protestantismus und Katholicismus oder die Werthschätzung des evangelischen Glaubens.* Fehrbellin: Im Selbstverlage des Verfassers, 1862.

Virchow, Rudolf. *Die Freiheit der Wissenschaften im modernen Staat.* Berlin, 1877.

———. *Glaubensbekenntnis eines modernen Naturforschers.* Berlin, 1873.

———. *Über die Erziehung des Weibes für seinen Beruf.* Berlin: T. C. F. Enslin, 1865.

———. *Über die nationale Entwickelung und Bedeutung der Naturwissenschaften.* Berlin, 1865.

———. *Über Wunder: Rede gehalten in der ersten allgemeinen Sitzung der 47. Versammlung deutscher Naturforscher und Ärzte zu Breslau am 18. September, 1874.* Breslau, 1874.

Vraetz, A. *Die Aufhebung der Katholischen Abteilung im preußischen Cultusministerium.* Mainz, 1871.

Wacker, Theodor. *Friede zwischen Berlin und Rom? Geschichtliche Erinnerungen aus der Blüthezeit des Kulturkampfes.* Freiburg im Breisgau, 1879.

Warmut, Christian. *Die evangelische Kirche als Hauptmacht des Staates gegen Rom.* Breslau, 1882.

Wasserschleben, Hermann. *Die deutschen Staatsregierungen und die katholische Kirche der Gegenwart.* Berlin: C. G. Luderitz'sche Verlagsbuchhandlung Carl Habel, 1872.

Weber, Carl Julius. *Die Jesuiten: Ihre Lehre und ihr Wirken in Kirche, Staat und Familie.* Cologne and Leipzig: E. H. Mayer, 1874.

Weber, Theodor. *Der Gehorsam in der Gesellschaft Jesu.* Breslau, 1872.

———. *Staat und Kirche nach der Absicht des Ultramontnismus.* Breslau, 1873.

Weicker, Gustav. *Das Schulwesen der Jesuiten nach den Ordensgesetzen.* Halle: Buchhandlung des Waisenhauses, 1863.

Wendt, Bernhardt. *Symbolik der römisch-katholischen Kirche.* Gotha: F. A. Perthes, 1880.

Werner, Karl. *Geschichte der katholischen Theologie: Seit dem Trienter Concil bis zur Gegenwart.* Munich, 1886.

Wider die Jesuiten. Elberfeld, 1872.

Wie werden in Preußen der Staat und die Katholiken gegenüber der neuen Lehre von der Unfehlbarkeit des Papstes sich verhalten? Düsseldorf: Julius Buddeus, 1870.

Wiskemann, Heinrich. *Die Lehre und Praxis der Jesuiten in religiöser, moralischer, und politischer Beziehung von ihrem Ursprung an bis auf den heutigen Tag.* Cassell: J. Georg-Luckhardt, 1858.

Zeising, Adolf. *Religion und Wissenschaft, Staat und Kirche: Eine Gott- und Weltanschauung auf erfahrungs- und zeitmäßiger Grundlage.* Vienna: Wilhelm Braumüller, 1873.

Zeller, Eduard. "Preußen und die Bischöfe." In *Eduard Zellers Kleine Schriften,* ed. Otto Leuze, 3:402–7. Berlin: Georg Reimer, 1911. Originally published in *Preußischer Jahrbücher* 28 (1871): 205–9.

———. *Staat und Kirche.* Leipzig: Fues's Verlag, 1873.

———. *Vorträge und Abhandlungen.* Leipzig: Fues, 1877.

Zentrums-Album des Kladderadatsch, 1870–1910. Berlin: A. Hoffmann, 1912.

Zöckler, Otto. *Der Jesuitismus nach seiner Stellung und Bedeutung in der Entwicklungsgeschichte des Mönchtums.* Eberfeld: R. L. Friederichs, 1867.

Secondary Literature

Aldenhoff, A. *Schulze-Delitzsch: Ein Beitrag zur Geschichte des Liberalismus zwischen Revolution und Reichsgründung.* Baden-Baden: Nomos, 1984.

Allen, Ann Taylor. *Feminism and Motherhood in Germany, 1800–1914.* New Brunswick: Rutgers University Press, 1991.

Allerhand, Jacob. *Toleranzpolitik und Kulturkampf.* Eisenstadt: Roetzer, 1982.

Allport, Gordon W. *The Nature of Prejudice.* Cambridge, Mass.: Beacon, 1954.

Altermatt, Urs. "Katholizismus: Antimodernismus mit modernen Mitteln?" In *Moderne als Problem des Katholizismus,* ed. Urs Altermatt et al., 33–50. Regensburg: Verlag F. Pustet, 1995.

Altgeld, Wolfgang. *Katholizismus, Protestantismus, Judentum: Über religiös begründete Gegensätze und nationalreligiöse Ideen in der Geschichte des deutschen Nationalismus.* Mainz: Matthias Grünewald Verlag, 1992.

Anderson, Benedict. *Imagined Communities: Reflections on the Origin and Spread of Nationalism.* London: Verso, 1983.

Anderson, Margaret Lavinia. "Interdenominationalism, Clericalism, Pluralism: The Zentrumsstreit and the Dilemma of Catholicism in Wilhelmine Germany." *Central European History* 21 (1988): 350–78.

———. "The Kulturkampf and the Course of German History." *Central European History* 19 (1986): 82–115.

———. "The Limits of Secularization: On the Problem of the Catholic Revival in Nineteenth-Century Germany." *Historical Journal* 38 (1995): 647–70.

———. "Piety and Politics: Recent Work on German Catholicism." *Journal of Modern History* 63 (1991): 681–716.

———. *Practicing Democracy: Elections and Political Culture in Imperial Germany.* Princeton: Princeton University Press, 2000.

———. "Voter, Junker, *Landrat,* Priest: The Old Authorities and the New Franchise in Imperial Germany." *American Historical Review* 98 (1993): 1448–74.

———. *Windthorst: A Political Biography.* Oxford: Oxford University Press, 1981.

Anderson, Margaret Lavinia, and Kenneth D. Barkin. "The Myth of the Puttkamer Purge and the Reality of the Kulturkampf: Some Reflections on the Historiography of Imperial Germany." *Journal of Modern History* 54 (1982): 647–86.

Anderton, Keith. "The Limits of Science: A Social, Political, and Moral Agenda for Epistemology in Nineteenth-Century Germany." Ph.D. diss., Harvard University, 1993.

Appel, Rolf Herbert. *Kirche und Freimaurer im Dialog.* Frankfurt am Main: J. Knecht, 1975.

Aschheim, Steven E. *Brothers and Strangers: The East European Jew in German and German-Jewish Consciousness, 1800–1923.* Madison: University of Wisconsin Press, 1982.

Bammel, Ernst. "Die evangelische Kirche in der Kulturkampfära: Eine Studie zu den Folgen des Kulturkampfes für Kirchentum, Kirchenrecht und Lehre von der Kirche." Ph.D. diss., University of Bonn, 1949.

———. *Die Reichsgründung und der deutsche Protestantismus.* Erlangen: Universitätsbibliothek, 1973.

Barrows, Susanna. *Distorting Mirrors: Visions of the Crowd in Late Nineteenth-Century France.* New Haven and London: Yale University Press, 1981.

Barth, Dieter. *Zeitschrift für Alle: Das Familienblatt im 19. Jahrhundert.* Münster: Institut für Publizistik der Universität Münster, 1974.

Barthel, Manfred. *Die Jesuiten: Legende und Wahrheit der Gesellschaft Jesu Gestern, Heute, Morgen.* Düsseldorf: Econ Verlag, 1982.

Bauer, Clemens. *Deutscher Katholizismus: Entwicklungslinien und Profile.* Frankfurt am Main: J. Knecht, 1964.

———. *Rudolf Virchow: Der politische Arzt.* Berlin: Staap, 1982.

Bauman, Zygmunt. *Culture as Praxis.* London: Routledge, 1973.

———. *Modernity and Ambivalence.* Ithaca: Cornell University Press, 1991.

Baumeister, Martin. *Parität und katholische Inferiorität: Untersuchungen zur Stellung des Katholizismus im deutschen Kaiserreich.* Paderborn: F. Schöningh, 1987.

Becker, Josef. *Liberaler Staat und Kirche in der Ära von Reichsgründung und Kulturkampf: Geschichte und Strukturen ihres Verhältnisses in Baden, 1860–1878.* Mainz: Matthias Grünewald Verlag, 1973.

Becker, Winfried. "Der Kulturkampf als europäisches und als deutsches Phänomen." *Historisches Jahrbuch* 101 (1981): 422–46.

———. "Kulturkampf und Zentrum: Liberale Kulturkampf-Positionen und politischer Katholizismus." In *Innenpolitische Probleme des Bismarck-Reiches,* ed. Otto Pflanze, 47–71. Munich: R. Oldenbourg, 1983.

———, ed. *Die Minderheit als Mitte: Die deutsche Zentrumspartei in der Innenpolitik des Reiches, 1871–1933.* Paderborn: F. Schöningh, 1986.

Beifang, Andreas. *Politisches Bürgertum in Deutschland, 1857–1868: Nationale Organisationen und Eliten.* Düsseldorf: Droste Verlag, 1994.

Bellmann, Dieter. "Der Liberalimus in Seekreis (1860–1870): Durchsetzungsversuch und Scheitern eines regional eigenständigen Entwicklungskonzeptes." In *Provinzialisierung einer Region: Regionale Unterentwicklung und liberale Politik in der Stadt und im Kreis Konstanz im 19. Jahrhundert. Untersuchung zur Entstehung der bürgerlichen Gesellschaft in der Provinz,* ed. Gert Zang, 185–263. Frankfurt am Main: Syndikat, 1978.

Berg, Christa. *Die Okkupation der Schule: Eine Studie zur Aufhellung gegenwärtiger Schulprobleme in der Volksschule Preußens 1872–1900.* Heidelberg: Quelle und Meyer, 1973.

Berlin, Isaiah. *Two Concepts of Liberty.* Oxford: Oxford University Press, 1959.

Bieberstein, Johannes von. *Die These vor der Verschwörung 1776–1945: Philosophen, Freimauer, Juden, Liberaler, und Sozialisten als Verschwörer gegen die Sozialordnung.* Bern and Frankfurt am Main: Peter Lang, 1976.

Birke, Adolf M. *Bischof Ketteler und der deutsche Liberalismus: Eine Untersuchung über das Verhältnis des liberalen Katholizismus zum bürgerlichen Liberalismus in der Reichsgründung.* Mainz: Matthias Grünewald Verlag, 1971.

————. "German Catholics and the Quest for National Unity." In *Nation-Building in Central Europe*, ed. Hagen Schulze, 51–63. Leamington Spa: Berg, 1987.

————. "Zur Entwicklung und politischen Funktion des bürgerlichen Kulturkampfverständnisses in Preußen-Deutschland." In *Aus Theorie und Praxis der Geschichtswissenschaft: Festschrift für Hans Herzfeld zum 80. Geburtstag*, ed. Dietrich Kurze, 257–79. Berlin: de Gruyter, 1972.

Björnsson, Páll. "Liberalism and the Making of the 'New Man': The Case of the Gymnasts in Leipzig, 1845–1871." In *Saxony in German History: Culture, Society, and Politics, 1830–1933*, ed. James Retallack, 151–65. Ann Arbor: University of Michigan Press, 2000.

Blackbourn, David. "The Catholic Church in Europe since the French Revolution: A Review." *Comparative Studies in Society and History* 33 (1991): 778–90.

————. "Catholics and Politics in Imperial Germany: The Centre Party and Its Constituency." In *Populists and Patricians: Essays in Modern German History*, 188–214. London: Allen and Unwin, 1987.

————. *Class, Religion, and Local Politics in Wilhelmine Germany: The Centre Party in Württemberg before 1914*. New Haven: Yale University Press, 1980.

————. *The Long Nineteenth Century: A History of Germany, 1780–1918*. New York: Oxford University Press, 1998.

————. *Marpingen: Apparitions of the Virgin Mary in Nineteenth-Century Germany*. New York: Alfred A. Knopf, 1994.

————. "The Problem of Democratisation: German Catholics and the Role of the Center Party." In *Society and Politics in Wilhelmine Germany*, ed. Richard J. Evans, 160–85. London: Croom Helm, 1978.

————. "Progress and Piety: Liberals, Catholics, and the State in Bismarck's Germany." In *Populists and Patricians: Essays in Modern German History*, 143–67. London: Allen and Unwin, 1987.

Blackbourn, David, and Geoff Eley. *The Peculiarities of German History: Bourgeois Society and Politics in Nineteenth-Century Germany*. Oxford: Oxford University Press, 1984. Originally published as *Mythen deutscher Geschichtsschreibung: Die gescheiterte bürgerliche Revolution von 1848* (Frankfurt am Main and Berlin: Ullstein Materialien, 1980).

Blackbourn, David, and Richard Evans, eds. *The German Bourgeoisie: Essays on the Social History of the German Middle Class from the Late Eighteenth to the Early Twentieth Century*. London: Routledge, 1991.

Blanke, Richard. "The Polish Role in the Origin of the Kulturkampf in Prussia." *Canadian Slavonic Papers* 25 (1983): 253–62.

Blaschke, Olaf. *Katholizismus und Antisemitismus im deutschen Kaiserreich*. Göttingen: Vandenhoeck und Ruprecht, 1997.

————. "Die Kolonisierung der Laienwelt: Priester als Milieumanager und die Känale klerikaler Kuratel." In *Religion im Kaiserreich*, ed. Olaf Blaschke and Frank-Michael Kuhlemann, 93–135. Gütersloh: Chr. Kaiser, 1996.

————. "Das 19. Jahrhundert: Ein Zweites Konfessionelles Zeitalter?" *Geschichte und Gesellschaft* 26 (2000): 38–75.

————. "Wider die Herrschaft des modern-jüdischen Geistes: Der Katholizismus zwischen traditionellen Antijudaismus und modernen Antisemitismus." In

Deutscher Katholizismus im Umbruch zur Moderne, ed. Wilfred Loth, 236–63. Stuttgart: W. Kohlhammer, 1991.

Blaschke, Olaf, and Frank-Michael Kuhlemann, eds. *Religion im Kaiserreich: Milieus—Mentalitäten—Krisen.* Gütersloh: Chr. Kaiser, 1996.

Blätter, Sidonia. *Der Pöbel, die Frauen, etc.: Die Massen in der politischen Philosophie des 19. Jahrhunderts* (Berlin: Akademie Verlag, 1995).

Blessing, Werner K. *Staat und Kirche in der Gesellschaft: Institutionelle Autorität und mentaler Wandel in Bayern während des 19. Jahrhunderts.* Göttingen: Vandenhoeck und Ruprecht, 1982.

Bloth, Hugo Gotthard. *Adolph Diesterweg: Sein Leben und Wirken für Pedagogik und Schule.* Heidelberg: Quelle und Meyer, 1966.

Böhme, Helmut. *Deutschlands Weg zur Grossmacht. Studien zum Verhältnis von Wirtschaft und Staat während der Reichsgründung, 1848–1881.* Cologne: Kiepenheuer und Witsch, 1966.

Bornkamm, Heinrich. *Die Staatsidee im Kulturkampf.* Darmstadt: Wissenschaftliche Buchgesellschaft, 1969.

Bramsted, Ernest. *Aristocracy and the Middle-Classes in Germany: Social Types in German Literature, 1830–1900.* Chicago: University of Chicago Press, 1964.

Brandt, Hartwig. "Forschungsbericht: Zu einigen Liberalismusdeutungen der siebziger und achtziger Jahre." *Geschichte und Gesellschaft* 17 (1991): 512–30.

Brück, Heinrich. *Geschichte der katholischen Kirche in Deutschland im neunzehnten Jahrhundert.* Münster: F. Kirchheim, 1905.

Buchheim, Karl. *Ultramontanismus und Demokratie. Der Weg der deutschen Katholiken im 19. Jahrhundert.* Munich: Kösel-Verlag, 1963.

Burckhardt, Jacob. *Die Kultur der Renaissance in Italien.* Stuttgart: Alfred Kröner Verlag, 1976.

Bush, Norbert. "Feminisierung der ultramontanen Frömmigkeit." In *Wunderbare Erscheinungen: Frauen und katholische Frömmigkeit in 19. und 20. Jahrhundert,* ed. Irmtraud Götz von Olenhausen, 203–20. Paderborn: F. Schöningh, 1995.

Bussemer, Herrad-Ulricke. *Frauenemanzipation und Bildungsbürgertum: Sozialgeschichte der Frauenbewegung in der Reichsgründungszeit.* Weinheim and Basel: Beltz Verlag, 1985.

Bussmann, Walter. "Preußen und das Jahr 1866." *Aus Politik und Zeitgeschichte: Beilage zur Wochenzeitung "Das Parlament"* 24 (1966): 19–27.

———. "Zur Geschichte des deutschen Liberalismus in 19. Jahrhundert." *Historische Zeitschrift* 186 (1958): 527–57.

Calhoun, Craig, ed. *Habermas and the Public Sphere.* Cambridge: MIT Press, 1992.

Casteras, Susan. "Virgin Vows: The Early Victorian Artists' Portrayal of Nuns and Novices." *Victorian Studies* 24 (1981): 157–84.

Cesaire, Jean. "Der Liberalismus und die Liberalismen: Versuch einer Synthese." In *Liberalismus,* ed. Lothar Gall, 134–46. Cologne: Kiepenheuer und Witsch, 1976.

Christian, William. "Provoked Religious Weeping in Early Modern Spain." In *Religious Organizations and Religious Experience,* ed. John Davis, 97–114. London: Academic Press, 1982.

Constabel, Adelheid, ed. *Die Vorgeschichte des Kulturkampfes: Quellen aus dem Deutschen Zentralarchiv.* Berlin: Rütten und Loening, 1956.

Craig, Gordon A. *Germany, 1866–1945.* New York: Oxford University Press, 1978.

Cubitt, Geoffrey. "Catholics and Freemasons in Late Nineteenth-Century France." In *Religion and Politics in France since 1789,* ed. Frank Tallett and Nicholas Atkins, 121–36. London: Hambledon Press, 1991.

————. *The Jesuit Myth: Conspiracy Theory and Politics in Nineteenth-Century France.* Oxford: Oxford University Press, 1993.

Dahn, Otto, ed. *Vereinswesen und bürgerliche Gesellschaft in Deutschland.* Munich: R. Oldenbourg, 1984.

Dahrendorf, Ralf. *Society and Democracy in Germany.* New York: W. W. Norton, 1967.

Davidoff, L., and C. Hall. "The Architecture of Public and Private Life: English Middle-Class Society in a Provincial Town, 1780 to 1850." In *The Pursuit of Urban History,* ed. Derek Fraser and Anthony Sutcliffe, 327–45. London: E. Arnold, 1983.

Dettmer, Günter. *Die ost- und westpreußischen Verwaltungsbehörden im Kulturkampf.* Heidelberg: Quelle und Meyer, 1958.

Ditscheid, Aegidius. *Matthias Eberhard: Bischof von Trier im Kulturkampf.* Trier: Paulinus, 1900.

Dittrich, Franz. *Der Kulturkampf in Ermland.* Berlin, 1913.

Dölle, Adalbert. *Der Kulturkampf und seine Auswirkung auf dem Eichsfeld und im Fuldaer Land von 1872 bis 1887.* Duderstadt: Mecke, 1987.

Dotterweich, Volker. *Heinrich von Sybel: Geschichtswissenschaft in politischer Absicht (1817–1861).* Göttingen: Vandenhoeck und Ruprecht, 1978.

Doyle, James Anthony. "The Image of the Society of Jesus in German Literature from Fischart to Hochhuth." Ph.D. diss., Boston College, 1976.

Ebertz, Michael N., "Maria in der Massenreligiosität. Zum Wandel des popularen Katholizismus in Deutschland." In *Volksfrömmigkeit in Europa: Beiträge zur Soziologie populärer Religiosität aus 14 Ländern,* ed. Michael N. Ebertz and Franz Schultheiss, 65–84. Munich: Chr. Kaiser Verlag, 1986.

Eckhard, Rudolf. *Die Jesuiten in der deutschen Dichtung und Volksmund.* Bamberg: Verlag der Handels-Druckerei, 1906.

Eisfeld, G. *Die Entstehung der liberalen Parteien in Deutschland, 1858–70: Studien zu den Organisationen und Programmen der Liberalen und Demokraten.* Hanover: Verlag für Literatur und Zeitgeschehen, 1969.

Eley, Geoff. "Bismarckian Germany." In *Modern Germany Reconsidered, 1870–1945,* ed. Gordon Martel, 1–32. London: Routledge, 1992.

————. *From Unification to Nazism: Reinterpreting the German Past.* Boston: Allen and Unwin, 1986.

————. "Liberalism, Europe, and the Bourgeoisie, 1860–1914." In *The German Bourgeoisie: Essays on the Social History of the German Middle Class from the Late Eighteenth to the Early Twentieth Century,* ed. David Blackbourn and Richard Evans, 293–317. London: Routledge, 1991.

————. "Notable Politics, the Crisis of German Liberalism, and the Electoral Transition of the 1890s." In *In Search of a Liberal Germany: Studies in the His-*

tory of Germany Liberalism from 1789 to the Present, ed. Konrad H. Jarausch and Larry Eugene Jones, 187–216. New York: Berg, 1990.

———. *Reshaping the German Right: Radical Nationalism and Political Change after Bismarck.* Ann Arbor: University of Michigan Press, 1991.

———. Review of *Windthorst: A Political Biography,* by Margaret Lavinia Anderson. *New German Critique* 32 (1984): 189–96.

———. "State Formation, Nationalism, and Political Culture in Nineteenth-Century Germany." In *Culture, Ideology, and Politics: Essays for Eric Hobsbawm,* ed. Raphael Samuel and Gareth Stedman Jones, 277–301. London: Routledge, 1982.

Elshtain, Jean Bethke. *Public Man, Private Woman: Women in Social and Political Thought.* Princeton: Princeton University Press, 1981.

Evans, Ellen Lovell. *The German Center Party, 1870–1933: A Study in Political Catholicism.* Carbondale: Southern Illinois University Press, 1981.

Evans, Richard J. "The Concept of Feminism: Notes for Practicing Historians." In *German Women in the Eighteenth and Nineteenth Centuries: A Social and Literary History,* ed. Ruth-Ellen B. Jones and Mary Jo Maynes, 247–58. Bloomington: Indiana University Press, 1986.

———. *Death in Hamburg: Society and Politics in the Cholera Years, 1830–1910.* New York: Penguin Books, 1987.

———. *The Feminist Movement in Germany, 1894–1933.* New Brunswick: Rutgers University Press, 1976.

———. "Religion and Society in Modern Germany." In *Rethinking German History: Nineteenth-Century Germany and the Origins of the Third Reich,* 125–55. London: HarperCollins, 1987.

———. *Society and Politics in Wilhelmine Germany.* London: Croom Helm, 1978.

Ewens, Mary. *The Role of the Nun in Nineteenth-Century America.* New York: Arno Press, 1978.

Eyck, Erich. *Bismarck: Leben und Werk.* 3 vols. Erlenbach and Zurich: Eugen Rentsch, 1944.

Faber, Karl Georg, ed. *Die nationalpolitische Publizistik Deutschlands von 1866 bis 1871.* Düsseldorf: Droste Verlag, 1963.

———. "Realpolitik als Ideologie: Die Bedeutung des Jahres 1866 für das politische Denken in Deutschland." *Historische Zeitschrift* 203 (1966): 1–45.

———. "Strukturprobleme des deutschen Liberalismus im 19. Jahrhundert." *Der Staat* 14 (1975): 201–28.

Farr, Ian. "From Anti-Catholicism to Anticlericalism: Catholic Politics and the Peasantry in Bavaria, 1860–1900." *European Studies Review* 13 (1983): 249–69.

Fehrenbach, Elizabeth. *Verfassungsstaat und Nationsbildung 1815–1871.* Munich: R. Oldenbourg, 1992.

Ficker, L. *Der Kulturkampf in Münster.* Münster: Aschendorff, 1928.

Fischer, Fritz. "Der deutsche Protestantismus und die Politik im 19. Jahrhundert." *Historische Zeitschrift* 171 (1951): 473–518.

Fletcher, Roger. "Recent Developments in West German Historiography: The Bielefeld School and Its Critics." *German Studies Review* 7 (1984): 451–80.

Foerster, Erich. "Liberalismus und Kulturkampf." *Zeitschrift für Kirchengeschichte* 47 (1928): 543–59.

Fohrmann, Ulrich. *Trier Kulturkampfpublizistik im Bismarckreich: Leben und Werk des Preßkaplans Georg Friedrich Dasback.* Trier: Paulinus-Verlag, 1977.

Ford, Caroline. "Religion and Popular Culture in Modern Europe." *Journal of Modern History* 65 (1993): 152–75.

Fout, John C., ed. *German Women in the Nineteenth Century.* New York: Holmes and Meier, 1984.

François, Etienne. *Die unsichtbare Grenze: Protestanten und Katholiken in Augsburg, 1648–1806.* Trans. Angelika Steiner-Wendt. Sigmaringen: Jan Thorbecke Verlag, 1991.

Franz, Georg. *Kulturkampf, Staat, und katholische Kirche in Mitteleuropa von der Säkularisation bis zum Abschluß des preußischen Kulturkampfes.* Munich: D. W. Callwey, 1954.

Fraser, Derek, and Anthony Sutcliffe. *The Pursuit of Urban History.* London: E. Arnold, 1983.

Frevert, Ute. "Bürgerliche Meisterdenker und das Geschlechterverhältnis: Konzepte, Erfahrungen, Visionen an der Wende von 18. zum 19. Jahrhundert." In *Bürgerinnen und Bürger: Geschlechterverhältnisse im 19. Jahrhundert,* ed. Ute Frevert, 17–48. Göttingen: Vandenhoeck und Ruprecht, 1988.

———. *"Mann und Weib, und Weib und Mann": Geschlechter-Differenzen in der Moderne.* Munich: C. H. Beck, 1995.

———. *Women in German History: From Bourgeois Emancipation to Sexual Liberation.* Trans. Stuart McKinnon-Evans. New York: Berg, 1989.

Gall, Lothar. "Der deutsche Liberalismus zwischen Revolution und Reichsgründung." *Historische Zeitschrift* 228 (1979): 98–108.

———. *Der Liberalismus als regierende Partei: Das Grossherzogtum Baden zwischen Restauration und Reichsgründung.* Wiesbaden: F. Steiner, 1968.

———. "Liberalismus und 'bürgerliche Gesellschaft': Zur Charakter und Entwicklung der liberalen Bewegung in Deutschland." *Historische Zeitschrift* 220 (1975): 324–56.

———. "Liberalismus und Nationalstaat: Der deutsche Liberalismus und die Reichsgründung." In *Bürgertum, liberale Bewegung, und Nation: Ausgewählte Aufsätze,* ed. Dieter Hein, Andreas Schulz, and Eckhardt Treichel, 190–202. Munich: R. Oldenbourg, 1996.

———. "Die partei- und sozialgeschichtliche Problematik des badischen Kulturkampfes." *Zeitschrift für die Geschichte des Oberrheins* 113 (1965): 151–96.

———. "'Südenfall' des liberalen Denkens oder Krise der bürgerlich-liberalen Bewegung?" In *Liberalismus und imperialistischer Staat: Der Imperialismus als Problem liberaler Parteien in Deutschland, 1890–1914,* ed. K. Holl and G. List, 148–58. Göttingen: Vandenhoeck und Ruprecht, 1975.

Gatz, Erwin. "Bischöfliche Einheitsfront im Kulturkampf? Neue Funde zum Kirchenkonflikt im Bistum Hildesheim." *Historisches Jahrbuch* 92 (1972): 391–403.

———. *Rheinische Volksmission im 19. Jahrhundert: Dargestellt am Beispiel des Erzbistums Köln.* Düsseldorf: L. Schwann, 1963.

Gay, Peter. "Probleme der kulturellen Integration der Deutschen, 1849–1945." In *Die Rolle der Nation,* ed. Otto Büsch and James Sheehan, 181–92. Berlin: Colloquium Verlag, 1985.

Geertz, Clifford. "Ideology as a Cultural System." In *Ideology and Discontent,* ed. David E. Apter, 46–76. New York: Free Press of Glencoe, 1964.

———. *The Interpretation of Cultures: Selected Essays.* New York: Basic Books, 1973.

Gerhard, Ute. *Unerhört: Die Geschichte der deutsche Frauenbewegung.* Reinbek: W. de Gruyter, 1990.

Gerteis, Klaus. *Leopold Sonnemann: Ein Beitrag zur Geschichte des demokratischen Nationalstaatsgedankens in Deutschland.* Frankfurt am Main: Kramer, 1970.

Gibson, Ralph. *A Social History of French Catholicism, 1789–1914.* London: Routledge, 1989.

———. "Why Republicans and Catholics Couldn't Stand Each Other in the Nineteenth Century." In *Religion, Society, and Politics in France since 1789,* ed. Frank Tallet and Nicholas Atkin, 107–20. London: Hambledon Press, 1991.

Gilman, Sander L. *Jewish Self-Hatred: Anti-Semitism and the Hidden Language of the Jews.* Baltimore: Johns Hopkins University Press, 1986.

Goldberg, Ann. *Sex, Religion, and the Making of Modern Madness: The Eberbach Asylum and German Society, 1815–1849.* Oxford: Oxford University Press, 1999.

Golde, Günter. *Catholics and Protestants: Agricultural Modernization in Two German Villages.* New York: Academic Press, 1975.

Götz von Olenhusen, Irmtraud. *Klerus und abweichendes Verhalten: Zur Sozialgeschichte der katholischer Priester im 19. Jahrhundert. Die Erzdiözese Freiburg.* Göttingen: Vandenhoeck und Ruprecht, 1994.

———. "Klerus und Ultramontanismus in der Erzdiözese Freiburg: Entbürgerlichung und Klerikalisierung des Katholizismus nach der Revolution von 1848/49." In *Religion und Gesellschaft im 19. Jahrhundert,* ed. Wolfgang Schieder, 113–43. Stuttgart: Klett-Cotta, 1993.

———. "Die Ultramontanisierung des Klerus: Das Beispiel der Erzdiözese Freiburg." In *Deutscher Katholizismus im Umbruch zur Moderne,* ed. Wilfried Loth, 46–75. Stuttgart: W. Kohlhammer, 1991.

———, ed. *Wunderbare Erscheinungen: Frauen und katholische Frömmigkeit im 19. und 20. Jahrhundert.* Paderborn: F. Schöningh, 1995.

Gould, Andrew C. *Origins of Liberal Dominance: State, Church, and Party in Nineteenth-Century Europe.* Ann Arbor: University of Michigan Press, 1999.

Grenner, Karl Heinz. *Wirtschaftsliberalismus und katholisches Denken: Ihre Begegnung und Auseinandersetzung in Deutschland des 19. Jahrhunderts.* Cologne: Bachem, 1967.

Groeteken, Autbert, ed. *Die Volksmissionen der norddeutschen Franziskaner vor dem Kulturkampf (1849–1872).* Münster: Alphonsus Buchhandlung, 1909.

Gross, Friedrich. *Jesus, Luther und der Papst im Bilderkampf 1871 bis 1918: Zur Malereigeschichte der Kaiserzeit.* Marburg: Jonas, 1989.

Gross, Michael B. "The Catholic Missionary Crusade and the Protestant Revival in Nineteenth-Century Germany." In *Protestants, Catholics, and Jews in Germany, 1800–1914,* ed. Helmut Walser Smith, 245–65. Oxford: Berg, 2001.

———. "Kulturkampf and Unification: German Liberalism and the War against the Jesuits." *Central European History* 30 (1997): 545–66.

———. "The Strange Case of the Nun in the Dungeon, or German Liberalism as a Convent Atrocity Story." *German Studies Review* 23 (2000): 69–84.

Gründer, Horst. "Nation und Katholizismus im Kaiserreich." In *Katholizimus, nationaler Gedanke, und Europa seit 1800,* ed. Albrecht Langer, 65–88. Paderborn: F. Schöningh, 1985.

Gugel, Michael. *Industrieller Aufsteig und bürgerliche Herrschaft: Sozioökonomische Interessen und politische Ziele des liberalen Bürgertums im Preußen zur Zeit des Verfassungskonflikts 1857–1867.* Cologne: Pahl-Rugenstein Verlag, 1975.

Habermas, Jürgen. "The Public Sphere." *New German Critique* 3 (1974): 49–55.

———. *Strukturwandel der Öffentlichkeit: Untersuchungen zu einer Kategorie der bürgerlichen Gesellschaft.* Neuwied: Luchterhand, 1962.

Habermas, Rebekka. "Weibliche Religiosität—oder Von der Fragilität bürgerlicher Identitäten." In *Wege zur Geschichte des Bürgertums: Vierzehn Beiträge,* ed. Klaus Tenfelde and Hans-Ulrich Wehler, 125–48. Göttingen: Vandenhoeck und Ruprecht, 1994.

Hackett, Amy. "Feminism and Liberalism in Wilhelmine Germany, 1890–1918." In *Liberating Women's History: Theoretical and Critical Essays,* ed. Berenice A. Carroll, 127–36. Urbana: University of Illinois Press, 1976.

Hafenkorn, Folkert. *Soziale Vorstellungen Heinrich von Sybels.* Stuttgart: Klett-Cotta, 1976.

Hamann, Brigitte. *Hitler's Vienna: A Dictator's Apprentice.* Oxford: Oxford University Press, 1999.

Hamerow, Theodore S. *Restoration, Revolution, Reaction: Economics and Politics in Germany, 1815–1871.* Princeton: Princeton University Press, 1958.

———. *The Social Foundations of German Unification, 1858–1871.* 2 vols. Princeton: Princeton University Press, 1969–72.

———, ed. *The Age of Bismarck: Documents and Interpretations.* New York: Harper and Row, 1973.

Harris, James F. "Eduard Lasker and Compromise Liberalism." *Journal of Modern History* 43 (1970): 342–60.

———. "Edward Lasker: The Jew as National German Politician." *Leo Baeck Institute Yearbook* 20 (1975): 151–77.

———. "Rethinking the Categories of the Revolution of 1848." *Central European History* 25 (1992): 123–48.

———. *A Study in the Theory and Practice of German Liberalism: Eduard Lasker, 1829–1884.* Lanham, Md.: University Press of America, 1984.

Harris, Ruth. *Lourdes: Body and Spirit in the Secular Age.* New York: Viking Penguin, 1999.

Hartwig, Wolfgang. "Von Preußens Aufgabe in Deutschland zu Deutschlands Aufgabe in der Welt: Liberalismus und borussianisches Geschichtsbild zwischen Revolution und Imperialismus." *Historische Zeitschrift* 231 (1980): 265–324.

Hausen, Karin. "Family and Role-Division: The Polarisation of Sexual Stereotypes in the Nineteenth Century; An Aspect of the Dissociation of Work and Family Life." In *The German Family: Essays on the Social History of the Family in Nineteenth- and Twentieth-Century Germany,* ed. Richard J. Evans and W. R. Lee, 51–83. Totowa, N.J.: Barnes and Noble, 1981.

———. "Öffentlichkeit und Privatheit: Gesellschaftspolitische Konstruktionen und die *Geschichte der Geschlechterbeziehungen.*" In *Frauengeschichte-Geschlechtergeschichte,* ed. Karin Hausen and H. Wunder, 81–88. Frankfurt am Main: Campus, 1996.

———. " '. . . eine Ulme für das schwankende Efeu': Ehepaare im Bildungsbürgertum; Ideale und Wirklichkeiten im späten 18. und 19. Jahrhundert." In *Bürgerinnen und Bürger: Geschlechterverhältnisse im 19. Jahrhundert,* ed. Ute Frevert, 85–117. Göttingen: Vandenhoeck und Ruprecht, 1988.

Healy, Róisín. "Anti-Jesuitism in Imperial Germany: The Jesuits as Androgyne." In *Protestants, Catholics, and Jews in Germany, 1800–1914,* ed. Helmut Walser Smith, 153–81. Oxford: Berg, 2001.

Heckel, Johannes. "Die Beilegung des Kulturkampfes in Preußen." *Zeitschrift der Savigny-Stiftung für Rechtsgeschichte* 50 (1930): 215–353.

Heilbronner, Oded. "From Ghetto to Ghetto: The Place of German Catholic Society in Recent Historiography." *Journal of Modern History* 72 (2000): 453–95.

———. "In Search of the (Rural) Catholic Bourgeoisie: The Bürgertum of South Germany." *Central European History* 29 (1996): 191–93.

Heinen, Ernst. "Antisemitische Strömungen im politischen Katholizismus während des Kulturkampfes." In *Geschichte in der Gegenwart: Festschrift für Kurt Kluxen,* ed. Ernst Heinen and Hans Julius Schoepe, 259–99. Paderborn: F. Schöningh, 1972.

Heller, Andreas. " 'Du kommst in die Hölle . . .' Katholizismus als Weltanschauung in lebensgeschichtlichen Aufzeichnungen." In *Religion und Alltag: Interdisziplinäre Beiträge zu einer Sozialgeschichte des Katholizismus in lebensgechichtlichen Aufzeichnungen,* ed. Andreas Heller and Therese Weber, 28–55. Vienna: Böhlau Verlag, 1990.

Herzog, Dagmar. *Intimacy and Exclusion: Religious Politics in Pre-Revolutionary Baden.* Princeton: Princeton University Press, 1996.

Hirschmann, Günther. *Kulturkampf im historischen Roman der Gründerzeit, 1859–1878.* Munich: Fink, 1978.

Hofstadter, Richard. "The Paranoid Style in American Politics." In *The Paranoid Style in American Politics and Other Essays,* 3–40. New York: Vintage, 1965.

Holborn, Hajo. *A History of Modern Germany, 1840–1945.* 2 vols. Princeton: Princeton University Press, 1982.

Hölscher, Lucian. "Möglichkeiten und Grenzen der statistischen Erfaßung kirchlicher Bindungen." In *Seelsorge und Diakonie in Berlin: Beiträge zum Verhältnis von Kirche und Großtadt im 19. Jahrhundert und beginnenden 20. Jahrhundert,* ed. Kaspar Elm and Hans-Dietrich Loock, 39–62. Berlin: W. de Gruyter, 1990.

———. "Die Religion des Bürgers: Bürgerliche Frömmigkeit und protestantische Kirche im 19. Jahrhundert." *Historische Zeitschrift* 250 (1990): 595–630.

———. *Weltgericht oder Revolution: Protestantische und sozialistische Zukunftsvorstellungen im deutschen Kaiserreich.* Stuttgart: Klett-Cotta, 1989.

Hölscher, Lucian, and Ursula Männich-Polenz. "Die Sozialstruktur der Kirchengemeinde Hannovers im 19. Jahrhundert: Eine statistische Analyse."

Jahrbuch der Gesellschaft für niedersächsische Kirchengeschichte 88 (1990): 159–211.

Homig, Herbert. *Rheinische Katholiken und Liberale in den Auseinandersetzungen um die preußische Verfassung unter besonder Berücksichtigung der Kölner Presse.* Cologne: Wienand, 1971.

Horstmann, Johannes. *Katholizismus und moderne Welt: Katholikentage, Wirtschaft, Wissenschaft—1848 bis 1914.* Paderborn: F. Schöningh, 1976.

Horwath, Peter. *Der Kampf gegen die religiöse Tradition: Die Kulturkampfliteratur Österreichs 1780–1918.* Bern: Peter Lang, 1978.

Huber, Ernst Rudolf. *Deutsche Verfassungsgeschichte seit 1789.* 4 vols. Stuttgart: W. Kohlhammer, 1981.

Huber, Ernst Rudolf, and Wolfgang Huber, ed. *Staat und Kirche im 19. und 20. Jahrhundert: Dokumente zur Geschichte des deutschen Staatskirchenrechte.* 2 vols. Berlin: Duncker und Humblot, 1973.

Hübinger, Gangolf. "Confessionalism." In *Imperial Germany: A Historiographical Companion,* ed. Roger Chickering, 156–84. Westport, Conn.: Greenwood, 1996.

———. *Kulturprotestantismus und Politik: Zum Verhältnis von Liberalismus und Protestantismus im wilhelminischen Deutschland.* Tübingen: J. C. B. Mohr, 1994.

Huyssen, Andreas. "Mass Culture as Woman." In *After the Great Divide: Modernism, Mass Culture, Postmodernism,* 44–62. Bloomington and Indianapolis: Indiana University Press, 1986.

Hyde, Simon. "Roman Catholicism and the Prussian State in the Early 1850s." *Central European History* 24 (1991): 95–121.

Iggers, Georg G. *The German Conception of History.* Middletown, Conn.: Wesleyan University Press, 1968.

Jaeger, Karin. "Die Revolution von 1848 und die Stellung des Katholizismus zur Problem der Revolution." In *Kirche zwischen Krieg und Friede: Studien zur Geschichte der deutschen Protestantismus,* ed. Wolfgang Huber and Johannes Schwerdtfeber, 243–91. Stuttgart: Klett Verlag, 1976.

Jansen, Christian. "Saxon Forty-Eighters in the Postrevolutionary Epoch, 1849–1867." In *Saxony in German History: Culture, Society, and Politics, 1830–1933,* ed. James Retallack, 135–50. Ann Arbor: University of Michigan Press, 2000.

Jarausch, Konrad H. *Students, Society, and Politics in Imperial Germany: The Rise of Academic Illiberalism.* Princeton: Princeton University Press, 1982.

Jarausch, Konrad H., and Larry Eugene Jones. "German Liberalism Reconsidered: Inevitable Decline, Bourgeois Hegemony, or Partial Achievement?" In *In Search of a Liberal Germany: Studies in the History of German Liberalism from 1789 to the Present,* ed. Konrad H. Jarausch and Larry Eugene Jones, 1–23. New York: Berg, 1990.

Jockwig, P. Klemens. "Die Volksmission der Redemptoristen in Bayern von 1848 bis 1873: Dargestellt am Erzbistum München und Freising und an den Bistümern Passau und Regensburg; Ein Beitrag zur Pastoralgeschichte des 19 Jahrhunderts." In *Beiträge zur Geschichte des Bistums Regensburg,* ed. Georg Schwaiger and Josef Staber, 41–407. Regensburg: Verlag des Vereins für Regensburger Bistumsgeschichte, 1967.

Joeres, Ruth-Ellen B., and Mary Jo Maynes, eds. *German Women in the Eighteenth and Nineteenth Centuries: A Social and Literary History.* Bloomington: Indiana University Press, 1986.

John, Michael. "Liberalism and Society in Germany, 1850–1880: The Case of Hanover." *English Historical Review* 102 (1987): 579–98.

———. *Politics and the Law in Late Nineteenth-Century Germany: The Origins of the Civil Code.* Oxford: Oxford University Press, 1989.

Johnson, Trevor. "Blood, Tears, and Xavier-Water: Jesuit Missionaries and Popular Religion in the Eighteenth-Century Upper Palatinate." In *Popular Religion in Germany and Central Europe, 1400–1800,* ed. Bob Scribner and Trevor Johnson, 183–202. New York: St. Martin's Press, 1996.

Jürgensmeier, Friedhelm. *Die katholische Kirche im Spiegel der Karikatur: Die deutschen satirischen Tendenzzeitschriften von 1848 bis 1900.* Trier: Verlag Neu, 1969.

Just, Herald. "Wilhelm Busch und die Katholiken: Kulturkampfstimmung im Bismarck-Reich." *Geschichte in Wissenschaft und Unterricht* 25 (1974): 65–79.

Kähle-Hezinger, Christel. *Evangelisch-Katholisch: Untersuchungen zu konfessionellem Vorurteil und Konflikt im 19. und 20. Jahrhundert vornehmlich am Beispiel Württemburgs.* Tübingen: Tubinger Vereinigung für Volkskunde, 1976.

Kissling, Johannes B. *Geschichte des Kulturkampfes im deutschen Reich.* 3 vols. Freiburg im Breisgau: Herder, 1911–16.

Klöcker, Michael. *Katholisch—von der Weige bis zur Bahre: Eine Lebensmacht im Zerfall?* Munich: Kösel-Verlag, 1991.

———. "Das katholische Milieu: Grundüberlegungen in besonderer Hinsicht auf das Deutsche Kaiserreich von 1871." *Zeitschrift für Religions- und Geistesgeschichte* 44 (1992): 241–62.

———. "Probleme der politischen Integration der Deutschen 1867 bis 1945." In *Die Rolle der Nation,* ed. Otto Büsch and James Sheehan, 118–36. Berlin: Colloquium Verlag, 1985.

Kocka, Jürgen. "Germany before Hitler: The Debate about the German *Sonderweg.*" *Journal of Contemporary History* 23 (1988): 3–16.

———, ed. *Bürgertum im 19. Jahrhundert: Deutschland im europäischen Vergleich.* Munich: Deutscher Taschenbuch Verlag, 1988.

Kopperschmidt, Enno. *Jesuiten Arbeiten: Zur Geschichte des Jesuitenordens in Deutschland von 1866 bis 1872.* Munich: Ludendorff, 1940.

Korff, Gottfried. "Heiligenverehrung und soziale Frage: Zur Ideologisierung der populären Frömmigkeit im späten 19. Jahrhundert." In *Kultureller Wandel im 19. Jahrhundert,* ed. Günter Wiegelmann, 102–11. Göttingen: Vandenhoeck und Ruprecht, 1973.

———. "Kulturkampf und Volksfrömmigkeit." In *Volksreligiosität in der modernen Sozialgeschichte,* ed. Wolfgang Schieder, 137–51. Göttingen: Vandenhoeck und Ruprecht, 1986.

———. "Zwischen Sinnlichkeit und Kirchlichkeit: Notizen zum Wandel populäer Frömmigkeit im 18. und 19. Jahrhundert." In *Kultur zwischen Bürgertum und Volk,* ed. J. Held, 136–48. Berlin: Argument-Verlag, 1983.

Koshar, Rudy. *Social Life, Local Politics, and Nazism: Marburg, 1880–1935.* Chapel Hill: University of North Carolina Press, 1986.

Kosselleck, Reinhardt. *Preußen zwischen Reform und Revolution.* Stuttgart: Klett-Cotta, 1982.

Kraul, Margret. "Bildung und Bürgerlichkeit." In *Bürgertum im 19. Jahrhundert: Deutschland im europäischen Vergleich,* ed. Jürgen Kocka and Ute Frevert, 3:45–73. Munich: Deutscher Taschenbuch Verlag, 1988.

Krieger, Leonard. *The German Idea of Freedom: History of a Political Tradition from the Reformation to 1871.* Chicago: Beacon, 1957.

Lamberti, Marjorie. "State, Church, and the Politics of School Reform during the Kulturkampf." *Central European History* 19 (1986): 63–81.

————. *State, Society, and the Elementary School in Imperial Germany.* Oxford: Oxford University Press, 1989.

Lange, Josef. *Die Stellung der überregionalen katholischen deutschen Tagespresse zum Kulturkampf in Preußen (1871–1878).* Frankfurt am Main: Peter Lang, 1974.

Langewiesche, Dieter. "Bildungsbürgertum und Liberalismus im 19. Jahrundert." In *Bildungsbürgertum im 19. Jahrhundert.* Part 4, *Politischer Einfluß und gesellschaftlich Formation,* ed. Jürgen Kocka, 95–121. Stuttgart: Klett-Cotta, 1989.

————. "Frühliberalismus und Bürgertum 1815–1849." In *Bürgertum und bürgerlich-liberale Bewegung in Mitteleuropa seit dem 18. Jahrhundert,* ed. Lothar Gall, 63–130. Munich: R. Oldenbourg, 1977.

————. "German Liberalism in the Second Empire, 1871–1914." In *In Search of a Liberal Germany: Studies in the History of German Liberalism from 1789 to the Present,* ed. Konrad H. Jarausch and Larry Eugene Jones, 217–35. New York: Berg, 1990.

————. *Liberalismus in Deutschland.* Frankfurt am Main: Suhrkamp Verlag, 1988.

————. *Liberalismus und Demokratie in Württemberg zwischen Revolution und Reichsgründung.* Düsseldorf: Droste Verlag, 1974.

————. "The Nature of German Liberalism." In *Modern Germany Reconsidered, 1870–1945,* ed. Gordon Martel, 96–116. London: Routledge, 1992.

Langlois, Claude. *La Catholicisme au féminin: Les congrégations français à supérieure générale au XIX siècle.* Paris: Cerf, 1984.

Lee, W. Robert. *Population Growth, Economic Development, and Social Change in Bavaria, 1750–1850.* New York: Oxford University Press, 1977.

Leontovitsch, Victor. "Das Wesen des Liberalismus." In *Liberalismus,* ed. Lothar Gall, 37–51. Cologne: Kiepenheuer und Witsch, 1976.

Lepper, Herbert. "Widerstand gegen die Staatsgewalt: Die Auseinandersetzung der Generaloberin der Franziskanerinnen Elisabeth Koch zu Eupen mit den Staatsbehörden um die Ausführung des 'Klostergesetzes' vom 31. Mai 1875." In *Lebensraum Bistum Aachen: Tradition—Aktualität—Zukunft,* ed. Philipp Boonen, 98–139. Aachen: Einhard Verlag, 1982.

Lepsius, Rainer. "Parteisystem und Sozialstruktur: Zum Problem der Demokratisierung der deutschen Gesellschaft." In *Deutsche Parteien vor 1918,* ed. Gerhard A. Ritter, 56–80. Cologne: Kiepenheuer und Witsch, 1973.

Liedhegener, Antonius. *Christentum und Urbanisierung: Katholiken und Protestanten in Münster und Bochum 1880–1933.* Paderborn: F. Schöningh, 1997.

Lill, Rudolf. "Die deutschen Katholiken im Spannungsfeld der Konfessionen." In *Probleme des Konfessionalismus in Deutschland seit 1800,* ed. Anton Rauscher, 29–47. Paderborn: F. Schöningh, 1984.

———. "Die deutschen Katholiken und Bismarcks Reichsgründung." In *Reichsgründung 1870/71: Tatsachen, Kontroversen, Interpretationen,* ed. Theodor Schieder and Ernst Deuerlein, 345–65. Stuttgart: Seewald Verlag, 1970.

———. "Die deutschen Katholiken und die Juden in der Zeit von 1850 bis zur Machtübernahme Hitlers." In *Kirche und Synagoge: Handbuch zur Geschichte von Christen und Juden,* ed. Karl Heinrich Rengstorf and Siegfried von Kortzfleisch, 2:377–94. Stuttgart: Klett, 1968–72.

———. "Kirche und Revolution: Zu den Anfängen der katholischen Bewegung im Jahrzehnt vor 1848." *Archiv für Sozialgeschichte* 18 (1978): 565–75.

———. "Der Kulturkampf in Preußen und im deutschen Reich (bis 1878)." In *Handbuch der Kirchengeschichte,* ed. Herbert Jedin, 28–47. Freiburg im Breisgau: Herder, 1973.

———. *Die Wende im Kulturkampf: Leo XIII. Bismarck und die Zentrumspartei 1878–1889.* Tübingen: Niemeyer, 1973.

———, ed. *Der Kulturkampf in Italien und in den deutschsprachigen Ländern.* Berlin: Duncker und Humblot, 1993.

Lindenberger, Thomas. "Berliner Unordnung zwischen den Revolutionen." In *Pöbelexzesse und Volkstumulte in Berlin: Zur Sozialgeschichte der Straße (1830–1980),* ed. Manfred Gailus, 49–77. Berlin: Verlag Europäische Perspektive, 1984.

Lindt, Andreas. *Protestanten, Katholiken, Kulturkampf.* Zürich: EVZ-Verlag, 1963.

Lipp, Carola. "Katzenmusiken, Krawalle, und 'Weiberrevolution': Frauen im politischen Protest der Revolutionsjahre." In *Schimpfende Weiber und patriotische Jungfrauen: Frauen im Vormärz und in der Revolution 1848/49,* ed. Carola Lipp and Beate Bechtold-Comforty, 112–30. Moos and Baden-Baden: Elster, 1986.

Lipp, Carola, and Wolfgang Kaschuba. *1848—Provinz und Revolution: Kultureller Wandel und soziale Bewegung im Königreich Württemberg.* Tübingen: Tübinger Vereinigung für Volkskunde, 1979.

Lönne, Karl-Egon. "Katholizismus-Forschung." *Geschichte und Gesellschaft* 26 (2000): 137–44.

Loth, Wilfried, ed. *Deutscher Katholizismus im Umbruch zur Moderne.* Stuttgart: W. Kohlhammer, 1991.

———. *Katholiken im Kaiserreich: Der politische Katholizismus in der Krise des wilhelminischen Deutschlands.* Düsseldorf: Droste Verlag, 1984.

Lowenstein, Steven M. "Jüdisches religiöse Leben in deutschen Dörfern: Regionale Unterschiede im 19. und frühen 20. Jahrhundert." In *Jüdisches Leben auf dem Lande,* ed. Monika Richarz and Reinhard Rürup, 219–30. Tübingen: Mohr Siebeck, 1997.

Lutz, Catherine A., and Jane L. Collins. *Reading National Geographic.* Chicago: University of Chicago Press, 1993.

Marrus, Michael R. *The Unwanted: European Refugees in the Twentieth Century.* Oxford: Oxford University Press, 1985.

Martel, Gordon, ed. *Modern Germany Reconsidered.* London: Routledge, 1992.

McLeod, Hugh. *Piety and Poverty: Working-Class Religion in Berlin, London, and New York, 1870–1914.* New York: Holmes and Meier, 1996.

———. "Weibliche Frömmigkeit—männlicher Unglaube? Religion und Kirchen im bürgerlichen 19. Jahrhundert." In *Bürgerinnen und Bürger: Geschlechterverhältnisse im 19. Jahrhundert,* ed. Ute Frevert, 134–56. Göttingen: Vandenhoeck und Ruprecht, 1988.

McMillan, James F. "Anti-Clericals and the Women's Movement in France under the Third Republic." *Historical Journal* 24 (1981): 361–76.

Meiwes, Relinda. *"Arbeiterinnen des Herrn": Katholische Frauenkongregationen im 19. Jahrhundert.* Frankfurt: Campus Verlag, 2000.

———."Religiosität und Arbeit als Lebensform für katholische Frauen: Kongregationen im 19. Jahrhundert." In *Frauen unter dem Patriarchat der Kirchen: Katholikinnen und Protestantinnen im 19. und 20. Jahrhundert,* ed. Anselm Doering-Manteuffel, Martin Greschat, Jochen-Christoph Kaiser, Wilfried Loth, and Kurt Nowak, 69–88. Stuttgart: W. Kohlhammer, 1995.

Mendus, Susan. *Toleration and the Limits of Liberalism.* Atlantic Highlands, N.J.: Humanities Press International, 1989.

Mergel, Thomas. "Ultramontanism, Liberalism, Moderation: Political Mentalities and Political Behavior of the German Catholic Bürgertum, 1848–1914." *Central European History* 29 (1996): 151–74.

———. *Zwischen Klasse und Konfession: Katholisches Bürgertum im Rheinland, 1794–1914.* Göttingen: Vandenhoeck und Ruprecht, 1994.

Meyer, Ernst. *Rudolf Virchow.* Wiesbaden: Urania-Verlag, 1956.

Meyer, Folkert. *Schule der Untertanen: Lehrer und Politik in Preußen, 1848–1900.* Hamburg: Hoffman und Campe, 1976.

Michels, Sigrid. "Die Auswirkungen des Kulturkampfes in Düsseldorf." Schriftliche Hausarbeit zur Ersten Staatsprüfung für das Lehramt an der Volksschule: Pädagogische Hochschule Rheinland, Abteilung Neuß, 1967.

Moeller, Robert G. "The Kaiserreich Recast? Continuity and Change in Modern German Historiography." *Journal of Social History* 17 (1984): 655–83.

Möller, Frank. *Bürgerliche Herrschaft in Augsburg, 1790–1880.* Munich: R. Oldenbourg, 1998.

Mommsen, Wolfgang J. "Der deutsche Liberalismus zwischen 'klassenloser Bürgergesellschaft' und 'organisierten Kapitalismus': Zu einigen neueren Liberalismustinterpretationen." *Geschichte und Gesellschaft* 4 (1978): 77–90.

———. *Das Ringen um den nationalen Staat: Die Gründung und der innere Ausbau des deutschen Reiches unter Otto von Bismarck, 1850–1890.* Berlin: Propyläen, 1993.

———. "Society and State in Europe in the Age of Liberalism, 1870–1890." In *Imperial Germany, 1867–1918: Politics, Culture, and Society in an Authoritarian State,* 57–74. London and New York: Arnold, 1995. Originally published as "Gesellschaft und Staat im liberalen Zeitalter: Europa 1870–1890," in *Der autoritäre Nationalstaat: Verfassung, Gesellschaft und Kultur des deutschen Kaiserreiches* (Frankfurt am Main: Fischer Taschenbuch, 1990), 86–108.

————. "Wandlungen der liberalen Idee im Zeitalter des Liberalismus." In *Liberalismus und imperialischer Staat: Der Imperialismus als Problem liberaler Parteien in Deutschland, 1890–1914,* ed. K. Holl and G. List, 109–47. Göttingen: Vandenhoeck und Ruprecht, 1975.

Moody, Joseph Nestor, ed. *Church and Society in Germany: Social and Political Thought and Movements, 1789–1950.* New York: Arts, 1953.

Moore, Barrington. *The Social Origins of Dictatorship and Democracy.* Boston: Beacon, 1966.

Mooser, Josef. "Katholische Volksreligion, Klerus und Bürgertum in der zweiten Hälfte des 19. Jahrhunderts: Thesen." In *Religion und Gesellschaft im 19. Jahrhundert,* ed. Wolfgang Schneider, 144–56. Stuttgart: Klett-Cotta, 1993.

Morsey, Rudolf. "Bismarck und der Kulturkampf: Ein Forschungs- und Literaturbericht 1945–1957." *Archiv für Kulturgeschichte* 39 (1957): 232–70.

————. "Die deutschen Katholiken und der Nationalstaat zwischen Kulturkampf und Ersten Weltkrieg." *Historisches Jahrbuch* 90 (1970): 31–64.

————. "Probleme der Kulturkampf-Forschung." *Historisches Jahrbuch* 83 (1964): 217–45.

Mosse, Werner E. "Introduction: German Jewry and Liberalism." In *Das deutsche Judentum und der Liberalismus,* ed. Friedrich-Nauman-Stiftung, 15–27. Sankt Augustin: Comdok-Verlagsabteilung, 1986.

Müllejans-Dickmann, Rita. *Klöster im Kulturkampf: Die Ansiedlung katholischer Orden und Kongregationen aus dem Rheinland und ihre Klosterneubauten in belgisch-niederländischen Grenzraum infolge des preußischen Kulturkampfes.* Aachen: Einhard, 1992.

Müller, H. "Der deutsche politische Katholizismus in der Entscheidung des Jahres 1866." *Blätter für pfälzische Kirchengeschichte und religiöse Volkskunde* 33 (1966): 46–75.

Müller, Leonhard. *Der Kampf zwischen politischem Katholizismus und Bismarcks Politik im Spiegel der Schlesischen Volkszeitung.* Breslau: Müller und Seiffert, 1929.

Murphy, Bartholomew J. *Der Wiederaufbau der Gesellschaft Jesu in Deutschland im 19. Jahrhundert: Jesuiten in Deutschland, 1849–1872.* Frankfurt am Main: Peter Lang, 1985.

Nicholson, Linda J. "John Locke: The Theoretical Separation of the Family and the State." In *Gender and History: The Limits of Social Theory in the Age of the Family,* 133–66. New York: Columbia University Press, 1986.

Nipperdey, Thomas. *Deutsche Geschichte 1800–1866: Bürgerwelt und starker Staat.* Munich: C. H. Beck, 1983.

————. *Germany from Napoleon to Bismarck, 1800–1866.* Trans. Daniel Nolan. Princeton: Princeton University Press, 1996.

————. *Religion im Umbruch: Deutschland 1870–1918.* Munich: C. H. Beck, 1988.

————. "Wehler's 'Kaiserreich': Eine kritische Auseinandersetzung." *Geschichte und Gesellschaft* 1 (1975): 539–60.

Noyes, P. H. *Organization and Revolution: Working-Class Associations in the German Revolution of 1848–1849*. Princeton: Princeton University Press, 1966.

O'Boyle, L. "Liberal Political Leadership in Germany, 1867–1884." *Journal of Modern History* 28 (1956): 338–52.

O'Brien, Susan. "French Nuns in Nineteenth-Century England." *Past and Present* 161 (1997): 142–80.

————. "*Terra Incognita:* The Nun in Nineteenth-Century England." *Past and Present* 121 (1988): 110–40.

Olliges-Wieczorek, Ute. *Politisches Leben in Münster: Parteien und Vereine im Kaiserreich (1871–1914)*. Münster: Ardey Verlag, 1995.

Oncken, Hermann. *Rudolf von Benningsen, ein deutscher liberaler Politiker, nach seinen Briefen und hinterlassenen Papieren*. Stuttgart and Leipzig: Deutsche Verlags-Anstalt, 1910.

Paletschek, Sylvia. *Frauen und Dissens: Frauen im Deutschkatholizismus und in den freien Gemeinden, 1842–1852*. Göttingen: Vandenhoeck und Ruprecht, 1990.

Palmowski, Jan. *Urban Liberalism in Imperial Germany: Frankfurt am Main, 1866–1914*. Oxford: Oxford University Press, 1999.

Paz, D. G. *Popular Anti-Catholicism in Mid-Victorian England*. Stanford: Stanford University Press, 1992.

Pflanze, Otto. *Bismarck and the Development of Germany*. 3 vols. Princeton: Princeton University Press, 1990.

Phayer, J. Michael. *Sexual Liberation and Religion in Nineteenth-Century Europe*. London: Rowman and Littlefield, 1977.

Planert, Ute. *Antifeminismus im Kaiserreich*. Göttingen: Vandenhoeck und Ruprecht, 1998.

Prelinger, Catherine M. *Charity, Challenge, and Change: Religious Dimensions of the Mid–Nineteenth Century Women's Movement in Germany*. New York: Greenwood, 1987.

Raab, Herbert. "Zur Geschichte des Schlagworts 'Ultramontan' in 18. und frühen 19. Jahrhundert." *Historisches Jahrbuch* 81 (1962): 159–73.

Rauscher, Anton, ed. *Katholizimus, Bildung und Wissenschaft im 19. und 20. Jahrhundert*. Paderborn: F. Schöningh, 1987.

————, ed. *Religiös-kulturelle Bewegungen im deutschen Katholizismus seit 1800*. Paderborn: F. Schöningh, 1986.

Real, W. "Die Ereignisse von 1866–1867 im Lichte unserer Zeit." *Historisches Jahrbuch* 95 (1975): 342–73.

Reiber, Hans Joachim. "Die katholische deutsche Tagespresse unter dem Einfluß des Kulturkampfes." Ph.D. diss., University of Leipzig, 1936.

Reif, Heinz. *Westfälischer Adel, 1770–1860: Vom Herrschaftsstand zur regionalen Elite*. Göttingen: Vandenhoeck und Ruprecht, 1979.

Rémond, Réné. "Anticlericalism: Some Reflections by Way of Introduction." *European Studies Review* 13 (1983): 121–26.

Rengstorf, Karl Heinrich, and Siegfried von Kortzfleisch, eds. *Kirche und Synagoge: Handbuch zur Geschichte von Christen und Juden*. 2 vols. Stuttgart: Klett, 1968–72.

Repgen, Konrad. "Klerus und Politik 1848: Die Kölner Geistlichen im politischen

Leben des Revolutionsjahres—Als Beitrag zu einer Parteigeschichte von unten." In *Aus Geschichte und Landeskunde: Forschungen und Darstellungen,* ed. Max Braubach, 133–65. Bonn: L. Rohrscheid, 1960.

Retallack, James. "Social History with a Vengeance? Some Reactions to H.-U. Wehler's 'Das Deutsche Kaiserreich.'" *German Studies Review* 7 (1984): 423–50.

Ritter, Gerhard A. *Die deutschen Parteien, 1830–1914: Parteien und Gesellschaft im konstitutionellen Regierungssystem.* Göttingen: Vandenhoeck und Ruprecht, 1985.

Ritter, Gerhard A., and Merith Niehuss. *Wahlgeschichtliches Arbeitsbuch: Materialien zur Statistik des Kaiserreichs, 1871–1918.* Munich: C. H. Beck, 1980.

Robertson, Priscilla. *Revolutions of 1848: A Social History.* Princeton: Princeton University Press, 1952.

Rohe, Karl. *Vom Revier zum Rhurgebiet.* Essen: Hobbing, 1986.

———. *Elections, Parties, and Political Traditions: Social Foundations of German Parties and Party Systems, 1867–1987.* New York: Berg, 1990.

Romeyk, Horst. *Die leitenden staatlichen und kommunalen Verwaltungsbeamten der Rheinprovinz, 1816–1945.* Düsseldorf: Droste Verlag, 1994.

Rosenberg, Hans, ed. *Die national politische Publizistik Deutschlands von Eintritt der Neuen Ära bis zum Ausbruch des Deutschen Krieges: Eine kritische Bibliographie.* Munich: R. Oldenbourg, 1935.

Ross, Ronald J. *Beleaguered Tower: The Dilemma of Political Catholicism in Wilhelmine Germany.* Notre Dame: University of Notre Dame Press, 1976.

———. "Enforcing the Kulturkampf in the Bismarckian State and the Limits of the Coercion in Imperial Germany." *Journal of Modern History* 56 (1984): 456–82.

———. *The Failure of Bismarck's Kulturkampf: Catholicism and State Power in Imperial Germany, 1871–1887.* Washington, D.C.: Catholic University of America Press, 1998.

———. "The Kulturkampf and the Limitations of Power in Bismarck's Germany." *Journal of Ecclesiastical History* 46 (1995): 669–88.

———. "The Kulturkampf: Restrictions on Controls on the Practice of Religion in Bismarck's Germany." In *Freedom and Religion in the Nineteenth Century,* ed. Richard Helmstadter, 173–95. Stanford: Stanford University Press, 1997.

Rost, Hans. *Die wirtschaftliche und kulturelle Lage der deutschen Katholiken.* Cologne: J. Bachem, 1911.

Ruhenstroth-Bauer, R. *Bismarck und Falk im Kulturkampf.* Heidelberg: C. Winter, 1944.

Rürup, Reihard. "German Liberalism and the Emancipation of the Jews." *Leo Baeck Institute Yearbook* 20 (1975): 59–68.

Sagarra, Eda. *A Social History of Germany, 1648–1914.* New York: Holmes and Meier, 1977.

Sanchez, Jose. *Anticlericalism: A Brief History.* Notre Dame: University of Notre Dame Press, 1972.

Sander, Michael. "Katholische Geistlichkeit und Arbeiterorganisation." In *Soziale Frage und Kirche im Saarrevier: Beiträge zu Sozialpolitik und Katholizis-*

mus im späten 19. und frühen 20. Jahrhundert, ed. Ingrid Mruk. Saarbrücken: Sarrbrücker Druckerei und Verlag, 1984.

Saurer, Edith. "Frauen und Priester: Beichtgespräche im frühen 19. Jahrhundert." In *Arbeit, Frommigkeit, und Eigensinn: Studien zu historischer Kulturforschung,* ed. Richard van Dülmen, 141–70. Frankfurt am Main: Fischer Verlag, 1990.

——. "Religiöse Praxis und Sinnesverwirrung: Kommentare zur religiösen Melancholiediskussion." In *Studien zur historischen Kulturforschung,* 213–39. Frankfurt am Main: Fischer Taschenbuch Verlag, 1992.

Schapiro, J. Salwyn. "Was ist Liberalismus?" In *Liberalismus,* ed. Lothar Gall, 20–36. Cologne: Kiepenheuer und Witsch, 1976.

Schauff, Johannes. *Die deutschen Katholiken und die Zentrumspartei: Eine politisch-statistiche Untersuchung der Reichstagwahlen seit 1871.* Cologne: J. P. Bachen, 1928.

——. *Das Wahlverhalten der deutschen Katholiken im Kaiserreich und der Weimarer Republik.* Mainz: Matthias Grünewald Verlag, 1975.

Schieder, Theodor. *Das deutsche Kaiserreich von 1871 als Nationalstaat.* Cologne: Westdeutscher Verlag, 1961.

Schieder, Theodor, and Ernst Deuerlein, eds. *Reichsgründung 1870/71: Tatsachen, Kontroversen, Interpretationen.* Stuttgart: Seewald Verlag, 1870.

Schieder, Wolfgang. "Kirche und Revolution: Sozialgeschichtliche Aspekte der Trierer Wallfahrt von 1844." *Archiv für Sozialgeschichte* 14 (1974): 419–54.

——. *Volksreligiösität in der modernen Sozialgeschichte.* Göttingen: Vandenhoeck und Ruprecht, 1986.

——, ed. *Liberalismus in der Gesellschaft des deutschen Vormärz.* Göttingen: Vandenhoeck und Ruprecht, 1983.

Schloßmacher, Norbert. *Düsseldorf im Bismarckreich: Politik und Wahlen, Parteien und Vereine.* Düsseldorf: Schwann, 1985.

Schmidt, Erich. *Bismarcks Kampf mit dem politischen Katholizismus: Pius IX. und die Zeit der Rüstung 1848–1878.* Hamburg: Hanseatische Verlagsanstalt, 1942.

Schmidt, Gustav. "Die Nationalliberalen—eine regierungsfähige Partei? Zur Problematik der inneren Reichsgründung, 1870–1878." In *Die deutschen Parteien vor 1918: Parteien und Gesellschaft im konstitutionellen Regierungssystem,* ed. Gerhard A. Ritter, 208–23. Cologne: Kiepenheuer und Witsch, 1973.

Schmidt, Martin, and Georg Schwaiger. *Kirchen und Liberalismus im 19. Jahrhundert.* Göttingen: Vandenhoeck und Ruprecht, 1976.

Schmidt-Volkmar, Erich. *Der Kulturkampf in Deutschland 1871–1890.* Göttingen: Musterschmidt, 1962.

Scholle, Manfred. *Die preußsiche Strafjustiz im Kulturkampf 1873–1880.* Marburg: Elwert, 1974.

Scholten, Bernhard. *Die Volksmission der Niederdeutschen Redemptoristen und Oblaten während des Kaiserreichs (1873–1918).* Bonn: Hofbauer-Verlag, 1978.

——. *Die Volksmission der Redemptoristen vor dem Kulturkampf im Raum der Niederdeutschen Ordensprovinz.* Bonn: Hofbauer-Verlag, 1976.

Schürmann, J. *Johann Bernard Brinkmann: Bischof von Münster in Kulturkampf; Erinnerungen von J. Schürmann.* Münster: A. Ostendorff, 1925.

Schütze, Yvonne. "Mütterliebe-Vaterliebe: Elternrollen in der bürgerlichen Familie des 19 Jahrhundert." In *Bürgerinnen und Bürger: Geschlechterverhältnisse im 19. Jahrhundert,* ed. Ute Frevert, 118–33. Göttingen: Vandenhoeck und Ruprecht, 1988.

Scott, Joan Wallach. *Gender and the Politics of History.* New York: Columbia University Press, 1988.

————. *Only Paradoxes to Offer: French Feminists and the Rights of Man.* Cambridge: Harvard University Press, 1996.

Segalen, Martine. *Mari et femme dans la société paysanne.* Paris: Flammarion, 1980.

Seier, Hellmut. "Liberalismus und Bürgertum in Mitteleuropa 1850–1880: Forschung und Literatur seit 1970." In *Bürgertum und bürgerlich-liberale Bewegung in Mitteleuropa seit dem 18. Jahrhundert,* ed. Lothar Gall, 132–229. Munich: R. Oldenbourg, 1997.

Sell, Friedrich C. *Die Tragödie deutschen Liberalismus.* Stuttgart: Deutsche Verlags-Anstalt, 1953.

Sheehan, James J. "Deutscher Liberalismus im postliberalen Zeitalter, 1890–1914." *Geschichte und Gesellschaft* 4 (1978): 29–48.

————. *German History, 1770–1866.* Oxford: Oxford University Press, 1989.

————. *German Liberalism in the Nineteenth Century.* Chicago: University of Chicago Press, 1978.

————. "Liberalism and Society in Germany, 1815–1848." *Journal of Modern History* 45 (1973): 583–604.

————. "Liberalism and the City in Nineteenth-Century Germany." *Past and Present* 51 (1971): 116–37.

————. "Liberalismus und Gesellschaft in Deutschland, 1815–1848." In *Liberalismus,* ed. Lothar Gall, 208–31. Cologne: Kiepenheuer und Witsch, 1976.

————. "Partei, Volk, and Staat: Some Reflections on the Relationship between Liberal Thought and Action in Vormärz." In *Sozialgeschichte Heute,* ed. Hans-Ulrich Wehler, 162–74. Göttingen: Vandenhoeck und Ruprecht, 1974.

————. "Political Leadership in the German Reichstag, 1871–1918." *American Historical Review* 74 (1968): 511–28.

————. "What Is German History? Reflections on the Role of the Nation in German History and Historiography." *Journal of Modern History* 53 (1981): 1–23.

————. "Wie bürgerlich war der deutsche Liberalismus?" In *Liberalismus in 19. Jahrhundert: Deutschland im europäischen Vergleich,* ed. Dieter Langewiesche, 28–44. Göttingen: Vandenhoeck und Ruprecht, 1988.

Shiels, Richard D. "The Feminisation of American Congregationalism, 1730–1835." *American Quarterly* 33 (1983): 46–62.

Silverman, Dan. *Reluctant Union: Alsace-Lorraine and Imperial Germany, 1871–1918.* University Park: Pennsylvania State University Press, 1972.

Smith, Helmut Walser. *German Nationalism and Religious Conflict: Culture, Ideology, Politics, 1870–1914.* Princeton: Princeton University Press, 1995.

————. "Learned and the Popular Discourse of Anti-Semitism in the Catholic Milieu of the Kaiserreich." *Central European History* 27 (1994): 315–28.

————. "Nationalism and Religious Conflict in Germany, 1887–1914." Ph.D. diss., Yale University, 1991.

————. "Religion and Conflict: Protestants, Catholics, and Anti-Semitism in the State of Baden in the Era of Wilhelm II." *Central European History* 27 (1994): 283–314.

————, ed. *Protestants, Catholics, and Jews in Germany, 1800–1914.* Oxford: Berg, 2001.

Smith, Helmut Walser, and Chris Clark. "The Fate of Nathan." In *Protestants, Catholics, and Jews in Germany, 1800–1914,* ed. Helmut Walser Smith, 3–32. Oxford: Berg, 2001.

Sperber, Jonathan. "Competing Counterrevolutions: Prussian State and Catholic Church in Westphalia during the 1850s." *Central European History* 19 (1986): 45–62.

————. *The European Revolutions, 1848–1851.* Cambridge: Cambridge University Press, 1994.

————. *The Kaiser's Voters: Electors and Elections in Imperial Germany.* Cambridge: Cambridge University Press, 1997.

————. *Popular Catholicism in Nineteenth-Century Germany.* Princeton: Princeton University Press, 1984.

————. *Rhineland Radicals: The Democratic Movement and the Revolution of 1848–1849.* Princeton: Princeton University Press, 1991.

————. "Roman Catholic Religious Identity in Rhineland-Westphalia, 1800–70: Quantitative Examples and Some Political Implications." *Social History* 7 (1982): 305–18.

————. "The Shaping of Political Catholicism in the Ruhr Basin, 1848–1881." *Central European History* 16 (1983): 347–67.

————. "The Transformation of Catholic Associations in the Northern Rheinland and Westphalia, 1830–1870." *Journal of Social History* 15 (1981): 253–63.

Stearns, Peter N. *1848: The Revolutionary Tide in Europe.* New York: W. W. Norton, 1974.

Sterling, Eleonore. *Judenhaß: Die Anfänge des politische des politischen Antisemitismus in Deutschland, 1815–1850.* Frankfurt am Main: Europäische Verlagsanstalt, 1969.

Strasiewski, Bernhard. "Die Dominikaner in Berlin, ein kirchengeschichtlicher Überblick." *Wichmann Jahrbuch* 21–23 (1967–69): 30–41.

Stürmer, Michael. *Regierung und Reichstag im Bismarckstaat 1871–1880: Cäsarismus oder Parlamentarismus.* Düsseldorf: Droste Verlag, 1974.

Suval, Stanley. *Electoral Politics in Wilhelmine Germany.* Chapel Hill: University of North Carolina Press, 1985.

Tal, Uriel. *Christians and Jews in Germany: Religion, Politics, and Ideology in the Second Reich, 1870–1914.* Trans. Noah Jonathan Jacobs. Ithaca: Cornell University Press, 1975.

————. *The Kulturkampf and the Jews of Germany.* Jerusalem: International Center for University Teaching of Jewish Civilization, 1980.

Trapp, Werner. "Volksschulreform und liberales Bürgertum in Konstanz: Die Durchsetzung des Schulzwanges als Voraussetzung der Massendisziplinierung und -qualifikation." In *Provinzialisierung einer Region: Regionale Unterentwicklung und liberale Politik in der Stadt und im Kreis Konstanz im 19. Jahrhundert;*

Untersuchung zur Entstehung der bürgerlichen Gesellschaft in der Provinz, ed. Gert Zang, 376–434. Frankfurt am Main: Syndikat, 1978.

Trzeciakowski, Lech. *The "Kulturkampf" in Prussian Poland.* New York: Columbia University Press, 1990.

———. "The Prussian State and the Catholic Church in Prussian Poland, 1871–1914." *Slavic Review* 26 (1967): 619–37.

Twellmann, Margrit. *Die deutsche Frauenbewegung im Spiegel repräsentativen Frauenzeitschriften: Ihre Anfänge und erste Entwicklung 1843–1889.* Meisenheim am Glan: A. Hain, 1972.

Valentin, Veit. *Geschichte der deutschen Revolution 1848–1849.* Cologne: Kiepenheuer und Witsch, 1970.

Verbeek, Anselm. *Die Kölner Bischofsfrage und die Beilegung des preußischen Kulturkampfes.* Frankfurt am Main: Peter Lang, 1989.

Vocelka, Karl. *Verfassung oder Konkordat? Der publizistische und politische Kampf der österreichischen Liberalen um die Religionsgesetz des Jahres 1868.* Vienna: Verlag der österreichischen Akademie der Wissenschaften, 1978.

Vogel, Berhard, Dieter Nohlen, and Rainer-Olaf Schulze. *Wahlen in Deutschland: Theorie, Geschichte, Dokumente 1848–1970.* Berlin: W. de Gruyter, 1971.

Volkov, Schulamit. "Antisemitism as a Cultural Code: Reflections on the History and Historiography of Antisemitism in Imperial Germany." *Leo Baeck Institute Yearbook* 23 (1978): 25–46.

Wassermann, Henry. "Jews and Judaism in the Gartenlaube." *Leo Baeck Institute Yearbook* 23 (1978): 47–60.

Weber, Christoph. *Aufklärung und Orthodoxie am Mittelrhein, 1820–1850.* Paderborn: F. Schöningh, 1973.

———. *Kirchliche Politik zwischen Rom, Berlin, und Trier 1876–1888: Die Beilegung des preußischen Kulturkampfes.* Mainz: Matthias Grünewald Verlag, 1970.

———. "Ultramontanismus als katholischer Fundamentalismus." In *Deutscher Katholizismus im Umbruch zur Moderne,* ed. Wilfried Loth, 20–45. Stuttgart: W. Kohlhammer, 1991.

Weber, Marie-Lise. *Ludwig Bamberger: Ideologie statt Realpolitik.* Stuttgart: F. Steiner Verlag, 1987.

Wehler, Hans-Ulrich. *Deutsche Gesellschaftsgeschichte.* Vol. 3, *Von der "Deutschen Doppelrevolution" bis zum Beginn des Ersten Weltkrieges, 1849–1914.* Munich: C. H. Beck, 1987–96.

———. "Deutsches Bildungsbürgertum in vergleichender Perspektive: Elemente eines 'Sonderwegs'?" In *Bildungsbürgertum im 19. Jahrhundert: Politischer Einfluß und gesellschaftliche Formation,* ed. Jürgen Kocka, 215–37. Stuttgart: Klett-Cotta, 1989.

———. *The German Empire, 1871–1918.* Trans. K. Traynor. Leamington Spa: Berg, 1985. Originally published as *Das deutsche Kaiserreich, 1871–1918* (Göttingen: Vandenhoeck und Ruprecht, 1973).

Weiss, Otto. *Die Redemptoristen in Bayern (1790–1909): Ein Beitrag zur Geschichte des Ultramontanismus.* St. Ottilien: Eos Verlag, 1983.

Welter, Barbara. "The Feminization of American Religion, 1800–1860." In *Clio's*

Consciousness Raised: New Perspectives in the History of Women, ed. Mary Hartmann and Lois Banner, 136–57. New York: Harper and Row, 1976.

Wendel, Friedrich. *Die Kirche in der Karikatur: Eine Sammlung anti-klerikaler Karakturen, Volkslieder, Sprichwörter und Anekdoten.* Berlin: Der Freidenker, 1928.

Wernicke, Kurt. "Der 'Moabiter Klostersturm.'" *Berlinische Monatsschrift* 3 (1994): 3–14.

Wertheimer, Jack. *Unwelcome Strangers: East European Jews in Imperial Germany.* Oxford: Oxford University Press, 1987.

Wettengel, Michael. *Die Revolution von 1848/49 im Rhein-Main-Raum: Politische Vereine und Revolutionsalltag im Grossherzogtum Hessen, Herzogtum Nassau, und in der Freien Stadt Frankfurt.* Wiesbaden: Historische Kommission für Nassau, 1989.

Windell, George C. *The Catholics and German Unity, 1866–1871.* Minneapolis: University of Minnesota Press, 1954.

Winkler, Heinrich August. "Bürgerliche Emanzipation und nationale Einigung: Zur Entstehung des Nationalliberalismus in Preußen." In *Probleme der Reichsgründungszeit, 1848–1879,* ed. Helmut Böhme, 226–42. Cologne: Kiepenheuer und Witsch, 1968.

———. *Liberalismus und Antiliberalismus: Studien zur politischen Sozialgeschichte des 19. und 20. Jahrhundert.* Göttingen: Vandenhoeck und Ruprecht, 1979.

———. *Preußischer Liberalismus und deutscher Nationalstaat.* Tübingen: Mohr, 1964.

———. "Vom linken zum rechten Nationalismus: Der deutsche Liberalismus in der Krise von 1878/79." *Geschichte und Gesellschaft* 4 (1978): 5–28.

Winkler, Jürgen. *Sozialstruktur politische Tradition und Liberalismus: Eine empirische Längsschnittstudie zur Wahlentwicklung in Deutschland 1871–1933.* Oplanden: Westdeutscher Verlag, 1995.

Wollstein, Günter. *Deutsche Geschichte 1848/49: Gescheiterte Revolution in Mitteleuropa.* Stuttgart: W. Kohlhammer, 1986.

Yonke, Eric. "The Catholic Subculture in Modern Germany: Recent Work in the Social History of Religion." *Catholic Historical Review* 80 (1994): 534–45.

Zalar, Jeffrey T. "The Process of Confessional Inculturation: Catholic Reading in the 'Long Nineteenth Century.'" In *Protestants, Catholics, and Jews in Germany, 1800–1914,* ed. Helmut Walser Smith, 121–52. Oxford: Berg, 2001.

Zang, Gert. "Die Bedeutung der Auseinandersetzung um die Stiftungsverwaltung in Konstanz (1830–1870) für die ökonomische und gesellschaftliche Entwicklung der lokalen Gesellschaft: Ein Beitrag zur Analyse der materiellen Hintergründe des Kulturkampfes." In *Provinzialisierung einer Region: Regionale Unterentwicklung und liberale Politik in der Stadt und im Kreis Konstanz im 19. Jahrhundert; Untersuchungen zur Entstehung der bürgerlichen Gesellschaft in der Provinz,* ed. Gert Zang, 307–71. Frankfurt am Main: Syndikat, 1978.

———, ed. *Provinzialisierung einer Region: Regionale Unterentwicklung und liberale Politik in der Stadt und im Kreis Konstanz im 19. Jahrhundert; Untersuchungen zur Entstehung der bürgerlichen Gesellschaft in der Provinz.* Frankfurt am Main: Syndikat, 1978.

Zeeden, Ernst Walter. "Die katholische Kirche in der Siche deutschen Protestantismus im 19. Jahrhundert." *Historisches Jahrbuch* 72 (1953): 433–56.

Zeldin, Theodore. "The Conflict of Moralities: Confession, Sin, and Pleasure in the Nineteenth Century." In *Conflicts in French Society: Anticlericalism, Education, and Morals in the Nineteenth Century,* ed. Theodore Zeldin, 13–50. London: Allen and Unwin, 1970.

Zielinski, Zygmunt. "Der Kulturkampf in der Provinz Posen." *Historisches Jahrbuch* 101 (1981): 447–61.

Zucker, Stanley. "Ludwig Bamberger and the Rise of Anti-Semitism in Germany, 1848–1893." *Central European History* 3 (1970): 332–52.

———. *Ludwig Bamberger: German Liberal Politician and Social Critic, 1823–1899.* Pittsburgh: University of Pittsburgh Press, 1975.

Index

Note: Page numbers in italics indicate figures.